Mr. New Orleans

Orleans

The Life of a Big Easy Underworld Legend

By

Frenchy Brouillette

Matthew Randazzo V

ISBN-13:
978-0692237489

ISBN-10:
0692237488

DEDICATION

<u>Frenchy</u>: To New Orleans, baby.

<u>MRV</u>: To Melissa and Jeannie in love and admiration, and in celebration of the city of New Orleans

Within A Shadow of
A Doubt

A note from Matthew Randazzo V

Mr. New Orleans is a memoir set in the 20th century New Orleans underworld, where the objective truth is a particularly conspicuous and lonely tourist. This book is an oral history of the berserk hedonism, conspiratorial intrigue, and unprincipled laziness that made New Orleans the most infamous city in America, as told by the men and women who earned that infamy the easiest way they could.

Though the stories of these supernaturally gifted liars may be easily dismissed, their stories are no less credible than the "legitimate" records of an era of Louisiana history when the police departments were compromised, the FBI was negligent, the politicians were venal, the crooks were too smart to leave paper trails to anything but patsies, and many of the accepted facts about the state's leading citizens were as bizarre and debauched as the myths once told about Greek gods.

Mr. New Orleans is thus an unapologetically imperfect historical document, where corroborated truth is filed next to hard-to-believe and impossible-to-verify stories of ancient gangland mayhem. It is written by me in the voice of legendary New Orleans gangster Frenchy Brouillette, a man whom I know well and interviewed countless times over a period of six years.

Mr. New Orleans also incorporates the testimonies of dozens of mafiosi, law enforcement officers, political hacks, and apparently innocent civilians, all in Frenchy's voice. This is a street history extracted from the remnants of the Louisiana Mafia Family and other assorted insiders with a stake in the quickly vanishing history of New Orleans.

The purpose of *Mr. New Orleans* is to preserve the spirit and culture of the near-extinct New Orleans outlaw and the orgiastic black market society that he created, inhabited, and made famous. No claims are being made about the objective truth of all of the tales told within; no pretensions of scholarly certitude have been entertained. To read *Mr. New Orleans* is to promise to go easy, enjoy yourself, and take nothing as gospel ... *especially* the quotations from the newspapers and FBI.

The Rising Sun Blues

The only thing a drunkard needs is a suitcase and a trunk
The only time he's satisfied is when he's on a drunk.
Fills his glasses to the brim, passes them around
Only pleasure he gets out of life is hoboin' from town to
town.

One foot is on the platform and the other one on the
train.

I'm going back to New Orleans to wear that ball and chain.
Going back to New Orleans, my race is almost run.
Going back to spend the rest of my days beneath that
rising sun.

Chapter I

The Devil's Walk

The Devil's Walk in New Orleans
"'Twas so cold in the North
That 'Old Nick' grew quote wroth,
So he called round his favorite fiends,
Says he, 'by my troth,
'I'll be off to the South,
'For they've plenty of Hells in Orleans.'"
Anonymous 1837 Poem

FOR GENERATIONS, IF YOU FLEW TO WHAT IS TODAY LOUIS ARMSTRONG AIRPORT, JUMPED INTO A CAB, AND TOLD YOUR HACK THAT YOU WERE IN THE MARKET FOR LOOSE WOMEN, NO-LIMIT GAMBLING, HOT JEWELS, CHEAP BOOZE, OR A PREMIUM HIGH, THERE WAS A GOOD CHANCE HE WOULD TAKE YOU TO SEE FRENCHY, BABY.

THAT DOESN'T MAKE ME EVIL; THAT MAKES ME MR. NEW ORLEANS.

Being Mr. New Orleans is not a job, but an art. It is the art of looking good doing bad and getting rich doing just about nothing. It's the art of making it big while taking it easy.

If I appear to be working, then I'm doing the city an injustice. Whenever I am not cheating, I am cheating.

The honor of acting as New Orleans's mascot comes with a profound responsibility to forsake stress, stability, sobriety, monogamy, respectability, and all manner of legitimate employment and lawful behavior. I am as slippery as fried chicken fingertips when it comes to responsibility.

As the reigning Mr. New Orleans, I have been on a working vacation since the summer of 1953. I was seventeen years old when I snatched my big brother's Harley Davidson and gunned that sucker all the way from Marksville, Louisiana, down Highway 61 to the Orleans Parish Criminal Court.

All I knew about New Orleans I learned from Sunday school — that it was the home of vice, gangsters, and fallen women. That was one heavy sales pitch, and it bagged me good. Like so many Cajun rednecks throughout the centuries, I fled to New Orleans to escape everyone that told me who I was and what I was supposed to be.

It took only one night in a New Orleans bar to give me a profession, a mission in life: to be a French Quarter character. To a bored and lazy hick with a hunger to rebel, the diamond-drenched characters I met in the French Quarter were cooler than Hollywood, cooler than Rock 'n' Roll, definitely cooler than Hard Work and the American Dream.

From then on, I have never lifted a finger with honorable intentions. New Orleans taught a no-nothing Cajun virgin the pleasures of wine, women, and the type of good time that gets you sentenced to hard time. Jail is a small price to pay for a life worth living. Y'all can have work and a good night's sleep; leave the mayhem, devilry, and the easy money to Frenchy.

For these lessons, I thank New Orleans — and, if the bitch could talk, she'd have the good sense to thank me, too.

Though I was hardly what you might call a good student, I learned the lessons New Orleans taught me backwards and forwards. Don't take the word of a bona fide degenerate: you can read every letter of my 1600-page FBI file, my dozens of Louisiana criminal indictments, and my various divorce settlements without finding a single reference to anything resembling respectable employment.

Outside of the few prison assignments I did not escape through green-palming guards and trustees, I have not done an honest day's work since I was a teenager. Nonetheless, I've owned strip clubs, bars, casinos, brothels, and even a goddamn bank.

The moral of my story is that crime doesn't pay, but *fun* pays and pays and pays.

I don't deal in crimes – those get you imprisoned or killed. I commit fun.

I don't deal in victims – you catch beefs and religion from them. I deal with willing customers.

You could call my specialty "victimless crimes" if you were in the mood to sound stupid. Be honest, baby: if there ain't no victim, there ain't no crime. Cops shouldn't arrest you just for living.

I made my bread exclusively through the sale of the sort of fun no one wants you to have. I have committed about a million so-called "crimes", and they were just about all the same: selling people a good time they desperately wanted. Only the brand names and charges were shuffled – the product has always been fun.

And to sell fun, you need to have fun, or at least look like it. For a half-century, my profession has been to party. When I raise hell, the wallets of everyone nearby somehow empty into mine. My secret to success is simple: I have fun, look good having fun, and am always open to share with company. I make a living bringing extra fun to every party so that I can cut the squares in on the action – for a price.

In my heyday, I was a superstar on the street: a good-looking, muscle-bound bodybuilder who tooled around town wearing Italian silk suits, unbuttoned fluorescent shirts, a diamond ring on every finger, and spit-shined alligator boots. I drove only new convertibles and would never show my face in public without a cheerleading squad of beautiful women at my side. For added flare, I took along either a steroid-jacked coal black German shepherd or a gigantic flaming red parrot with a Cajun accent worse than my own.

I guess you could say I was cool.

Others might have called me a walking fiasco, or a stumbling fiasco depending on the time of night. As far as *I* was concerned, I was a work of art. Without meaning to be, I was probably a masterpiece of advertising. My appearance gave degenerates confidence that I was the sort of gin-soaked Moses who could lead them to whatever sick Promised Land they had a mind to visit. It's no surprise that I've spent my adult life being followed by a mob of whores, johns, junkies, gamblers, gangsters, go-go dancers, and G-men, who all march after me like I am leading the Devil's own Mardi Gras crew on parade.

I bet that you could take a peek behind me and follow the trail of empty wine bottles, discarded lingerie, and crumpled up citations all the way back to the Absinthe House — the centuries-old French Quarter bar where, in 1953, Mafia bookmaker Dutch Kraut bought a nobody nicknamed Frenchy his first beer. That beer was the ruin of me; until then, I had never found the courage to put my bad judgment into action. I had a gentle heart but a weak will and worse work ethic, which is the perfect recipe to create a town wino, not a gangster kingpin.

Then again, I sure was paid like one.

I hate the misconception that all underworld characters corrupt and hurt people. We just sell a customer something he may use to hurt himself, no different than a priest or a door-to-door knife salesman. Whenever I hear a politician talk about gangsters corrupting the innocent, I think they must have lost their mentality somewhere on the campaign trail.

You think you need to *sell* drugs, gambling, or sex?

Really?

Baby, I don't even know what marketing *means*. I can't string twenty words together without someone to spot me a syllable here and there. I'd starve if I had to rely on manipulating and corrupting the innocent.

The marks have always come to me. Never in my goddamn life have I had to hustle like a used car salesman to convince some unsuspecting pedestrian to buy a piece of ass or play a game of craps or smoke a little dope.

That's what I call science fiction. Supply never has shit on demand in the underworld, and that's the lay of the land north, east, south, and west. I am just a salesman whose workday ends at sunrise.

Though there are police station riff-raff who will call me a pitch-black predator and a ruthless killer, they are all wrong. They are being selfish, ruining my name to puff up their own. The only thing I've ever shot was booze, that and a damn sparrow I shot off her nest when I was a lil' redneck kid.

That damn sparrow and her starving-mouth chicks have haunted my nightmares for *seventy consecutive years.* Baby, I had a nightmare about that big-mouthed bird last night!

But the cops would have you believe I've been dropping human bodies helter-skelter since the Eisenhower administration. The cops will transform every crook they arrest into Al Capone if you give them the leeway, and Lord knows I've given them a couple hundred chances to smear my name over the years. I've worn handcuffs so often that some people look at me strange when they see me without them, as if they were my favorite piece of jewelry.

In general, you'd be better off forgetting whatever the cops have to say. You can't listen to those sorts of people and ever expect to make sense of the world. I am a criminal of the decent sort; I'd never hurt anyone with my wits about me. I am the kind of hopeless romantic who sometimes wakes up in a jail cell with heavy charges pending and no memory of anything but that first sip of wine the night before . . . or the week before. This makes me a victim of a weak constitution, not a criminal mastermind, and the only person I tend to hurt is myself.

And despite the sixty years I've spent boogieing down the lumpy streets of New Orleans, I don't think of myself as having changed much from the seventeen-year-old hick that sped out of Marksville, Louisiana on his big brother's motorcycle. Yes, the decades of violence, drinking, and drugging have taken their toll on my looks — baby, Michelangelo would have thrown down his brush and taken up pottery after he saw me — but deep down, I'm just as soft and simple as I ever was.

I'm the same bumpkin who feels more comfortable with horses and dogs than people, who can't keep a dollar in his wallet for more than a day, who can't pass a church without performing the Sign of the Cross, who still gets nervous and refuses to speak blue in front of ladies, who'd rather eat jail time than sit at a desk, who has been haunted by a murdered sparrow since the 1940s.

Unless you're a bottle of champagne, I don't mean you no harm. I'm just a happy-go-lucky, shiftless, shy redneck who tools around well-dressed and well-pickled to hide my true nature. Far from being some tough guy, I just happened to be carried away to this life by the strong current of fun that has dragged small-town hayseeds down the Mississippi to New Orleans for centuries.

If I had been born in the deserts outside of Hollywood, I believe I would have become an actor; if I grew up in Nantucket, I'd have been carried out to sea, and I'd be writing this story by dipping the big silver hook on my wrist into ink. Lucky for you, it just so happens that I grew up in the shadow of the vice capital of the South, and thanks to that coincidence, you a have much more interesting story on your hands.

I come from the same grand New Orleans tradition as the pirates Jean and Pierre Lafitte. Though I wouldn't put myself in the same category as the Lafittes, my associates included three men who could go toe-to-toe with them any day: New York's Frank Costello and New Orleans's own Carlos Marcello and Sylvestro "Silver Dollar Sam" Carollo.

When those legendary Mafia godfathers had big fish in town who needed to be treated right, they gave Frenchy a call and let me take care of business. I gave the whale gamblers reasons enough to stay in town until they lost their money; I made sure the labor union bosses were too eager to get back to their girls to haggle over how much money they loaned the Mob from their pension funds; I drowned them politicians in good times until the favors seemed like the least they could do as gentlemen.

Some politicians were easier than others. The easiest was the most powerful of all: four-time Louisiana governor Edwin Edwards, a coonass conman from Marksville who just happened to be my very own cousin. Life is as easy as a paid date when your own family runs the state.

"He's the strongest sonfabitchin' governor we ever had. He fuck with women and play dice, but won't drink. How do you like dat?"

<u>Carlos Marcello</u>
On Edwin Edwards

Forget what people say about me — Cousin Edwin was the finest pimp Louisiana has ever known. If Huey Long had been born a few decades later, Edwin would have twisted the Kingfish's mind, turned him out, and had him happily tweaking johns all around Baton Rouge. Edwin ran the state of Louisiana like a chaotic whorehouse for two decades, and he did it with the style and flash of a rap music video.

When Edwin went down, he took the leadership of the New Orleans Mafia, two of John Gotti's most powerful lieutenants, and the owner of the San Francisco 49ers NFL team with him. As you can tell, Edwin never saw any sense in doing things half-ass; if he was going to fall, he wanted to put Nixon in the shade.

My cousin's four high-rollin' terms as governor of Louisiana turned a whoring musclehead named Frenchy into the unlikeliest of political powerbrokers. If there was a problem too knotty for Carlos Marcello's network of political and police puppets to squash, then the most powerful man in the South called to ask me to intercede with my pipsqueak cousin Edwin. This commerce worked in both directions: like any Louisiana politician, Edwin needed a trustworthy liaison to stalk the shadows of the New Orleans underworld.

If you can't trust your blood, who can you trust?

Though Carlos Marcello appreciated my work on his behalf with my cousin, I think he was most grateful for my volunteer work as his babysitter. I'm talking about one 350-pound baby with a passion for pills, thrills, and bellyaches.

Shortly after I came to New Orleans, Carlos made a lifelong enemy in Robert F. Kennedy, the chief counsel of a Senate committee that was interrogating him. RFK would never forget how the uneducated, red-faced, icebox-shaped Sicilian with the streak of grey in his black hair had mocked him in front of dozens of news cameras. As Carlos muttered a couple thousand recitals of the Fifth Amendment, he wore a (pardon me, ladies, there ain't no other way to say it) "Go fuck yourself" smirk that another little big man like RFK could not forgive and forget.

After his brother Jack's crooked rise to the presidency — unlike most Mafia bosses, Carlos bet heavily on Nixon in that election — RFK allowed this personal vendetta to get in the way of his family's safety.

As an illegal alien, Carlos had been afraid that the government would deport him to Italy like they did to his predecessor Silver Dollar Sam, so he had obtained a forged Guatemalan birth certificate. Unimpressed with Carlos' scheme, RFK ordered Immigration to kidnap the Mafia boss of New Orleans, toss him into an empty military plane, and dump him — not in Italy — but in the jungles of his supposed homeland of Guatemala.

Judging by the Wile E. Coyote smarts on display in that decision, it's surprising RFK managed to live for so long without walking off cliffs or using his toaster in the bathtub. As far as safety precautions go, deporting Carlos Marcello to a nearby country was like locking your screen door as the Klan burned crosses on your lawn. RFK's little plot would only have been worth a nickel if the last step involved Carlos "resisting" and getting shot.

That's one thing I think the Italians can teach the Irish: never *wound* a dangerous enemy. What's the point? To make him angrier? When RFK put the screws to Carlos, Carlos should have needed a miracle on par with Lazarus to come back — not a plane ticket and a good lawyer.

And Carlos had a good lawyer: crack immigration hack Dean Andrews. Unfortunately for Carlos, his legal lucky charm was a friend and client of mine, which meant that Dean was a degenerate lecher, pillhead, wannabe black soul man, and party maniac with a seriously compromised life span. At any moment, this jive-talking mountain of cholesterol was liable to nosedive into the grave and take Carlos' freedom with him.

Contrary to the opinion of Dean's colleagues and life insurance actuary, Carlos actually thought it was *good news* when Dean's wife tossed him out on the street and told him to move in with me. With Dean as my roommate, Carlos could rest easy; his courthouse rabbit's foot would be safe.

Carlos knew I wouldn't let anything come between us. Once Carlos told me that I was going to be held responsible if anything happened to his attorney, I made sure that our good friend Dean was pampered and protected like a newborn. Baby, my life depended on it.

It was this drunk-babysitting-the-drunker arrangement that led to a confrontation that nearly killed all of us. It was the greatest showdown in the history of the New Orleans underworld: the day Carlos Marcello met Satan.

"Report of: Special Agent John C. McCurnin, II
Office: New Orleans   Date: November 25, 1968
Carlos Marcello has been seen in company [sic] with Frenchy
Brouillette, known pimp in New Orleans area."
F.B.I. Surveillance Document 92-2713

I named my firstborn daughter Satan because it suited her personality. She was deadly pretty, a well-made 100-pound black girl with a charming face and bad intentions. Though she was sweet-natured with friends, Satan was an extra helping of evil with strangers. She was my bodyguard, best friend, and my all-time bottom bitch — a black German shepherd who would kill anyone who even sniffed at me wrong.

I would trade every second I spent with any of my ex-wives to get a clone of that dog. I took on the New Orleans Mafia for that goddamn dog!

One morning in the early 1960s, I took my girl Satan out for breakfast. We were dressed to the nines at nine in the morning: me with my eight diamond rings, black cowboy boots, and open-collared suit exposing my muscular chest, and Satan with her jeweled collar made of gold. I took my girl out to The Snake Pit, a bar run by semi-retired French Quarter pimp Snake Gonzalez, who could be hospitable when he wasn't stabbing you.

I was sitting in a booth with Satan, who was uppity since we had both just taken a dosage of the steroids that made us the two best-built specimens in Louisiana in our respective weight classes and species. At the bar, I was watching a Mafia enforcer named Big Pete make a drunken ass of himself: he was tossing "a Caesar salad" in a big bowl using his roll of cash and a jar of mayonnaise as the only ingredients.

Fat, greasy, and disheveled, Big Pete was an obese clown whose too-small clothes barely covered the catheter and piss bag he wore at all times. Big Pete was a ridiculous character, but he was also a professional killer. He murdered like a plumber tightening a faucet – it was nothing to him.

Big Pete finished making his cash salad, and, as pimps and thieves started reaching over to pick up the mayonnaise-drenched bills, Pete teetered onto his feet and announced to no one and everyone that he was going "straight the fuck home." His piss bag sloshed as he veered to the right and left, trying to keep his balance; finally, the big meatball steadied and began rolling in my direction.

"Lemme through, God fucking dammit," Big Pete belched as he careened toward Satan like a tourist stumbling through a mickey haze.

My girl Satan gave this wino the evil eye, but Big Pete was Little Stevie Wonder at that point. He wasn't reading nobody's body language, let's just say that. A roaring tyrannosaurus rex wouldn't have caught his attention.

Before I could act, I saw my German shepherd fly, fangs first, at the Mafia enforcer. In a blink, Satan had ripped off one of Big Pete's cheeks and shredded the top of one of his arms; I pulled her back as she was wringing a bloody catheter back and forth in her jaws.

Satan slid on bloody paws as I dragged her out of Snake Gonzalez's dive, barking and growling like a fat Italian wife the whole way out. I tossed the crazy bitch in the back of my Cadillac convertible, told her that she was banned from licking me with her catheter mouth, and hightailed it in search of a good restaurant.

I wasn't hungry — I was dead.

I had been told that a man condemned to death gets to order his favorite meal before he's executed, so I wanted some chicken fricassee on the double, baby. Time was shorter than a Cajun jockey.

I knew that, within hours, Pete would plug in his piss bag, grab his big-ass revolver, and come looking for Satan. I'd be spared as one of "Carlos' boys," but there would be no potential happy ending after I whipped out my gun to stop Big Pete from hurting my goddamn dog. I wasn't about to live with Satan's blood on my hands.

Sure enough, I woke up the next day to the rumbling of a gigantic, drunk mummy pounding on my door. Covered in bandages, an arm dangling in a sling, and shitfaced as a blue-blooded debutante, Big Pete was waving his .45 with his good arm as I looked through my peephole. I threw a robe over my shoulders, locked Satan away in my bedroom, stuffed my pistol into my boxers, and kept a grip on the handle as I opened the door.

"Frenchy, I come to kill that fuckin' dog," the fat man grumbled out of the corner of his mouth.

"Pete, that dog didn't mean it, ya understand?" I said with a voice like a switchblade flicking open. I was talking like Clint Eastwood while feeling like I needed a catheter and piss bag of my own.

I've never been the courageous type. I'd like to say that I'm a lover, not a fighter, but in general I'm just too lazy to be bothered with either. Both are hard work. I'm more of a drinker.

Pete looked at me as hard as he could with his bleary, toilet-bowl eyes and decided that I was for real. If you believed the police and my street rep, I had a couple skeletons tucked away in my closet, too. Besides, given Piss Bag Pete's recent luck, I think the poor one-armed fatso realized that it wasn't the day to stake his life on a roll of the dice with Mr. New Orleans.

Big Pete grunted and shuffled to my couch. He sighed, which triggered a juicy fit of coughs. Clearing his throat, the disappointed killer mumbled, "At least you gotsta give me a puppy of dat bitch when you breed 'er."

I was in no position to refuse the fat man his request. When Satan had her next litter, Big Pete got the second toughest brawler in the bunch. I kept the toughest: the other canine love of my life, Malcolm X, who I named for being even blacker and meaner than his mom.

Some pain-in-the-asses have argued that Malcolm X was hardly a tougher name than Satan, so I had to admit that I started out too ambitious with the first name. The only name legitimately scarier than Satan was Silver Dollar Sam, and I damn sure wasn't going to risk giving that name to a *black* dog while that old Sicilian coot was still alive.

Even with one of Satan's brood, Big Pete was never satisfied. When Edwin became governor, Pete bugged me all the goddamn time: he wanted me to convince my cousin to grant him a license to carry his .45 pistol into government buildings! I don't even know if such a license existed, but I sure as hell wasn't going to find out on Pete's behalf. I was nervous, given the Marcello organization's record of shooting public officials.

After kicking the shit out of a giant Mafia thug, Satan became the most infamous dog in Louisiana. She was so popular that crooked bar owners started making her a special plate of burger or steak or bacon whenever I took her on my rounds. A generation later, French Quarter characters still told their fighting pitbulls that they'd better win, or a match with a long-dead German shepherd named Satan awaited them in Hell.

As much as I loved Satan, the bitch got a big head. All the acclaim made her feel invincible, but soon she confronted a beast who would have ended her life without hesitation if she got too cocky.

Early one morning, no more than an hour after I had gone to sleep after a typically long night, a rock crashed through my bedroom window. I heard Satan barking like a LSU football fan on the front lawn, and in one gymnastic motion I kicked up from my bed and landed feet-first in glass from the broken window. Hopping in pain, I bounced to the window and saw Satan drooling with rage and tensing her muscles. At any moment, she looked ready to jump on a short, stout man in a black suit who stood with his arm cocked back like Sandy Koufax, ready to fling another rock.

In between the two opponents, a meathead in a T-shirt bounced on the balls of his feet trying to warn off Satan like a hokey pro-wrestling referee. Before my sleep-drunk eyes could focus, I recognized the nervous, baby-talking voice trying to reason with Satan.

It was Sam LaBruzzo — Carlos Marcello's bodyguard and driver. Behind LaBruzzo stood the godfather of the New Orleans

Mafia, the richest crime boss in America, staring down Satan. If my dog jumped, all of us were dead: Carlos for crossing Satan, Sam for failing to protect Carlos, Satan for killing Carlos, and, of course, Frenchy for harboring that mafioso-mauling mutt.

As I was gawking in terror out of my window, Carlos slowly raised his barreling black eyes to me. "Frenchy, git the fuck down here, man," he hissed with glowing red cheeks. "I don't wanna be seen knocking on dat goddam door, ya hear you fuckin' mutt?"

This was Carlos' excuse. I'll admit - I've heard worse lies, usually from my own attorneys, but not often. Throwing rocks through my window and acting a fool on my front lawn in broad daylight was not exactly less conspicuous behavior than just ringing my doorbell. We both knew Carlos had been throwing rocks through my window in a bizarre Mafia rendition of *Romeo and Juliet* solely to avoid trying his luck by trying to pass by Satan.

Panicking over the imminent combat between Satan and Carlos, I became so clumsy that I nearly fell out of the broken window while wrestling on my robe. In those days, they didn't make clothes for men with roided-up python arms like mine, so putting on my sleeves was like stuffing my fists down two garden snakes. I sprinted out of my bedroom and out of the door, past a room full of prostitutes dozing in an opium-addled slumber and Dean Andrews splayed half-naked and half-dead on my couch.

I padded out onto my lawn in my cut-up bare feet, my half-on robe billowing in every direction, calmly yelling to Satan to "Goddammit, stand down, girl! Friends, girl, friends! Friends, baby, friends!"

More civilized than any of my wives, Satan immediately ceased her growling and relaxed her muscles. Though Carlos was clearly apprehensive of her, Satan also knew the score — she would have been busy shitting out the remains of anyone else who dared to throw a rock through my window, but on a primal level, Satan knew that Carlos was more wolf than man.

Never a fan of small talk, Carlos ignored my greeting and surged like a gator to the point. "Man, git fatass Deano to git his fat fucking ass down here before I fuckin' go git his fuckin' fat ass myself," Carlos spat with his thick, calloused hands in my face.

Despite his fine suits, Carlos was a pretty hard-shelled character. He was one of the few people I knew who spoke with as little class and education as me, which isn't surprising since I grew up lugging crates of potatoes around Marksville, and Carlos grew up lugging tomatoes around the New Orleans French Market. If you threw in Dean Andrews' black jazz hep cat routine, a normal American from anywhere else in the country wouldn't understand a word of our conversation.

"He gonna come wit' us," Carlos continued in his redneck guido jive. "He gonna git girls; he gonna git all da food he wants. Anything he wants, he gonna git — just no pills. Ya hear me, man? No pills ... fuck dem pills. Dey for the birds!"

Carlos knew his attorney well: Dean was a miserable insomniac whose greatest love affair was with sleeping pills. Dean might spend twenty-four hours in a mumbling, drooling blur after shotgunning a half-dozen high-caliber pills, and Carlos was driven to violent rage whenever he sought out his expert attorney and found a chicken-brained junkie instead.

I spared a moment to think about poor Dean, who was higher than the Holy Trinity in his sleeping-pill coma on my couch as we spoke. Carlos had a couple fishing camps where he regularly held Dean hostage, and Dean hated all of them. Though he loathed his stays at Carlos' camp on Grand Isle, once the site of the Lafitte brothers' pirate kingdom, Dean's least favorite destination was the camp in the tiny town of Venice, in the extreme southeastern corner of Louisiana where the Mississippi flushes into the Gulf of Mexico.

Dean said that visiting Venice, where you could practically see Cuba just over the horizon, reminded Carlos of the millions he had lost when Castro had stolen his gambling empire. Carlos was unforgiving with Dean under the best of circumstances, ranting and nagging him like an impossible-to-please Archie Bunker, but getting Carlos started on Castro and the Kennedys put him in that fire-and-brimstone Devil mindset so native to vengeful Sicilians.

"I need 'im for dat deportation talk, man. I need to kidnap Deano to the fishin' camp," Carlos continued, actually explaining himself like a normal person.

Usually, Carlos didn't explain shit to nobody. The man didn't talk – he demanded, and if he didn't get what he wanted he de-manned you. Satan must have unnerved him.

While I contemplated this, Carlos contemplated me.

"Frenchy," Carlos said with his slow, dripping-with-anger tone. "I *said...go git the fat ass!*" I ran back inside while Satan licked her lips and gave Carlos an inquisitive stare.

Dean was planted face-first on my drool-soaked couch, his mountainous ass cheeks wearing his ratty underwear like a thin, translucent coat of snow. It had only been a few hours since he swallowed a week's worth of sleeping pills; I was worried the big fat baby wouldn't be able to wake up. I dead-lifted the jelly-belly off the couch using my best weightlifting form, but Dean just melted to the floor and murmured and cooed like a girl putting up a fake fight.

Determined not to piss off Carlos, I juggled, lifted, and twisted the huge, hairy, sticky fat dumpling into the food-stained clothes lying on the floor. As I stretched a shirt over Dean's belly like a balloon over a basketball, he started moaning and doggy paddling on my chest. For a moment, I lost my temper and stooped to lift Dean onto my shoulders, fully intending to carry him to the lawn and dump him before Carlos' thousand-dollar shoes.

But I hesitated; a tickle of mercy stirred in my heart. A guy like me understood all too well that no junkie deserves to wake up from a high to the terror of an irate Sicilian murderer.

I shook Dean like a champagne bottle until he coughed himself awake. "Listen up, Dean, you got Carlos Marcello and Sam LaBruzzo out there waiting for you. Don't act like a goddamned fool."

Delivered in my harsh, scratchy Cajun accent, my warning pulled Dean out of his chemical dunk tank. Dean blinked, his pouting face confusedly accusing me of some type of betrayal, as if I had waited until he passed out and rushed out to call Carlos to prank him. Finally figuring out the gravity of the situation, Dean sped past all the intermediate steps between junkie stupor and wide-awake; Dean was suddenly ready for action, as in control of his senses as a stupor-mouthed junkie could ever be.

Dean was a smart cat. He knew he was tap-dancing on the edge of a blade. Like most of my straight friends, he loved the danger and actively sought it out. Dean was a hippie attorney who just wanted to be next to gangsters. For some of his underworld clients, Dean worked for free food, girls, or access. The only way Dean could keep his life interesting enough to be worth living was to wager his existence on his legal ability.

In a moment of profound drunken stupidity, Dean had given Carlos his word that he'd never have to leave American soil for the rest of his life. Carlos was not a maniac; he would not have held Dean's failure to out-muscle the Justice Department's against him under normal circumstances. Now that Dean had given his *word*, however, I gave even odds that Carlos would whack out his pilled-up attorney the second things looked bleak.

Sicilians are always obsessed with other people keeping their word ... while they lie like each one comes with a free pizza.

Dean was marked, anyway: he was "coincidentally" the attorney to Lee Harvey Oswald, a mutual acquaintance of both Carlos' and mine. As the time went by, I began to doubt the "deportation" cover story; since Carlos had the best deportation lawyers in Washington, D.C., why did he need to spend all of his time powwowing with a bohemian con man like Dean? Maybe Dean's real job was helping Carlos figure out how best to pull the puppet strings of his other client, Lee Harvey Oswald.

I'm hardly Sherlock Brouillette — a lot of people shared my suspicions. Over the years, Dean would be grilled about his part in the supposed Mafia conspiracy to kill John F. Kennedy by every dick with a notepad and tape recorder in America. Local wiseguys bet each other on how long Dean would last before he got clipped.

Baby, don't worry: I'll get to that whole mess about my friends murdering the president later. All you need to know now is that Dean feared for his life long before his client, Lee Harvey Oswald, got plugged by another Marcello Family goombah, Jack Ruby.

If he faltered at any point in doing right by Carlos, Dean told me he was sure that he would end up fed to alligators or dissolved in a vat of lime and dumped in the swamps —the supposed fate of countless of Carlos' enemies. Of course, I was tied up in the same wager: a twenty-seven-year-old Cajun pimp who unwillingly staked his life on his ability to keep Dean Andrews's suicidal addictions from compromising Carlos Marcello's plans. Too stupid to fear anything besides an immediate in-my-face threat, I didn't pay too much mind to the long odds against Dean behaving himself.

Facing the man he figured would be his future murderer, Dean slowly paced into the excruciatingly bright sunlight, a sweating fat man surrendering himself to the humidity and sleeplessness of a weekend in the swamp with Carlos. So much of Louisiana history went down like that: a sweaty fat man with book smarts kowtowing to a sweaty fat man with a gun.

Dean knew he would get to party and romp with as many prostitutes as he could handle at one of the Marcello family's vast secret camps, but he also knew that most of his weekend would be spent pouting in a quiet funk, listening to the operatic Hitler rants of Louisiana's most powerful man.

I scratched Satan behind her ears as Carlos, Sam, and Dean drove away in Carlos' bronze Cadillac. Bon voyage, you lovebirds!

"Girl, time for breakfast!" I said as I stooped down to hug my welterweight, homicidal monster. Satan galloped ahead of me like a frat boy within sight of a $1 beer night, barking for me to hurry up. I tossed two filet steaks stolen from the supermarket by one of my booster friends into a pan and poured out two glasses worth of brandy. I flipped one rare filet to Satan and washed down the other one with the brandy. Breakfast taken care of, I whipped out our steroid syringes and dosed daddy and daughter up.

Ready for the day, we tooled out to the New Orleans Athletic Club so I could lift weights, and she could bark down skittish bodybuilders. After a good workout, we had a $300 lunch with various judges and city councilmen at their restaurant of choice, Mandina's, and took a joyride that eventually ended up in the Quarter — where my days truly began and ended. Thanks to the Quarter, I expected to live fast and leave behind a young, tan, immaculately developed corpse.

That was forty-seven years ago, give or take a step in either direction. Just about everyone else is long dead. The Mafia is gone; even the New Orleans I knew is gone. The only characters left are the Brouillettes: me and my cousin Edwin, whose mother is a Marksville Brouillette like me. Edwin is in federal prison, and last I heard I'm a fugitive with outstanding warrants, but at least we're both still here.

We're no longer menaces to society.

We're just historical landmarks, baby.

Sometimes I ask myself: how did the two wildest tomcats from the last golden age of Sodom end up as the only survivors?

I came to the same conclusion as Edwin as to why God has spared us: he wants us to hand down our memories to a world that cannot possibly imagine the way Louisiana used to be. I'm told my eighty-one-year-old country cousin just finished pecking out his memoirs in Oakdale Federal Correctional Complex in Allen Parish, Louisiana. I hope he no longer has any campaigns left to run and tells the truth; he'll be more legendary than all the Rolling Stones put together if he cops to half his exploits.

As a tight-lipped gangster who never ratted once in his life, the thought never occurred to me to share my memories until the last few years. Then I realized: why not? The cops will have to go to the cemeteries and dig up my old partners in crime, and they'd better bring a couple thousand paddy wagons to carry them all. Let's be real: you can't flip on corpses who committed crimes against other corpses in a city that pretty much no longer exists.

Baby, you might as well charge me in the Supreme Court of Atlantis.

After the beating Katrina laid on New Orleans, I decided that the only way to bring the ghettos and ruins back to life was to tell the truth about what was once the most exciting city in America. New Orleans only has a future if it smartens up about its past. The Crescent City may or may not be gone, but I'll be damned if it's going to be forgotten — not after you read the stories I'm about to tell.

How's that for a sales pitch, baby?

Chapter II

Drugstore Cowboy

1936-1953

> "I neglect nothing to turn the attention of the inhabitants to agricultural pursuits, but in general they are worthless, lazy, dissolute, and most of them recoil from the labors necessary to improve the lands."
>
> ### Jean-Baptiste Le Moyne de Bienville
> The Founder of New Orleans

BABY, I'M SO COUNTRY I WAS BORN MY OWN FIRST COUSIN.

If you think that sounds like a bum rap, just try being a crook born in a town called Marksville.

In case you don't get the gag, being a crook from Marksville is like being a wolf from Sheepsville. "Marks" are a criminal's customers, victims, and dupes. Marks are the lily-white, churchgoing, average folk who make up the client base of every whorehouse, drug dealer, bookmaker, and loan shark in the world. Contrary to what television will tell you, criminals generally sell their goods to genuinely "good people", not other dirtbags.

Baby, take it from me: everybody's got their kink. If you're reading this and think that you don't, take my word that you just haven't been introduced to it yet. Call up Frenchy sometime, and get ready for a journey of discovery. Don't worry, it'll be expensive, but it'll be worth it!

Crime is the only business where the customers think that their salespersons should be sent to jail. That hypocrisy is the reason I feel like I've made an honest living in a dishonest world. I'd like to think I've done mostly good in my life; the vast majority of my sins made people smile. Nonetheless, sometimes I am overcome with doubt and shame, and for that I can thank the miniature versions of Mama and Papa Brouillette that have paced around the back of my mind for the last fifty-five years.

I believe my parents were lovingly handmade by God to ensure that I felt guilty for things I honestly don't feel are wrong. They were not hard-case, strict Catholics like you see with the Irish — I could have shook off humorless prudes like that without a second thought. My ma and pa were unbelievably sweet, laidback country folk with good hearts, which means the shame I caused them remains a bur under my saddle.

They were not particularly worldly, as you would expect from folks who raised children within spitting distance of places called Niggerfoot and Dry Prong. They could make do with little and often did. All they really held dear was their family and their good name. They didn't ask too much of me besides bringing no stain on the clean white linen of our family's reputation in our gossipy small town.

Needless to say, I let them down, and in that I was not alone.

It's not easy for my family to understand how their simple, churchgoing clan produced three of the most infamous crooks in Louisiana history. Of the three of us, they feel most humiliated by me; at least my cousin Edwin was elected Governor four times before *he* went to federal prison, and his brother Nolan had the good sense to get shot before the feds caught up with him and splashed his sins all over the newspapers.

In the mind of my parents and siblings, our family now rivals the Longs, the Lafittes, and the Marcellos for the title of the most crooked family in Louisiana history. This made Marksville a suffocating place to live for self-conscious and proud country folk.

Marksville really was nothing more than four square miles of swampy pastureland in central Louisiana. A couple thousand cow paddy-scented French Creoles, barefoot black sharecroppers, and glum Tunica and Biloxi Indians lived in Marksville, just standing around waiting for the Apocalypse to deliver them from boredom. The place can be summed up by the Marksville logo: a wagon wheel missing a spoke, which is a colonial French version of the old "a few fries short of a Happy Meal" or "a few bricks short of a load" joke.

Marksville was interesting only in that it was the northernmost home of the Cajun and Creole French, where the Mediterranean world sat on the barstool next to the redneck Deep South. Call it the Louisiana Mason-Dixon Line: the border between Catholic Louisiana and the southern part of Arkansas that happens to reside in the state of Louisiana. Go any further north than Marksville, and you were liable to get bored to death by run-of-the-mill Southern Protestant rednecks, as opposed to Marksville's equally boring French Catholic rednecks. The border really only marked the point where you could no longer get decent food and where the locals changed how they prayed and mispronounced words.

Separated by only about 150 miles from the mythical Sodom of New Orleans, Marksville residents were self-righteous about how little the honest, upstanding, hardworking country folk like them had in common with Big City People. Due to the lack of anything to do, Marksville prided itself on the idea that its citizens did nothing but go to church and work themselves to exhaustion. If you listened to what Marksville people said, you'd believe they actually thought fun was a frivolous "Big City value" unknown in those parts.

When huckster politicians barnstormed in Marskville, folks would come from miles away to see New Orleans take a good beating from the stump. Standing out in a field with their Sunday-best clothes, picnic baskets, and "sugar-tit" homemade pacifiers for their babies, the crowds would hoot and spit and holler as the politician raised hell about "them pretty boy politicians" in the Big City with their tailor-made suits, stinking cologne, and flashy "Jew-financed" campaigns. Even the New Orleans politicians would talk and dress like rednecks when in Marksville, hitching up their formless potato-sack pants real high and rolling up the sleeves of their checkered farmer's shirts and sticking their thumbs under their suspenders as they talked.

To give you an idea how alienated Marksville felt from the glamour and excitement of New Orleans, my family was ecstatic when countrified governor Huey Long called in the Louisiana National Guard to place New Orleans under martial law and crush his political opponents in the city. My father was so excited that I don't think he would have hesitated to enlist to serve in an open war between "real Louisiana" and the Crescent City.

A town like Marksville was hardly any fun for a kid born with a touch of devilment. A wild time was riding a horse; a good party was drinking in a field; a big shindig was Sunday mass or some hoedown with carefully chaperoned kids dancing to banjo pluckers and fiddlers on grass turned to tar from chewing tobacco. The nicest things about Marksville were outside town: the dusty paths along Coulee Noire, Bayou Bourbeux, and Lac Grand Bayou, perfect for fishing, mud bank crawfishing, and watching the hundreds of white pelicans mill about like drowsy hookers waiting for a call.

The best times of my childhood and adolescence were spent taking my Tennessee walking horse and later my Harley Davidson down these dusty country roads. Of course, if you didn't have a horse or a motorcycle in Marksville, you didn't have a single goddamn thing to do besides drink and screw, and I never learned how to do either until I came to New Orleans.

"Hard work is damn near as overrated as monogamy."
Huey Long

When I entered the world in 1936, I became the baby of my family in every meaning of the word. Good looks ran in the Brouillette clan, but I had the sort of looks that make everything else optional. Marksville had nothing that could compare to me; even the pelicans got insecure and started preening their feathers when I came around.

Even as a small child, I had full plump lips, creamy skin, and beautiful hair. Look at the youngest photos of me in this book: you don't think that masterpiece stuck out in the middle of the countryside? It made life very easy since my striking mom, Lilly Belle, had a weakness for beauty that she passed on to me. As her youngest and prettiest, I was always her greatest love and her most expensive and prized fashion accessory.

My sweetheart of a mom was the town clotheshorse and flirt, though as far as I know she was always strictly proper. Lilly Belle was a kind, vivacious, lovely girl whose guiltiest pleasure seemed to be dolling herself up and vamping in front of the entire congregation at Mass every Sunday. I realized pretty quick she wasn't going to church for the religion, which made me less than attentive to the Martian, I mean Latin, nonsense coming out of the priest's mouth.

Judging by my life, my ma might have gotten herself in trouble if my dad had given her the chance. Lucky for the both of them, my mom was positively queer over my old man, Percy. As long as I can remember, I was uncomfortably aware of the sexual chemistry between my parents. Even after four kids, Percy and Lilly Belle flirted so much in raunchy Cajun French that I picked up the language — well, only the blue parts.

Sometimes the French girls ask me where I learned to talk "like that," and they'd think I'm even sleazier than I look if I told them the truth — that I learned it from Mother Dearest.

Though I was my ma's little pet, my father was no mark. Percy believed that it was the duty of any man with a little brawn and a little go-get to find himself a fertile wife, a honest job, and a piece of land where he could build a house with his own two hands.

Percy constructed a large, unpainted house of the finest local cypress for his family on a grassy, cricket-filled lot, and he set about giving the prettiest girl in town a litter of babies. I was the youngest of four and the family favorite.

Having proven himself a worthy man by Marksville standards, Percy moseyed in to fatherhood like Moses carrying stone tablets. He was comfortable. He didn't ask questions and didn't brook complaints. Everybody in my family damn sure stuck to the letter of his laws. Since we never challenged him, my father was a gentle boss, and I don't recall him ever having to raise his voice or argue. He was as relaxed and hands-off as a country pops could be in those days.

Combined with my mom's indulgent temperament, you couldn't find a safer, calmer, or more stable household in the world. Even during the Depression, we lived well. I always had second servings at supper, new clothes for every school year, plenty of toys, and room in our huge backyard to kick up ant piles and hunt for frogs. I never remember wanting for a thing besides excitement.

Of course, there was a catch – the worst one.

Hard work.

My dad had to earn this secure lifestyle through manual labor. He built up a moving business from scratch by rambling around our parish, haggling over leftover crops with the local farmers, and then lugging them to the school board for a few dollars profit per load. It was the sort of elbow-grease business that an illiterate country boy with the work ethic of a pack mule can make a fine living at, and my dad soon enough owned three big sputtering moving trucks.

The problem with being the son of a pack mule is that it's inevitable you'll be harnessed up and set to work as well. Pack mules don't sire Clydesdales, after all. As soon as I was old enough to lift without breaking in half, I was hauling sacks of potatoes on and off those goddamn rigs. I hated my pa's trucks then, and in retrospect I hate them more now: I can't help but resent the only hard work I've ever done outside of a gym or a bedroom.

The moving job was bad enough on principle, but the real torture came from the weather. If you are lucky enough to have missed Marksville during your travels, take it from me: Marksville's climate is so hot that you can pull crawfish from the mud already boiled. Even the mosquitoes and alligators get lazy in that humidity. After about an hour, I was ready to dump the school lunches into the bayou and let all the sweating little kids starve as an act of mercy.

But I never said a word. My mother and the rest of my siblings were so polite, obedient, and easygoing that I really would have felt like the devil himself if I had tried to act up. It would have been unthinkable. Even as a kid, I realized that I did not have any real reason to protest; it was hardly mean of my family to expect me to work like everyone else in the family.

Besides, whenever I dared to whine, my saintly older brother, Percy Jr., pounced on the opportunity to display his superiority. That good-for-everything overachiever was liable to become Pope if my mom said it would make her happy. I always had a feeling that Percy was jealous of me since he was half good-lookin', and I was one-and-a-half good lookin'. Percy Jr. was always drawing attention to my laziness with his tirelessness, and it was only thanks to my movie-star face that I escaped harsher criticism.

My pa tried to foster my work ethic by actually paying me a fair wage for the hours I put in on those sweatbox trucks. "I'm big on rewarding a hard day's work," my smiling dad would tell me as he wiped his sun-scarred forehead with his sleeve. My father was a good, respectable, sweat-and-dirty-fingernails redneck with an appreciation for hard labor and the men who did it; he paid his men fat checks during the lean Depression years.

I tried to make my pa proud, but I was never good at playing the prince. With my good little boy crewcut and shy manner, my parents were convinced I'd make a darling altar boy, and, under compulsion, I was sent right off to Catholic school. Of course, the time our priest spent trying to transform the easily bored, deadly shy Brouillette kid into an altar boy would've been better spent trying to turn water into wine. I had a better chance of beating the Soviets to space than I did of learning Latin and satisfying that grumpy old priest and his wart-nosed, potion-brewin' nuns.

Sometimes I think I ended up a crook for no better reason than I figured a real job had to be as boring as church and Catholic school. I am like those Catholic schoolgirls who bust out and become boy-crazy at eighteen; I was so repressed and quiet growing up under those nuns that I eventually just exploded.

But how I turned out was never my ma and pa's fault, and it hurt me to know that in later years they believed that my crookedness was somehow due to their shoddy handiwork as parents. My old man and my ma should have looked at how well the rest of my siblings turned out and realized I was just a freak of nature. I never committed a single wicked act to spite my parents or to rebel against their values.

Like most people, I am wicked because it is easier and more entertaining than being good.

The only thing I could ever hold against my parents was that they named me Kent, the most horrible, white-bread name in the world. When they offered me a book deal for my life story, I said it was a goddamn line-in-the-sand deal-breaker if they intended to put that name on the cover.

History could do without the story of "Kent Brouillette."

I don't think I could have ever built a business for myself in New Orleans with a name like that. Can you imagine the incredulous looks I would've gotten if I introduced myself to some humorless, knife-scarred Sicilian prick in the French Quarter as "Kent from Marksville?"

They would've mugged me just on principle.

"The condition I let [casinos] operate on was jobs. [...] They had to give a job to anybody I sent to them. I practically ran an employment agency.
But that's politics. You got to have jobs to give."
Frank "King" Clancy
Sheriff of Jefferson Parish (1928-1956)

Baby, Louisiana has its own word for a crime boss: sheriff. I can't say I've known any Louisiana sheriff to be more straight than crooked, and I damn sure have known some gangsters who were downright gentlemanly in comparison.

I've always been a bit backwards when it comes to cops and criminals. One of my first memories came when I was a ten-year-old playing with some Lincoln Logs on the floor of our living room, and my dad told me that Al Capone had died. Old Percy spoke with this somber voice as if the news would really bother me, like the death of Roy Rogers or Mickey Mouse. Frankly, I didn't have the slightest idea who Al Capone was — I was a Louisiana country boy born many miles and a few years from Prohibition Chicago.

"Who's Al Capone, Pop?"

"Why, Al Capone was a gangster! A big time gangster," my father said, as if it shocked and somehow disappointed him that his own son did not know the name of the great Al Capone. From that point on, I had an instinctual respect for any gangster I heard about on the radio. My father gave me the impression they were real heroes of the people, Robin Hood types.

Nonetheless, I was never the sort of kid who idolized bank robbers and "Public Enemies." Like most country boys of my generation, my hero was good old Roy Rogers, the "King of the Cowboys" who I followed through his films, radio show, and later his TV program. In imitation of Roy and his animal helpers

Trigger and Bullet, I developed a lifelong affection for palomino horses and German shepherds.

Naturally, I fancied myself Roy Rogers's successor and begged my parents to arrange lessons in trick-riding for me. During my very first lesson, some ornery horse tossed me right onto my tailbone with what sure felt like homicidal intentions. As my spine buzzed like a tuning fork, I cursed for the first time of my life: "Well, fuck *this* shit!" For a future heavyweight boxer, I had no liking for pain — which is probably why I turned out to be as much of a bust as a fighter as I was as a rodeo star.

Though I had no future on horseback, I continued to leisurely practice with a gentler Tennessee walking horse. All the cool kids with money had walking horses because they were such a comfortable and smooth ride; it was like driving a Jaguar. By the time I was thirteen or fourteen, I had developed a decent hand with horses thanks to my Tennessee, and, to this day, whenever a square asks me what I do for a living, I say I'm a horse trainer.

That isn't exactly a lie. For years I did train horses — to run in fixed races. I made a lot more fixing horse races than I ever would have as a rodeo star.

One day as I was gingerly riding my Tennessee around town, a brand-new Oldsmobile Rocket 88 pulled up alongside my apprehensive horse. "Boy, that's one fine Walking Horse you have there!" said the tall man in the driver's seat, tipping his big police hat in my direction. One word brought on another, and I made my first friend in law enforcement.

Sheriff Jack Jeansonne was a fanatic about Tennessee walking horses, and he mistook my fear of the grumpier breeds of horses as a connoisseur's preference for the walking horse's smoother ride. For a kid who had already been held back twice in school, I was lucky that my good looks and shyness gave me the air of a strong, silent, mature type. Within minutes of meeting me, the man in his big sheriff's hat asked me to come on down to the police house and "Help ole T-Jack out."

Everyone knew the sheriff as T-Jack or "Little Jack"— the 'T' is short for *petit* in Cajun slang. Since I remember T-Jack being taller than most of the little red Cajuns slouching around Marksville, I have to figure that he earned his *petit* through having the same name as his daddy or some truly gigantic Cajun.

Or maybe the T stood for a secret square name - I rather be "T-Jack" than "Sheriff Trevor."

When I first shuffled into the police station like a kid stepping onto the set of a TV show, I was in complete awe of T-Jack and the title of sheriff. For a boy raised on cowboy stories, working under a real-life sheriff who moseyed around town with a revolver during the day, pimped around at night in his Rocket 88, and kept a stable of prize Tennessee walking horses was unbelievably exciting. I entertained all sorts of heroic notions about T-Jack and his gun-slinging escapades with Marksville's invisible criminal element.

I've never been a good judge of character. Even for a Louisiana sheriff, T-Jack turned out to command a shamefully lazy and disorganized police department. It was like a gang of potheads giggling in a bachelor pad. Within moments of my first visit, T-Jack placed me behind a desk and told me to answer the phone and just say "Sheriff's Department." That was my training; besides those two words, I had no idea whatsoever what to say or what to do if someone called.

As T-Jack and his deputy headed out the door, he reassured me, "Don't ya worry nah, kid, we'll jus' be down the street strappin' one on. If someone calls, jus' keep'um busy till we get back. Won't be long nah."

That afternoon, the entire on-duty staff of the Avoyelles Parish Sheriff's Department was future Public Enemy Frenchy Brouillette — barely out of junior high, too shy to answer the phone, and completely panicked. When T-Jack returned with a redder face than usual, he tipped his hat at me and said with a fine smile, "G' job, boy. Looks like we got a new hon'rary dep'ty," and tipped me a few coins.

I felt like a young Cajun Earp brother.

Overnight, I became double-tight with Sheriff T-Jack as his unpaid secretary. I'd answer the phone any old way I liked — "Hey! We're the police!"— and hand it off to whoever was nearby if it sounded serious, which was rare. If it didn't sound important, I'd blow the people off, which always pleased T-Jack. "Good 'nitiative, boy. We don't want nah people wastin' our val'ble time nah!" he'd say with his muddy boots on his desk.

Sheriff T-Jack was something of a guru to me. By TV standards, he was an embarrassment as a sheriff, but by Louisiana standards he was a class act. When it came to the criminal element in town, as far as I could tell he was the gang boss and called the shots and kept order — which is the exact job description of a traditional Louisiana sheriff. They just keep the action quiet enough not to inconvenience the businessmen or scare the mothers.

Until I met T-Jack, I thought when adults referred to Marksville as "wide open" they were talking about the lack of things to do. It was only after listening to T-Jack and his deputies that I began to realize that it was *abnormal* in 1950s America for there to be slot machines in the Main Street pharmacy, jukeboxes in the gas station, and dirty magazines in the grocery store.

I had no idea that Avoyelles Parish was supposed to have "blue laws" against the sale of alcohol, which seemed preposterous considering every adult I knew besides my parents were tanked round-the-clock. It never occurred to me that the police would decline to enforce the law until I saw Sheriff T-Jack send his friends, campaign supporters, and relatives home with a hat-over-heart apology whenever they were mistakenly dragged down to the station.

Working with T-Jack brought me to a devastating, mindblowing revelation: Marksville was an outlaw town! Of course, it was a *boring* outlaw town, but still the entire city operated according to a careless contempt for the laws of God and man. The hellfire and brimstone guilt trip my parents and the nuns were laying on me clearly wasn't the real scoop. If even the heroic Sheriff was a wicked old horndog, then what hope did a flunked altar boy like me have?

It was the police station, not Catholic school or church that made me understand that we are all hopeless sinners. In polite company, everyone talked about sin as if it was a disease that infected everyone else. In the police station, it was clear that sin infected *everyone* — Sheriff T-Jack most of all. Every week, I saw some relative or teacher or fellow churchgoer or friend of my pa's marched past my desk for something shameful.

One of the well-known ne'er-do-wells was my Uncle Morris, which my family pronounced "Myrus" since we didn't know how to talk in Marksville. In fine country style, Uncle Morris was my uncle on both sides of the family. Uncle Morris was my dad's brother, and he married my mom's sister — a pair of brothers marrying a pair of sisters, which gave our family tree a creepy mirror effect.

My mom and dad were their own in-laws, and, as I mentioned earlier, that makes me my own first cousin. That wasn't exactly unusual in Marksville; the white folks were one big family, and so were the black folks and the Indians. It's not like Marksville was a regular Ellis Island for immigrants. Visitors seemed reluctant even to stop for gas.

When my aunt died, Uncle Morris went outside the family and married a schoolteacher named Mildred. Morris was Mildred's pimp, which doesn't mean Mildred sold sex to anyone; she just worked her ass off to support Morris' lazy, carousin' ass. He was an inspiration through and through, my Uncle Morris.

Morris was smart enough never to ask Mildred to turn any actual tricks; they would have starved to death. The woman looked like an ostrich — thin neck, thin legs, sparse hair on her head, a little beaky nose, and a sour face she would pinch like she was laying an egg whenever Morris embarrassed her.

Speaking of laying eggs, that was Uncle Morris's secret to having fun. Since Mildred gave Uncle Morris hell over his booze habit because it made him feral, Morris would hide his wine bottle under his setting hen. Morris spent all day and all night concocting excuses to sneak out of the house and dig that wine bottle out from under that hen. Morris was always "checkin' on the birds," "scarin' away a coyote," "shooin' away a hawk," or "fetchin' some eggs." Since Morris went out to take a nip so often, poor Mildred thought Uncle Morris was romancing those pretty little hens, which wasn't that unlikely since it *was* Marksville and my Uncle Morris she was thinking about.

Once Uncle Morris noticed that I was turning out pretty rotten and shiftless, he took an interest in me. Morris took me "hunting" along the bayou, which was basically an excuse for him to slam liquor and tell me dirty stories. I was in awe; Uncle Morris had the perfect life! He let a girl do the work for him, drank all the time, and partied whenever he wanted. He was a countrified swinger! As you can probably tell, Sheriff T-Jack and Uncle Morris were far greater influences on me than my parents ever could have hoped to be.

"Boy, never feel sorry for havin' a good time," T-Jack would say as he swaggered out the door to raise hell with his mistress, often leaving me as the sole agent of Law & Order in our town. Those were truly words to live by.

Sheriff T-Jack and I became known as "The Drugstore Cowboys" around town since we'd mill about in riding boots in the drugstore and bullshit all afternoon. Sometimes, we'd take our Walking Horses over and tie them out front like real cowboys, which tickled me pink. Though I didn't realize it at the time, I was a perfect wingman for the hot-blooded sheriff: I was handsome enough to attract female attention but too young and shy to close the deal, leaving the job to cocky, smirking ole T-Jack. T-Jack was hardly shy about reminding all the local ladies that he carried "high-caliber" weaponry as he nonchalantly flicked his cigarette ash on the floor.

The most exciting and confusing time at the sheriff's office was "shape-up day." That was the day when T-Jack sat in his office with me and eagerly sorted through potato sacks full of coins delivered by his deputies. Each deputy would be given a list of drug stores, bars, restaurants, and country stores that contained "Indian Head" slot machines, pinball machines, pool tables, jukeboxes, and other illegal coin-operated gaming devices.

After emptying the machines, the deputies brought T-Jack the loot, which was then separated into two piles: one for T-Jack and one for "Carlos." At the end of the day, T-Jack called his most trusted deputy into the office and said, without blushing, "Take dis' bag here to Carlos' people on de double."

At the time, I thought Carlos must have been some big police official in Baton Rouge or Spanish gambling entrepreneur. Only years later would I realize that "Carlos" was Carlos Marcello and that Sheriff T-Jack was actively collecting gambling proceeds for the New Orleans Mafia and its allies, Frank Costello's mob in New York. Marcello had made his fortune as a young man by distributing Costello's slot machines throughout Louisiana and Texas using a simple marketing pitch: "We'll make you rich, or we'll make you disappear."

Later, Carlos realized that if he cut the sheriffs in on his profits, he never had to stick out his neck; anyone who refused to take his machines was raided by the police until they were run out of business or made good with Carlos. "Call in the fuckin' cavalry," I later heard Carlos mutter to one his brothers when he wanted the police sent as his muscle.

When we became friends, Carlos always had the nicest things to say about T-Jack. In retrospect, so do I. I'm sure T-Jack would have blasted away any legitimate public menace in Marksville, and I like that he never wasted time on bullshit that hurt nobody. Besides, he was partial to Carlos Marcello and Tennessee Walking Horses, and any friend of Tennessee Walking Horses and the Marcello family is a friend of mine.

❧ ❧ ❧ ❧ ❧

"Now, if you ask me, Kent should be ashamed of hisself.
The pain he put our parents through when they heard
about him carrying on with the Mafia and the loose women....
It was pitiful. Shameful. We darn near heard ev'rythin' he was up
to. That boy had a solid gold mother and father, and he broke
their hearts. For what? To carry on like a fool, that's what."

Percy Brouillette Jr.

Sometimes you can judge a book by its cover, but my good
friend Bill Elder was like a porno mag slipped into an edition of
the *New York Times*. For a majority of my years in New Orleans,
my Marksville high school buddy Bill was the Walter Cronkite of
the Crescent City, the TV newsman who knew how to read his
cue cards as if they were notes slipped to him by God. Bill even
looked trustworthy, like a wise and serious owl: round face, beady
eyes, and beakish nose.

Appearances aside, Bill was wilder and more unpredictable
than a wounded nutria rat, but he had this squinty serious look
about him that convinced folks that he could never tell a lie. Bill
used to laugh about this misconception —"Frenchy, how come
you're the infamous crook when you're a damn altar boy
compared to me?"

When I reached the public high school, I was a gorgeous
sixteen-year-old specimen in a freshman class of fourteen-year-old
puberty victims. To be honest, I never should have made it to the
public high school; the junior high school I had occasionally
attended only graduated me since I would still be there today if
they hadn't given me a free ride. I entered high school two years
behind the other boys my age, but I didn't mind; schoolwork was
easier when your friends can just give you their old homework.

I had to attend class with fourteen-year-olds, but I sure as hell
wasn't going to be seen with them outside of class. I hooked up
with a junior crew of wannabe bad boys made up of Bill Elder,

future Louisiana legal luminary Chris Roy, and Billy Guillot, who would become a professional wrestler — well, midget wrestler. Poor Billy was about knee-high, but as tough as any of my other friends, because he was not above punching a fella square in the Johnson.

That was his martial art, and an effective one it was.

Though I was still far too meek to flaunt bad behavior in my parents' faces, I decided I could at least look the part of a teenage rebel. Without the nuns to scare me, I was free to grow out my crewcut until it could be greased and slicked back and use my money to buy a Harley Davidson. When it came to fashion, I was dangerously ahead of my time: there were very few motorcycle greasers in 1952 Marksville, a couple years before a little Sicilian in New Orleans recorded Little Richard's first records and gave birth to rock 'n' roll.

My mentor Bill Elder was something of a genius as a prankster, so I studied up and tried to one-up Bill to prove my bad boy bona fides. Though I was more cowardly and less creative than Bill, I had the advantage of knowing all the town gossip from working for T-Jack. For example, I heard one Italian guy in town had a real battle-axe of a wife, so I put lipstick on the back of his collar while he was playing pool. That night, T-Jack was called because the old lady was assaulting that tubby Italian with tin cans.

A few months later, my gang decided to capitalize on the UFO craze sweeping the nation. We wrapped cotton around one end of six strips of haywire and then tied the other end of the haywire around the legs of six buzzards that we had captured in traps. Before we released the buzzards in the middle of the night, we soaked the cotton in gasoline and lit it on fire. As the panicking buzzards swarmed back and forth through the air, the entire town saw the night sky illuminated by inexplicable balls of fire. My deeply religious mom swore to her death that she had actually seen "little green men" looking at her through the windows of their spacecraft that night.

Years later in New Orleans, Bill pulled me aside. "You ever think how lucky we were that we didn't burn down that entire goddamn town?"

No matter how tough Bill and I acted around boys, we weren't exactly swashbucklers when it came to the ladies. I fled at the sight of any creature that threatened to be pretty, and, when ambushed, I couldn't muster a single syllable. Unfortunately, this silent act gave me the appearance of a brooding, mysterious, misunderstood teenage rebel, which made me completely irresistible. Girls hunted me down like there was a bounty on my head, but none of them wild bitches collected. My motorcycle was too fast.

No matter what you hear about Catholic schoolgirls or the supposedly prim and proper women of the 1950s, them girls were *hardly* ladies. Them Marksville girls made *me* feel cheap and exploited; they were only after one thing! One local beauty queen, who failed to convince me to corrupt her, threw a fit and shrieked, "Either something's wrong with me, or something's *very* wrong with you!"

The only girl I graced with my attention was a pretty little thing named Mary, who I slipped the tongue under extreme duress. Our romancing was strictly a product of compulsion. Mary had taken a ride with Bill, Chris, and me in Bill's truck out to the countryside around the Indian reservation with the intent of forcing her tongue down all three of our throats. Though I wasn't interested, to turn her down in front of the boys would have been no different than slipping into a dress and changing my name to Sue-Ellen. I sucked up my fear and took to kissing like a naughty dog having his face rubbed in the crap he took on the carpet.

Of course, afterwards we all carried on like we had really achieved an impressive conquest that night, which was pretty funny because it turned out that loose Mary would become a hooker of great infamy as an adult. We were like Columbus planting our flag on land that I later found out was already plenty populated.

Though I only necked with Marksville's foremost future whore, I did manage to stand up the only United States Senator in Marksville's history. Her name was Elaine, and she was the college-age wife of my cousin Edwin Edwards. Now, don't get the wrong idea: the future First Lady of Louisiana and United States Senator did not come on to teenage Frenchy *sexually*.

No, Madam Senator did something far worse: she tried to make me dance with her at a local hoedown! I would have signed up for the seminary before agreeing to shuck and jive on that dance floor for the entire goddamn town to see. Instead, I pawned Elaine off on the only gay kid I knew in Marksville, who incidentally could dance like Ginger Rogers.

Though we tried our rotten best, in general, the quality of me and Bill's hell-raising was so poor that the devil wouldn't have taken our souls if we had offered him a 2-for-1 discount. My high school report card gradually became a rap sheet, but it was all strictly misdemeanor beefs. I made sure my schoolyard hijinks never interfered with my family life. To be honest, there wasn't any percentage in being a bad kid at home; being good paid too well. I needed my family to subsidize my fleet of horses and motorcycles.

To the eternal fury of my old maid of an older brother, Percy, my family never missed an opportunity to spoil me. Whereas Percy had to buy his own Harley Davidson himself, my parents kicked in a little cash when I purchased mine. When I crashed that Harley before the factory polish wore off, my parents insisted that Percy give me one of his souped-up Harleys, which I also promptly crashed. Handyman Percy was then asked to repair the bike so I could give totaling the thing another try.

This turned my big brother pretty sour on me. Percy was Jan Brady before Jan Brady came on the scene. It became thin, prematurely balding Percy's crusade to convince my parents that I shouldn't be allowed to pilot any contraption with a fossil fuel engine, especially a motorcycle. My sweet-natured, indulgent parents of course ignored him.

Desperate to stomp on my toes, Percy tried to report me to Sheriff T-Jack for riding my motorcycle without a license. My fellow Drugstore Cowboy and I enjoyed a good laugh. "Sumpthin' wrong with that brother of yours, huh, boy? He ain't no fun," T-Jack teased in between swigs of afternoon whiskey.

Unlike his notorious brother, Percy would stay in Marksville and live with my parents until their death. If you know where to look, you'll still find him at the Brouillette homestead, which he has left completely unchanged under a coating of dust ever since my ma and pa's deaths decades ago. Despite being roughly the same age as Teddy Roosevelt, Percy still works seven days a week — without pay and without complaint. He is the sort who believes hard work heals the soul.

Percy Jr. is a good man who never understood me and whom I will never understand either, but I hope that he knows that I love him nonetheless. Sorry about your Harley, Percy, and also about that Cadillac of yours that I totaled, and for missing ma's funeral, and for just about everything else besides. None of it was personal.

⚜ ⚜ ⚜ ⚜ ⚜

"Rounders and ramblers and gamblers and hoboes and wayfaring strangers and unfortunate rakes hurtling toward siren-song cities that shine atop distant plateus at the end of the line ... New Orleans. The road to possibility, rendered in steel and steam and thunder."

<u>Ted Anthony</u>
Chasing the Rising Sun

You can blame my criminal career on good old Jack LaLanne. Poor clean-living Jack LaLanne: I feel I let him down worse than my family. If I were to join any religion, I'd follow Jack LaLanne's clean-living gospel — hands down. When it comes to the rules of healthy living that Jack LaLanne taught me, never have my beliefs and my behavior been further apart.

Bodybuilding turned out to be my life's great passion. Nothing else has inspired me to voluntarily consent to hard work. I first became aware of Jack and the 1950s bodybuilding subculture when a muscled-up kid from Brooklyn was sent down to live with relatives in Marksville.

Not since Lucifer fell from Heaven to Hell has someone took a spill quite like that. I can't imagine what he did to deserve *that* fate — putting the poor kid down would have been more humane.

My life was changed by one of my new friend's bodybuilding magazines, which happened to contain a story on fitness guru Jack LaLanne. Though Jack was nearly three times my age, he was performing superhuman stunts like swimming from Alcatraz to San Francisco while handcuffed or whipping off 1000 pushups in a row. For a shy and square kid like me, seeing this wholesome American guy parading around with all these massive muscles and incredible world records was a life-changing revelation.

Jack LaLanne was my rock star. He was Elvis. Other kids of my generation were inspired to pick up guitars to make themselves cool - I picked up dumbbells.

Though I was too tongue-tied to speak for myself, Jack taught me that I could let my *body* speak for me. I was sure that people outside of Marksville would take one look at a muscular man and think of toughness, discipline, and self-confidence. Since I kept my mouth shut, it would take a long time for a stranger's first impression of my character to be erased by reality.

Jack was just an average, approachable guy who worked so hard that he managed to turn himself into a god amongst men. Jack honestly made your everyday pipsqueak think he could become the coolest and toughest guy around. Hard work made sense to me on these terms, so I decided to lift and sweat my way up the food chain.

To Percy's steaming outrage, my wonderful parents did not hesitate to embrace my new obsession and encouraged me to become the best freak of nature I could be. My ma mail-ordered me a professional barbell and chin-up set, and my dad spent a weekend building a tin-roof shed in our yard as my own personal gym.

It took my poor mom weeks to find the weird muscle magazines I wanted. Don't forget: bodybuilding was a new and bizarre fad, a bunch of oiled-up, damn-near-naked men showing off their muscles to each other like fruitcakes. The few stores that stocked bodybuilding magazines hid Jack LaLanne under the counter with Betty Page and naughty Tijuana comics.

A lot of good Catholic mothers in Marksville would have thought their son was going a little queer on them, but my mom just thought my beefcake obsession was funny. She couldn't help but laugh and shake her head every morning as she watched me drinking my raw eggs and protein powder cocktail.

Cajun people love to eat, so the bodybuilder's diet creeped my family out more than the fruitiness. Percy looked at me across the dinner table as if I was desecrating the communion host by eating healthy, but his scowls were my inspiration to lap up my bland food like it was dinner at Antoine's. I insisted on eating broiled calf liver while everyone else was gobbling down fried chicken, pork and beans, buttered biscuits, and tall glasses of creamy café au lait. They teased me every night, going on and on about how tasty their slice of pie or drumstick was.

I spent every free hour, day or night, in my workout shed. With nothing more than free weights, a chin up bar, and plenty of eggs and liver, I constructed a body that compared favorably to the jacked-up steroid monkeys of the past forty years — myself included. I had a prison physique: a body honed to perfection out of lack of anything else to do.

I quickly discovered, however, that my awesomely overdeveloped build had no effect on my social life. I was still scared of girls, still didn't know how to talk to strangers, still couldn't find anything interesting to do in Marksville, and still couldn't muster the courage to have any sort of fun that might get back to my family.

I just looked like Hercules now.

Unfortunately, my brain was not keeping pace with the growth of my muscles: my dad barely saved my little buddy Billy Guillot's life when he walked in on me suspending Billy from my chin-up bar with 150 pounds of weights tied to his ankles. My dad was not impressed when I told him that I was just trying to do Billy a favor by "stretching the midget out."

In retrospect, that sounds dirtier than I understood at the time.

A few weeks later, my friends Bill Elder and Chris Roy had a school exam that they were panicked about. "Don't worry about it," I told them, portraying the stone-cool leader of the pack.

Eager to impress my pals, that night I snuck over to our school and jimmied the window to the teacher's classroom. I tiptoed to her desk, pulled out two copies of the test from her files, and exited the way I entered. With the test in hand, Bill and Chris figured they were made; they filled out the answers with their books at home and carried their copies into class to substitute with the real thing.

There was only one problem: those two dummies didn't check to make sure the test I grabbed was really the one they were given. I either grabbed the wrong test, or the teacher changed her mind; the test she gave Bill and Chris' class was definitely not the one I stole. They received a perfect score on both tests 100% on the test they turned in and 0% on the actual test given to the class that day.

Even for two brilliant kids, there was no way for Bill and Chris to talk their way out of that scheme. They were caught dead to rights for cheating, burglary, and first-degree stupidity. Bill Elder and Chris Roy were dragged into the principal's office in front of the entire school, and expulsion seemed like the only reasonable punishment for cheating twice on the same test.

That wasn't going to work for me — Bill and Chris were great students with lots of potential. They didn't deserve to be kneecapped over a silly quiz. I went to the bathroom, slicked back my hair, threw on my leather coat, and shouldered my way into the principal's office.

"Brouillette, what do you think you're doin'?" the principal shouted as I clomped into his office.

"I'm not goin' to let these two kids take the fall. I put them up to it and made them do it, see? I broke into school and stole that test myself. These two weren't gonna say no to someone like me..." I paused, trying to think of what a legitimate bad apple would say. "Uh, ya hear? That's right, see."

Of course, this story was pretty far-fetched — why would a bully force two kids in higher grades to cheat on their own tests? Besides, everyone knew that Bill, Chris, and I were all tight, double-tight. But look at it from the principal's perspective: he could have lost two of his best and most promising students, or he could have blamed a muscled-up biker who was going to fail out of school anyway. That afternoon, I was expelled, and Bill and Chris went on to successful careers.

At first, my expulsion was a relief — I was paroled from school two years early. I remember running out of that damn high school, feeling that hot humid breeze on my face and rejoicing that I was done listening to teachers for the rest of my life. I was free to bullshit all day with T-Jack, ride horses, and blast around town on my motorcycle. If I told the Sheriff of my desperate circumstances, maybe I could become an official, on-salary deputy. Working for the Louisiana police meant that my life would be a paid vacation, a crime spree with a regular paycheck courtesy of the tax payers.

I was halfway down to the police station when an awful blues crept over me. I may have been free from school, but I was not free of my parents and the grip they maintained on my spirits. I had let them down; I had wasted their money, wasted their time, and laid waste to their good reputation.

My conscience has always been a sneaky pickpocket snatching away my joy before I suspect a thing.

Marksville was a small town and a small-minded town; my misbehavior would become common knowledge by sundown, and my parents would be blamed. I had ruined the Brouillette name. Now my parents would hear whispers in church that the Brouillette boy was a bully, a cheater, and a teenage delinquent; they would become notorious failures as parents.

I thought that this would be the end of my parents' patience and gentle treatment of the family's black sheep. I couldn't face their anger; the idea made me sick. I hid out in my workout shed and lifted weights until I nearly passed out, listening hard for one of my dad's big trucks to pull up the driveway. Surely, someone would tell him before the night was over, and I would *really* get the ass-kicking I had deserved for years for being lazy and shitless.

Finally, I heard a rap on the shed, and there was a holler to come inside. My brother Percy, his eyebrows bunched low and to the middle, escorted me to the gallows. I was so dehydrated from sweating that I was slipping and stumbling into the house like a wino. I'm sure I cut a pretty pathetic figure to my mom and pops, who were standing close together in a corner of the kitchen like two cops hashing out a line of questioning before an interrogation.

I knew I had it coming. I sat down at the kitchen table, hung my head down almost to my knees, and waited. I looked like I was about to cry since my eyes were pinched and burning from the sweat mixed with hair grease that had poured down from my scalp.

I looked pitiful enough to shoot, which made it even easier than usual for my good-hearted parents to let me off. "It's not like a diploma was ever going to do you any good, Kent," my dad started. That woke me right up, both because it was the truth and the sort of truth that you never hear parents admitting.

I couldn't believe it: my parents let me off *again*. It was easy for them in this instance; my family was made up of pragmatic country people who had prospered for generations without resorting to "sissy shit" like diplomas and book learning.

As far as my ma and pops told me, their son becoming the town disgrace was all for the best: I wouldn't waste any more of the school's time, the school wouldn't waste any more of my time, and I could work full-time on my dad's trucks and make an honest living. My parents even seemed optimistic, as I had to have a better chance of redeeming myself by delivering lunches to the schoolhouse than I ever did filling out quizzes inside the schoolhouse.

I was destroyed — the only thing worse than school was those damn hellbox trucks. A lifetime spent carrying potatoes back and forth in 100-degree swamp heat was worse than a death sentence. With a life like that, the only way I'd ever be able to notice when I had died and gone to Hell would be when my fellow potato-haulers suddenly became guys like Stalin and Jack the Ripper. No matter how big a coward I was, I could never allow this life to happen to me.

Worse than my fear of decades spent as a potato-jockey was the heartsickness I felt at my ma and pa's response. I can't explain it, but my parents' gentle, understanding attitude shattered my state of mind like a Bourbon Street beer bottle. All at once, I couldn't take it anymore.

The guilt was too much. If my dad had given me a good ass-kicking, today I'd probably be lugging potatoes with Percy Jr. or enjoying life as the retired sheriff of Avoyelles Parish. However, when my parents went on being saints even after I copped to being a burglar and cheat, I realized I could never stand living around people *this* good. It would be a drag. I would always feel like a bum in comparison, no matter how much I matured.

At that moment, I decided that I would sooner drive Percy's Harley straight into the bayou than spend every day living in the shadow of my suffering, saintly parents. It would be like watching one of those "kids are starving in Africa!" TV commercials on a loop forever, just a lifetime guilt trip.

So I ran away. With decades of going back and forth across Marksville in a vegetable truck as my future, the decision to take a chance on a new life as a highway tramp was easy. I jumped on Percy's pieced-together Frankenstein of a Harley Davidson and set off for New Orleans. I was seventeen years old. It was 1953. I was about to suffer a bout of culture shock that I'm not sure has ever ended.

Not since Huck Finn took a ride down the Mississippi has an innocent country boy gotten himself into more unexpected trouble.

Chapter III

Frenchy Arrives

1953-1954

> "Night is the sick man's day,
> For the soul wakens as the body fails. ...
> And, loosed as if the school-time of a life
> Were over, with its spirit-checking toils,
> We to the fields stray — following where'er
> Fancy, the vagrant, calls us!"
>
> **N.P. Willis**
> *The Daily Picayune*
> New Orleans
> 11-26-1848

IT CAME AS NO SURPRISE TO ANYONE IN MARKSVILLE THAT I MADE FOR ORLEANS PARISH CRIMINAL COURT AT TOP SPEED. It was the tradition for Marksville's dropouts, tramps, runaways, and crooks to head for the Big City via Highway 61, which came to a stop at the steps of New Orleans' grim criminal courthouse.

This was seen as a positively profound coincidence in Marksville and New Orleans alike, since natives of both towns agreed that Highway 61 was the pipe that drained the toilet bowl of the countryside down to the sewer of Sin City. In the mind of just about everyone, I was just another ignorant, starry-eyed, redneck shitkicker on my way to being flushed and forgotten in New Orleans.

Technically, Highway 61 didn't lead all the way down to New Orleans — they decided to complicate my story by naming the last stretch Airline Highway at old Huey Long's suggestion. Supposedly, Governor Huey got tired of driving the winding, carsick route down from the state capitol in Baton Rouge to all of his favorite bars, clubs, and brothels in New Orleans, so he had a new straight-shot road built to lessen his travel time and stress. This road was so level, straight, and empty that it reminded him of an airport runway — and that's where Airline Highway got its name.

This supposed airport runway didn't lead up and away; it was a gradual nosedive from the comparable high ground of Baton Rouge down to the stagnant, steaming, pestilential, below sea-level mud bowl of New Orleans. That's all southeast Louisiana is: a few feet of muddy, rockless river silt spread thinly over the sea like a layer of chocolate icing. That entire section of the state has been sinking and dissolving away into the Gulf of Mexico ever since we dammed up the Mississippi River to prevent flooding — which hasn't proven particularly effective last I looked around what's left of this town.

And trust me, when you rode down to New Orleans for the first time in those days, it felt like you driving on a mud-covered water bed. The roads became bumpy, wavy, potholed, and cracked. In my first week in New Orleans, I saw an entire car fall into a pothole and stick out like a duck diving ass-up for fish. With globs of mosquito and dragon fly splattered all over my face, I blasted down Airline Highway, bobbing and weaving past the mud puddles, gravel hills, and gaping caverns that defaced the road at irregular intervals like acne.

As both the approach and the escape route for the sleaziest tourist city in the South, Airline Highway was sort of a bum's row of fast food joints, motels, honkytonks, pawn shops, and eyesore businesses. Compared to how ghetto the area would become during the '70s and '80s, when disreputable folk like televangelist Jimmy Swaggart and Frenchy Brouillette would regularly get busted there, Airline was positively ritzy in 1953, but it still chilled me to my bones.

I had never been outside of my tiny hometown, so the great sprawling mess of motels and businesses seemed like a bona fide metropolis. Coming from religious country, just *the idea* of all those roadside motels full of vacationing unmarried couples, husbands and their mistresses, and highway ladies of the night made me feel nervous and perilously close to deadly temptations.

On my way into New Orleans proper, I passed the Town & Country Motel at 1225 Airline Highway, the headquarters of Carlos Marcello and the New Orleans Mafia. The Town & Country complex was inconspicuous, nothing more than a plain roadside motel building, a low-ceilinged diner, and a little shitbox brick office in the back for Carlos. Even its location was intentionally humble; you would not figure that the Mafia, with all of the state to choose from, would pick a dumpy Airline Highway motel just over the Orleans Parish line. I zipped by the Town & Country without the slightest idea that it was where Sheriff T-Jack sent all the jukebox and slot machine loot from Marksville.

That was one of the quirks of the New Orleans Mafia: besides the French Quarter, the crime family's operations were primarily based outside of New Orleans in the suburbs and boondocks. The Mafia flourished along the West Bank of the Mississippi (so backward it's locally known as "The Wank") and in Jefferson Parish, a narrow strip of largely swampy land directly to the west of Orleans Parish. In honor of former barkeep and bootlegger Carlos Marcello, Jefferson Parish is fittingly shaped like a bottle opener standing upright. Carlos owned over 6000 acres of swampland in the area, and whole towns along the Gulf of Mexico and its inlets survived off his smuggling ("shrimping") businesses.

You couldn't do a damn thing in Jefferson Parish without Carlos. His cronies infested the parish government and police department, allowing his soldiers to establish local criminal monopolies in all of Jefferson's towns: Metairie, Gretna, Kenner, Terrytown, Grand Isle, Avondale, Westwego, Marrero, Harvey, and Jean Lafitte. If you live in Jefferson Parish today, just about everything around you can be traced directly back to Carlos' money: contractors he put in business, banks that made their profits off his money laundering, bars and restaurants that lived off his jukeboxes and slot machines, swamps cleared and rivers dammed and levees built thanks to his bribery of the state government.

You can especially thank Carlos for the fact that you can get better greaseball Italian food on the outskirts of New Orleans than in the city itself. New Orleans would kill for restaurants as good as joints like Tony Angello's, Mosca's, Impastato's, Carmine's, and Sal and Judy's.

Within a minute or two of passing by Carlos' headquarters, I entered Orleans Parish and found my way to Canal Street, the road a gas station attendant told me led to the legendary French Quarter nightlife district. It was on Canal Street where New Orleans first delivered a "You're not in Marksville anymore, Dorothy" smack upside my pretty head.

I slowed down my sputtering Harley in confusion. I was reluctant to stop, but my curiosity overruled my fear when I saw what appeared to be a voodoo temple in the middle of a Christian cemetery in which every spot was filled by imposing above-ground vault. The tombs I knew in Marksville were just thin concrete slabs lying on the ground like baseball cards, but these New Orleans tombs were actual *homes*, or even mansions.

As any tourist will tell you, the dead in New Orleans are buried in aboveground tombs, half out of European tradition and half because you can't bury bodies in three feet of river silt and expect them to stay buried. In fact, they say it's impossible to "bury" a body in New Orleans; all you can do is *sink* a corpse by drilling holes in the casket and standing it on one end to make it fill with water. I wouldn't know – I swear, honest injun, I've never had to bury a body.

The shallow Earth explains why New Orleans cemeteries are aboveground affairs, but only big city stupidity can explain why people spend tens of thousands of dollars building marble temples to house their melting corpses in pestilential heat. They say the heat is so bad in those "oven" tombs that the bodies just explode after a few days, after all.

I parked my bike on the street and strolled over, with my jaw flapping, to a huge burial complex. The "tomb," if you want to call it that, had three levels: a columned marble mausoleum with a bronze door on the bottom, a large dirt mound sitting atop the mausoleum like a grassy toupee, and then a gigantic bronze statue of an elk atop the mound.

This triple-decker reefer madness hallucination could not be real; surely I was suffering from heat stroke. As best as my little mind could figure, the only way to justify the cost of building a marble building, covering it with dirt, and then topping it off with a giant elk statue was that the zoo had a star-attraction elk that had died. It never occurred to me that the statue might be commemorating members of an Elks Lodge — or that some ratty elk sweating its fur off in the Louisiana heat was unlikely to become a star zoo attraction.

I stumbled over from tomb to tomb in disbelief, weary and unsettled by the fact that what I was seeing was real. I marveled at the graves built with tons of granite and polished marble, surrounded by fine sculptures, and fortified with Gothic-style gates of curlicue black iron.

I felt like Indiana Jones stumbling upon the ruins of some great, lost city of maniacs. I figured most of these wealthy, old fuddy-duddies had probably been buried after their kids killed them when they heard that their inheritance was being spent at the cemetery.

That cemetery was my first impression of New Orleans, and it left me in no doubt about the truth: New Orleans was stone crazy, and I was a dirt-poor nobody with absolutely no idea how life worked in the Big City.

Canal Street was called "Dead Man's Street" by some of the local characters since it began in a mess of nineteenth century cemeteries and ended at the Mississippi River, where all the other bodies were dumped. Revving my Harley and following Canal Street into the center of the town, I discovered that New Orleans was incomprehensibly wealthier and more cosmopolitan than I had imagined *any* town could be. In those days, the last stretch of Canal Street with its *eight lanes of traffic* was maybe the most cosmopolitan thoroughfare you could find in America outside of Manhattan or Chicago. On either side of the street were three bumper-to-bumper lanes heading in opposite directions; the middle two lanes, for New Orleans's famous streetcars, were decorated with rows of tall bronze Parisian lampposts.

You have to remember, as strange it sounds, New Orleans was one of the wealthiest cities in 1953 America. In those days, only New York could boast of richer port traffic, and Las Vegas hadn't yet caught up in gambling and drug commerce. New Orleans was a tropical underworld boomtown greater than the Havana of its day.

On Canal Street, it looked the part. Celebrities and royalty stayed on Canal Street, rooming at the Hotel Monteleone or the Roosevelt Hotel, taking in shows at the Saenger Theater, drinking at the swanky Sazerac bar, and dancing at the lavish Blue Room nightclub frequented by stylish Mafia millionaires like Frank Costello, "Dandy" Phil Kastel, and Meyer Lansky – men the press called "sportsmen." The women walking along the sidewalks clip-clopped in leather high heels and finely flowing red dresses; the men tooled around with their jeweled fingers shamelessly squeezing their dates' asses.

By the time I got to the heart of this avenue of riches, it was nightfall, which meant that the streetlamps were flaming, and the storefront signs sparked up, glowing with electric light. The buildings on both sides were all huge, multi-story, boxlike buildings — department stores, hotels, movie theaters, concert halls — that were decorated with large, illuminated signs to catch the eye.

The parallel lines of glowing lampposts gave Canal Street the appearance of an interstellar landing strip for UFOs, and, baby, that sure fit. Driving down that road made me feel like I had been abducted and dumped in an alien civilization. I couldn't believe my eyes: the size of the buildings and the mega-wattage of electricity and the clothing styles of the pedestrians bore no sign of the human society I knew from Marksville.

And hallelujah for that! I was a shiftless, sexless, bored country boy who had the good fortune to obliviously stumble into the neon hellfire of the sexiest, dirtiest, most glamorous underworld city in America. All of my prayers had been answered; finally, life was interesting.

And life was about to get devilishly interesting. I hung a left at the end of Canal Street onto Decatur Street and entered the French Quarter.

⚜ ⚜ ⚜ ⚜ ⚜

"I have to tell you, in the '40s and '50s, the French Quarter was elegant. Most of the women would wear hats and furs and beautiful dresses to watch the burlesque shows. It was not uncommon for me to put on a lovely evening gown after performing and waltz out to dine with celebrities and millionaires at 'Diamond' Jim Moran's."
Kitty "Evangeline the Oyster Girl" West
Burlesque Legend

Kids in Marksville learned about the French Quarter about the same time they were told about the bogeyman and the dire need to say a Hail Mary before bedtime. The French Quarter was where innocent souls were ruined: where Big City dads bought their sons hookers on their thirteenth birthday; where high school kids took their dates to get liquored up and corrupted; where sleazy tourists searched in vain for the "live sex shows" spoken of so frequently in local lore.

That this snake pit of sleaze had infested the most historic neighborhood in Louisiana only added to its infamy and shame. Everyone in upstate, uptight Louisiana shook their judgmental heads at the idea that an entire district of irreplaceable centuries-old French and Spanish colonial architecture was being helplessly desecrated by every manner of perverse vice operator. Go-go joints, bordellos, porno shops, honky-tonk dance lounges, and rip-roaring bars inhabited the ruins of Old New Orleans, and these businesses, as shameless and gaudy and neon and colorful and dirty as they were, were as classy and classic as the Parthenon compared to the carny dirtbags that infested them like a horde of masturbating spider monkeys.

"Hey, Mac, yah wanna party?" one swarthy Spanish cabbie called out to me as he leaned lazily on his curbside parked taxi.

"Hey there...ah, kid, you look like you need to party *bad*, man!" sneered a fat, red-faced hack lounging on the next taxi parked along Bourbon Street.

"Man, don't worry about dese fools none, boy," said the next hack, a wiry Italian with a pencil mustache and greased hair, as he hopped next to me on the sidewalk with quick spidery legs. "Besides, dese cats couldn't find ya a *real* party if dey were locked up in a women's prison, ya hear?"

"Hey thar, ya fuckin' hacks!" bellowed the fattest and sweatiest man I've ever seen, a splat of mashed potatoes wrapped in a New Orleans Police Department uniform. "Stop steerin' that Vidalia! Stop pandrin'! Don't ya know that ya fucks can't park out 'ere on Ber-bonn no mah?"

Outside of a zoo, I don't think I've ever seen larger animals than the pigs that worked for the NOPD in the 1950s. Back in those days, the Mayor distributed patronage to his supporters by sending paychecks to 3000 roustabouts and bums as "rat catchers," so you can imagine how crooked the contemporary

NOPD hiring policies were. As far as I could tell, the qualifications for becoming a French Quarter beat cop were poor health, alcoholism, and a close family relationship with a bookmaker in the neighborhood. The only "crime" these tubs of shit fought was NITQ — Nigger In The Quarter.

The enormous walrus cop blasted me with his shitty beer breath and threw his arm around my muscular shoulders to keep upright. As he sidled over, I notice that his shirt was untucked, his pants piss-stained, and his zipper completely down. "List'n nup nah, boy," the cop slurred into my ear. "Dontcha trus' those hacks, nah. These fleece ya good; mickey you right up!"

My head was suddenly jerked into a headlock, my jaw crushed up against the cop's warm, sweaty bosom. "Nah, if you wanna par-tay, boy..." he said with a dirty, rotten whisper. "I kens take care of dat!"

I squirmed free and hustled across the busy street. The only thing more unsettled than my mind was my stomach, which was agitating against me like an inmate clanking his tin cup against the bars of his cell. I was brushing my bottom lip with my teeth and pawing at my belly, thanks to the aromas steaming out of every restaurant I passed.

Coming from the country, I had never smelled food that made its point with such fury; the flavors were temperamental. One patch of sidewalk was sweltering with the scent of crawfish simmering in a dark roux sauce, the next with the musk of peppery andouille sausage in smoking tubs of gumbo, the one after that with fresh oysters char-grilled with a glaze of garlic butter and a powdering of Romano cheese.

I did not feel safe or worldly enough to brave a French Quarter restaurant on my first night, so I sought simpler comforts. At a safe distance from the cop and the cabbies, I zeroed in on a Lucky Dog hotdog stand and decided to take a moment to calm myself down. By the way, it should come as no surprise that the world record for Lucky Dog consumption is held by a French Quarter NOPD officer!

I ordered myself a dog and a Coke. I dabbed my forehead on my sleeve and looked around nervously. "Hot, ain't it, Mac?" asked the friendly young guy making my hotdog. I smiled — finally, a normal, sane person to talk to!

"Yeah, ya...ugh, boy, it sure is, really hot," I said, shy and stumbling over my words as always.

"Damn right, it's hotter than a two-dollar pistol out here!" the hot dog jockey said as he tonged pounds of toppings onto my dog without asking. I had no idea what that phrase meant; I figured a "two-dollar pistol" must have been hot because it was recently fired, not because it was stolen.

"Yeah, hot as a pistol alright!" I squeaked with a dumb smile.

"Yeah, you know what's good for the heat?" he asked with a smirk. I figured he'd say a root beer or lemon ice. "A good lay. You in the mood to get laid, huh? You look like a stud, alright," he said encouragingly.

"Uh, nah, not tonight. Already had some," I mumbled, grabbing the hot dog with a shaky hand.

"You ain't queer, are ya?" the hot dog vendor asked, suddenly pushy. "Because, if ya are," he continued with a hooked eyebrow. "I can take care of *dat* too. I know a hot dog boy who would put that sausage to shame. All it would cost..."

I walked away in one hell of a hurry. Everyone in this goddamn town was trying to get me laid, and I was so stupid that I didn't take them up on it! You ain't never seen a more pimped out place than the French Quarter in the 1950s; every bellboy, beat cop, cabbie, cashier, and hot dog vendor had commission arrangements with local pimps and bordellos.

You'd walk down Bourbon Street in prime hours and see bums raiding hotdog stands that were left completely abandoned. A vendor would be in too much of a hurry to run off with a big-money john to close up shop, and his wares would be left undefended while he waited for hours at a bordello for his mark to finish up. Once the mark finished, then the hotdog boy could calculate his commission and receive it immediately from the madam — and immediately write a check to the Lucky Dog people for the lost inventory.

You didn't mess with the Lucky Dog people. They employed more violent ex-cons than Carlos.

All these pimps and assistant pimps were called "procurers" and "steerers" in those days, and their prey were called Vidalias. I was *definitely* a Vidalia: a no-nothin' out-of-town sonofabitch beggin' to be fleeced.

There are two stories about how the term Vidalia for a tourist came into use. The true story is that there was a rich lumberman from the tiny town of Vidalia, Louisiana, who would regularly travel down to New Orleans to carouse with gamblers, dealers, and whores until his cash ran out. This mark spent dough like he was a counterfeiter afraid to hold on to the stuff.

Because they all received a commission on his swinging, the town's procurers staked out prime locations whenever the word was out that the man from Vidalia was on the prowl. The procurer who "hooked" the lumberman could retire off his share of a weekend partying spree. Soon enough, all the madams and bar owners started promising bonuses to their procurers and barkers if they brought in "a Vidalia"— which gradually changed its meaning from a rich mark to any old out-of-town dummy.

The other explanation for the term Vidalia is a total hype-job engineered by the best hype artist the Quarter has ever seen — my good friend and mentor, Norma Wallace, the infamous New Orleans madam. Norma sought an opportunity to burnish her legend by naming one of her many little yappy dogs Vidalia; she then told all of her young and gullible associates that the age-old term was derived from her puppy. Generations grew up listening to that bullshit and eventually it became "the truth."

As I shuffled around the Quarter with a Lucky Dog in my mouth, I was one overwhelmed Vidalia.

The sidewalks in the Quarter resembled one long row of carnival attractions. In a dazzling procession, I passed by blind bluesmen, three-card monte scammers, redneck coonasses selling live crawfish and iced shrimp, mimes, acrobats, hobo clowns, shuck and jiving dancers, deformed circus freaks shaking tin cans, a toothless drooling old mongrel dancing wildly with a cane and sunglasses, and an old Spanish lady crawling on her knees holding a giant cross and a statue of a saint.

Everyone was shabbily dressed and prematurely weathered, dried, and burnt down by the New Orleans sun. It was as if every raving mad, outlaw carny ever kicked out of a circus had been forcefully resettled down in one neighborhood, like a leper colony that referred to the condition of your soul instead of your skin.

And it sounded like the circus, too. The street was an insane orgy of overlapping rackets, music of a dozen different genres blasting out from the clubs and lounges at teeth-cracking volumes. All along Bourbon Street were neon-lit go-go joints that showcased world-famous showgirls, and each one of these palaces of sin employed a house band that was amplified beyond reason to deafen and confuse the passerby. It was the sound of sin tuning up: the headboard-slamming of a walloped drum, the braying trumpets, wild switchblade licks of blues guitar, and the fuzzy electric holler of a foamy lipped singer.

To add this hellacious racket, each go-go joint employed a carnival barker on the sidewalk to yell over this metallic mess and convince pedestrians to step inside. In front of each club's glowing, buzzing, electric door-signs and red awnings stood the barker, dressed to impress, pouring sweat, and red-faced from overexertion.

"Come one and all to see the incredible, the glamorous, the exotic, the world renowned femme fatale of the French Quarter — Evangeline the Oyster Girl! *Only* at the internationally famous GUNGA DEN club!" called out one barker. "This temptress of the deep emerges on a giant oyster shell like Venus, the goddess of love, and, boy, does she live up to the comparison, ladies and gentleman!"

"Tonight, an exclusive superstar revue at the CASINO ROYALE!" spit out another barker; this time with the speed and tone of a racetrack announcer. "A full night's slate of entertainment, from hilarious comedy to stupefying magic to velvety crooning that will leave the ladies swooning, all topped off by the most seductive and electrifying stage performer in the *world* today, Alouette LeBlanc! The CASINO ROYALE paid top dollar to convince the toast of Parisian society, the tassel-twirling Alouette LeBlanc, to abandon her exclusive spot with the Folies Bergère in Paris— Paris, *France!*" the barker clarified, worried that they would mistake Alouette for a showgirl from the Folies Bergère in Paris, Texas, I guess.

"Why waste your time with all these other low-class joints?" the most grizzled, loud, and fierce barker howled into the night. "In those places, you see it *all* before. T'night, at the world renowned SHO-BAR, we got the only one-of-a-kind act in all of creation: Divena the Aqua-Tease, the only showgirl in history to perform her seductive act *completely under water!* Divena the Aqua-Tease has gills to go along with her thrills!"

One after another these barkers regaled pedestrians with tall tales and exaggerated descriptions of all the great showgirls of the day, the gigantic stage props they used, and the freakshow stunts they performed. None of the girls just danced and stripped; they all had carnival gimmicks and expensive costumes to give "polite" audiences an excuse to claim they weren't paying to look at a striptease.

Between the carnival gimmicks and the assorted vaudeville entertainers who performed before each showgirl act, the moral whitewashing appeared to work. The crowds outside the 500 Club or Sho-Bar were stuffed with well-dressed, well-off, middle-aged couples or tour groups. This gave an air of class to the French Quarter burlesque clubs, which was helped by the fact that many of them inhabited old colonial-style brick buildings with white façades and ornate balconies on the second and third floors. How bad could a go-go joint be if it was housed in a historical landmark and patronized by good middle-class folk in sports coats and modest dresses?

Pretty bad, I decided. I pored over the full-color posters that decorated the walls of each jiggle joint with growing arousal and horror. I was wide-eyed and faint from fear of damnation (and the blood draining from my brain) after only a few moments of looking at these interstellar floozies. Take my word for it: these girls looked like strange and sexy Martians. I had never seen anything like them.

Subtlety certainly was not the strong suit of the burlesque stars of 1953 Bourbon Street. They flew their freak flag pretty damn high. Their candy-colored wigs were the size of wheelbarrows; their fake eyelashes were larger than dragonfly wings; their makeup looked like house paint applied with a roller; their stockings were as thick as wind socks; and the courageous girls who sprung for Eisenhower-era breasts implants were literally walking science experiments.

To be honest, a lot of those showgirls would look pretty damn bizarre to modern eyes. Thanks to the incredible advances made by mankind over the past half-century in the fields of cosmetics, plastic surgery, wig-making, fashion, and exercise and nutrition, the glamorous go-go bombshells of the 1950s, in retrospect, resembled gruesome Mardi Gras cross-dressers.

As a seventeen-year-old born during the Depression, I certainly didn't notice the resemblance to drag queens at the time. In fact, I *loved* how gloriously sleazy and tawdry the showgirls looked. I was a complete innocent living in a comparatively innocent era. Women in those days were under so much pressure to act prim and sexless that the showgirls with their Brides of Frankenstein look became supercharged with sexual appeal simply by advertising themselves as available. Eye candy was too hard to come by for men to be finicky.

Like millions of suckers every year in the French Quarter, I was enticed by the posters outside of the go-go joints to peek inside and dirty-up my eternal soul. I was lucky that I looked poor and shiftless, because otherwise an obvious Vidalia like me would have had a rough night.

Fleecing the stupid and the innocent was what go-go joints like the Mafia-owned Sho-Bar (run by Carlos' brother Peter Marcello) and 500 Club (run by Carlos' lieutenant Frank Caracci) were all about. Most of them were b-drinking establishments or, as they were popularly known, "Venus Flytraps." B-joints were places that paid the burlesque dancers, waitresses, or plain-clothes female employees commissions on each cocktail or bottle of booze they duped suckers into buying them in the hope of getting the girls drunk enough to take the party behind closed doors.

That wasn't quite how things turned out in places like the Sho-Bar. Invariably, the girls would go home sober, and the men would wake up in some piss-stinking alley very hungover, very sore, and completely broke. The girl's drinks were generally heavily diluted with water or completely nonalcoholic to keep them sober, and the suitor's cocktails were mixed stiffer than paint thinner.

If a b-girl was invited to share a bottle of liquor with a man, then she would simply dump the contents of her glass or even the entire bottle right onto the floor whenever he looked away. Then it would be time to order another bottle! This little trick made the floors of most go-go bars so sticky that each step almost unscrewed my cowboy boots from my feet.

Within a couple hours, the blind-drunk Vidalia would be lured to a "private room in the back" by a b-girl who was very accomplished at acting drunk, vulnerable, and rarin' to screw. Before the drunk could drop his pants, a thug would emerge from a hiding spot and smack him in the back of the head with a blackjack. The thug would confiscate the KO-ed drunk's wallet, watch, and jewelry before carrying him outside to be tossed next to piles of trash bags. If a customer refused to get drunk enough to be rolled, then the girls ordered him the "house specialty"— a "Mickey Finn" cocktail laced with the knockout agent chloral hydrate.

And if you called the police, the paid-off French Quarter beat cops would arrest you for getting "handsy" with the girls, who were obviously acting in self-defense, and force you to bribe them to be released.

Luckily for me, either I looked too cheap to be worth rolling, or some pretty waitress took pity on a fine lookin' specimen like me, and I made it out of those go-go joints with no harm done to anything but my soul.

I remember clenching my teeth and leaning forward as that red satin curtain parted before my first showgirl act. I felt like I was dripping with ice-cold sweat with eyeballs as big as golf balls as I saw my first naked lady in person. There are no words to describe my joy as I stared at the jiggling of two pendulous, creamy breasts with their areola half-covered by sparkly tassels. As I watched those tassels twirl, I forgave myself for being expelled from high school, running away from home, and abandoning my family. I forgave myself everything.

At that moment, Kent Brouillette died, and the creature known as Frenchy took his place. I resolved that moment that, Marksville be damned, I was going to be a New Orleanian until the city sunk into the sea.

That turned out to be a conservative estimate.

"The notorious Frenchy Fay ... is again in trouble. Scarcely a week or a month passes but what he is in trouble with the police [...] (Frenchy) was in the saloon about half-past 7 o'clock Sunday morning, drinking. A dollar was lying on the counter and seemed to want an owner, and Frenchy grabbed at it. The bartender objected and insisted upon Frenchy returning the dollar. Frenchy grabbed a bottle of Three-feather whisky, the lightest of the bunch, and shied at the bartender (...) Then Frenchy took hold of a 'Green River,' then a bottle of 'Black Label,' and finally a bottle of 'Old Crow,' determined not to discriminate in the brands, all of which he thought were warranted to kill if they hit."

The Daily Picayune
New Orleans
12-18-1906

I moved into the YMCA on Lee's Circle in downtown New Orleans, spending my days weightlifting at Ajax Gym and my nights exploring the French Quarter.

Ajax Gym was the first gym opened by Joe Gold, the Jewish bodybuilding pioneer who later mentored Arnold Schwarzenegger and founded the Gold's Gym and World Gym chains. I had first learned of Ajax from bodybuilding magazines — they reported that it was supposed to be the most cutting-edge bodybuilding gym in the world. To be among a clique of devoted, serious bodybuilders was a dream come true; finally, I was in a social circle that understood my obsession.

Thanks to my godlike build, I was quickly accepted as a regular at Ajax, and Joe Gold took a liking to me. With his immaculately tanned body and slicked-back black hair, Joe was not only the boss at Ajax but also the undisputed coolest guy in the local bodybuilding community. A little bit older than the rest of us, he protected me from the bullies in the bunch and ensured I didn't make too much of an ass of myself in the Big City.

That's not to say Joe himself took it easy on me. While I would be doing my curls, I would be surprised to hear a message like, "Will Tex from Marksville report to the barn, please? It's milking time!" reverberating through the gym's crackling PA system.

It was at the gym that I met my first two New Orleans friends: Neil Gautier and Jacques LeGrand. For three New Orleans muscleheads of French ancestry, Neil, Jacques, and I could not have been more different.

Jacques was the lovechild of Pepe LePew and Mr. Miyagi, a heavily accented lothario from Paris obsessed with becoming a gentle master of the martial arts. With the heavy-jawed looks of a classic movie star, Jacques was an athletic phenom who was both a world-class swimmer and a black belt master of judo. Jacques used his credentials as a former star on the French national swimming team to secure a job at Pontchartrain Beach in New Orleans as a lifeguard, which was one of the most sought-after jobs in a city full of oglers and horndogs.

Jacques spent his entire "workday" parading his physique up and down the beach for the enjoyment of the bathing beauties of Louisiana. Neil and I would head down to the beach, watch Jacques from afar, and, as soon as he got close to picking up a girl, run into the water and pretend to be drowning. He'd have no choice but to "save" us, and we'd do our best to make him look like an incompetent jackass as he did it.

It was one thing for a committed virgin like me to cock-block Jacques, but for a sex demon like Neil Gautier to get in the way was downright hypocritical. I've known old-ass Neil for over fifty years, and, over that time, it was rare to ever see him when he wasn't on the way to or from getting laid. With a few thousand conquests dating back to the 1940s, Neil has a little black book that is a coat of yellow paint away from being able to pass for a phone book.

"Best Lay" Gautier is the sort of biological freak who can have sex fifteen times a day if you give him the chance. If most men carry muskets that take an eternity to reload, Neil walks around with an AK-47 with a full banana clip of rounds at the ready.

Every few years, I play a trick on Neil and call him up pretending to be on my way to some far-off state where a degenerate orgy is about to go down. Before I finish the sentence, Neil is in his car, flooring the gas pedal. Eight or ten hours later, Neil will give me a call from a quiet, empty motel in Jacksonville or San Antonio or Memphis sounding very, very sad. "Where's the party, Frenchy? What happened to the *party*, Frenchy?"

Back in 1953, Neil had no problem making his own sex parties from scratch since he looked like a young Tony Curtis wearing fifty pounds of ripped muscle. Being friends with Neil was like having the Marquis de Sade as my older brother. I had never had a girlfriend, yet my best friend was convincing *Leave It to Beaver*-era Catholic schoolgirls to try out orgies and leather play.

Neil was the sort of perv who reveled in asking me to sniff his fingers after he came back from a date. Neil offered to "break me off a piece" of his girlfriends to "pop my cherry," but that wasn't my style. Though I was even better looking than Neil, it didn't make no difference; he could talk, and all I could do was stutter, stare, and run away.

Instead, I tried to deal with all of my pent-up sexual aggression by going to St. Louis Cathedral regularly and praying away my evil. Yes, I was still that gullible; the Marksville Sunday school still had a mark in me. The courage I felt on my first night in New Orleans was gradually decaying, and the old Catholic guilt and shame were creeping back in.

I can't tell you how many times I saw country folk spit in disgust when someone mentioned that you could buy a piece of ass within sight of St. Louis Cathedral, the oldest Catholic church in America. To me, it made perfect sense; with ready and willing adult women nearby, maybe the priests would stick to run-of-the-mill sins and not be driven by desperation to do anything too creative. To Marksville people, of course, there was no sin greater than a priest getting a righteous hummer.

Little did they know that some of the priests of St. Louis

Cathedral were buying those hummers with money from the church poor box. That wasn't how Marksville liked to picture the holy men of the Quarter. Instead, the priests were portrayed as besieged loners, exiles within their own community like the Jews in Nazi Germany. Surrounded by every manner of sin and vice, the poor priests clutched their rosaries and huddled in corners, fearful of mob violence.

They were no more under siege than I was, of course. Mass didn't stop me from consorting with the worst sort of folk that would tolerate me. Since church wasn't curing me of my raging hormones, I turned to a teenage boy's last option: violence. After working myself ragged all morning at Ajax and sunning myself at Pontchartrain beach during the afternoon, I finished off the last reserves of my energy at a bar called Murray's Tavern in the French Quarter.

Murray's was a ramshackle dump, one of the worst places in the French Quarter, but we weren't interested in class, or alcohol for that matter. My buddies from Ajax and I would march into Murray's shoulder-to-shoulder to force everyone to clear out of our way. We took our bodies far too seriously to drink; we came to fight, and Murray's was basically a brawl with a bar built around it.

The violence was so spontaneous and total it seemed choreographed, as if there had been an agreement at a certain time for everyone to start kicking each other's ass. At Murray's, you'd see everyone talking like old friends, and then a fight would break out on the other side of the bar, and, for no reason, all the smiling drinkers would just start punching each other with murderous intent. They would shrug, as if to say, "Hey, nice talking to you, but I guess it's time to fight," and then just wail on you.

Every night this routine happened at Murray's Tavern.

I mean *every...single... night.*

That was Murray's entire marketing plan: it was where you went in the French Quarter for a drunken brawl. It delivered on its reputation, and it gave a nervy, uptight virgin like me a nightly excuse to exhaust frustration by using pot bellies for punching bags.

After I bruised up my pretty face, I felt macho enough to hang around the more swanky nightlife hotspots in the Quarter. In the bars and lounges where all of the city's gamblers, gangsters, and politicians talked crooked with each other, I was the strange, awkward James Dean-looking teenager standing in the corner, talking to no one but listening to everyone very intently. It did not take long for me to become well known in my own right as a member of the French Quarter troupe of freaks and eccentrics.

In a community defined by drink, sex, and bad behavior, the presence of an extremely shy, teetotaling country boy with the body of Hercules was an amusing curiosity. Everyone would ask each other how the hell did a good-looking boy like me spend so much time in the French Quarter without *ever* seeming to have any fun?

Soon enough, thanks to my huge, out-of-style cowboy boots, dumb hayseed grin, and bar brawler bruises, I was given the nickname "Tex" by the French Quarter regulars. Because of my inability to speak and my exploits at Murray's Tavern, the locals had mistaken me for a real, wild, shitkickin' redneck. Since I had left Marksville specifically to escape the country, I loathed the nickname "Tex" even more than my old name and finally began to speak up and tell everyone to cut the shit.

"The next shitass to call me 'Tex' is gonna get plastered, y'all hear?" I'd shout like Popeye over the din of the bar. I'd wait a moment for everyone to act scared, but instead the entire crowd would erupt into laughter.

I got what I wanted, but for the wrong reason: as soon as the assorted drunks and characters heard my Cajun French accent, they settled on a new and more appropriate nickname. "Alright, Frenchy!" and "Go on, now, Frenchy!" the drunks sitting along the bar would hoot and shout.

I loved my nickname the moment I heard it, and from that

point on I introduced myself to strangers as "Frenchy." It sounded exotic, cosmopolitan, cool, even dangerous. The funny thing is that Quarter regulars meant it to be even more offensive than "Tex."

I had earned the nickname because my countryside Cajun French accent was so thick that *no one* could understand whatever the hell I was trying and failing to say. "Frenchy" was no more than a more colorful way to call me a Cajun redneck, but that didn't matter to me. All that mattered was that I was no longer "Tex."

Now that I was on a roll, I didn't waste any time earning my third nickname. The "Tex" crisis had forced me to begin talking to some of the barkeeps and club owners in the Quarter, and the only thing I knew enough to talk about was bodybuilding. In my early months in the city, no matter if you met me in a sophisticated beatnik bar or rowdy honky-tonk, all you heard from me was that I was training for the Mr. New Orleans bodybuilding contest and that I was determined to win.

Everyone heard so much about that damn Mr. New Orleans contest that I became "Mr. New Orleans," again as a joke. "Hey, Mac, let me introduce you to my friend, Frenchy, the *reigning* Mr. New Orleans!" the characters would say to their friends with a wink.

Which leads me to a "if a tree falls in the forest" sort of question: if you lose a bodybuilding contest that no one cares about in the first place, does that mean you even lost?

Well, I can answer that question: no, it means you never lost.

As far as the French Quarter tall tales go, I have been the reigning Mr. New Orleans contest winner since 1953. The actual result of that bodybuilding contest has about as much influence on who gets to wear the title of "Mr. New Orleans" as getting the most votes has in determining the winner of a New Orleans city election. In New Orleans, the spoils go to the liars and the cheaters, and fair elections are for fairy tales.

That's why they call them fairy tales, y'know?

Chapter IV

Exile on Bourbon Street

Mid-1950s

> "I'm so thirsty that I'm blue,
> Old friend Booze I long for you,
> I never knew that I'd miss you,
> The way I do
> Boohoo, Boohoo!"
> **Carl Zerse**
> "I've Got the Prohibition Blues (for My Booze)" (1919)

THE HEART OF THE FRENCH QUARTER IS THE OLD ABSINTHE HOUSE, AND THAT HEART HAS PUMPED OUT LIQUOR FOR CENTURIES. You couldn't invent a more perfect place for Mr. New Orleans to drink his first glass of beer and receive his crown.

No building has a longer history of maintaining a fashionably bad reputation in all of America. The Old Absinthe House is the ancient bar where Andrew Jackson and the pirate Lafitte brothers supposedly made their under-the-table deal to defeat the English before the Battle of New Orleans, saving Louisiana from prim English values and Victorian morality.

The bar was definitely the birthplace of the Absinthe House Frappe, the 19th century cocktail that created the craze for the illegal psychedelic alcohol in America. In the 1950s, the rumor was that there was a subterranean canal under the bar where all of the local smugglers and boosters paddled their goods to be sold to the Absinthe House's shadow owners in the underworld.

It is only fitting, baby, that I was baptized with booze in the drinking hole favored by such legends as Mark Twain, Oscar Wilde, Franklin Roosevelt, and my hero Jean Lafitte. It's not like the last of the Big Easy legends would be made around the bar of your local Applebee's. You know what they say: rarely is fine wine aged in a shitty barrel.

There is only one problem; I did not take my drink at that famously ratty old brick bar at 240 Bourbon Street. No, I took my first drink at 400 Bourbon Street, the temporary home of the Old Absinthe House for around eighty years. That's how you know the *Old* in Old Absinthe House is no joke: can you think of another bar where *eight decades* is nothing more than a brief interim in its history?

You see, during Prohibition, the infamous outlaw tavern was raided so many times that the owners smuggled the historic absinthe fountain, topped off with the statue of Napoleon, and the bar itself to an empty warehouse down the street, where they operated the Absinthe House in exile as a speakeasy. Once Prohibition ended, the owners saw no point in moving again, and it wasn't until 2004 that the Old Absinthe House was returned to its original location.

In other words, the surroundings of my first drink weren't as historic as I'd like to be able to tell you. Nonetheless, history was still being made at the Absinthe House in 1954; the occasional house pianist was none other than Louis Armstrong himself.

It was late one extremely balmy night, and the Absinthe House was packed like a 5 p.m. streetcar. I was standing against the brick wall of the bar desperately trying to stay conscious, Hercules with a pale face and a sweat-drenched muscle shirt. As usual, the doors and windows to the bar were all open, but the foul air was in no mood to leave.

I was dangerously dehydrated since I was too scared to drink anything but the sweat dripping down into my mouth. In a hopping joint like the Absinthe House, no one was going to stop the party to bring me an emergency glass of ice-water or drag me to a doctor if I took a floor dive.

Empty-handed, empty-headed, and nearly blacking out, I tried to distract myself by listening to the chatter in what was one of the ultimate New Orleans insider hangouts. It was one of those "Only in the French Quarter" melting pots where governors, police chiefs, celebrities, and blue-bloods got merrily drunk alongside pimps, whores, gangsters, and plug-ugly day laborers. Everyone who has ever mattered in the state of Louisiana at one point or another spent a night mattering in the Old Absinthe House, baby.

I was eavesdropping on the grossly sexual storytelling of a man who I believed to be the mayor of New Orleans when a voice even more accented than my own called from the bar. "Hey dere-rah, boy!" bellowed a cherry-nosed, potbellied fossil in a beautiful suit, which his shaky hand was busily soaking with beer from his overflowing mug.

The old boozehound sounded like a Nazi villain from the movies with this thick, fake-sounding accent. I thought he was putting everyone on talking like that, and I ignored him, figuring that he must be some sort of a wise guy.

He was, but a different sort of wise guy.

"I said...uh...ugh, vut is the name? Gott, I know it...Ah, yah, French boy! Frenchy, I'm speaking to you, meathead!" Well, I figured wrong. I had never seen the man before, yet he knew my name and wanted to talk. I was so weak from the heat that I looked like a weary POW stumbling over to this Colonel Klink in his silk suit. Up close, you could see dry skin flaking off around his fleshy pink head, and his eyes were honey-dipped from the booze.

"Uh, yes?" I said sheepishly as I stood next to the fossil at the bar.

"Boy, vut my name is, it is Dutch, Dutch Kraut," he explained.

As far as names went, this sounded a little queer to me, like introducing yourself as "Limey Dago" or "Jap Spic." A moment later, I realized this way of thinking was silly for a guy named Frenchy to entertain.

"Listen 'ere, vut you got is a good built, and you got the looks. Are you a figh-tah?" Dutch asked, licking his booze-dried cracked lips.

"Well, I like to fight, sir," I said dumbly, thinking of my brawls at Murray's Tavern.

"Yah, yah," the old man laughed, misting my face with beer. "And vut I like is to drink, how do you say, but I ain't vhat you call no fish, ya? Understand, yah? Are you a boxer, or you just a fighter, yah see?"

"Well," I mumbled, getting shy. "I've never trained in boxing, no."

"Nah, nah, with face like yours, you could make good money, yah," Dutch said between long slurps of beer. "Feed ya a bunch of stiffs vile you train and learn the ropes, and then see vut you can do, ya get me? Vould you train?"

"I already train at a gym all day, weightlifting."

"Nah, boy!" Dutch yelped, panting with laughter again. He was very drunk, and my hick ways amused him greatly. "I'm not talking no nancy shit; I'm talking boxing! Sweet science! Not sissy science! Vould you drop vut ever you call it and train to be a boxer? If I gave you a job and a nice apartment to make it vort your vile?"

My eyebrows nearly shot off my goddamn forehead in shock. Was this guy actually offering me a place of my own to live in and a real honest job? I would have done anything on Earth besides going to a job interview and working a real job to escape sleeping in a YMCA bunk bed. I was sick at heart from writing letters to everyone I knew in Marksville begging for cash.

"All I gots to do, you're saying, is work out at a boxing gym, and you'll give me a job and a place to stay?"

"Shit, boy. Vit a look like yours, I'll give ya a top-of-that-line apartment in the French Quarter, a new car, and thah easy-ass job in the world if you-a fightin' for me. Vut is it that you say to dat?" Dutch asked with a smile and an encouraging slap on my shoulder.

My own car? A job and a place to stay were nice, but a car might as well have been a crown and my own kingdom. I was already woozy and lightheaded, and this outlandish offer made me feel like I was suffering a full-blown fever dream. I had just come from Murray's, where I got punched in the face for fun. How bad could boxing be, especially at that pay scale?

"Dutch, you got a deal."

Dutch clapped his fat mitts in joy and slapped me on my back so hard that my chest collided against the bar. It seemed like I made old Adolf's night even more than he did mine!

"Barkeep, two lagers, on your double!" Judging by the lightning speed with which our drinks were delivered in a lazy French Quarter bar, Dutch was a man of some power and reputation. I stared down at that sudsy, ice-cold, overflowing mug of golden beer, and I was conflicted. On the one hand, I feared for my immortal soul, and on the other, I was hotter and thirstier than a fat man working in the sugarcane fields. Besides, I could not risk offending my new boss, who was loudly and incoherently making some toast.

Without thinking, I clinked mugs and took one long gurgle, my first ever sip of alcohol. My second, third, fourth, fifth, sixth, seventh, and eighth sips of alcohol followed in close succession, and within three minutes I had ordered my first refill.

Finally, it had happened: my life had begun. I was named Frenchy; I was Mr. New Orleans; and now I was drinking beer with a gangster.

Within a few months, I would count the two most powerful Mafia bosses in America as personal friends, and I ate at the best restaurants in the city for free. Instead of sharing bunk beds at the YMCA, I lived with my pothead stripper girlfriend in a furnished apartment above one of the city's most glamorous burlesque clubs.

One day I'm a clean-living, law-abiding, god-fearing Christian boy, and the next day I'm an adult who thinks he knows better. All it took was one beer to make me a gangster. That's one hell of a drug.

"I remember that old man with the crazy accent and the silver in his hair when he was the barman at Gasper's—Dutch, right? And I definitely remember old Frenchy. He was short and very muscular, very friendly —devilishly handsome to be honest. He was always at the racetrack. I remember one day seeing Frenchy sitting with Sam Saia, and all these bags of money were being brought to them in their seats. The bagmen would say, 'This one is from Chicago, this one from Kentucky,' and so on. I asked them what race they had won the cash from, and they told me the name of a race that hadn't started yet! They left before the race even started! That was a pretty good hint that old Sam Saia fixed that race."

<u>Evangeline the Oyster Girl</u>

Let me tell you why any criminal-minded individual should respect Dutch Kraut: you never heard of him until I shone the limelight on his name. *Everyone* who mattered in the underworld knew Dutch Kraut, but nosy people like you had no idea he existed.

Dutch was the perfect gangster: he was the best friend of everyone who could give him money and power, and he was a stranger to anyone who could hurt him. I saw Carlos Marcello and New York godfather Frank Costello treat Dutch like a big-time powerbroker, yet at the same time I know for a fact that there were district attorneys and police officials in Louisiana who thought he was nothing more than some kooky old German drunk. Very few suspected that Dutch was a gangster, and that's why he died free, rich, and happy.

Contrary to what you see in Hollywood depictions of the golden age of the Mafia, the Mob was overflowing with non-Italian gangsters in its heyday. The reason the non-Italians are largely forgotten by history is because they were less reckless, ambitious, and violent than the Italians. They made less news. They could never reach the top of the Mafia pyramid since their names didn't end in vowels, so what was the point in taking risks if there was nothing to gain?

I knew lots of Mafia racketeers like Dutch: non-Italian, nonviolent, mild-mannered businessmen who made their fortunes without ever hanging a headline on their name or visiting a jail cell. After all, there were only a couple dozen Italian "made" guys in the Marcello Family, yet the organization controlled hundreds of businesses and made Fortune 500 money every year. There were countless white-collar "managers" keeping the syndicate operating while the Italians bloodied their knuckles, fed each other to alligators, and racked up years behind bars.

Ironically, many of the non-Italians understood the point of a secret criminal society like the Mafia better than the Italians: it's supposed to stay a secret that you're a criminal so that you're never caught! Dutch took that concept of secrecy to almost ridiculous lengths, especially for a lawless and laidback town like New Orleans. Dutch was then and continues to be a legitimate international man of mystery.

He was one sneaky German, assuming that he was actually German and not Austrian or Dutch or Polish. I was never sure of his background. I saw him answer to the name Joe to some people, John to others, and Dutch to everyone else, yet I'm pretty sure he was born under none of those names. Sometimes he claimed to be a native born Louisianan with an inexplicable accent and Crout as his real last name, but then again there were times he told me that he was named "Dutch" because he immigrated to America from Holland and "Kraut" because he was German, a native of Hamburg or Munich depending on his mood — thus, Dutch Kraut.

Dutch's position within the New Orleans Mafia was the French Quarter lieutenant of Sam Saia, the kingpin of sports betting in the South. Sam Saia was Carlos Marcello's highest grossing underling, and I've heard it said that he was maybe the single richest bookmaker in America in the 1950s. Headquartered in the backrooms of the working-class Felix's Restaurant and Oyster Bar in the French Quarter, Saia managed the central clearinghouse for every illegal sports bet made in the gambling-mad city of New Orleans and the surrounding territories from Dallas to Mobile. Saia controlled so much cash that casinos in Las Vegas would call into a rowdy oyster bar on Iberville Street to lay off millions of dollars of wagers that they were unable to cover.

Saia was one of the smartest gangsters I ever met. He made sure that you would never have guessed that "Mr. Sam" was a crime boss by his appearance and behavior. Sam was just a jowly-faced, balding, frowning, working class Italian with salt-and-pepper hair who never drew attention to himself or made a scene. You could sense that he was important only because of the constant stream of runners and messengers rushing in and out of Felix's, but he never acted like a swinging dick.

Like so many multimillionaire mobsters I've known, Sam could never come to terms with the idea that a criminal should have to *pay* for clothes, so he wore whatever suits he could get for cheap or for free. The result was that he looked like a schlub sometimes, which was always funny to me since Dutch, his lieutenant based only a few blocks away on Bourbon Street, *operated out of a tailor's shop.* That's why a tubby old drunk like Dutch dressed so nicely.

The difference between Sam Saia's wealth and prestige and his average appearance occasionally led to some confusion among visitors to the French Quarter. Next door to Saia's headquarters Felix's at 739 Iberville Street was La Louisiane Bistro at 725 Iberville Street, which happened to be the home of *another*

Mafia multimillionaire. Unlike Sam Saia, however, "Diamond" Jim Moran wore his wealth on his sleeve ... and everywhere else on his body.

"When you walk into a certain Italian eatin' house here you are greeted by James Brocato. He smiles at you through eye-glasses that are studded with diamonds around the rims. Jim now goes by the name of 'Diamond Jim Moran.' He is the only man I ever knew who wears diamond-studded shoe-strings and has a diamond zipper in his pants. [...] [Y]ou will find him wearing $210,000 worth of diamonds. His pride and joy, though, are mink ties [...] 'No other human bein',' he said, 'has as many mink ties as me.'"
Harman W. Nichols

Diamond Jim had one of the most incredible pedigrees in the history of the New Orleans underworld. A tough heavyweight boxer, Diamond Jim was hired as the bodyguard and bagman of Governor and later Senator Huey Long in the 1930s. When Long made a deal with New York crime boss Frank Costello and New Orleans godfather Silver Dollar Sam Carollo to open up New Orleans to national Mafia gambling interests, Diamond Jim was deputized to oversee Long's joint gambling ventures with the Mafia.

Moran made so much money working for this trio that he began to decorate himself from his glasses to his shoestrings with hundreds of diamonds — hence his nickname. Even his teeth sparkled with diamonds. Rappers would have loved this guy.

The civilians of New Orleans were wowed by Diamond Jim's display of his wealth, but the gangsters took a completely different message from Jim Moran's flashy style. Only a truly dangerous man could walk around New Orleans, of all cities, wearing $100,000 worth of diamonds without *any* fear of getting robbed.

Debonair, flashy Diamond Jim was the official party host whenever Silver Dollar Sam or Carlos Marcello needed to entertain outside powerbrokers. Diamond Jim's camp on Lake Pontchartrain was the meeting place whenever the national Mafia leaders visited Louisiana. In one meeting attended by New York Mob boss Joe Adonis, Frank Costello's New Jersey underboss Willie Moretti, Las Vegas kingpin Bugsy Siegel, and many others from across America, Diamond Jim deputized his son to act as a waiter since he could trust no one else to keep quiet about what was discussed.

During the meal, Bobby Moran tripped and dumped a plate of food on Moretti. Terrified of "disrespecting" the other kingpins, Diamond Jim leapt over the table and started to slug the shit out of his son, hoping to save both of their lives. Moretti quickly pulled Diamond Jim off his son.

"Hey, hey, what the fuck over here!" Moretti shouted. "Whatta's matta wit' you, Jimmy? Who gives a shit? This jacket," Moretti said, pointing to the stained silk coat, "it only cost me $200. What is $200 to me? That's nuthin' to me." To demonstrate that he was being serious, Moretti whipped out two one-hundred-dollar bills and set them on fire, letting them burn away to ash before letting them float to the ground.

"*That's* what I think about $200," said Moretti with a laugh. "Now, Jimmy, kiss your son, and Bobby, kiss your father. Who gives a shit? Don't let anything get in between you. Life is too short." After dinner, Bobby told his dad that he wished Moretti had just let him get his ass kicked and tipped him the $200 instead.

As he aged, Diamond Jim decided that his nice restaurant behind the Casino Royale burlesque club was too modest for his talents and wealth. Looking to build a palace that would put the rest of the Quarter to shame, Diamond Jim purchased La Louisiane Bistro on Iberville Street. La Louisiane was an old restaurant that Diamond Jim with his white suits and diamond-studded eyeglasses quickly remodeled as the most ridiculously decadent Mafia hangout in the city. He stuffed the joint full of chandeliers and fine paintings and drop-dead classy broads in evening gowns.

To make sure everyone knew that La Louisiane was the fanciest hotspot in the city, Diamond Jim had his chefs occasionally plant diamonds in the food as a tooth-popping publicity stunt. New Orleans politicians were infamous for hanging out around La Louisiane in the hope of getting a sparkling bribe stuffed into their meatballs.

Naturally, when out-of-town crooks, whale gamblers, and cops came to check out the evil genius of bookmaking and gambling on Iberville Street, they usually mistook Diamond Jim for Sam Saia. Certainly, the bejeweled owner of the palatial La Louisiane looked more like America's gambling kingpin than the poorly dressed guy in the raw oyster bar next door.

Though I wished that I could spend more time amidst the glitz and glamour of La Louisiane, I did not have the juice to hang with that crowd, and it fell outside of Dutch's jurisdiction. Dutch only collected the bookmaking business of the French Quarter establishments that weren't Mafia-run. This meant, sadly, that many of the big go-go joints were not his territory, either.

On the other hand, Dutch's fiefdom did include all of the major French Quarter bordellos, which were run by madams who were only loosely affiliated with Carlos, as well as a few dozen restaurants, hotels, bars, stores, and apartment buildings.

Working for Dutch was basically like being a postman who delivers cash instead of letters. All day long, the runner would earn his title, hustling back and forth between the tailor shop and each stop on his daily rounds, delivering cash payouts and picking up new bets. In the early evening, when all the sporting events had begun, and no more bets could be taken, Dutch invited his favorite runners to drop off their last delivery over dinner and drinks at Kolb's on St. Charles Street, the city's most popular German restaurant.

Kolb's was a New Orleans institution, a 19th century restaurant famous for the whitewashed ironwork on its balconies, the electrified white-on-blue "Kolb's" sign hanging over St. Charles Street, and its claim to be the first restaurant in history to showcase live jazz bands. Kolb's was also famous because everyone mispronounced its name — it was supposed to sound like "Cobb's."

After that very first night with Dutch in the Old Absinthe House, I ate supper for five or six years straight at Kolb's. I was Dutch's best friend more or less immediately; the ancient Hun was fixated on the idea that I would make him millions as a pretty-boy boxer, and it endlessly amused him to watch me struggle to keep up with his drinking. Dutch began every meal by downing three "double-strong" martinis and then three Löwenbräu beers, in addition to the additional beer he needed to wash down the thick German food. Since I tried not to lose face by being out-guzzled by a feeble old man, Dutch was working on killing me by dessert.

After supper at Kolb's, Dutch would take me to meet Sam Saia at his nightly card game on Decatur Street, where the boss would have high-stakes fun before inevitably returning to Felix's. Like most gaming kingpins, Sam was a gambler himself. Dutch and I would usually part ways for the night around 9 or 10 p.m., usually to visit different bars around the Quarter. We usually got a few hours of sleep apiece before meeting up again at the tailor shop in the morning.

I owe my long-lived alcoholism, my criminal career, and my love of German food to those years of conversations at Kolb's with Dutch. I barely said a word to Dutch during the rest of the 1950s; our relationship was one long, drunken lecture from him to me. And don't get me wrong: I was grateful! I desperately needed the old man's help. I would have never survived in New Orleans and in the Mafia without the crash course given to me by Dutch.

The time I spent as Dutch's protégé was close to the happiest period of my life. *Everything* in my life was easy besides getting laid, which I still didn't know how to do since that was the one thing a crotchety lush like Dutch couldn't teach me. Everything else about my life was a free ride.

Whenever I made my rounds as the official representative of the Mafia, I was treated as if I was Carlos Marcello himself. It was my right to eat for free at all of the fancy restaurants where I picked up the bets, including New Orleans classics like Arnaud's, Brennan's, and Antoine's. It was a rule that a wiseguy could not be charged more than "bar prices" anywhere in the French Quarter, which meant I spent somewhere between $0-$1 on every drink I purchased.

Since I had to work in the Quarter, Dutch ensured that I lived in such style that it reflected well on him. I was given a penthouse apartment above the Gunga Den burlesque joint at 325 Bourbon Street. In that apartment, you damn well knew that you were in the diseased heart of the French Quarter. All night I could hear the men whoop and holler for Linda Brigette, the "Cupid Doll," and Bert Ferguson's house band always played loud and bombastic when "good" would have sufficed for me. When the shows stopped, the party never did; I was treated to a symphony of breaking beer bottles, ugly brawls, out-of-tune street musicians, babbling drunks, and rebel-yellin' college kids well into the morning hours.

After growing up in Marksville, where everything was so quiet you could hear the mosquitoes fart, the constant hubbub of Bourbon Street was the most comforting soundtrack imaginable. At all times, I was reminded that something was going on, that excitement was mine to have on request. I slept enough during my boring years in the countryside to make up for the sleep I lost living in the Quarter.

"The police department was the stepchild of the municipal budget, and the focal point of graft and corruption. ... Patrolmen reported for the duty or not as they pleased, paraded the streets in full uniform with prostitutes, and engaged in drunken carousals in public resorts, while many were the open accomplices of burglars, pickpockets, and crooked gamblers."

Herbert Asbury
The French Quarter

In 1954, the French Quarter was a beautiful place to live if you didn't mind sharing your neighborhood with hundreds of freaks, gangsters, and crazies. Personally, I was always partial to that sort of company, probably because I *was* that sort of company.

Unlike today, the Quarter was not just a tourist trap. In those days, if you lived in the Quarter, you felt like you actually belonged to a real, permanent community — a tiny, homey, and somewhat deranged 19th century European village in the center of a modern city. There were still ancient immigrants around who spoke broken English, cursed you with the Evil Eye, and suspiciously watched the street traffic from the windows of the homes they had owned since before Teddy Roosevelt's balls had dropped.

The Quarter contained a number of mom & pop corner groceries with soda fountains, Jewish tailors and haberdashers and shoe-menders, hole-in-the-wall cafes and delis, well-attended churches of various dominations, even offices for various quacks like chiropractors and lawyers. If anything, the Quarter was more habitable and convenient than your average neighborhood since, unlike most places, high-quality strip clubs, bordellos, and bars were all within short walking distance.

Quarter natives acted as if they were living on an island of street-smart geniuses in a great ocean of dumb marks. We all felt like we were in on the great joke that the neighborhood played on the world. Each morning, the locals would gossip to each other about the dumb Vidalias that fell for the latest stunts and scams conceived by the promoters and club owners. It was quite the spectacle, watching a new horde of tourists and weekenders fall for the same tricks and make the same mistakes night after night.

Since we were surrounded by thousands of fools and marks, the Quarter natives actively sought out and befriended the other regulars in self-defense. We figured that the time may come when a full-scale riot would erupt, and we'd have to band together and repel the swarms of blind-drink outsiders. The whole appeal of the Quarter, after all, was that the parties were always right on the edge of becoming riots, and the old-timers told stories about a long-ago revolution where a band of armed rowdies barricaded themselves in the Quarter and overthrew the city government.

The ultimate French Quarter insider was the mafioso, who justifiably felt like he was in on yet another joke played on American society. To Marcello Family insiders, everyone in New Orleans was a mark, someone who lived according to rules that only guidos knew were imaginary. None of the traffic laws, zoning laws, parking laws, bar cover charges, restaurant menu prices, and posted ticket prices applied to a Mafioso — and we loved that we got away with it.

I didn't fully comprehend the power I had as a member of Sam Saia's network until Dutch arranged for me to get my first car: a 1949 Mercury convertible. Since I was a car nut, I hated the idea of parking my pristine Mercury outside of my apartment on Bourbon Street, the busiest and wildest street in the South. I would spend as long as thirty minutes precisely positioning that Mercury on the street outside of the Gunga Den to ensure that it was as far away from other cars and the overcrowded curb as possible. Then I would take the time to lovingly cover my Mercury with a tarp, which I would try to nail down into the cracks in the sidewalk.

It turned out to be illegal to park your car damn near in the middle of an extremely busy road and then pitch a tent on top of it. I was pretty grumpy when I saw that expensive ticket taped onto my car tent, but Dutch didn't seem to be bothered and snatched the paper from my hand. "Yah yah, I'll take care of *dat!*"

The next day, I got a visit from Junior and Louis, the French Quarter beat cops, who apologized for ticketing me and gave me their home numbers in case I ever wanted to have the police tow a car from Bourbon Street. "All it takes is one call, Mac, and we'll toss any car you want right into the fucking Mississippi! We don't give a fuck! You call, we do!" Junior told me.

Soon afterwards, I upgraded to a brand-new Oldsmobile convertible. When Junior and Louis saw my new car, they suggested that I stop worrying myself with the tarp and just build a garage for my Oldsmobile right on Bourbon Street! That's how great it was to be a wiseguy in the 1950s: not only did the police ignore my completely illegal carport on the city's most important street, they were the ones who suggested that I build it. When I came home every night, it wasn't rare to see Junior or Louis standing guard by my garage, shooing away the rubberneckers who couldn't believe what they were seeing.

Junior and Louis weren't doing me any favors; Sam Saia and Carlos Marcello were amply compensating them through weekly envelopes full of cash. Paying off the police was the cost of doing business in New Orleans, and the Marcello Family always made sure to give so generously that they secured what passed for the self-interested "loyalty" of the crooks in blue. Though Dutch wanted me to train as a boxer, he never would have used me as muscle; the bribes he paid were a down payment on the use of the police department as his personal collection service and terror squad.

Unfortunately, the incompetent punks the NOPD hired generally were no better qualified to be criminals than law enforcement officers. In the year of my arrival in New Orleans, it seemed like a new police scandal broke every week; one team of police safecrackers was caught stealing $300,000, and shortly after that, two cops were arrested for violently raping a deaf mute. I cannot begin to communicate how incompetent the average criminal had to be to get arrested by the NOPD in the 1950s, so it's mindblowing to think of how stupid a NOPD officer must have been to get busted by *other* NOPD officers. . . let alone thanks to the testimony of a deaf mute!

When Dutch had a job that was too important to risk giving to the fuzz, he had another option besides troubling and possibly incriminating Carlos Marcello. Dutch was one of the elite New Orleans gangsters who were trusted enough to receive The Sheet: a weekly menu of criminal acts offered for sale by a local brotherhood of mercenary leg-breakers and head-busters.

The Sheet was one page, no frills, circulated every Monday: around $25 for a broken nose, something like fifty dollars for collecting a small debt, $100 for a snapped limb, much more for permanent facial disfigurement or loss of limb, maybe $1000 or so for a serious program of torture ... and then murder was negotiable depending on the person.

I know it's easy to dismiss a story like this, but The Sheet would be such an outlandish lie that I wouldn't waste my time trying to make anyone believe it. Though I didn't see The Sheet after the late 1950s, before that time I regularly saw both Dutch Kraut and Sam Saia perusing a given week's offering of criminal delicacies. What I never found out was precisely who was publishing that damn thing, or why the prices changed from week to week. I wish I would have kept some copies to sell at auction; I imagine I could make a killing.

❧ ❧ ❧ ❧ ❧

"The Little Mayor is the law on Bourbon Street and throughout a large section of the Old French Quarter... The Little Mayor is almost as much of an institution here as crab gumbo and jambalaya, both of whom he vaguely resembles. Everyone on Bourbon Street adores him—and, if they fail to do so, they are more than liable to get a belt in the snoot."

<u>George Dixon</u>

I can't say that I was too impressed with Dutch's managerial skills. What's the point of picking a boxer for his looks and then throwing him into the ring completely untrained, all but guaranteeing he'd get his Hollywood smile pummeled ugly?

Why didn't he concentrate on making me a movie star instead? Granted, I couldn't speak, which didn't bode well for my acting career, but the fact that I couldn't box was a pretty bad omen for my boxing career.

Dutch didn't understand that a fighter could not become a boxer in only a few months. I was a pretty mean hombre to tussle with in a bar brawl, but, with no training to speak of, I wasn't going to be worth a shit dancing around a boxing ring and trying to pelt some jackrabbit-nimble kid who had been sparring every day since he was potty trained.

Since I was still only a teenager, I guess I could have someday become a half-ass professional, but I never developed the work ethic for boxing that I did for weightlifting. The reason was obvious: pumping up muscles was way more pleasing for a narcissist than getting punched really hard over and over directly in the face. For a few years in the mid-1950s, I sucked up the pain and gave professional boxing a shot, mostly out of fear that Dutch would abandon me if he didn't think there was money to be made in the ring.

Like just about every business venture in the French Quarter, the first step to making me into a star boxing attraction was a visit to Gasper Gulotta, the man who had launched Dutch's criminal career. Gasper was a swarthy, sweaty, bite-size Italian – you know, a central casting guido. Gasper was a go-go joint owner who traveled about town enveloped in a cloud of cigar smoke. Back during the Lincoln administration, he hired an off-the-boat Dutch Kraut as a bartender and later manager at Gasper's, his go-go joint across from Frank Caracci's 500 Club on Bourbon Street.

When Dutch's raids on the club's liquor inventory reached startling proportions, Gasper neatly took care of business. Instead of firing Dutch and making an enemy, Gasper slipped Dutch a wad of cash the size of a toilet paper roll and told him it was his startup bankroll as a bookmaker. Gasper then walked Dutch over to Felix's and hyped him up to Sam Saia, who was happy to take the trustworthy alcoholic off Gasper's hands. Instead of breaking Dutch's heart by firing him, Gasper received his lifelong loyalty and appreciation.

That was Gasper, master operator; his hand was always surgically precise and smoother than a sip of Bailey's. Gasper earned his nickname as the "Little Mayor of Bourbon Street"— only my country cousin Edwin could compete as a pure politician. Gasper was a magician: never satisfied with merely getting his way, he would somehow leverage and engineer and hustle and pimp out every situation in order to receive maximum lagniappe.

You know the phrase "have your cake and eat it, too?" Well, Gasper always had his cake, ate it too, conned the baker out of his bakery, and then burned it down to collect the insurance money.

Recognized by all levels of society as a good ole boy and square dealer by New Orleans standards, Gasper was the last of the great French Quarter saloon bosses and underworld fixers. Thanks to his unique ability to make his name golden with bluebloods, rednecks, and blackhands alike, Gasper was able to position himself as the backroom boss of the French Quarter, the Little Mayor who neutrally governed the most lawless and profitable district in the city.

Presiding over the French Quarter, Gasper cultivated the image of a disinterested government bureaucrat taking pains on everyone else's behalf — even though he was clearly getting richer all the time. Gasper skimmed off the top of all his financial duties: collecting the bribes for the police and the politicians from the local vice rackets, negotiating the transfer of girls between go-go clubs and brothels, and impartially ruling whenever there was a turf dispute between the local cabbies or barkers or barkeeps. Gasper's sure hands made him the indispensable mechanic who could keep the machinery of the city greased and running like a brand-new Cadillac, and he amply compensated himself for the work.

Among Gasper's many unofficial jobs was the underworld's boxing boss, so Dutch and I visited him at his go-go joint. The Little Mayor blew cigar smoke in my face as he patted down the muscles on my arm and looked my chin over.

"Looks like the kid can roll!" he announced suddenly, which made Dutch giddy with dreams of million-dollar paydays. Since Gasper had close ties to every gym, sporting venue, bookmaker, and fight fixer in the city, we thought he could have turned Mamie Eisenhower into a title contender with a few phone calls.

Before Gasper could sign off my career, however, he had to bring me to see his brother, the man from whom he inherited the post of boxing rackets boss. Gasper's brother was Peter "Pete Herman" Gulotta, one of the greatest world champions in the history of the bantamweight division. Blinded by repeated blows to his eyes, Pete Herman was so gifted in the ring that he won his last world title *after* he had lost most of his eyesight; he bragged that he could "box by Braille."

At the end of his career, Blind Pete settled down as the manager of Pete Herman's Ringside Bar and Lounge at 938 Conti Street, which was well known for its larger-than-life neon sign that depicted the owner in his boxing regalia.

Pete Herman was the only superhero I ever met. With his

sight, Pete Herman was one of the greatest athletes in history; as a blind man, he was still a world champion fighter. As he aged, Pete honed his other senses to godlike intensity. I would walk into his club and see the old blind man setting records on his pinball machine.

Really, I ain't shittin'!

Every once in a while, he'd lumber over to you, raise his pant legs, and ask, "What color are my socks?" Inevitably, you'd look down and see two socks of identical make but different colors. Once you told him that his socks were mismatched, Pete would smirk and grumble out of the corner of his mouth. "Dat fucking nigger that dresses me," he'd say as he shook his head, "he don't never learn dat fucking colors *feel* different to me."

Whenever a heckler fucked with one of Pete's performers, the old man padded over to the table and introduced himself. "How 'bout we take a walk and talk 'bout all 'dis?" Inevitably, the starstruck drunk would follow Pete to the men's room. Once all the stalls were empty, Pete would lock the bathroom door and lean against it. The drunk would try to explain why he was heckling, but Pete would start insulting the drunk as much as he could. Pete would push and push the heckler until he inevitably told the old man, "Listen, sir, I don't want to fight an old blind man."

As soon as he heard those words, Pete would smile, crack his knuckles, and pop his neck. "Blind, right? It would be unfair to fight a blind man, right?" Suddenly, Pete would flick down the light switch, and the bathroom would descend into total darkness. "Guess who's blind now, you motherfucker you?"

No heckler ever emerged from that bathroom on his own two feet.

I had heard so many stories about Pete Herman that I was seriously underwhelmed by the legend in the flesh. To say the least, Pete was no longer an imposing physical presence. Pete was just a tiny little bowling ball of swarthy flesh with a flat nose, a gorilla face, and his pants tucked up to his tits in classic old guido style. He did not look particularly scary. Seeing that Pete really was completely blind, I couldn't imagine how he planned to size me up.

I never found out.

As he was introducing himself, the little Italian gnome overheard a patron mouthing off to his bartender. Pete Herman turned in the direction of the man and, in the sweetest old geezer voice, asked if he could feel the man's face to "see him." When the loudmouth came closer to let Pete feel his face, the former world's champion knocked him out cold with a right hook.

When Pete turned back around as if nothing had happened, he was in such a good mood that he gave me his blessing as a boxer without further ado and invited us to have a drink with him at the bar.

While we were drinking, Dutch asked Pete which gym would be suited to my skills as a complete novice. "Well, there are two gyms worth talking about," said Pete Herman. "There is Whitey Esneault at St. Mary's Italian Gym in the Quarter, and there is Curly's Gym on Poydras Street. Whitey's a tough, no-bullshit guy who makes great fighters; you can tell he's a good trainer because the bastard only has one leg, but his students are known for their footwork! Figger that out!" wheezed Pete, laughing.

"Curly, on the other hand, is a crooked, mobbed-up old dago who has a full bar installed right in the fucking gym..."

"Well, shit," I interrupted, "I don't care what y'all say, I'm going with Curly!" This comment caused a round of laughter, and Pete toasted my wisdom.

My instincts turned out to be correct; Curly was the boxing coach for me. Since I was never going to amount to dick in the fight game, it was much better that I train under a lazy old bullshitter like Curly who would let me slack off than a real ball-buster who would ruin my life. Hanging around Curly's gym, showing off my muscles while I ordered drinks from the bar, I made a number of very powerful friends in the Mafia. For wiseguys, watching the fights at Curly's was second in popularity only to betting on the gruesome cockfights held in LaPlace, twenty-five miles west of New Orleans.

The downside of my half-ass training was that, in my sixteen fights as a professional, I had my nose broken seven times against comically poor competition. I've never been as pretty again.

Though I won all of my fights at Curly's Gym, I did so simply by overpowering and out-cheating my much smaller, much flabbier, much less-connected opponents. When I could not simply bull rush and out-muscle my opponents, I relied on the knowledge that Curly's crooked referees would let "Dutch Kraut's boy" get away with anything. I'd bite, headbutt, elbow, knee, and stomp on the toes of my opponent – I was as shameless as a Republican banker at church. I could have melted my opponent with a flamethrower, and Curly's ref would have ruled it a clean technical knockout in my favor.

Despite my unbeaten heavyweight boxing record, no one remained under the impression for very long that I would amount to anything. After my last fight, which I fancied a pretty decent performance, Dutch Kraut walked over, squeezed me on the shoulder, and shook his head as if to say, "Sadly, no." I think we were both relieved not to have to continue on with that charade.

Without my time in the ring, I returned to visiting raucous honky-tonk bars for my violent kicks. Having outgrown Murray's Tavern, I graduated to the club run by my boxing cronies, the Conforto family. I knew four Confortos: Papa Joe and his sons Joe Jr., Angelo, and Jerome. They were all boxers, and they were all wannabe wiseguys who acted more like shitkicking rednecks. They liked to drink, raise hell, and beat the shit out of their customers in bar fights. Their club was a raucous ancestor of today's biker bars. The Confortos were my sort of guys — so crazy that they were never boring.

I was returning home to my Bourbon Street apartment early one evening when my French Quarter acquaintance Joe Conforto Jr. sped around a corner in his convertible at an outrageous speed and nearly careened into me. Junior was a dangerous man, but he looked scared shitless.

A moment later, as Junior's car was swinging out of sight, gunshots rang out, and I heard bullets whiz by my head. I dropped to the ground and turned to see the gunman, who turned out to be the prettiest damn redhead to ever start a French Quarter shootout in high heels. It was Junior Conforto's wife, Janet, a well-known burlesque star who went by the name of Jada and danced at The Sho-Bar, the go-go joint owned by Carlos Marcello's most vindictive brother, Pete Marcello.

"Sorry, Frenchy!" Jada called out nonchalantly as she clip-clopped down the street in her heels, her makeup running down her cheeks and her long red hair flowing wild in the wind. Pedestrians whistled and screamed "You go on, girl!" as shots blasted out again.

"Wow, Junior must've been fooling around again," I thought to myself. This was not the first time I had heard of Junior driving his rabid redhead to gunplay. Once, when Joe was about to hit Jada during a fight in the kitchen, she pulled her pistol on him and humiliatingly made him prepare her dinner at gunpoint.

"Frenchy," Junior told me later, "if only I could've gotten six inches closer, I could've knocked that bitch right out. But dammit if Jada don't know my range! She always kept me just out of reach, teasin' me like hell, smirkin' like a jaybird. She cocked the hammer on dat damn pistol and told me to put some extra garlic on her goddamn salad. Boy, I was steamed, but I knew better than to press my luck with dat crazy bitch, man, so I made her one hell of a salad and kept my fuckin' mouth shut!"

As I was getting up from the pavement and brushing off my soaked and muddy clothes, I heard Joe's car screech back around the corner. He pulled up alongside me. "Frenchy, is dat crazy whoo-ah comin' up behind me?"

Pissed off about my ruined clothes, I looked around, saw no one, and dropped to the deck again anyway. I screamed, "She comin', Joe, she a-comin'!" as Junior floored his car into a street sign, rebounded, and then hung a left ... right into Jada's line of fire. She barely missed his head.

Despite his good luck to survive his marriage to Jada, Junior was always grumbling that he got a raw deal in life. Junior and the other Conforto boys were all obsessed with earning Carlos' trust, but they were too wild and primitive to be "made."

I remember a night when twelve Arkansas Razorback football players were raising hell in Papa Joe's bar, disrespecting the staff and acting like fools. I could see the Confortos start fuming and cracking their knuckles, so I came over and asked if I could help get things under control. Papa Joe looked at me, scoffed, and just said, "Get the door. *We* got *dis!*" Those four Confortos beat the accents off those twelve Arkansas football players.

There was another time when the son of an electrician who serviced the sound systems of the French Quarter bars came back from Korea and picked a fight with the Confortos. The GI went to his dad and asked why he wasn't collecting on a $35 bill owned by Papa Joe Conforto, but his dad told him to let it go. "It's not worth it for $35," he said.

Instead, the GI went to the Confortos bar and walked right up to Papa Joe and told him that he was delinquent in paying a $35 bill for fixing the microphones on the bar's stage. Papa Joe snorted and said that he'd have his wife send a check in the mail.

"No," said the GI as he leaned across the bar, "you don't understand. I'm not leaving without my $35."

"Alright," said Papa Joe with fire in his eyes. "I'll do you better dat! I'll give you 45!" Papa Joe Conforto whipped out a .45 caliber pistol, shot it into the ceiling, and then pointed it at the GI. Whatever action that boy saw overseas was insufficient preparation, because he ran out of that bar like the French retreating from the Nazis. He had to intercede with Casino Royale MC Frank Pirelli, whom the Confortos owed a favor, to save his life.

There's a funny story how Frank "Frankie Ray" Pirelli earned that favor from the Confortos. One night, Papa Joe called Frank over to authenticate the story of a hot stripper drinking at the bar who said that she was so famous that world-renowned columnist Walter Winchell would give the Confortos press if she performed in the club. Frank took one look at the showgirl and nodded, "It's a celebrity, all right, but not a she."

"What the fuck you talkin' 'bout?" asked Joe Conforto in confusion.

"That's Christine Jorgensen. First man ever to get an operation to become a woman!" said Frank.

"You mean to tell me that pretty thing is a man?" screamed Joe far too loud for Frank's comfort level.

Frank was getting ready to duck bullets, but he was totally wrong. Joe turned to Christine, offered his hand, and said, "You're hired!" Turning back to Frank, Conforto grabbed him with his strong hands and said, "You gotsta come over and MC for me when *this thing* performs. I don't want my shitty MCs introducing a legit star!"

Supposedly, old Papa Joe Conforto fell pretty hard for Christine. He/she even caught Papa Joe drilling a hole in the dressing wall to "try to sneak a peak at her snatch." Papa Joe would spin and twirl Christine on the dance floor while his long-suffering wife sighed indifferently at the cash register and his meathead sons had shit-fits watching from the bar. "Holy shit, man!" Junior Conforto said to Frankie Ray the first time he saw this display. "Did my dad go fruit, or what?"

"I dare *you* to go tell him that," Frankie responded. Over the years, Christine would pay for plane tickets for Papa Joe and his wife to visit in New York; it became one of the oddest friendships in the world.

It may have been stories like this that made it impossible for Carlos Marcello to take the Confortos seriously as wiseguys. Dancing and taking vacations with transexuals wasn't exactly Carlos' style. The Confortos were good for paying tribute, knocking people around, and installing Carlos' jukeboxes in their bar, but the godfather saw little advantage in dealing with them on a more intimate basis than that. Junior Conforto was always scheming up cockamamie ideas for winning Carlos' trust and affection.

Finally, fate intervened and gave the Conforto brothers their chance. One year, Carlos Marcello chose to attend the Tarpon Rodeo thrown in Grand Isle, a tiny barrier island where Carlos maintained a fishing camp. When Carlos was asked by the press about the possibility of being deported to Italy like Silver Dollar Sam, he made all of his friends laugh by responding, "I ain't never been there. And don't want to go there. I wish they would deport me to Grand Isle where I could do some fishing."

Like a politician, Carlos viewed Grand Isle's annual rodeo as an opportunity to charm, glad-hand, and make an impression on as many otherwise hard-to-reach rural powerbrokers as he could. Counter to his secretive and paranoid reputation, Carlos made a point to regularly appear in crowded public places to remind everyone that he was scared of no one and that he was a friendly, stable businessman that could be trusted to deliver a square deal — unless you dicked around with him.

At this rodeo, Carlos was swaggering around a muddy pasture to the side of the rodeo ring, happily shaking hands with strangers and sampling the carnival food on offer. To make a point of how little he had to fear from anyone, Carlos was alone, unaccompanied by a bodyguard, a completely vulnerable Mob boss in a sweat-soaked suit, chomping on a corndog.

Two big Cajun redneck boys happened to clip Carlos' shoulder as they walked past. Without hesitating, the short and tubby Carlos reeled around at those two Paul Bunyans with blazing red eyes and, with a mouth stuffed with corndog, told them to go fuck themselves. The two Cajuns looked at each other, smiled, and whipped around to kick Carlos' ass. Before they threw the first punch, Carlos barked, "You know who da fuck I am, you dumb country cocksuckers?"

"Nope!" the Cajuns said as they started to lay into the most dangerous criminal in the South.

Luckily for Carlos, Junior and Angelo Conforto happened to

be attending this rodeo, and they naturally shadowed Carlos in the hope of getting noticed. When they saw Carlos was in trouble, the two rough-and-tumble boxers rushed in and dumped a ferocious ass-beating on the Cajuns.

Grabbing Carlos by either hand, they pulled the bruised, muddied, busted-lip gangster up from the ground and tried to pat him off. Carlos slapped their hands away, grabbed Junior Conforto by the back of the head and yanked him close, then whispered into his ear, "I won't never forget dis, man. Anything you and your brother ever want, lemme know, man. It's fuckin' *done*."

"Frenchy, we gots that golden ticket, boy!" Junior crowed to me every night for weeks. "Carlos, he said *anything* we ever want; we gotsta favor, a free pass, from *dah Man*, man. We gots it made."

Junior and Angelo were fucking tap-dancing around the French Quarter, thinking their decades of going underappreciated and underutilized would end. Junior debated for months over what to ask for, and he decided that requesting too much would lead to bitterness and resentment from Carlos. Junior didn't want a handout since that would make him look like a welfare case; all he wanted from Carlos was an opportunity to prove himself.

Finally, Junior and Angelo agreed to ask for a loan to build a new dance lounge that they would co-own with Carlos, giving them an excuse to work closely with the godfather and impress him with their business acumen and trustworthiness. Once Carlos got to know them, the Confortos naturally figured that they would quickly become Carlos' personal bodyguards and trusted confidants. They never imagined that multimillionaire Carlos would turn them down on an inconsequential $10,000 or $20,000 loan.

"Well, boys," Carlos said from behind his big desk at the Town & Country Motel, "it's tough times right now."

"Carlos, we know; we'd really appreciate the loan," Junior

Conforto continued his pitch with a begging tone. "We'll show you it's a good investment."

"Boys, boys," Carlos laughed. "You must not been listenin'. I done *said* dat times are tough. What else can I say?"

The King Midas of Jefferson Parish, the owner of tens of thousands of acres of property and dozens of businesses, was pleading poverty. Carlos smirked, shrugged, and dismissively motioned with his hand for the Confortos to leave. Junior and Angelo had been turned down. Their "golden ticket" favor from Carlos Marcello had proven to be a ticket to go fuck themselves. The Confortos would never be Carlos' boys.

"That muthafuckah!" Junior screamed as he punched the walls of his family's bar and kicked over stools. "That muthafuckah said *anything! ANYTHING!* Anything we fuckin' wanted. Cheap, Jew-ass cocksucker!" I was pretty damn happy that the other Confortos had seen fit to close the doors to the bar and let Junior vent privately among friends. If Junior had talked that sort of shit in front a crowd, I would have had no choice but to save my ass and run to Carlos. Junior Conforto would have talked himself from a golden ticket to a one-way ticket into an alligator's colon.

Chapter V

Mr. Tux

Mid-1950s

"Dat stuff? It's like one of them fairy tales. Like *Sleepin' Beauty an' de Seven Dwarfs*."

Carlos Marcello
Reviewing *The Godfather*
As reported by John H. Davis in *Mafia Kingfish*

"FRENCHY, TONIGHT'S THE NIGHT YAH BEEN VAITING AND VAITING FOR; I'M TAKING YOU TO SEE THE MAN THEY CALL THE LITTLE BIG MAN," Dutch Kraut told me with a sleepy drunk smile from across our usual table at Kolb's. His words were swimming in the usual gargle of Löwenbräu. Seeing the puzzled look on my face, Dutch rushed to correct my impression that I was about to lose my virginity to a fat midget. "Frenchy, I'm takin' yah to see *The* Little Big Man, that's vut. That's Carlos, Frenchy, Mister Carlos Marcello. I'm taking yah to see the man in charge in this town, Carlos Marcello."

I had heard a great deal about Carlos Marcello; I will go as far as to say that he had become an inspiration to me. Everything I heard about Carlos sounded exactly like me.

As far as I could see, I was practically Carlos Jr. Like me, the godfather was raised in a backwater Louisiana village, given a shitty name he hated, spent his childhood lugging vegetables around for his dad, got the reputation as the black sheep of the family, ran away to move to the French Quarter as a teenager, and made up for his incomprehensible accent with his muscles. With so much in common, clearly we would become best friends, and he'd see to it that my career was an incredible success.

Coincidentally, my naïve fantasies about Carlos and I relating to each other turned out to come true. Very few people earned the trust of the paranoid and secretive Mafia boss of Louisiana, but somehow an obviously disreputable goon like me maintained a close friendship with him until he went senile.

After a dinner and drinks at Kolb's, Dutch instructed me to go back to my apartment and get dressed for a "formal" night on the town. "I can't be introducin' you to thah Little Big Man in vat shirt and blue jeans, Frenchy!"

This threw me into confusion. Besides sacraments of the Holy Catholic Church, I had never attended any sort of function that called for formal dress. I was liable to show up with an Abraham Lincoln hat on my head and tap-dancing shoes on my feet. Too embarrassed to ask Dutch, I hustled out of Kolb's intent on asking a complete stranger what "formal" meant and heading to the nearest department store.

Without time to visit a tailor, I purchased an off-the-rack tux completely unequal to the task of handling a muscular frame such as mine. As a result, I was unable to lift my arms, spread my legs, and walk at a normal pace without the risk that I would explode clean out of my clothes like the Incredible Hulk and find myself naked mid-stride. The collar was so tight around my throat that I was being very slowly suffocated, so my already incomprehensible accent obtained a desperate wheeze to add to its charm.

Still, the mere fact that I was wearing such a fine-sounding piece of clothing convinced me that I must have been a picture-perfect model of class—even if the tux fit like a surgical glove. I almost purchased an honest-to-god top hat to complete the ensemble.

When I returned to Kolb's with an affected stroll and a regal bearing worthy of Cary Grant, Dutch spit his Löwenbräu all over the table. I nearly gave the poor old kook a stroke. Choking on an unstoppable laughing fit, Dutch could not form a comprehensible syllable for around fifteen minutes.

Finally, the old man collected himself, had the maitre d' bring his sports coat, and walked me to his car. The fact that Dutch himself was only wearing a sports coat, slacks, and a business shirt should have been a hint that this wasn't exactly a top hat and cane affair. "Formal" to a French Quarter bookmaker probably wasn't Prince-of-Wales formal.

Dutch had a grand ole laugh at me as we waited for our limousine to arrive. On the verge of delirium, Dutch was harping on how my tiny tux reduced my normal stride to a tight-assed, straitjacketed waddle. Dutch damn near collapsed to the sidewalk, wiping tears from his eyes and mumbling the word, "Penguin! Penguin!" I was redder than a baboon's ass as I pulled him up, and only my fear of my suit popping off my limbs stopped me from running away at top speed.

Finally, a limo courtesy of Carlos Marcello arrived outside of Kolb's to take us to The Beverly Country Club, the Mafia's luxury casino in Jefferson Parish. This was not a perk for Dutch and me—anyone in southeast Louisiana could call The Beverly and order a free limo ride to the casino. It was all on Carlos, and it was a great scam. Think about this for a second: once the marks were trapped at The Beverly as Carlos' hostage audience, how long do you think they were kept at the bar waiting for their ride home, drinking and cranking those slot machines to pass the time?

The Beverly was New York crime boss Frank Costello and Carlos Marcello's local response to the new casinos of Las Vegas and Havana. The charm of the place was that it was every bit as luxurious, ambitious, and ostentatious as those other casinos — despite being built in a state where casino gambling was illegal. How do you hide a sprawling palace of chance that serves tens of thousands of customers and employed hundreds of people?

As far as Carlos was concerned, you *didn't*. He planted that architectural middle finger right in plain sight in suburban Jefferson Parish and built it fancy enough that it could be seen from space. That should give you an idea what Carlos thought about the American government and its laws — and why a rebellious teenager like me came to idolize him.

They don't make criminals like that anymore; Carlos was the sort of prick who would've interrupted Judgment Day to tell God that his attorney was filing a motion for a change of venue. Carlos was so bold that he could *credibly* be accused of being arrogant and daring enough to "order a K" on President Kennedy.

That boldness occasionally cost Carlos, and the Beverly Country Club was one obvious instance. With a construction cost in the millions, the lavish casino was shut down in 1950 due to attention from Senator Estes Kefauver, whose Senate committee declared Carlos "the evil genius of organized crime in Louisiana" and ridiculed the local sheriff for allowing The Beverly to operate wide open. The Beverly was eventually reopened when the heat wore off, but it was a quieter affair and voluntarily shut its doors whenever Carlos was in the news.

I very slowly and cautiously exited Carlos' black limo, worried about the possibility of a sudden tear in what New Orleans black girls call "cat cruncher" tight pants. I had been far too self-conscious to enjoy my first limo ride. Dutch was sweating heavily from the combination of booze and laughter, so he looked even more ragged and disreputable than usual. "Be veh-wee careful, thah, Frenchy. Ha, ha, you must vatch that poor outvit; it looks like it is holdin' on for its dear life!" That fossil was still stumbling and crying from the laughter when he exited the limo, and I thought I had no chance of avoiding a massive embarrassment.

Stepping inside The Beverly momentarily distracted me from my cat-suit tux. In my first year in New Orleans, I had sworn that I had seen everything, but my jaded attitude was dismantled in a moment. This place was grander than anything I had ever seen in a movie: golden door handles, enormous sparkling chandeliers, eruptions of roses in antique vases, monogrammed silverware, miles and miles of pristine oriental carpets, walls draped in silk, and cocktail waitresses serving flutes of champagne.

As rich as French Quarter characters like Diamond Jim Moran and Sam Saia were, The Beverly was proof that Carlos Marcello and Frank Costello were operating with Midas' checkbook. Their resources were closer to royalty than crime bosses, and it came as no surprise to me when the FBI later claimed that Carlos' Mafia empire was by far the biggest industry in the state of Louisiana. Carlos had ample cash to spare — just not for the Conforto brothers.

Thanks to the flurry of nods, winks, and hand gestures that spread contagiously across the Beverly's staff as we walked onto the brightly lit gaming floor, I could tell that Dutch Kraut was recognized as a man of importance. This display seem to sober Dutch up instantly; he became more concerned with playing the Big Shot than laughing at how deep my pants were wedged into my ass-crack — and, baby, they were as deep as they could get without compromising my innocence before God.

I painfully shuffled behind Dutch without an idea of where we going, when I sensed that someone was staring at me. Looking around, I spotted two fuming black eyes over Dutch's right shoulder. I immediately recognized the owner of that deathly stare as The Little Big Man, Carlos Marcello.

Carlos Marcello was known as The Little Big Man because he was a five-foot-four, Humpty-Dumpty little dago with silver-and-black hair who stood with the erect, hulking posture of a Goliath. Dressed simply in a beautifully tailored black suit, Carlos so forcefully radiated power and aggression that I felt myself grow smaller with each step I took toward him. Even with Dutch walking ahead of me, I had that same "holy shit, I'm not prepared for this" feeling I got when the bell rung for the first round of a boxing match.

As he cordially shook the hand of his old pal Dutch, Carlos focused intently on my face, trying to place me in his enormous catalogue of acquaintances. His gaze was so intimidating that I felt good and ready for a nice faint. With his ragingly intense eyes, oil- black eyebrows, and sharp beak nose, Carlos had this feral look about him like an eagle staring down a rabbit. I felt a heat wave across my skin as he sized me up.

Dutch introduced me with glowing enthusiasm and explained that I was working with Sam Saia, which earned an appreciative nod from Carlos. The hand I extended to the Boss was shaky, clammy, and cold as a blue crab salad. With snapping turtle reflexes, Carlos snatched my hand and gave it a squeeze that could have crushed an apple.

"Carlos Mar-sella, nice to meet-cher, man!" Carlos spit out with a gruff voice and dirt-poor, country-ass accent that contrasted to an absurd extent with our swanky surroundings.

I immediately liked Carlos with a passion when I heard that voice; here was one operator who was every bit as country as me. I felt my body calm and my senses return; it felt as if cataracts had been scraped from my eyes, huge peanut butter scoops of wax removed from my ears, and a crippling case of the stupids lifted from my tongue.

"Hallo there, Mr. Carlos, my name is Frenchy Brool-yet. It's suh honor to meet ya after all dat Mr. Kraut here has told me about ya." Carlos nodded graciously and smiled far more brightly and charmingly than you would ever have expected from a man with his devilish reputation. He looked downright friendly.

"Hello there, Frenchy," said a quiet, croaky, strained voice from Carlos' side. The small, aging, big-nosed gentleman who extended his hand to me was the meekest and most unobtrusive person I had yet met in big-talking, cocky New Orleans. He looked like a professor or an IRS agent in a narrowly tailored suit. As I shook his soft, manicured hand, I stole a glance at his gorgeous blue silk tie and the perfectly crumpled, white silk handkerchief popping out of his left breast pocket like a rose.

"It's truly a pleasure to meet you," the gentleman continued, "my name is Frank Costello."

I felt my hand flinch, unintentionally putting a righteous squeeze on Costello's hand as I heard his name. I was eye-to-eye with the most famous gangster in America, the protégé and successor of Lucky Luciano, the legend who had been crowned "The Prime Minister of the Underworld" by the press. Known for his classy Wall Street–style approach to organized crime and his appearances at high-society charity balls, Costello's courtly manner and strained voice would be imitated by Marlon Brando for the role of Don Corleone in *The Godfather.*

Costello's introduction evaporated my temporary calm and rendered me bolt-stiff and nervous in my suffocating tuxedo. Carlos may have been a Louisiana hick like me, but Frank Costello sure seemed as classy and blue-blooded as a Roosevelt.

As Dutch was making animated small talk with his old pals Carlos and Frank, a tall and stately black waiter in a tuxedo approached and nodded to us. "May I offer you some refreshments, gentlemen?" he asked with painstaking enunciation.

"Nothing for me, thank you, young man," coughed up Frank Costello.

"Coffee, hot!" grunted Carlos out of the corner of his mouth.

"Ahh, vell, you have Löwenbräu, no? Oh, good, Löwenbräu then!" said predictable Dutch.

The black waiter craned in my direction and inexplicably shot me a demented smile. This guy was shining porcelain at me like we were long-lost brothers; I had no idea what was going on.

"Sir, if you don't mind me asking, I do not recognize you, and I thought I knew everyone in town in our profession," the waiter asked as he eyed my tuxedo, which was identical to his. "Where is it that you wait?"

"Dressing formally" turned out to mean that I was wearing the same tuxedo as a black waiter. As humiliated as I was at that moment, I must credit myself for not projectile vomiting all over poor Frank Costello.

There was an awkward, lip-biting pause while I pondered whether the waiter's comment had been heard by the rest of my party, but my confusion was quickly dispelled. "*Holy shit,*" gasped Carlos, "dat's *cold,* man!"

Even prim Frank Costello could not help but chuckle, and I am pretty sure Dutch Kraut may have sprayed Lowenbrau all over his boxers. Carlos gave me a friendly punch on my shoulder and smiled, as if to encourage me for being a good sport.

"C'mon, nah, Frenchy, lemme show you mah office," Carlos said, placing a hand on my shoulder and damn near squeezing my lat muscle off the bone. "I gots the nicest office you ever saw. It's all fuckin' electric, man. I press a button, and walls disappear, blinds open, a bar comes out of the fucking wall! It's like magic, man! Damndest fucking shit you ever saw!"

From that moment to his death forty years later, Carlos Marcello never saw me without an immediate smile for "Mr. Tux." Though he never said it, I think he had a soft spot for me thanks to that bumbling first impression. Carlos had once been an eighteen-year-old hick who ran away from home to live a life of adventure in the French Quarter, and he forever pictured me as the same lovably clueless Cajun teenager he met in the Beverly Country Club.

Sometimes a first impression is the only impression you ever get to make.

It wasn't really a surprise Carlos liked me. Even at the height of their power, most Mob bosses were not exactly Rhode Scholars and society cocktail party fixtures. They were uneducated violent criminals and drug dealers who got powerful. Though the police chiefs and politicians would have loved to become their close friends, most of those crooks loathed being in the company of "white" people who made them feel self-conscious about their lack of culture, education, and breeding. Most mobsters preferred the comfort of associating with pimps, stickup kids, and degenerate gamblers — the sort of people whose culture and attitudes they *understood*.

Carlos' personality, conversational style, experiences, sense of humor, and outlook on life all had far more in common with a humble hick like me than they did with any congressman or business tycoon. We were just two black sheep, Catholic country boys pursuing lives that we knew would most likely end badly. No matter how much trouble we got into for being each other's friend — and we both paid for it at one time or another — we stuck together from that first night at the Beverly County Club.

And if Carlos and his brother Joe weren't long dead, you wouldn't be reading this book, baby — believe *dat*!

"I'm successful because I'm the everyman. I'm *every* man."
Carlos Marcello

Baby, don't believe the hype; Carlos Marcello was the first African-American Mafia boss.

Before you think I'm being cute like the people who say the first black president was Bill Clinton (whose rich uncle supposedly financed Clinton's early career using money he made with Carlos), let me tell you that Carlos Marcello was literally born in Africa. Culturally, Carlos also happened to be as black as Fats Domino — or at least as black as a Mafia boss could be in the Jim Crow South and survive.

For most of his life, Carlos Marcello's biography could have fit any small-time black crook. He was the uneducated son of a field hand on a sugar plantation who was given a new name by the plantation owner. He was a stickup kid as a teenager. He did hard labor on the prison plantation with blues singer Leadbelly and made his name in the underworld as a marijuana dealer and moonshine retailer in a Negro bar.

As an adult, Carlos talked jive, partied in jazz clubs, drove golden Cadillacs, wore enormous black sunglasses in the dead of night, and knew more black folk on a first-name basis than any pandering politician. He had a more intimate understanding of black culture than any wiseguy I ever met.

Even as a Mafia boss, Carlos had soul. The blues spread across the South largely thanks to Carlos' decision to include "Negro" records in the jukeboxes he forcefully installed throughout the South.

The man known as Carlos Marcello was born Calogero Minacore in 1910 to a poor Sicilian family in Tunisia. As a baby, the young Carlos journeyed with his family to Louisiana and a new home: Algiers, a swampy village across the Mississippi from New Orleans named after the African pirate city. The young family had its name changed to "Marcello" by a plantation overseer, and baby Calogero was given the less difficult name of "Carlos." I always sensed that Carlos didn't appreciate having his very Sicilian name replaced with a name more fitting of a Puerto Rican cab driver.

After a few years of field-hand labor, the Marcellos purchased a family farm in the swampland and settled down to raise tomatoes, turnips, and kids. Mama Marcello squatted out six more sons and two daughters, all of them American citizens — unlike their unnaturalized big brother, Carlos.

Carlos' parents were so poor that they could not afford the proverbial "turnip truck," and they were unlucky that the Brouillette family vegetable-towing business didn't service Algiers. Instead, young Carlos spent his youth lugging vegetables around in the pestilential swamp heat in the back of a horse and buggy. Known as the ornery kicking mule of his family, ignorant redneck Carlos abandoned his family at the age of eighteen to move to the French Quarter. He had a very rough time.

Carlos looked up to the French Quarter hoods like I idolized Roy Rogers. Carlos had watched the Mafia his entire life since it was his job to sell his family's produce in the French Market in the Quarter, which was run by "Silver Dollar" Sam Carollo's gang. Carlos began engineering daring armed robberies in the hope of impressing the wiseguys.

He failed.

At the age of nineteen, Carlos was convicted of robbing a grocery and sentenced to seven-to-ten in the worst prison in America, the converted slave plantation known as Angola — another African name. Angola earned its name by brutally whipping its prisoners as they toiled in the sugarcane fields. When I was kid, a gang of Angolan prisoners made headlines when they took razor blades to their Achilles tendons to cripple themselves and get out of the backbreaking slave labor. The press called them "The Heel String Gang."

Having proven himself a stand-up guy in Angola, Carlos was released in 1934 by gubernatorial pardon. Carlos served four years in Hell, and, baby, if you ask me, I bet that death stare he used to such effect over the years was developed as a handsome, undersized teenager in Angola. Carlos may have gotten physically soft as he aged, but there is no doubt that he had to have the thick skin and bite of a gator to emerge from that prison with a reputation as a stone-cold convict.

Almost immediately after his release, Carlos was recruited by the reigning French Quarter Mob chieftains of the day, Frank Todaro and Baptiste Pecoraro. Always a master politician, Carlos quickly married Frank Todaro's daughter and was consequently inducted into Silver Dollar Sam's Family.

If his stint in Angola did not prove Carlos' toughness, his overnight rise in Silver Dollar Sam's Family certainly did. Silver Dollar Sam was more Wild West gunslinger than a typical Mob godfather, and he ran a crime family that had more in common with modern cocaine cartels than the gentleman mobsters you see in the movies.

After scheming his way to the title of Mob boss by his mid-twenties, Sam built a reputation as a complete maniac by personally committing his own murders and traveling in broad daylight with a sawed-off shotgun hanging from a sling around his shoulder. In a few months in 1930, Silver Dollar Sam was arrested both for the shooting of the top bootlegger in New Orleans *and* the shooting of a federal narcotics agent who had dared to go undercover against him.

That penchant for assassination was a unique characteristic that only the New Orleans Mafia, the oldest Family in America by decades, shared with its relatives in Sicily. Only in the Big Easy would crooks openly go after feds, judges, cops, and even Presidents; every white boy was fair game. The old wiseguys loved to tell the story of how the Family whacked out New Orleans Police Chief David Hennessy in 1890 for doing his job.

In my day, the old blues and jazz musicians still sang songs about the murder of old Chief Hennessy. Usually, it was the contemporary wiseguys who were requesting the song. They dedicated the song to their favorite cop or President Kennedy, hollered along with every lyric, clinked glasses, and threw twenty-dollar bills on the stage.

Ex-con Carlos set up his first headquarters in The Brown Bomber, a dumpy black bar where he sold marijuana and moonshine. In a viciously racist Mafia family in the segregated South, Carlos' decision to associate with black folk was a little bit queer. His marijuana racket was also curiously "black" since pot was an almost exclusively hepcat black drug in those days. Carlos was no small-time peddler, either; in 1938, he sold an undercover FBI agent twenty-three pounds of marijuana in one sale, which might as well have been a ton for that era.

When Senator Huey Long, Frank Costello, and Silver Dollar Sam made their deal to open up Louisiana to the national gambling syndicate, it was this hardcore ex-con drug dealer who was the unlikeliest beneficiary. Handpicked by Frank Costello to distribute his slot machines in the South, Carlos organized his six younger brothers and some cousins and muscled Costello's machines into every available storefront from Grand Isle to Marksville. Once he had established the relationships with the local police departments and business owners, Carlos expanded his business to include the distribution of jukeboxes, pinball machines, and cigarette dispensers — all steady-income, no-work rackets.

By the time Silver Dollar Sam was deported to Italy in 1947, there was no one in Louisiana who could challenge Carlos' bankroll and muscle. In a symbolic move, Carlos called a Mafia conclave at —what else —a segregated Negro bar called the Black Diamond owned by New Orleans pimp Henry Muller. Carlos always had a soft spot for pimps, another common trait with black hoods.

At the Black Diamond, Carlos had himself formally recognized as acting boss of the New Orleans Family until Silver Dollar Sam could have his deportation order reversed. Carlos would be the boss and later official godfather of New Orleans until his death nearly a half century later.

During his long reign, Carlos cultivated closer ties to black America than any other Mafia boss in history. Carlos was a friend to dozens of black ward bosses, crooked preachers, business leaders, entertainers, and average folk over the years, and he treated them beautifully to their faces. When Carlos needed to launder money and property by registering countless cars, houses, businesses, and real estate properties, he ignored Italians and put his loot in the names of black families he had "adopted" and financially supported. I know black women who grew up revering their "Uncle Carlos," the jolly Italian who bounced them on his knee and dropped off expensive Christmas presents every year.

Because of this, Carlos was in constant danger of being seen as a "nigger lover" in the underworld, which would have been a death sentence. Silver Dollar Sam surrounded himself with men who would pull a trigger as casually as they would rip a fart, and the idea that Silver Dollar Sam's successor was a "race traitor" would have been ample excuse to clip him.

To compensate, whenever Carlos was around white folk he acted like black people gave him hives. "Nigger" was used like commas in Carlos' sentences. Carlos made a point to brag that he hated black people so much that he regularly donated money to the Ku Klux Klan — which also hated Catholics, Italians, and illegal aliens, three minority categories which obviously applied to Carlos.

Carlos also constantly talked about whacking out Martin Luther King, and, after the assassination, he occasionally would hint around with a smile that he had "taken care of" King. It's commonly said that his associates were meeting with supposed assassin James Earl Ray shortly before Dr. King's murder, so I wouldn't dismiss the possibility if someone gave him enough money.

Despite all that, I guess what I am tap-dancing around saying is the feeling that Carlos had a soft spot for black people in his heart. Compared to the venomous hate he spit at real enemies like the Kennedys, his racist talk seemed half-hearted.

If you ask me, Carlos was probably every bit the racist and every bit the hepcat. He was a poor illegal alien and ex-con who was cool with some blacks but hated and feared "niggers," the breed of "uppity" blacks that a lot of Southerners defined as their own separate race. Those blacks threatened the status quo – the status quo where Carlos reigned as king.

Carlos was a pretty good representative of 1950s New Orleans, where the locals idolized black musicians as superstars...and also applauded when those same musicians were beaten and robbed by the cops whenever they walked around Bourbon Street without prominently displaying their instruments. They didn't want them getting "too big for their britches."

"She used to say she hoped her death would be that her husband caught her in bed with a sixteen-year-old and shot her."
Wayne Bernard
Ex-husband of Norma Wallace
As quoted in *The Last Madam* by Christine Wiltz

Around the time that I goofed into charming the most powerful man in Louisiana thanks to a tiny tuxedo, Dutch sent me on a mission to the most powerful *woman* in Louisiana. Once again, I acted the fool so well that I earned myself another lifelong mentor, guardian, and friend. I just had the knack for dummying upwards.

I am speaking of the legendary Norma Wallace, Queen of the French Quarter, the last great New Orleans madam and the most spectacular woman that ever had the good taste to want to have sex with me. In 1954, Norma was probably the most infamous criminal in New Orleans, more so than even Carlos Marcello. The Mafia was still a mysterious tall tale in those days, and the wiseguys were well camouflaged by the fact that every single public official in the state was a criminal as well. On the other hand, there was *no* woman like Norma Wallace, and very few men.

Long before women got around to getting liberated, Norma lived freer than every man I knew, and I knew plenty of outlaws and free-spirited French Quarter gypsy types. To say that Norma was a man born into a woman's body would be giving undue credit to men. I never had the balls that she did, and I can't think of anyone I ever met besides Carlos and Silver Dollar Sam who could compete with her.

Norma was notorious for not giving a good goddamn about any rule that was supposed to govern women's behavior. A voluptuous, forty-something lady when I met her, Norma had been in the sex rackets since her mom turned her out as a small child in the French Quarter, yet she had never seen the inside of a jail cell. This was considered one of the greatest achievements in New Orleans history since *no* criminal besides Silver Dollar Sam invited the attention of the press and police more than Norma Wallace.

Norma loved the spotlight, and she loved what the spotlight did for her bordello's business. Norma mocked police officers and district attorneys in the press, vamped for newspaper photographers on her way into courtrooms, discarded husbands like toothpicks, openly conducted passionate affairs with celebrities and gangsters, and made a scene in all the swanky nightlife joints by appearing in opera diva gowns with a gaggle of gorgeously turned-out hookers.

With her cocked fedora, platinum hair, and dangerously low-cut dresses, Norma cast herself as a celebrity and filled the role so well that even the blue-bloods treated her like one.

When Dutch Kraut told me that he was reshuffling my duties so that my route included Norma's renowned "Green House" bordello at 1026 Conti Street, I was far more intimidated than when I had been told I would be meeting Carlos Marcello. Carlos was a murderous gangster, but I did well with murderous gangsters.

On the other hand, Norma appeared to be the most extraordinary woman in the world, and I was a catastrophic failure even with completely ordinary women. My nervousness and fear of visiting that bordello was mightily intensified by the presence of Norma's dozen or so girls, all young and beautiful, who I had been trained by the movies to picture as sex-mad harridans. As a scared-shitless Catholic virgin, I trembled at what would be done to me by these hungry lionesses.

Needless to say, I spent about two hours doing my hair and selecting my outfit on the first morning that Norma Wallace's bordello was added to my route. If I was to be damned, I decided that I should undertake to fall in style. I also felt like I somehow owed it to Norma's house full of prostitutes to be sexier than I normally was. (And baby, that took some work.) I don't feel comfortable using the phrase "thought process" when it comes to me, but what passed for mine was similar to people who try harder to be funny when talking to a comedian.

I was, of course, being a damn fool. Until you've lived my sort of life, you cannot imagine anyone less sexy-feeling than a working whore in the early morning hours after a full shift. I could have walked into Norma's place with Paul Newman and Marlon Brando in tow, and the ladies' only concern would have been to remind us to keep down the racket so they could sleep.

Standing outside Norma's bordello, I was pretty unimpressed. This narrow, three-story tenement with black ironwork balconies on the second and third floors certainly did not look like Hell's embassy on Earth, and it wasn't exactly glamorous in comparison to the many splendid homes I knew in the French Quarter. I was expecting sensual decadence on the scale of the Beverly Country Club.

I was relieved to be visiting Norma Wallace's bordello with a credible, full-proof alibi. I was no pervert and degenerate: just an organized criminal doing my job. I felt like I was getting a free shot to gawk and take in the sights without being self-conscious, as if bookmaking was somehow a less sinful and embarrassing activity than paying for a piece of ass.

I rapped on the front door of the quiet building. Nothing. I pounded on the door a few more times. Nothing.

Finally, I got a good rhythm going on the rickety old door, which suddenly opened the tiniest slit. A young black girl's face appeared in the crack. "Sorry, sir," the young girl said politely. "Miss Norma is not available to receive gentlemen callers at this hour. You *must* excuse us." The door shut.

Embarrassed to be mistaken for a john, I shouted in my best attempt at a gruff and businesslike underworld voice, "Open up! I've been sent by Dutch and Sam, let me in!"

The door cracked open again. "Boy, I don't care who referred you," the pretty girl said quite assertively with a leer that implied that I was mentally incapacitated in one fashion or another. She quickly collected herself and restored her studied, proper tone, continuing, "Miss Norma is not receiving visitors at the moment. This is not an appropriate hour to be calling."

"No, clearly, *you* don't understand," I said, getting grumpy since anyone passing by would have thought I was a sex freak like Neil Gautier begging to get laid at 9 a.m. in the morning. "I'm not a customer, mam! I am the new runner who picks up all the bets and delivers the payoffs! You know, sports bets?"

"Boy," the girl said as she whipped open the door to reveal a prim maid's outfit. "Why didn'tcha say somethin'?" she said with a smile, her impression of a movie governess replaced by a country black accent. "You people owe me two dollars on yesterday's race at the Fairgrounds." I was escorted inside. "I guess you want to meet Miss Norma, bein' the new boy and all!" the girl said with what may have been a wink.

The girl knew that she was serving her boss a prime cut.

If Norma's bordello seemed a letdown from the outside, on the inside it was reassuringly bonkers. Fine antique lamps, carpets, and furniture were used as mattresses by a mess of marauding monkeys, parrots, and yappy dogs. The place smelled like a zoo sprayed with expensive perfume and potpourri. I would learn that working as Norma's maid was one of the most stressful jobs in New Orleans: besides the police harassment, any maid had to deal with Norma's incessant demands to keep the house immaculate despite her own refusal to restrain her menagerie of exotic pets.

Norma's more ornery girls raised hell about those damn pets and the number they did on everyone's living quarters, but Norma dismissed their objections with queenly disinterest. "Girls," Norma would drawl, "rest assured that my pets are not the wild animals I would kick out of here if given the choice!"

As I walked into Norma's surprisingly small office, little did I suspect that I had been set up by Fate. On a normal morning at 9 a.m., I would have seen Norma with sore red eyes, her hair in rollers, her face covered in bright neon facial cream, and her busty body swathed in a frumpy silk robe. She was susceptible to blinding headaches in those early morning hours when the sunlight burned her night-accustomed eyes, and I often would see her splayed on a couch with a rubber ice bag on her head. On an average morning, in other words, Norma was anything but a sexually intimidating presence.

However, it was just my luck that Norma had a court date scheduled for an hour after my first visit to the bordello and was thus in peak condition. Dolled up to please New Orleans's newspaper and TV photographers, Norma was introduced to me as the Goddess of Love in all of her glory. I had never been so physically attracted to a woman in my life, especially a woman thirty years older than me. She dressed like a fashion model and had the presence of a movie star.

Squeezed into a form-fitting, narrow-waisted lady's business suit, Norma had painstakingly chosen an outfit that pulled, yanked, propped up, and redistributed her voluptuous figure in the most charming fashion. Her brightly painted toes and fine calves were well showcased by open-toed high heels, and she wore a fashionable Parisian hat cocked to the point that it was almost falling off of her head.

Her blond hair flickered like no human hair I had ever seen before, and I swear to you that not a single strand was not exactly where it was meant to be. She had the most disciplined head of hair I have ever had the honor to admire.

I could see through Norma's large, ostentatious sunglasses that she liked what she was seeing, as well. I later learned that Norma's preference in sexual partners was very convenient: she liked 'em very young, very naïve, very muscular, and very Mediterranean. In other words, I might as well have been wearing a big red bow.

"Why, hello, young man, how may I help you?" Norma said with a lilting, affected voice that, to me, sounded like how queens and duchesses must have spoken at grand balls. Norma had a perfect mark in me; I never would have suspected that she had grown up a starving poor French Quarter street urchin and child prostitute. "It is most unusual to receive visitors at this time of the day, but I assume my maid must have had a pressing reason to escort you to my room."

"Uh. Uh?" Those two grunts were about all I could muster for half a minute. Every moment I stood tongue-tied and awestruck flattered Norma's ego and raised my stock in her eyes — she never tired of displaying her sexual dominance over young men. If I had never made a single intelligible sound, we probably would have been married within days. As far as I could tell, this was the strategy used by her last husband with great success; it was only when he began to speak and ruin his dumb, dark, and handsome appeal that things went bad.

"Calm down, honey," Norma reassured me as she gently placed a bejeweled hand on my shoulder. "Let's walk out onto the patio and enjoy some demitasse."

My eyes grew wide and panic-stricken. Behind her sunglasses, Norma fixed a searching look on me, trying to deduce what in her offer could have possibly scared me so. After a moment, Norma found me out. "Oh, boy, there is nothing to worry about. *Demitasse* is just a small cup for coffee or espresso, just a saying, nothing untoward!"

"Oh," I said as my tensed shoulders slumped with relief. *Demitasse* sounded far too French and suggestive for my comfort. "It's okay...I mean, I'm okay. It's just been, well, a long night for me," I improvised, concocting a lie that made me look like a degenerate drunk or drug addict.

"Do tell me about it, honey," Norma said warmly, clearly enjoying my embarrassment.

"Uh, no, I don't think...that, uh...interesting...at all." I cleared my throat. "I'm actually, believe it or not...I am here on business. Someone...actually...hired me. I work for Dutch Kraut and Sam Saia, and I'll be picking up the, uh, money and bets around here, uh, now and then continuing from now."

"Well, that's excellent news," Norma cooed, leaning in and poking a finger into my chest with the intention of flustering me. "That means we'll be seeing each other every...single...day," Norma whispered, licking her lips between each word. Snaking a soft and lovely arm around my shoulder, Norma pressed her perfumed body next to mine and sighed. "We can't *help* but get to be great friends."

I'll be honest with you: it is to my eternal discredit as Mr. New Orleans that I managed to fumble the opportunity to lose my virginity to the most notorious madam in Louisiana history. I saw the lady every goddamn day for years, and it was no secret to anyone that she had her eye on me. If she had made the first move — as was her style — I would have surrendered with great relief.

Being defiled by Norma would have been a favor to my soul as well as my body. I was going to commit the sin of fornication eventually, but being seduced by Norma would have exonerated me from all responsibility. God is a sensible sort, and He must understand that it would be unfair to expect a guileless fool like me to resist the French Quarter's most devilish temptress. Clearly, I would have been the helpless victim; the sin would have been *hers*.

Unfortunately for my soul, two obstacles appeared in the way of my destiny to become the third or fourth Mr. Norma Wallace. The first problem was that I only saw Norma in the early morning, when she typically felt as sexy as a rabies-infested nutria. The other issue was that someone told the poor girl that her ex-husband Pete Herman, who had originally bankrolled Norma's bordello when she was a young floozy on the make, owned a piece of my career as a boxer.

Suspecting that I may have been off-limits, Norma hesitated to strike a defenseless target like me just long enough for us to fall into the routine of being friends instead of lovers. By the time that she learned that easygoing Pete couldn't have cared less,

Norma thought of me more as a helpless country cousin than a strapping teenage bodybuilder with a bad case of blue balls.

Instead of mentoring me in the art of sex, Norma ended up teaching me the ways of the vice racket. In the same way I was Dutch Kraut's understudy in the world of gambling and the Mafia, I became Norma Wallace's protégé in the skin trade.

I was honored to be her student, but I was destined to disappoint Norma as I had every other female who ever blundered into my life. It was to Norma's great annoyance that I found other teachers to help show me the ropes.

"Old Hyp Guinle liked to drink, but the older he became the more of a family man he became. He was basically all right as an old man. As a young man, though, he had the reputation of being a royal asshole – just as soon to kick your ass as shake your hand."

Evangeline the Oyster Girl

I owe my pimp hand to the Godfather of Jazz, Hypolite "Hyp" Guinle. Hyp made his name as a French Quarter "fancy man" and "business manager" in the 1930s, and as was then fashionable for New Orleans pimps, he invested his loot in the jazz racket.

French Quarter bordello hang-arounds and street musicians had invented jazz music in Hyp's infancy, and this outlaw ghetto music naturally attracted black market investors like rap does today. Many characters tried to follow the path blazed by French Quarter pimp, cardsharp, and piano genius Ferdinand "Jelly Roll" Morton, who achieved riches and stardom in the jazz racket.

Without the musical genius to cut it as a recording artist, Hyp sought to emulate Jelly Roll by becoming a jazz promoter. In 1934, he leased the premises of a 19th century pharmacy at 339 Bourbon Street for $50 and renamed it The Famous Door. Hyp stocked The Famous Door's dance floor with the most beautiful fallen women in the South and hired the top hootenanny jazz acts to play wild, loose, and fast.

Unfortunately, as I can attest, pimps make poor businessmen. We are too inclined to play Big Shot, adopting stray bar tabs like Baptists adopting Chinese babies. Like me, Hyp Guinle was a regular genius at shitting away cash to no good purpose besides looking cool, and, unlike me, he was a degenerate gambling fool to boot. By 1940, the word was that the owner of the most popular jazz club in the city was in danger thanks to his outstanding debts.

Enter Hyp Guinle's blushing new bride, Genevieve, who supposedly had the money to make right Guinle's debts and save his life. A strong-willed and mercilessly practical woman from a real spaghetti-and-meatballs family, Genevieve gave old Hyp an ultimatum: turn over The Famous Door's books to her and leave the pimp game, or face Silver Dollar Sam's debt collectors as a penniless bachelor. Though New Orleans knew no greater "good time man" than old Hyp, he paroled himself into the custody of his no-bullshit Italian bride.

He spent the rest of his life under a type of house arrest.

No longer a player, Hyp became a spectator. After a lifetime as a gangster, Hyp suffered severe withdrawals as a normal mark. In desperation, he conceived of a plan to place himself as near to the street game as legally possible. With Genevieve's blessing, he opened a secret hole-in-the-wall social club behind The Famous Door called The Spot, to which only bona fide underworld characters were allowed entrance.

You never saw an uglier, tougher, and more credentialed group of thugs in Christendom than the lineup of creatures in The Spot on an early weekend morning. The only regulars at The Spot who did not boast demonic rap sheets were me and old Genevieve herself.

The only condition that Genevieve set on Hyp's plan to surround himself with gangsters and pimps was that she must be allowed to be present at all times. During my hundreds of visits to The Spot, I do not recall a single time when matronly Genevieve was not situated right in the center of the action, happily and permanently chopping garlic for the kitchen. Though she never looked up from her cutting board or said a word, you could see a smirk of amusement and satisfaction on her face as she listened to all of the characters regale the room with their tall tales.

Even more so than her husband, Genevieve got one hell of a contact high from being around crooks; after all, she had married Hyp!

The only person who could detach Genevieve from her cutting board and her crusade to dice every garlic bulb below the Mason-Dixon Line was Carlos Marcello. If Carlos had not been married to Frank Todaro's pretty little daughter, I have a feeling that he would have made Genevieve Guinle the next inductee into the Marcello family. He loved Genevieve with a love purer and sweeter than any other: the love of a fat Italian for good Italian food.

I've known my share of hungry guidos, but I do believe that no animal ever born to a mortal woman nursed a more ravenous hunger for greasy Italian food than Carlos Marcello.

That is one reason why I became a close friend; as a constantly training bodybuilding and boxer, I was always hungry and always itchin', in my nervous way, to hijack every social gathering and redirect it to the nearest restaurant. In my forty years of friendship with Carlos, he never turned down an invitation to a restaurant — even if he was presently eating *at another restaurant.*

Carlos' passion for food was ultimately his tragic flaw — and the saving grace of many other wiseguys. If you were in Carlos' doghouse, it was an open secret in the New Orleans Mafia that the only way to survive was to do whatever you could to distract Carlos from your mistakes by getting on the topic of food. Like a pregnant woman, Carlos was susceptible to hypnosis via induced food cravings. Whenever I heard Carlos angrily lecture his lieutenants, they would begin in the most comical fashion to plant subliminal reminders of Carlos favorite foods into their responses.

"I know, Carlos, I'm sorry; I'm redder than Mosca's red gravy over here!"

"Carlos, there's no excuse for what I did; I deserve to be barbecued like an alligator for letting you down!"

"Sorry, Carlos. I'm torn up about what I done. My stomach is tied into knots like Italian sausages."

Eventually, Carlos' tongue would begin licking his lips, and his brain would short-circuit. "Aw, fuck it, man!" Carlos would grumble. "Let's go get sumptin' to fuckin' eat over here. I'm fuckin' starvin'!"

When the FBI finally took down Carlos and sent him to jail, it was thanks to the undercover work of agents who had earned his trust through constant invitations to his favorite restaurants. It was Carlos' deeply held belief that no limp-dick G-man could sit at a dinner table and eat like a real man through course after punishing course at restaurants like Tony Angello's or Impastato's. Until he saw their faces at court, Carlos never could believe that his heavyweight dinner pals — who had shared such meaningful culinary memories with him — could really have betrayed him.

Carlos' dilemma when it came to Genevieve and The Spot was a matter of image control and risk management. Carlos felt it was beneath his station in life to associate with the street-level characters who patronized The Spot, and, in his experience, even momentary exposure to average petty crooks resulted in serious hassles from beggars and rats.

Nonetheless, Carlos was constantly complaining of his inability to enjoy a peaceful meal at Hyp Guinle's joint. The source of The Spot's allure was Genevieve's Old Country recipe for *braciole*, the fried beef-roll dish commonly used by wiseguys as a nickname for their cock. Displaying the unmistakable genius of Louisiana Italians to mispronounce anything with a syllable,

Carlos mangled the Sicilian *braciole* (brah-zhole) into something resembling *booshaloni*.

"Frenchy, man, I'mma needin' some of dat booshaloni right 'bout now, ya hear me?" Carlos would grumble with crazed eyes. "Goddam dem fuckers at The Spot. Dat old battle axe Genevieve won't give my man Provino [Provino Mosca, the personal chef to Mob luminaries from Al Capone to Carlos Marcello] dat goddam recipe, man! Fuck it! Let's go!"

Carlos' solution to his frequent *booshaloni* cravings was to park his Cadillac or his black limousine outside of The Spot and send in his driver to tell Genevieve to get cooking. Genevieve would throw that busy garlic-dicing knife down and damn near sprint into the kitchen to get to work for her favorite customer.

Braciole is a time-consuming dish to prepare, so it became something of an embarrassment to Carlos that he would twiddle his thumbs for an hour or two in a car parked in full view of Bourbon Street's pedestrian traffic. Everyone in The Spot recognized Carlos' driver and his heavily tinted rides, but Carlos slunk back in his seat and refused to show his face and confirm that he had nothing better to do with his time.

Of course, Carlos could have sent his driver alone to pick up his precious *booshaloni* and bring it back to him, but that would have involved eating lukewarm *booshaloni*. Carlos needed to dig in while it was still *sweating*.

I may have first visited The Spot as a *booshaloni* runner for Carlos, who sent me to get Genevieve cooking while he visited the Quarter. In those days, Carlos occasionally liked to take in the shows at the go-go joints — but he wasn't ogling the showgirls. Whatever his faults, I don't think I met a single man in New Orleans more devoted to his wife and more monogamous than Carlos. He sincerely seemed uninterested in other women.

On the other hand, Carlos was fucking *obsessed* with acrobats and flamenco dancers, two breeds of entertainers that frequently performed as warm-up acts in the burlesque bars. After an acrobat or Spanish dancer performed, Carlos would deafen the entire room with his whistling, clapping, and rabid shouts of approval. Afterwards, you could see him cornering an acrobat and peppering him with questions like an eager schoolboy. "Man, how do ya even get *dat* limber?"

While Carlos quizzed acrobats, I would rush over to get Genevieve cooking. Since there were few more prestigious professions in New Orleans than gofer for Carlos Marcello, old Hyp pulled me aside and practically insisted that I make The Spot my nightly home in the French Quarter. Seeing that his clientele were the ugliest gang of ne'er-do-wells this side of an 18th-century pirate bar, I decided that this would be a wonderful place to study the New Orleans underworld and accepted his offer.

Like most French Quarter characters, I designated The Spot as the last stop on my nightlife adventures. The Spot's primetime was from 3 a.m. to 8 a.m. since its clientele consisted of creatures of the night who preyed on marks during the hours when civilians went out to party. Only when the tourists dispersed did the pimps and wiseguys repair to The Spot to share stories, gamble, and order up snacks.

Hyp invited me to sit at his side at his regular table every night so that he could have a naïve, ignorant, and agreeable audience to listen to the 1930s anecdotes he had told everyone else in the French Quarter decades ago. The fact that I alone out of The Spot regulars was gullible enough to occasionally bankroll Hyp in the night's card games was another point in my favor. My cash was Hyp's one lifeline to gambling; he could never convince his tightwad old lady to let him waste their money.

We were usually joined by Steve Valenti, another retired French Quarter pimp from the Jurassic Era who also had become a famously pussy-whipped jazz club owner. Valenti had opened Steve Valenti's Paddock Lounge at 315 Bourbon Street and promptly surrendered all control of its operations to his domineering wife. Henpecked relentlessly, Steve and Hyp got together at The Spot every night to relive the good times when they were two of the most notorious outlaws in town.

Steve and Hyp were good friends going back decades, and they got along beautifully as long as they avoided one subject — the one subject they never avoided. Rarely did a night go by at The Spot without the two of them engaging in a fierce, spit-spraying, table-slapping, shoe-flinging argument. These arguments never, ever had anything to do about their competition as two of New Orleans's foremost jazz club owners; I never heard them debate the skills of their bandleaders Sharkey Bonano and Papa Celestin or anything remotely to do with music or business.

Steve and Hyp's only topic of dispute was over which of them had the most skilled and profitable hooker in their stable back in the day. To call it a friendly rivalry would be too generous; this was a life-or-death religious dispute that ended in shoving and wrestling matches. With the dogged professionalism of their best musicians, Hyp and Steve delivered the millionth rendition of their standard argument with the same passion, fury, and hatred as the first.

I always laughed myself silly at the idea that these two old coots had so much pride and ego invested in the skills of ancient, long-forgotten hookers. At the time, as an unmarried bachelor, I could not comprehend why they were always bragging about long-dead hookers and never about their own wives. Now, as a veteran divorcé, I realize where they were coming from.

Inevitably, the debate would begin with Valenti making a quiet dig, almost as an aside, at the sexual skills of Hyp's "old lady," the legendary Chinese hooker whose memory he jealously guarded like the Holy Grail. This would agitate Hyp greatly, and he would retaliate by condemning Valenti's favorite Old Lady as a "toothless, nickel-a-blow, old hop-smoking hag." From there, general combat would ensue until someone took pity on me and intervened. Genevieve never bothered; she had suffered through the argument too many times to care about another replay and was too secure in her absolute domination of Hyp to be jealous.

With their nightly debate checked off the list, Hyp and Steve reconvened their warm friendship and together sought to tutor me. Though I did not realize it at the time, both of these men were so nostalgic for the pimp game that they were evangelizing for me to follow in their footsteps. They saw that I had what it took. My looks, style, boxing skills, underworld connections, and naturally shy personality all combined to make me an ideal candidate to become a pimp.

Shyness, in many ways, was the key.

The art of the pimp, as taught to me by Hyp and Steve, was the art of playing hard to get permanently with a group of women. Prostitutes seek out pimps for three reasons: to enlist a protector in the underworld, to purchase a place of stability in their chaotic lives, and to find an outlet for all of the emotions normal girls throw at their daddies and husbands.

A whore will pay a pimp less for his protection than for his approval and affection, to fill the hole left by her usually negligent dad. A girl with daddy issues usually has little respect for anyone who treats them too well — which is one reason I was so frequently scammed, stabbed, and shot by girls who did not appreciate my genial disposition. To maintain a prostitute's willingness to spend her money on the same pimp, a pimp must be able to stay always distant enough to keep her "chasing." The second she feels like she has "conquered" her pimp, then she leaves.

Emotional distance may seem easy to fake, but in practice it is very hard to live and work with a beautiful woman for years without growing intimate. As Hyp and Steve knew, a successful pimp therefore needs to either be a naturally shy, reclusive person or a merciless sociopath. I was no sociopath, but I found it easy to befriend people but impossible to get too close to them. I was calibrated just right to live the easy life of a pimp, and Hyp and Steve were dying to show me the way so that they could live through my success.

At the time, I had no idea what they were doing. I thought their lessons about the skin rackets were delivered solely because they were two nostalgic old bastards lamenting that their lives had passed them by — which was also true. Regardless of their intentions, I loved hearing the stories about legendary characters like Ernest "Snake" Gonzalez, the pocket-sized, knife-wielding bogeyman whom the FBI wanted for allegedly dismembering misbehaving hookers, and the Anselmo family, who had contributed three generations of French Quarter pimps to the underworld, each one going by the nickname BeBe.

At the time, the Anselmos had quite a feud going with Norma Wallace, the self-proclaimed Enemy of All Pimps. Norma banished all pimps from the premises of her bordello and would threaten to fire any girl she caught wasting her money on the Anselmos, whom she denounced viciously. Her propaganda had an effect, though not the one she intended. Instead of avoiding the Anselmos, Norma's girls took to attempting to murder them. Allegedly, one of Norma's girls stabbed BeBe the Second, and another one shot BeBe the Third in a bar owned by the Schwegmann grocery family.

In addition to maintaining an elite stable of girls, Hyp and Steve taught me that the other factor in a pimp's success was his friendship with the noble brotherhood of cabbies. "Hacks, Frenchy! The pimp game is all 'bout dah hacks! Goddam, shitty, awful, foul-smelling hacks!" Hyp snorted. "They's barely human, but, if you wanna be a pimp, then you gotta make friends with the hacks by hook or by crook. Some pimps, like dat Snake Gonzalez, even become hacks on the side to make dem feel more comfortable. You gots ta do whatever it takes; when in Rome and all dat shit!

"Bribe 'em, give 'em free lays, give them bigger cuts of the action; don't mattah. All dat mattahs is dat, when some Vidalia hops into a cab and asks where dee girls at, then they take dem right to you."

I had plenty of opportunities to study and befriend the subhuman race of hacks at The Spot, which naturally catered to them. As an expert on the quirks and flaws of cabbies, Hyp understood that an underworld dive offering nightly crooked card games could find no better species of gullible, mark-ass degenerate gamblers. Hyp generously built a six-car cabstand outside The Spot for his customers to use, which, like a hummingbird feeder, was also an investment in our entertainment.

Hyp selected a table by the window as his own to ensure a front-row seat to the cabstand entertainment. The hacks parked their rigs at the stand whenever they snatched a mark looking to get laid and needed to use the payphone to call a pimp or madam to see if they could be accommodated. Naturally, the sight of a primed and ready mark left unguarded in a taxi would cause the other hacks to rush out of The Spot in a feeding frenzy. The screaming matches, fistfights, and pleas for camaraderie that would ensue were endless entertainment.

One night when Hyp, Steve, and I were sitting at our usual table by the window, we witnessed the most stupendous display in the history of the New Orleans hack. For the first time since the days of the Confederacy, an army paraded down Bourbon Street in full regalia with the triumphant General Angelo Pecoraro at the forefront.

Though there was frenzied competition for the title, Angelo was universally recognized as a contender for the sleaziest, slickest, and sharpest hack in all of cab-driving New Orleans. From our table at The Spot, we heard the barking voice of General Pecoraro pierce the night long before we saw his army. *"ONE and a TWO! ONE and a TWO! C'mon you mutts, ONE and a TWO!* TO NORMA'S WE GO TO SCREW!"

A crowd gathered along The Spot's windows to see Angelo with a Navy officer's hat upon his head and an improvised baton bobbing up and down in his hand. In beat with the hack's stomping feet followed twenty-five foreign sailors in perfect marching order, chanting some gibberish in a language I did not recognize. Angelo was not about to risk losing this gigantic haul of Vidalias by transporting them one carload at a time, so he was marching them straight down Bourbon Street all the way to Norma's place on Conti.

For once, the competition between the hacks disappeared, and the entire audience of The Spot poured out onto Bourbon Street and cheered. Of course, while The Spot was empty, someone rushed to the card table and cleaned out all of the unattended cash and undrunk beers.

The next morning, I visited Norma on my daily rounds and asked her about how she did that night with the sailors. "Let's just say I could not retire on their business," drawled my friend as she slumped in her office chair, sipped on a coffee, and rubbed her forehead. "I like to keep prices no lower than thirty a throw, but, with those numbers, bulk pricing just comes with the territory, honey. That would be fine if those Mediterranean types didn't want to fuck for so long and kiss so much."

I nodded with a great air of knowledge for a virgin. I had already heard Norma lecture about the mercilessly strict rules she enforced on her girls: no kissing, no extra-long sessions, no service of customers with extraordinarily large penises or STDs, no drug use, no pimps or boyfriends on the premises, no flirting with Norma's friends and business visitors (this included me), and no appearing in public in anything but pristine condition.

If Norma saw a girl come down the stairs with lipstick smudged from kissing, she would scream, "Not in my house! This is not romance!" A girl with chipped toenail polish, a run in her stockings, or poorly done hair who showed herself before Norma was liable to get paddled.

"Norma, you should have seen dem people in The Spot," I said, smiling eagerly at the thought of how much amusement the story of Angelo marching down Bourbon Street would bring Norma. "I was sittin' wit' Hyp Guinle and Steve Valenti..."

"Oh, fuck them two old pimpin' cocksuckers," Norma hissed with unprecedented venom in her voice. For all her class and charm, the woman talked like a Mack Truck when angry. You could hear her old-fashioned French Quarter street urchin accent in her flashes of rage. "I hear you're sitting at the knee of those two shit-for-brains, and it'll be the ruin of ya!"

"Uh, Norma," I stammered, with my bottom lip trembling. "I...uhh...."

Seeing the pathetic state that her anger had reduced me to, Norma returned to her maternal, aristocratic tone of voice. "Oh, honey, I do not mean anything against you. Steve and Hyp are good enough men these days now that they chopped off their balls and handed them to their wives, but I don't have any patience for pimps, past or present or, God forbid, future!"

"Norma, that reminds me," I ventured cautiously. "I have always wondered. Steve and Hyp seem like good guys, and I don't think they would just hurt people. What's so bad about pimps?"

Norma pulled her head back, and I could see in her eyes that sunken look she adopted whenever I said something unfathomably stupid. I sighed.

"Pimps are parasites, Frenchy," Norma said directly and emphatically. "You know what that word means, Frenchy? They're leeches. They're mosquitoes. They prey on foolish girls who don't know any better, feed off their work without doing anything, and hook them on drugs.

"Pimps are bad people who contribute nothing to society but misery and want," Norma said with uncommon emotion, as if recalling long-ago abuse. As far as I know, Norma had trifled with bootleggers and gangsters like Al Capone's enforcer Sam "Golfbag" Hunt, but as a young woman she had never worked for pimps, only madams and her mom and herself. Maybe Norma was so proud that she would never admit to being dumb enough to be abused by a pimp.

"But, Norma," I continued, more persistent than usual. "What is the difference between what a madam does and what a pimp does?"

"Everything in the world, Frenchy!" she whinnied at me, tapping her long fingernails on her desk like a teacher summoning me to pay attention. "Before I get to that," she said, showing sudden annoyance on her face, "no one says 'madam' besides Vidalias, Frenchy. I am a landlady. I want to smack you when you say that word. Don't embarrass me like that. I can't be seen next to you if you talk like a fool.

"That said, what does a landlady do that a pimp doesn't?" she said with the self-righteous fury of a wife. "Let's see: I give my girls a place to live, food to eat, free weekly doctor care, defense against all the other operators, protection and bail money, and guidance in this world. I teach them how to talk, dress, walk, dance, and eat like proper women; I prepare them for life.

"If a girl is ready to leave me, I do my best to help them get started. I reshape these girls. After I'm done with one of these barn animals, she makes a wonderful wife, and many of my girls are now married to millionaires. You'd be lucky if I set you up with one of my girls one day," Norma said with a change in her tone of voice and some of that old seductive teasing edge. She still sized me up every once in a while, and her carnivorous stare still made me feel like an awkward, helpless thirteen-year-old.

"Compared to all of that, what does a pimp do besides bribe the police and procure drugs?" Norma asked with an upturned nose. "Nothing! They do nothing! You'll never see me let a pimp into this house. Not over my dead body!"

I'd prove Norma wrong within a few years — and have a hell of a time doing it.

Chapter VI

The Four Whoresmen of the Apocalypse

1956-1960s

> "Madame, I wish to inform you that I possess in the highest degree every vice of a gentleman!"
> **Bernard Xavier Philippe de Marigny de Mandeville**
> The Last Great Creole Gentleman of New Orleans

SOMEWHERE BETWEEN MAN AND BEAST IS THE CREATURE KNOWN AS THE ITALIAN HOUSEWIFE. Baby, trust me, when it comes to Italians it's the women you have to fear. Behind just about every take-no-prisoner guido is an Italian wife holding him prisoner; behind every ball-breaker is a wife breaking his nuts. I knew many Italian gangsters like Hyp Guinle and Steve Valenti who were fearless criminals on the streets and fearful husbands at home.

Unlike Italian guys, you can't really get away with shooting an Italian broad — no matter how much they deserve it. Most do, but it's just not done. I'm not saying it's right, just that it's the way it is. In the Mob, you're not even supposed to get divorced, let alone clip your wife.

I know one infamous New Orleans wiseguy from the Carollo side of the Family, who is still around, who went nuts beating his head against that rule. He got so exhausted listening to his wife's bullshit that he pulled his gun and whacked out one of her exotic pets. "Wanna keep pushing your luck?!" he hissed with the gun still fuming in his hand.

The wife looked at the gun, laughed, and did not even hesitate to continue tearing him new assholes. She got away with it, and he had to buy her a new pet.

Italian women are scary, baby.

The first Italian housewife to do her damndest to ruin ole Frenchy was the mother of my first wife. She had the look of a hippo dressed up as a woman for Halloween and the personality of Carlos with constipation. This woman did the impossible: she turned a virginal gangster into a miserable married man in a matter of a few days. I was just like Hyp Guinle and Steve Valenti, only I skipped the "having fun" stage.

The year was 1956, and I was a twenty-year-old virgin. This was a miraculous achievement; I am sure that never before in history has there been a good-looking gangster who survived three years in the French Quarter without getting laid. It was not an intentional achievement; I was just too shy to let the girls take me that final step and too embarrassed to let one of the wiseguys set it up for me. I kept holding out hope that Norma would change her mind about me, but a girl who fancies you as her friend never fancies you any other way. I was stuck.

Finally, my bodybuilding pal Neil "Best Lay" Gautier took matters into his own hands — I don't mean that literally, of course. Though Neil liked to mock my terror of women, it made him paranoid to be seen in public with a guy as good-looking as me who never got laid. He was afraid it would start rumors spreading that we were more than just weightlifting pals. So Neil decided to force me to take the dive.

He had the perfect bait: a Catholic schoolgirl who I'll call Isabella to protect her reputation. Neil was smarter than he looked — he knew that the girl that finally convinced me to give in to sin had to be sinless herself. Isabella was the dream girl for a failed altar boy: a prim, devout, drop-dead gorgeous Catholic virgin who modeled at local department stores. You could sum up Isabella by the fact that she might as well have been the mascot of her school, Holy Angel High.

Though I was a hardened gangster by the age of twenty, I was still stuck in junior high when it came to girls. Isabella was younger but more mature, and she nursed me through my first relationship like I was thirteen years old. I was so innocent that the idea of holding hands was a stomach-twisting terror; I didn't dare go in for a kiss until Isabella went Gorgeous George on me and physically manhandled me into a lip-lock.

Soon afterwards, pretty young Isabella insisted that I meet her family. I should have known I was in trouble by the look of her dad — not even in prison had I ever seen a man so broken and hopeless. I was expecting the mom to be a pretty lil' thing like Isabella, but this lady looked more like Dom Deluise than Isabella. Momma She-Beast weighed as much as a Cadillac and had all the feminine grace of an old bull toad.

Before I could even introduce myself, this mustached sumo grunted at me with a fierce look in her eye. "Whatta yo intentions wit' ma daughta, mistuh Broo-lay?!" she rumbled like she was barely holding back from spontaneously combusting into flames.

"Uh..." I didn't know what to say. I never had intentions, with her daughter or anyone. Every day, I sort of got up in the morning and stumbled around for sixteen hours without any particular plan in mind. Finally, I came up with an answer. "I like to have fun with your daughter. She is...nice?" I said with terror in my eyes.

"You betta do whatsa right! Isabella a very good girl! DO WHATTA RIGHT!" the merciless mama roared at me with a meaty finger pointed at my chest.

"JESUS CHRIST!" I shrieked, sweat dumping down my face like a grievous head wound. As you can imagine, taking the Lord's name in vain in a traditional Catholic household was not a good political move. I was too terrified that night to remember what happened next, but I imagine Isabella's dad had to restrain that Sicilian slugger from getting off her fat ass and knocking me out.

So, we were engaged before the pasta was served at the next night's dinner. I was not overly bothered. It takes a lot to really depress me. I had gone my entire life without getting laid, so the idea of having sex with Isabella for the rest of my life was no great sacrifice. In fact, the realization that I was now guaranteed to get laid on my wedding night erased any thought of changing my mind. I could not see past that spot on my calendar where sex was waiting for me.

I was excited to get married! That's how innocent I was.

The only person heartbroken seemed to be Neil Gautier. Poor Neil. He was never much of a strategist; if he had gone to war in Korea, he would have ended up leading the Red Chinese and North Koreans to the city limits of Washington, D.C. He tried to turn a virgin into a player, and instead he managed to turn a virgin into an engaged virgin. To a sex maniac like Neil, the only thing more shameful than virginity was marriage, so I was something like the superhero of the stupid to him.

At least single virgins had hope!

Taking up the other side of the debate, my family in Marksville conceived a fantasy that I may not have been a hopeless fool for the first time in my life. My parents, Percy Jr., and my sisters came down to New Orleans for the wedding, and they were very impressed by my choice of a truly devout, classy, and beautiful Catholic girl to be my wife. They could not have asked for more.

The fact that I had managed to make such a good living as, ahem, a "waiter at Kolb's" was even more miraculous to the Brouillettes. What can I say? Mr. Tux came out of mothballs. I already had a waiter costume thanks to that useless tuxedo that I wore to The Beverly Country Club, so it was the easiest lie to tell. Besides, I spent more time at Kolb's with Dutch than the actual waiters.

The wedding was a beautiful affair — I had Dutch arrange for St. Louis Cathedral, New Orleans's most iconic building and a bona fide basilica of the Catholic Church, to host the holy union of Frenchy Brouillette and Isabella the Foxy Catholic School Girl. Through the entire ceremony, I stood in my too-tight tuxedo thinking the same thing every traditional groom thinks over and over: Jesus Christ, hurry up so I can ball this girl.

After the priest pronounced us man and wife, I practically threw the bitch over my shoulder like Tarzan and sprinted back down the aisle.

I shouldn't have been in any rush. Seriously, we should have had dinner, took in some shows, played checkers. There was no reason to be hasty.

It was on my wedding night that I discovered that not all Catholic schoolgirls are lionesses in the bedroom. The Church only makes bad girls worse; it has the opposite effect on good girls.

If a girl had a little bit of wildness in her, a lifetime of Catholic denial, guilt, and repression would nurse that wild side into a feral, bloodthirsty, full-fledged sexual hysteria. On the other hand, Catholic school turns girls who are not sexual by nature into stubborn enemies of the penis.

It must have been ninety degrees outside, but I think the tip got frostbite. I got the feeling that Isabella had spent so much time modeling at department stores that the mannequins had turned into a bad influence. A blow-up doll would have been more dynamic.

The "marriage" lasted three months before Dutch Kraut interceded with the diocese and arranged an annulment. Isabella had lost interest in me as well, but her mother was fuming over her lost virginity. She sent Isabella's daddy after me in some type of Sicilian blood feud war, but the old man just sat me down, asked for a drink, and shared stories about "the old battle-axe" for a few hours. "I'm leaving the bitch too, so I can't blame ya, Frenchy!" he confided before pounding a shot.

So ends the story of marriage number one. Looking back, it was my best.

"I was [always] susceptible to young and beautiful people."
<u>Norma Wallace</u>

Norma Wallace could stand no more. A veteran of her fair share of doomed marriages, Norma was embarrassed that I nearly damned myself over the charms of a witless, frigid schoolgirl. "Frenchy, honey, don't you understand?" she drawled with that look of ridiculing disbelief that no one could match.

"You've got it made, child. FUCKING MADE, YOU SHIT!" she shrieked. In my experience, only two topics brought the devil to Norma's tongue: pimps and my relationship mishaps. Norma wanted to live vicariously through me. Both as a lover and a gangster, I could do everything that, as a woman, she could not do.

"You are beautiful, young, connected, and male," she said with her dark eyes pinning me down like a hand on my throat. "What I would do to be in your shoes!" she whispered as if she was sharing her deepest secret. "Frenchy, don't fuck this up, boy! Don't go ruin yourself and get married! HAVE FUN!"

After my annulment, I was an even bigger joke in the Quarter than before. Between Norma, Neil, Dutch, and the other bodybuilders and wiseguys, everyone let me know that I was the squarest gangster in the history of the Quarter and a disgrace to the title of Mr. New Orleans.

Clearly, this could not stand. To compensate, I turned to alcohol in greater and greater quantities to embolden myself. Soon, I was drinking old Dutch under the table, and, unlike Dutch, I had enough good looks to keep pretty young things from holding my inebriation against me. Thanks to booze, I was able to confront women in earnest.

My next step was to enlist Neil Gautier as my tutor and tag-team partner. He devised an ingenious pickup routine: we would wear our tightest muscle shirts and ask a table full of pretty young women if they wanted to "judge our bodybuilding contest." An hour later, we'd be posing in our underwear at my apartment, and within minutes we'd be in separate bedrooms, taking on as many bodybuilding judges as we could handle.

As you can imagine, French Quarter floozies were more spirited lays than prim Catholic schoolgirls. I realized that sex, while not quite as enjoyable as drinking and bodybuilding, was a respectable third place in life's pleasures.

Wait, I forgot about horses and motorcycles.

Anyway, after a year or two of practice, one of the French Quarter floozies I picked up with Neil unexpectedly turned into my first "character" girlfriend. Latashma was like a photo negative of Isabella: black everywhere angelic Isabella was white. Latashma was a stripper, a drinker, a chain-smoker, and most terrifying of all, a devoted pothead.

Though a pothead stripper is probably the least exotic creature in modern America, this was some heavy shit for me. Pot, cocaine, heroin, speed: it was all in the "evil, insanity-causing drugs" category to most white Americans. It was total Reefer Madness; you were led to believe that one hit from a joint could send a normal person on a cannibalistic murdering spree.

Despite the fact that Carlos Marcello himself had once been one of the biggest pot dealers in the South, pot was considered strictly "nigger shit" by any respectable wiseguy in those days. Discovering that a pretty white girl like Latashma smoked pot would have been no less surprising and terrifying to me than discovering that she was a vampire or a werewolf. I figured I had no choice but to dump her; I would not stoop that low.

Actually, I would stoop that low — more or less continuously for fifty years now. It was a great shock to my system to learn that, once we got romantic, Latashma's depravity was the biggest turn-on I had ever experienced. The Catholic boy who thought he wanted a Madonna turned out to want nothing less than a whore. My awareness that I was committing the sin of fornication with a sinful, debauched, fallen woman made that sin the sweetest of any I had ever experienced.

One taste of "dangerous" ass converted me from my fascination with virgins, good girls, and conventional women. Since Latashma, I have not dated or slept with a single woman who did not have an underworld job or a criminal record. I can't get up for it; it holds no interest for me. I need the danger, the shame, and the chaos. I had seen what happened to old Hyp Guinle and Steve Valenti: straightlaced women rob crooked men of their mojo.

Though I loved having sex with Latashma, I feared sleeping with a "dangerous" pothead. In fact, I literally couldn't sleep with her. I lay awake all night, tense as a cobra, waiting for the devil weed to possess her and convince her to carve me up like a fried turkey. The same Frenchy who would later sleep like a Chinaman in a hop daze while imprisoned with literal murderers could not sleep for a second with a tame pothead stripper.

I was not the only person disconcerted by Latashma's habits. Norma Wallace was hot and bothered. "Frenchy, are you touched in the head or somethin'?" she asked with a venomous drawl as I walked into her office one morning. "What is it with you Catholic country boys?"

I was baffled as to what the judgmental landlady was talking about. I was doubtlessly guilty of doing something wrong, but I never would have guessed that Norma Wallace of all people would moralize about bed partners.

"Frenchy, really now, hun, a stripper? A druggie? You don't need to go cheap to get laid! Look at the girls in my place!" In other words, Norma wanted me to avoid sleazy girls like strippers in favor of more classy dames like prostitutes.

"Norma, I wish I could!" I grumbled. "You keep dose girls away from me like I got yellow fever or somethin'! C'mon, nah, you won't even let 'em talk to me! Whaddya think I'm going to do to them?"

"Frenchy, that's for your protection, you silly ass," she laughed. "My girls may not drink or do drugs or carry on like fools, but they would eat you up for breakfast and be starving by lunch. They'd tie you up in pretzels!"

Norma began to laugh again, but then her eyebrows shot straight up and her face turned serious. It was an obvious "Eureka!" look. She had devised a solution that fixed more than one of her problems.

"Except for one girl..." Norma said with a look of mischief in her eyes.

Though it was the last thing in the world she ever wanted to do, Norma Wallace was about to turn me into a pimp.

"I'd rather try touching the moon than take on a whore's thinking."

Al Swearengen
Deadwood

Excluding carnal relationships of brief and dubious character, Norma Wallace was not by nature a matchmaker.

Norma preferred for her girls to be celibate when not on the clock — or at least dykes. Norma herself, though she hid this information from her memoir, was known to carry on with her favorite girl, Rose, who ironically was just about the most troublesome and least accommodating hooker in New Orleans history. When Norma retired, Rose inherited Norma's priceless black book of clients, the Holy Grail of the sex rackets, and did little business worth noting.

When Norma's girls did bother with men, it was a matter of great consternation for her. Decades of experience had taught her that whores who are henpecked to death by a motherly landlady almost always seek out a pimp, both to "rebel" and to obtain imaginary leverage against their domineering female boss. Since Norma brooded over pimps like a rooster obsessing over hawks, she suspected every man who was not a loyal paying customer of being a pimp on the prowl.

A professor would probably call it irony that the one man Norma Wallace set up with one of her girls turned out to be the most notorious pimp in New Orleans history. I speak, of course, of myself.

Norma would never hold it against me; she knew it was her fault. "I should have known better to put a good-looking boy like you with a working girl! What else was going to happen?" she'd sigh. She never stopped being my friend.

The girl who Norma used to lure me away from Latashma was a tiny, bony, mousy little thing with blond hair whom I'll call "Sarah" since I'd rather not use her real name. Sarah was truly the most mild-mannered, classy, well-educated, and innocent working girl I would ever meet; she belonged in a library, not a bordello. Knowing that I had developed a taste for the exotic, Norma was smart to accentuate the one unique edge to Sarah's personality: she was a middle-class Jewish girl from New York City.

To a Marksville boy born in 1936, Judaism was a satanic cult of international bankers and Christ killers. Besides the whole Jesus-crucifying angle, I did not know a thing about the Jewish people, so the idea of dating a Hebrew hooker was exponentially more thrilling and mysterious than bedding some pothead stripper. She might as well have been Tibetan or Navajo.

I took Norma up on the offer to escort Sarah to breakfast at the end of her long workday. I arrived at the Green House on Conti Street at 4 a.m., right as the last customer was stumbling cross-eyed down the steps, and was introduced to Sarah by a beaming Norma. Thinking that I was dealing with a high-falutin' New York society girl, I bowed and kissed her frail, childlike hand. Both Norma and Sarah were charmed; it is rare to find a gentleman who will treat a hooker like a princess mere minutes after she serviced her twelfth customer of the night.

I drove Sarah in my shining, new convertible to The Snake Pit, the late-night diner owned by Ernest "Snake" Gonzalez, the most feared New Orleans pimp of the '50s through the '70s. It only took a few minutes for Sarah and I to fall into puppy love; no two more naïve and gentle-natured people have ever worked in the French Quarter rackets. Sarah was a girl who would blush at the mere mention of sex, and it was clear by the repulsed way she looked over The Snake Pit's criminal clientele that she was a civilian at heart.

After breakfast, Sarah insisted on picking up the bill; I was appalled by the idea, but she actually argued the fight out of me. She paid; I was too green to understand that on the street this meant I was accepting her as my old lady. That night, after I took Sarah back to her room at the John Mitchell Hotel, she pecked me on the cheek and asked if we could see each other again. I looked at the hotel hallway carpet, boiling with nerves, and mumbled out something or other.

Norma was a very clever woman. In setting Sarah and me up, she had given two vulnerable, easily misled kids a safe haven. I needed a good girl who had an edge of wickedness to keep me excited, and she needed a jaded street character who could overlook her profession and treat her like the lady she was deep down. By falling in love with each other, we achieved Norma's ultimate goal of keeping us both free from public embarrassment and exploitation — and ensuring that we both remained under her influence.

People always ask me how I can be romantically involved with women who have sex with other men on a nightly basis. The answer is that the French Quarter ruined me. Spending my formative years in that sex-drenched district killed any sense of conventional relationships. Every wiseguy I knew had a stripper mistress, and my biggest influences were an alcoholic German bookmaker, a tiny sex maniac bodybuilder, two retired pimps, a madam, a Mafia boss, and a family of crazy guido boxers whose patriarch was in love with a post-op transsexual.

By the time I became sexually active, I was completely and utterly cynical about everything sex-related besides the act itself. Jealousy was never a factor.

Sarah's love for me was not the love of a girlfriend for a boyfriend. It had a weirdly childish note to it; she treated me like her daddy and her lover. She became clingy, desperate, sentimental. In other words, she loved me with a bottom bitch's love for her pimp. I had no idea that this sort of relationship existed, and I had no comprehension of what Sarah was doing when she asked me to "hold" $300 for her.

I honestly thought the poor girl wanted to use me as a bank! By the time her nest egg passed the astronomical 1958 sum of $5000, I was beginning to feel guilty for reasons that I could not detect. When I asked Sarah to take her five grand and put it in a real bank, a strange smirk snaked across her face.

"Baby, when I want it back, I'll ask for it," she purred with devilment in her eyes. Sarah was anything but a devilment-in-the-eyes sort of girl, so I was very unnerved. My vague feeling that I was doing something wrong became an unmistakable sense of guilt.

Despite my guilt, I refused to let Sarah move into my apartment on Bourbon Street. I was quite happy with living separately since I could have all the joys of bachelorhood during the French Quarter's nightlife hours and wifely pleasures with Sarah when she got off work. Sarah was insistent, however, and every night for months she would ask to move in, and I would slap it down by asking her to take her money back.

One day, long after the money under my mattress had ballooned to tens of thousands of dollars, Sarah came down with appendicitis. Though she underwent surgery at the local hospital, she came down with a serious infection and booked a flight home to convalesce with her family and consult New York doctors. I insisted that she take her savings with her, but she accepted only $200 as her traveling cash. "Don't worry, I'll be back for the rest," she cooed with the same inexplicable wink.

Later that week, I received a phone call from my beloved in New York. She told me that she was healing well and, after an awkward pause, asked once again if she could move in with me when she returned. I hemmed and hawed and eventually deflected with a "Later, baby, later."

I never heard from Sarah again, and neither did Norma Wallace.

Contrary to the stereotypes I had been told, the Jewess never came back for her fortune. Though I had never known it, little Sarah had told every working girl at Norma's how "that pretty boy Frenchy is my old man," and every hooker within a hundred mile radius knew that she gave me her money. My reputation as the lily-white gangster was forever after stained. I was just one more exploiter, user, and predator. A pimp.

Sarah's story was the most mundane imaginable: a fragile hooker disappears after being used up by her pimp. The only mystery was why Norma Wallace made an exception and allowed a pimp like me to visit her Green House.

Though Norma knew the truth, no one else in New Orleans would accept that I was not Sarah's pimp. Trust me, baby: "pimp" is a stain that cannot be easily washed from a gentleman's reputation. There is no hope — especially when the hooker in question disappears, and you respond by blowing $20,000 in cash on clothes, cars, jewelry, and rounds of drinks for the bar.

Maturity is something that comes, if it ever does, with age. I'm still waiting for it to arrive. It appears to be takin' its sweet ass time.

The result of all this infamy was that every call girl in the New Orleans area was eager to make my acquaintance and possibly join my team. Why wouldn't they be? I was the new status symbol in the hooker community! Any girl attracted by the allure of a pimp naturally would seek the youngest, best looking, most connected, and most exclusive operator in the bunch.

And, boy, was I exclusive: only one girl made the cut, and she had been given to me by Norma Wallace, who wouldn't even talk to any other pimp!

I was quite troubled by all of this nonsense. Barely comfortable with the idea of being the boyfriend of a single girl, I had no idea what to do as the pimp and master of scores of them. I emphatically rejected every girl who sought to enlist my services, and I swore up and down Bourbon Street that Frenchy Brouillette would never be a pimp.

And then Dutch Kraut died.

⚜ ⚜ ⚜ ⚜ ⚜

"I used to give [Police Chief Beauregard] Miller $50,000 in cash every few months. I used to stuff de cash in a suitcase and carry it over to his office....I used to give 'em all cash money. I'd go out in de mornin' with my pants pockets full and say, 'Hello, here's a twenty for ya, pal.... Here's a hundred bucks.... Here's a fifty.' I took care of everybody."

<u>Carlos Marcello</u>

To Carlos Marcello, Mafia was just Italian for Money. The Mob usually handled civilians by using persuasion and purchase power. Carlos tossed around cash like crumbs to pigeons, and in return the cops, the district attorneys, and the politicians would do what he asked with no fuss and no muss. Carlos liked to say that the secret to his success was that he always remembered just how everyone "liked dey coffee."

One police chief received precious antiques, real estate, and historical collector's items from famous gangsters; another had free goods funneled to his family restaurant; another ran wild at Carlos' gambling houses and feasted at the Marcello family restaurants. Everyone with a police title or political office received jobs and bags of cash to hand out to supporters and family. Carlos knew how to listen and give a person just what they needed to feel appreciated.

The problem with a crime family that pays for survival is that it relies on long-standing friendships and business relationships with the people in power. Anyone can stick a gun to someone's head and get them to do what they want, but high-caliber bribery and racketeering requires trust and connections and some sort of backroom political genius. It requires the right sort of people, and when those people die, the Family falls apart.

During the last golden age of the French Quarter, Carlos had assembled just the right cast of characters to run it: Gasper Gulotta, Diamond Jim Moran, and Sam Saia, with his lieutenant Dutch Kraut. These men knew everyone there was to know and knew just how they "liked dey coffee." They kept everyone in line. They paid everyone off so that no one messed with business in the Quarter. It was like an aquarium, where all the sharks are so well fed that they don't bother eating the other attractions.

When Gasper, Diamond Jim, and Dutch died, one after another, in the late 1950s, they took the peace, the glamour, and the money in the French Quarter with them. The New Orleans Mafia's domination of the district was never as complete or as lucrative. Everyone messed with business. The police, the politicians, and the district attorneys got greedy.

The greatest blow was the death of old Gasper Gulotta, the last great saloon boss of New Orleans. You could tell how important Gasper was to the city by the identity of his celebrity pallbearers: the Mayor, the Superintendent of Police, and Sam Saia. That captures Gasper completely. He was the last man who could unite everyone in New Orleans behind a single goal — making money.

Without Gasper's political know-how and decades of piled up favors to call-in, the Mafia was unable to keep the various factions within the police department, district attorney's office, and political machine from breaking the peace and going into business for themselves. The Quarter was robbed blind from every angle. It quickly became the hot spot for penny-ante police shakedowns, sham vice squad raids, and extortionate indictments by the district attorney's office. Every "legitimate" agency of government and law enforcement in the city opened up protection rackets in the Quarter.

The subsequent death of Diamond Jim Moran had the side effect of killing off the French Quarter's glamour and appeal to mobsters. Without Gasper and the diamond-decorated prince of La Louisiane to host the parties, the wiseguys stopped coming to the Quarter for pleasure or business.

The wiseguys were making too much money elsewhere to risk doing business with a city government that was out of control. To them, the New Orleans government was an unprofessional and incompetent crime family that needed to get its house in order before it could be trusted as a business partner again. Without the Mob's administrative supervision, the Quarter went to hell. Burlesque clubs, bars, and lounges began to close, and the ones that didn't close became less extravagant, less clean, and less profitable.

The Golden Age ended abruptly, and the Quarter quickly skipped passed the Silver, Bronze, Iron, and Tin Ages to arrive at the Everything Smells Like Piss and Vomit Age.

The sudden death of Dutch Kraut was the most catastrophic event that had occurred to me in my life. Though I was caught by surprise, I can't say that his death should have been unexpected. The man lived like a pig and looked half-dead from the moment I met him. He really was a queer old fossil, and it's a miracle that he lasted as long as he did.

Dutch's daily routine of huge meals at Kolb's, constant heavy drinking and smoking, relentless partying, and sleep deprivation was not conducive to a long life. He lived well and died with a full belly, a full-on drunk, a full bank account, and something pretty close to a clean record. I raise my glass to him.

It didn't immediately occur to me that Dutch's death might jeopardize my standing in the New Orleans Mafia. If anything, I figured I would get bumped up the ladder; after all, there was an opening for a heavily-accented drunk to oversee Sam Saia's

French Quarter operations. I did not suspect that a multimillionaire Mob chief would be hesitant to bet his freedom and security on my ability to manage a complicated bookmaking operation.

My meeting with Sam Saia at Felix's Oyster Bar was devastating. Not only was Sam reluctant to inform me that a twentysomething Cajun from Marksville lacked the maturity, connections, and street credibility to manage the French Quarter beat, but he also had no choice but to let me go altogether. The increased police presence in the Quarter spooked the rich old bastard, and he saw no reason to risk getting arrested if he didn't have wise old fixers like Gasper and Dutch to shield him. Sam Saia had enough cash already, so he shut down his French Quarter operations until the heat cooled down.

My career was deader than a crawfish with a straight tail. If this had happened in my later years, I would have driven my convertible down Airline and visited Carlos at the Town & Country and asked for a gig. At the time, however, I was too obsessed with staying in my comfort zone of the French Quarter to risk appealing to Carlos and receiving an offer I couldn't refuse to work in St. Bernard or Plaquemines Parish. I chose to tackle the French Quarter by myself.

Without Dutch as my hookup, I had no choice but to vacate my apartment on Bourbon Street above the Gunga Den. I approached Chris Owens, a famous burlesque dancer, and rented out a penthouse apartment that she or one of her sugar daddies owned by her house. I rented the place for only one reason: it had a pool, and I had visions of sunning myself by the water as dozens of bikini-clad girls rubbed oil all over my body. After I moved in, I threw on my swim trunks and made my way to the pool, only to be greeted by a growling, drooling attack dog standing guard.

Apparently, Chris had decided that only she would be allowed to use the pool.

So I moved out the next month and found myself another

penthouse apartment in the Quarter. Thanks to my savings, courtesy of Dutch Kraut and Sarah, I was not exactly hurting for cash, but I would eventually need a job to support my Mr. New Orleans lifestyle. I had no intention of surrendering my right to eat out at nice restaurants and drink champagne every night, even if I was no longer receiving the huge discounts afforded to Sam Saia's representative. I needed a new job, so I circulated word around the Quarter.

I didn't expect to get my dream job during my first day on the market. The offer came from Tony Rabina, the mobbed-up owner of the Chez Paris b-drinking nightclub on Bourbon Street. The Chez Paris was one of the nicer b-drinking joints in the Quarter, which means that it relied more on the b-girls' charm than knockout drops to fleece the customers. Tony figured that a guy named Frenchy was the perfect manager for a place called the Chez Paris, especially since my supposed "strong pimp hand" and friendship with Carlos would give me added leverage to control the girls.

"It's the role I was born to play!" I told Tony Rabina as I accepted his offer. It was not hard to convince me to take command of a fully stocked bar and a group of pretty girls. Besides, I thought it would do my reputation good to let everyone know that I was the manager of a major French Quarter establishment, not some street pimp.

Unfortunately, I did not understand the b-drinking business. Instead of being a pimp, the manager of the Chez Paris was nothing more than the pimps' agent. Only about two-thirds of the Chez Paris's profits came from the overpriced cocktails and bottles of champagne that the b-girls convinced the marks to buy them from the bar. The rest of the money came from arranging for the tourists to get laid through the house pimps.

Whenever one of the b-girls approached me behind the bar and told me that her mark was lookin' to get laid, it was my job to call up one of three major pimps who had arrangements with us. In the late '50s and early '60s, the real power players in the New

Orleans pimp game were Sherman Keaton, Mike Roach, and Ernest "Snake" Gonzalez, with his partner Cody Morris. Between the four of them, they controlled upwards of seventy or eighty hookers and over a million dollars in business a year.

The 1960 New Orleans pimp was an interesting creature. Since the madams and Carlos' boys generally aspired to class instead of flash, the pimps of the day were generally clean-cut gentlemen dressed in black sports coats. They operated bars and lounges as the headquarters for their operations, and a number of them owned taxicabs to appeal to the hacks who referred them business. Following Gasper Gulotta's example, the pimps made a point to socialize and befriend each other; their motto was "there's plenty of money to go around!"

Their market was well-defined and separate from the madams' business. The bordellos of the classic French Quarter landladies like Norma Wallace, Dora Russo, Marie Bernard, Bertha Anderson, and Gertie Yost did not compete with pimps for customers. The landladies serviced the needs of the best and brightest, the high-class locals and tourists.

The visitors to the bordellos were like the men who claim to read Playboy for the articles. Most bordello customers were paying for the atmosphere and experience rather than the sex. The bulk of the landladies' profits did not even come from turning tricks. As soon as the john was escorted into the drawing room by a maid, the landlady hit him up for a $5 glass of champagne or worse, and she dragged out hours of flirting so that he kept drinking. As soon as the john took a girl up to a room, the leisurely pace was reversed; he was lucky if he got ten minutes to pump before he was dumped.

The average visit to a bordello was closer to a consultation with a doctor than a romantic rendezvous. The john was escorted into a room and immediately instructed to strip. The call girl would then inspect his pubes for crabs, milk his dick for a moment to check for signs of venereal disease in his ejaculate, and then give it a good scrubbing over a washbasin. Once the john was judged clean, the call-girl yanked off her gown, threw herself on the bed, and gave him five or ten minutes to get it over with. No kissing was allowed, and heaven help you if you smudged her makeup.

As you probably can tell from this description, the bordello was not the place of choice for real sex connoisseurs. The bordellos were great places for rich squares to hang out, network, make witty conversation with pretty girls, and feel like tough guys. Norma's was the safe haven where Louisiana Governor Earl Long held campaign meetings and movie star John Wayne visited when filming in the city. Al Capone himself, along with his brother Ralph, unwound at Norma's after he was released from prison.

As opposed to the bordellos, the pimps sold sex, not an experience. Forget all the window-dressing: the pimps got you fucked. They might send you to a dreary motel or studio apartment, but everything was on the table — from passionate romantic role-play to orgies with all the lagniappe. Better yet, the pimps delivered girls to your house or hotel room, and they had a girl for every price range. For the poor, the perverse, and the paranoid johns in the New Orleans sex rackets, the pimps provided the best bang for the buck.

I gradually became close with the pimps at the Chez Paris. Mike Roach was the nicest — a dumpy, wheezing, old white guy who was close to Carlos and liked me because I was comparatively in Carlos' inner circle. He liked to bullshit with me and share wiseguy stories about the days when the deported Silver Dollar Sam ruled the city. Roach was always trying to get me to go visit his bar and drag some of Carlos' boys along, but I had hotter places to hang out.

Sherman Keaton was a much heavier presence. Sherman was the owner of the Black Door Lounge, and he could barely fit through that black door. A huge man for that era at 5'11" and 240 pounds, Sherman was a mean Tony Soprano–looking icebox with a bulldog face and thick, calloused fists. Sherman was nice to me, though, because I could steer him business.

Last, and physically least, was Ernest "Snake" Gonzalez, a swarthy Creole Spanish knife-fighter with devilish black eyes and the reputation of a voodoo priest. Snake had a mysterious air about him; he looked haunted. Though he was a tiny, thin guy with a little mustache, Snake projected enough menace to stand down any street gang.

To give you an idea of Snake's mojo, the FBI once yanked me off the street and pressed me to give up information about some girls that Snake had allegedly chopped up into little pieces. When Snake's Nola Cab Company taxi pulled up to a lounge, people would start quietly slithering out of the back entrance.

Along with his business partner Cody Morris, who handled the accounting and bribery aspect of their affairs, Snake managed a stable of thirty-two girls in the early 1960s, and every one of those hookers would have chosen to cross Satan before Snake. Snake lived up to his other nickname: The Boss. A lot of the hacks and peddlers visited Snake at his after-hours bar, The Snake Pit, as a sign of respect.

Though Snake was always polite to me, he represented all of the most violent stereotypes that kept me away from wanting to become a pimp. While at the Chez Paris, I did my best to steer business to Mike Roach and Sherman Keaton, who gave me forty percent of whatever the Vidalia spent — a fantastic rate, ten percent higher than the city average. It was the happiest part of my night when Mike Roach drove up in his '59 cherry-red Cadillac convertible with custom fins and handed over a big bag of loot.

My time at the Chez Paris turned out to be an unexpected financial bonanza. Within weeks of taking on the job, my favorite b-girl and I set the all-time New Orleans record for the most money fleeced from a Vidalia at a b-drinking bar. In a few hours, we convinced some out-of-town tycoon to buy fifty-two bottles of champagne at $32 apiece and countless rounds of drinks for the other bar patrons.

When we ran out of booze to sell this guy, I had the clever

idea to encourage him to make takeout orders from all of the restaurants where I knew the manager would give me a cut.

By the end of the night, the Chez Paris was offering a complimentary buffet stocked with lobster and Oysters Rockefeller from Antoine's, Chinese food from Dan's International, char-grilled oysters from Felix's, sausages from Kolb's, and hamburgers from some place like Bud's Broiler — all courtesy of the Vidalia. The b-girl and I received a taste of the purchase price from every dish in this spread, and we naturally took our usual commission from all the drinks. We both went home with well over a thousand dollars.

After that night, I figured my future was settled: manager at the Chez Paris was the life for me. I pictured myself building up a fortune over the next few years and eventually buying a French Quarter bar to run myself like Hyp Guinle, Steve Valenti, Joe Conforto, and so many others had done before. It was the French Quarter's version of a conventional career path.

In the meantime, I had no intention of leaving a job where my only responsibilities were to crack open new bottles of champagne while I drank and partied with my underworld friends. As manager of the Chez Paris, I already held court like I owned the place, and folks like Norma Wallace and Sam Saia were very impressed by how quickly a young man with no discernible talents had made it big.

The drawback of success is that I've found it to be very easy for me to attain and impossible for me to sustain. I always seemed to get tripped up on my strolls down easy street.

The culprit in this case was none other than Jim Garrison, the damndest hypocrite ever to live.

❧ ❧ ❧ ❧ ❧

"The moment insiders heard Jim Garrison had chosen Pershing Gervais as his chief investigator. [...] Well, let's just say that led to what could politely be called 'suspicion' of his motives and judgment."

Harry Connick
Orleans Parish District Attorney (1973-2003)

It was a mystery to me that my tenure at the Chez Paris was during the last days of b-drinking in the French Quarter. I was the bartender of the French Quarter apocalypse. The first three horsemen of the apocalypse were Gasper Gulotta, Diamond Jim Moran, and Dutch Kraut — and the fourth and final horseman was none other than the new district attorney, Jim Garrison.

Garrison is better known as Kevin Costner's heroic character in the JFK movie— or, if you are just about any New Orleans powerbroker, "that lying cocksucker Garrison."

District Attorney Jim Garrison was a mistake that never would have happened in Gasper Gulotta's days. The problem with Garrison was not that he was a clean, honest civil servant — the problem was that he was just shitty at being crooked ... just like the Kennedys. For such a half-ass politician, you have to give it to Garrison for pulling off the coup of conning Oliver Stone and other brain-damaged glue-sniffers into believing that he was an American hero.

Garrison was one of nature's authentic strange birds: a 6'7" bisexual sex maniac with a big melon head and an obsessive hunger for hookers, swinger orgies, and picking up drag queens in the French Quarter.

How do I know? Because he was my customer for years.

The hookers called him "The Jolly Green Giant" due to his enormous size in all areas and unhealthy pallor, and the police called him "The Mickey Mantle of the DA's Office" - not because he swung a veritable Louisville Slugger, which was also true – but because he was a "switch-hitter" in the bedroom. Without an expert like Gasper to size him up, the local characters felt comfortable electing Garrison DA in 1962 since he had so many skeletons in his closet. After all, voracious bisexuals usually were the easiest politicians to handle, and Norma Wallace assured everyone that Garrison was not only her attorney but one of her few outcall clients.

The wiseguys were further comforted by Garrison's choice for his campaign deputy and head investigator: Pershing Gervais. I am not speaking lightly when I say that Pershing Gervais was the single crookedest crook in the history of New Orleans.

Let that claim sink in for a moment, baby. It might take a while for your brain to come to grips with such an achievement.

Pershing's résumé as a backstabber and sleazeball was humbling. A sample would read: ballot-stuffer, dirty cop, professional informant, sexual deviant, male prostitute, gay bar owner, political bagman, crooked chief investigator for the District Attorney's office, and finally an informant in the Witness Protection Program who later double-crossed the government.

With his pencil mustache and greasy hair, Pershing was so disreputable that I immediately assumed everything he said was a lie, and most of the time I was right. Pershing was a real compulsive case: he could not help but lie, and he could not help but steal. Willpower and forethought played no part in his life, and it is a miracle that he survived until old age without getting clipped. He was just lucky, a little rodent who scurried from scam to scam.

As the lisping son of two deaf mutes, poor old Pershing looked physically pained when he spoke, so I always felt bad for him for being born such a relentless babbling bullshitter. Being a pathetic compulsive liar with a lisp made him a natural New Orleans Police Department officer, but he was kicked off the force when he stole $150,000 from two thieves he arrested and went on a prolonged orgiastic bender in New York City. Pershing's conduct in Manhattan was so outlandish that the rumors spread all the way back down to New Orleans. The son of a bitch actually managed to get fired from the NOPD!

Pershing rebounded by working as a rat against the pigs for the Metropolitan Crime Commission. I guess you could call that poetic justice. To make ends meet, Pershing also opened up a side practice as the most expensive gigolo in New Orleans; he claimed to earn $1500 a lay thanks to his ability to muster a long-lasting foot-long erection for anything living or dead.

The joke was Pershing's going rate was "$100 per inch," which is classic Pershing: he was such a liar that he had to stretch an authentic foot-long dick into a fifteen-inch dick. Pershing invested his whoring profits in the purchase of a gay bar aptly called The Dungeon, which had a reputation for rolling and blackmailing closeted businessmen and politicians.

As you can imagine, the news that the Uptown "reform" candidate Jim Garrison had chosen a five-alarm scoundrel like Pershing Gervais as his deputy inspired confidence in Garrison's corruption and stupidity across the New Orleans underworld. Surely, no DA's office with Pershing Gervais on staff would be a particularly formidable proponent of cleaning up the streets.

Gervais collected campaign donations and bribes from every go-go joint, bordello, casino, and b-drinking bar in the Quarter, and in return he promised immunity from all prosecution when Garrison was elected. Rumors abounded in the Quarter that Garrison and Gervais, two well-hung sex freaks who had served in the army together, were partners in more than that campaign.

After Garrison's election, the Jolly Green Cocksucker set about killing the French Quarter for once and for all. It was common knowledge that Garrison had ambitions to higher political office, which was ridiculous since no candidate has less of a prayer in statewide elections than a crooked New Orleans district attorney. Looking for some good publicity in the uptight parts of the state, Garrison went after the obvious target: the French Quarter. The asshole who "cleaned up the Quarter" would naturally become a superstar in places like Marksville.

Garrison was presented with a strategic problem, however. There were very few available targets that he could get away with hitting. He could not move against the Mafia bookmakers and gaming rooms because he was terrified of Carlos, and he could not attack the bordellos because of his past history. All that were left were the b-drinking bars, which were "in the backyard" of the Superintendent of Police, Joe Giarrusso, who collected tribute as if he had invented and patented Mickey Finns. Surely, the district attorney would not go to war with the Superintendent of Police.

What can I tell you? Garrison was nuts. Minutes after being elected, Garrison dropped his pants and went after every b-drinking club in the city with no Vaseline. As Garrison let the rest of his caseload fall into disarray, he became a fixture on the front page of the Times Picayune, crowing about his latest French Quarter bust. In a desperate ploy to gain the approval of the upstate redneck and Uptown blue-blood voters, Garrison even called out Superintendent Giarrusso as a corrupt do-nothing.

As I said, none of this silliness would have happened in Gasper's days as the Little Mayor. Unfortunately, Gasper was no longer around, and Carlos was too distracted in 1962 to intervene. With his reputation and career on the line, the normally placid Giarrusso had no choice but to strike back and seize some publicity of his own. In a bid to cut off Garrison's funding and recreational opportunities, Giarrusso waged a full-on war against the bordellos.

The bordellos were always the obvious choice: they were high-profile sitting ducks good for millions of dollars worth of glowing publicity. Unlike Carlos or the Confortos, the landladies also had no muscle and no history of vengeful violence against public servants. It was a no-lose situation for the police.

After over thirty years of continuous operation, Norma Wallace was indicted using an undercover sting. After Norma was driven out of her French Quarter business, Carlos extended the courtesy of letting her run girls out of his untouchable string of motels along Airline Highway in Jefferson Parish. After conferring with Carlos' army of attorneys, Norma saw no hope of escape and did the unthinkable: she pled out and served hard time in women's prison. The last Queen of the Underworld had been dethroned, never to be replaced.

It was a stupid coup that would do lasting damage. The world would never again be as safe for New Orleans working girls.

Giarrusso and Garrison's war paralyzed business in the French Quarter, and the exodus of money that began in the late 1950s quickly took on catastrophic proportions. It was incredible; you could see the glamour and the cash drain away from the Quarter by the day. Soon, Bourbon Street was no longer competition for the Las Vegas Strip; it was just a sleazy row of strip joints and dive bars.

The Chez Paris was just one victim among dozens. I was comparatively lucky. I had been moseying around with a lucky horseshoe up my ass for the previous eight years, during which I had not suffered a single arrest. I was long overdue to get collared, and everyone at the Chez Paris knew that Garrison's people were coming. Since the job of the b-drinking manager was to take the fall for the owner and the girls, I started asking the advice of all the ex-cons in the Quarter about how to survive in jail. Neil Gautier started teasing me mercilessly about the imminent loss of my "ass cherry."

To Neil's disappointment, my ass cherry survived. The night the undercover agents infiltrated the Chez Paris, one of them happened to overpay me at the bar. As the only honest Catholic boy to ever work behind a French Quarter bar, I dutifully rushed over to the agent's table and returned his extra cash. As he looked up at me in disbelief, my favorite b-girl leaned over and sarcastically explained to him that I "was a real good kid just putting himself through college."

Five minutes later, the entire staff of the Chez Paris was lined up against the wall with their hands behind their backs, and I was instinctively clenching my ass cheeks. The agents went from one side of the line to another handcuffing everyone, but, when they came to me, the cop whose money I had returned just patted me on the shoulder and whispered in my ear, "Get out of here, college boy."

When I stepped outside onto Bourbon Street, I saw my favorite b-girl waiting for me.

"It looks like we were nice to the right cop!"

I was still lucky, but it was hard for me to see the truth in that. Dutch was still dead, I was unemployed again, and the French Quarter was a war zone. I had no idea what to do with my life.

Just like after Dutch's death, opportunity did not wait long to pay old Frenchy a visit. My favorite b-girl swung by a few days after our non-arrest with a message. She was passing word from Mike Roach and Sherman Keaton that they had nowhere safe to room six high-class hookers they had ordered from out of town for a big convention. Since everyone knew that I had a huge penthouse apartment, they asked if I would let the hookers stay in my spare rooms while they were in town in exchange for a fat payoff.

This sounded like a fine idea to me. With no other way to pay my rent, I would be happy to get top dollar to keep a bunch of pretty hookers company. It's not like this was particularly taxing work; making pretty girls smile came naturally to me.

The six girls arrived in good spirits and very fine form: some blonds, some brunettes, even a redhead. They all looked me over with surprise and satisfaction; they had clearly suffered through far less pleasant roommates. I was flirting with them and offering to invite Neil Gautier over for a big slumber party when I received a phone call. I debonairly excused myself and strutted over to the phone, making sure to flex my biceps as I picked it up.

"Baby, what's doin'?" I said.

"Frenchy, you won't believe it," my b-girl said in a panic. "They got 'em!"

"Got who, baby?"

"Sherman, Mike, Snake...they got all the pimps! Giarrusso or

Garrison just busted all of 'em!"

I remember my exact thought at that moment: Well, fuck!

Watch as a handsome country boy from Marksville grows up into a seasoned, wary New Orleans Mafia associate.
(Photos from the author's collection)

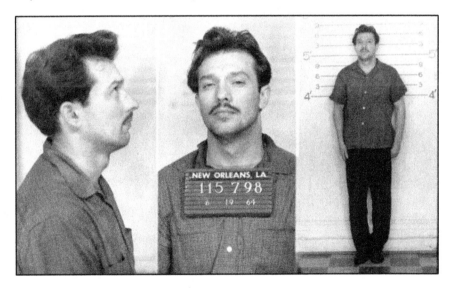

This is the booking photo of my very first arrest from June 19, 1964. It never amounted to anything, thanks to my lazy old buddy Jim Garrison. I resent the NOPD for pulling me off my couch and dragging me to the station looking like this. If I had known the photo would survive, I would have bribed them to let me get dressed up for my first mug shot.

On the left is the Kingfish himself, Huey Long, the governor and senator who let New York godfather Frank Costello expand his gambling empire to Louisiana.

On the right is "The Jolly Green Giant," New Orleans District Attorney Jim Garrison, who did his best to always look the other way from such underworld business.
(Photos courtesy of New Orleans Public Library)

The three Mafia godfathers I have known: on the left is dapper Frank Costello of New York, who conspired with Huey Long to expand his gambling empire to Louisiana; in the middle is the devilish, knife-scarred Silvestro "Silver Dollar Sam" Carollo of New Orleans (pictured here in 1930); and on the right is their protégé Carlos Marcello as a 29-year-old drug and gambling kingpin in 1939.

This is the New Orleans French Quarter roughly around the time I arrived in the late 1950s. You can get an idea of the sort of colorful, ethnic character of the neighborhood. (Photo by Marion Post Wolcott courtes of the Library of Congress's Farm Security Administration)

A fresh oyster truck making its delivery to Felix's Oyster Bar, the headquarters of Sam Saia's Mafia gambling network.

In the middle is my cousin and partner in crime, Edwin "The Silver Fox" Edwards, four-time governor of Louisiana and present-day federal prisioner. (Photos courtesy of New Orleans Public Library)

On the left is Sammy Marcello, Carlos' prostitute-interviewing, goat-herding brother. The second and third photos are of Carlos' most trusted and likable brother, my greatest wiseguy friend Joe Marcello. (First two photos courtesy of the 1979 U.S. House Select Committee on Assassinations)

The sickly man on the left is Sam LaBruzza, Carlos Marcello's longtime bodyguard, years after his physical peak. In the middle is Sherman Keaton, one of the most powerful pimps of the 1950s and 1960s. On the far right is the wildest go-go dancer of her day, the stone-crazy sharpshooter Janet "Jada" Conforto.

Here we see three of the many alleged conspirators in the assassination of John F. Kennedy. The top guy is obviously my old buddy, Lee Harvey Oswald, whom I chatted with in Carlos Marcello's office. The two guys below were also associates of the Marcellos: goofball go-go joint manager Jack Ruby and hairless sexual deviant David Ferry.

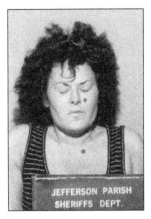  

Well, sometimes booking photos can be unflattering. On the left is my ultimate bottom bitch Jackie, who was a beautiful woman when she wasn't being arrested looking like a cavewoman. Next to her is "The Asshole", her son who stole my transsexual parrot and got me falsely charged with attempted murder. On the right is the lovely Renee, who nearly partied me to death in the 1980s.

On the left, you can see that Neil "Best Lay" Gautier still looks dirty-minded as can be. Next you can see the love of my life, Dusty, both before and after her wild lifestyle and drug abuse began to take its toll. (Left photo courtesy of Melissa Randazzo, middle photo from the author's collection)

On the left, you can see me enjoying the company of a beautiful young lady in the late 1970s. The next two photos are of me from a very profitable day at the fairgrounds in 1981.
(Photos from author's collection)

Here we see the best team of car-jacking, safe-cracking, jewel-heisting highwaymen in the history of modern America: Farish "Tex" Cody on the left and Dale on the right. I don't know who the girl is, but I wish we had been introduced.
(Photo from the author's collection)

Much like the city itself, time has not been kind to the superficial façade of Mr. New Orleans. Here are a couple of my mugshots from the 1990s.

Mr. New Orleans on one of the most iconic corners in the city.
(Photo courtesy of Melissa Randazzo)

This is the home that my dad built for our little family in Marksville, Louisiana. He was square as they come: responsible, respectable, hard-working, and honest. In other words, I am proof that, sometimes, the apple falls very, very far from the tree.

Here you see both the brains and brawn of this operation -- this is me with the writer of the fine book you are holding in your hands.
(Photos courtesy of Melissa Randazzo)

Chapter VII

A Regular Humanitarian

1960s

"Mr. Brouillette emphatically stated that due to his 'respect for the Federal Bureau of Investigation' he would never ever think of violating Federal Prostitution Laws."
FBI Document 31-8777
Filed February 8, 1971

PIMPS ARE PEOPLE TOO. My profession has never lessened or meddled with my humanity. Far from it, I believe the pimp game has taught me patience and a great deal more about human nature than I ever cared to learn.

The job itself is no more evil than any other gig in the service industry. I've done bad things which I regret as a criminal, but none of them were as a pimp. As a pimp, I introduced women who wanted to get paid for sex to men who wanted to pay for sex — ensuring that both parties got exactly what they deserved out of the deal. Sin need play no part in the transaction.

I'll admit that I was a reluctant recruit to the sex rackets. As a repressed Catholic schoolboy at heart, I had to approach my destiny by degrees: first as the friend of wizened old operators Norma Wallace, Hyp Guinle, and Steve Valenti; then as the boyfriend and banker of a prostitute; and, finally, as the procurer for all of the city's pimps at the Chez Paris.

By the time I had six all-star hookers camped out in my apartment with no one to procure tricks for them, the sex game had been largely robbed of its mystery and voodoo. Prostitution wasn't the terrifying "white slave trade" that I had imagined in Marksville, and call girls definitely were not the blood-sucking sex cannibals I feared or fantasized them to be. It was just a criminal racket as boring as any other. As usual, the real victims were voluntary and destined to get victimized somehow anyway.

Still, I hesitated out of fear of what my family in Marksville would say when they heard that I was a whoremonger. If I decided to cause my dear old family any more trouble, I would need an excuse.

And baby, I ended up getting plenty. When I finally came out as a pimp, events had conspired to make my decision feel entirely selfless and involuntary. For a moment, the entire health of the New Orleans tourist industry depended on whether I chose to become a pimp.

With no help from me, it came to pass that every major pimp and madam in the city was jailed or in hiding during a major tourist week. The livelihoods of hundreds of bartenders, bellhops, taxi drivers, hot dog salesmen, and prostitutes who supported themselves via referrals to or from pimps were in jeopardy. Carlos Marcello had VIPs traveling from across the country for an underworld summit, and he depended on giving them the full "New Orleans treatment" in order to get the terms he wanted out of them. Worst of all, I had six hookers, twelve breasts, twelve tearful eyes, and sixty sharp-nailed fingers stranded in my apartment with nothing to do but make me feel guilty for not getting them the money they *desperately* needed.

New Orleans was a city built on tourism and the port, and both of these industries traditionally required pimps and prostitutes to thrive. With the entire pimp brotherhood out of action, the city was crying out for a savior who could keep the sex trade rolling. With my already established street cred, underworld connections, pimp reputation, and hooker-enthralling good looks, it was clear that I was the only man qualified for the job.

Still, I needed to be pushed. I resisted the initial appeals to my greed and lust by the hookers in my place, who offered all sorts of perks if I put them in business. Since these women made their living manipulating and flattering a man's ego, they quickly hit on a more successful manner of persuasion: the Catholic guilt trip.

As soon as I heard all of the tragedies that would befall these innocent women if I did not energetically pimp them out — children that would starve, mothers that would die for want of expensive medication, pimps that would lay down hellacious beatings in lieu of their expected cash — I felt like becoming a pimp would make me a hero...so a hero I became. I was the world's first humanitarian pimp.

"I love the white girl and the black,
and I love all the rest,
I love the girls for loving me,
but I love myself the best."
"A Little Apple Cider"
Louisiana Minstrel Song

From the very beginning, I was the biggest pimp in New Orleans. I made a few phone calls to spread the word, and within hours, my initial tally of six hookers rose to twenty-four. All of Sherman Keaton's and Mike Roach's girls hustled over to me so that they could get back to hustlin'. In the weeks that followed, my stable reached forty and, on the busiest nights, even fifty girls. There was a vacuum that needed to be filled — which, when you think about it, is the entire point of the sex rackets.

Since I had been apprenticing for the role of sex-trade operator ever since I first met Norma Wallace and Hyp Guinle, I did not make a single false step when I started up my own operation.

The best move I made was to pattern myself, not after the

many pimps I knew from The Spot and Chez-Paris, but instead after Norma Wallace. She had lasted for forty lucrative years, much longer than any pimp, so I figured that she clearly knew the secrets to mastering the sex trade. Later in my career, I would meet a female pimp, but I think I may have been the first male madam. I followed none of the rules of the pimp.

Like Norma, I never beat anybody, never hooked anyone on drugs, never stole money owed to a working girl, and never disrespected anyone who treated me with respect. When the time came, and a call girl decided to quit, I put together a pile of cash and jewels as a "retirement package" and wished her the best.

This code of honor is why Norma never had anyone rat on her, and that's why I only had a couple girls rat on me in over forty years of breakneck operating.

I've always said, "If you have to beat a girl, you don't want her. If you have to hook her on drugs, you don't want her. If you need to mistreat a girl to keep her, you're not good enough at what you do; you're cheating." Most pimps end up in jail because the girls they treat like shit rat them out at the first opportunity.

My determination to follow in Norma's high-heeled footsteps went so far as hiring her doctor, Edwin Miller, to give my women weekly checkups and free comprehensive healthcare. If you got sick working for me, Dr. Edwin gave you the medicine you needed, and I supported you for as long as you were kept from working.

Dr. Miller also did me the favor of saving my life three times when I was seriously wounded. Once, a Mafia hitman stabbed me in the gut for firing his girlfriend. It was all a big misunderstanding. We were good friends who just didn't see eye to eye on that issue, and I was sorry to hear of his mysterious death when I went out of town on vacation some time later. On two other occasions, I was ambushed and shot by unseen assailants; if I had seen those cowards, they wouldn't have gotten the chance to shoot me.

I did my best to keep my ladies drug-free, which was like

taking a roll of absorbent paper towels to the Gulf of Mexico and trying to scrub your way to dry land. I told Dr. Miller to check my girls for signs of abuse and nag the junkies to quit. It was hopeless, but I never bought them drugs, and I did my best to keep my girls from overdosing or becoming pathetic.

Granted, my definition of "drugs" is pretty narrow: just poison like crack cocaine, crystal meth, PCP, and heroin. Snake Gonzales used to lecture me and try to convince me that heroin helped to control a working girl and keep her docile, but I always thought that was stupid. The drugs get all the money in the end, and you pay for it on the witness stand.

Another difference between Snake and me is that I did not headhunt women, very far from it. I used to watch Snake Gonzales and Mike Roach try to turn every single pretty girl they met, and it both sickened and amused me. I could never get over how greedy those two rich men had to be to expose themselves to such constant humiliation and rejection. I also laughed to myself that they were such bad pimps that they felt the need to *recruit*.

I was different; I not only refused to recruit but also turned down girls who tried to sign on with me. From the very beginning, the whores came to me and won *me* over. If a veteran came to me looking for "representation," I told her to get out while she still had her life and the looks required to get a husband. The fresh-faced rookies who came to me got such a stern talking-to that I'm sure I made more nuns than a traditional Catholic girls' school.

Besides all the behavioral guidelines, I made sure not to forget Norma's most important business rule: Mind the Cops. Norma always used to say, "Without the police, I'd never had made it for forty years," and, now that I've been in the sex business for even longer than her, I can't say that my experience has been any different.

To get my relationship with the flatfoots started off on the right foot, I approached a former NOPD officer whom I knew from The Spot. This poor guy had been kicked off the force for bribery, which was like a fish being booted from the sea for having gills, and was making a living as a lowly driver for the Bell taxi company. I have never seen a happier man than that ex-pig when I bought his cab for $2000 cash and hired him full time as my bagman and police liaison. My new PR flack visited each cop in the First District once a week with a $10 bill in his hand, which purchased my paperless operating license in the state of Louisiana.

If there's anything I learned from the pimps, it was Hyp Guinle's commandment to always Mind the Hacks. I took my newly purchased taxi, #1669 Bell, on a grand total of one drive: from my place to the Spot's cabstand, where it was parked permanently as an advertisement. I sat inside that cab with the door open and held court, the Don Corleone of hacks, granting favors and listening to grievances.

I made them an offer even idiots like them could not refuse: every cabdriver who agreed to "go on the record" with me as their go-to operator received a new transmission in their car, free drinks at the Spot on my tab, and the money to pay off their petty gambling debts. Within days, I had 250 hacks acting as my personal sexual Amway team, procuring johns from all four corners of the South.

Hyp Guinle was right; the hacks were a goldmine. The affection of the taxi brotherhood was worth $1500-$3000 a day in pure profit for me in 1960s dollars. In case you don't understand that, I made around a *million dollars* in my first year as a pimp, and those were the days when a million dollars could buy you five new cars, five new boats, five new mansions, and five new trophy brides.

The secret to this windfall was volume. My 250 taxi drivers asked every customer they ever picked up, "Whatchoo looking for, man?" If that customer answered with *anything* that was illegal, I received a phone call at my penthouse apartment or at my late- night headquarters at the Spot, where Hyp Guinle and Steve Valenti watched my success with pride mixed with disbelief.

Once the hack had me on the phone, he would usually request his favorite girl — the girl he believed could best run up the bill, since he got paid on commission. I'd send the hack's favorite girl, or a reasonable replacement, to meet the hack and the mark outside of my penthouse or a major hotel. My girl would negotiate the services and the price in front of the hack so that he could be assured that he received his full cut, and, if successful, she'd then call to let me know the terms of the deal. The hack would then drive the lovebirds to a cooperating hotel. After they were done, the hack would return my girl to my place, and I'd divvy up the proceeds.

As you can imagine, there was a lot of sleight of hand that went along with the turning of the average trick. If you deal, you deal double. Once in the hotel room, the girl would always try to renegotiate with the john to convince him to pay more so that she could skim the difference between the original price and the actual price.

I was no better; I always made sure to scam the cops — who did nothing — on their share of the proceeds. Theoretically, the split was supposed to be: 30% to the girl, 30% to the hack, and 20% apiece for the pimp and the house detective at the hotel. In reality, I always kept 35% and handed the pig 5%, which was still more than he deserved.

Life as the benefactor of every taxi driver in New Orleans came with some fringe benefits. There is a common misconception that pimps wear a great deal of jewelry because of their vanity or to impress girls. Though that may be the motivation today, originally a pimp's jewelry collection was the result of his friendship with his hacks, who in the olden days rolled every mark that got into their cab naïve enough to be sporting a nice ring or watch.

If a pimp wanted to keep the taxi drivers' loyalty, he needed to act both as their call girl provider *and* as their hot-jewelry fence. If you didn't buy their stolen jewelry, some other pimp would be happy to oblige and, in the process, steal your hack. So, pimps naturally got overburdened with so much hot jewelry that they could never move all of it. Instead, they wore it.

I was no different. I sported a diamond or ruby ring on every finger, a diamond-studded gold watch on my wrist, a jumble of gold necklaces around my throat, and a jeweled belt buckle. I sparkled so much that I looked like the constellation of Hercules walking down Bourbon Street at night.

To protect my hoard of jewels, I bought my infamous bodyguard dog Satan, and, to make use of the new billboard space, I slapped a couple pounds of jewels on her dog collar. I was always reprimanding that mutt and telling her that she couldn't chew on a diamond dog collar without ruining her teeth. A guard dog with Cajun-grandma teeth would do me no good.

The cab driver who procured the lion's share of my jewelry was probably Larry Levine, nicknamed "The Chicken Picker" for his nimble fingers. Larry was just about the friendliest con man you'd ever meet. He'd drive you around all night, give you discounts and free drinks, show you all the hotspots around town — and keep driving until you eventually passed out drunk in the backseat of his cab. You'd wake up the next morning in the middle of a swamp wearing nothing of value.

Larry got bold with me over the years since he was the husband of one of Norma's girls and figured that gave him license to act the fool. Larry once came up to me when I was minding my own business and asked me to come see a mark in his cab. I figured he wanted to negotiate a lay, so I agreed. Once I sat down next to the mark in the backseat, Larry turns on the guy in anger and screams, "GIVE ME YOUR FUCKING MONEY!" With one look at my muscles and my pimp jewels, the mark tossed his wallet to Larry.

That was a pretty low trick as far as I was concerned, but Larry stuffed some hot diamonds in my palm and made us friends again.

Powdered in jewels like a Fabergé beignet, I became by necessity something of an expert fence. This made my dealings with the incredibly impatient and ignorant hacks extremely frustrating, because *now* I knew when they were losing me money.

For example, very late one night Angelo Pecorara came to me with an immaculate diamond the size of a testicle. This stone was museum showpiece quality, so I told Angelo to hold onto it until the next day and to meet me and my expert at Canal Jewelry in the morning. The next day, I walked over to Canal Jewelry with a hop in my step, only to see my expert jeweler examining Angelo's diamond with a devilish grin on his face.

"Hey dere, Frenchy!" that jewel-studying cocksucker said to me. "Dat hack Angelo don't know *shit* about diamonds, man! You won't believe what I paid for dis here beauty!" Thanks to Angelo's impatient and greedy decision to head to the jeweler without his agent, we both lost $8000 or $9000 on the deal.

One night Angelo got his just desserts. He picked up one of my oldest fleabag girls and brought her to a motel room where she had an appointment. Angelo parked his cab outside to wait for his cut and found himself waiting for twelve straight hours. This was theoretically a *good* thing because a twelve-hour tab would give him a huge commission.

Each hour, the girl came to the window and blew Angelo a kiss, which was the signal that the mark was continuing to add to his tab. After twelve kisses at the window, each time with the girl looking progressively sweatier and hard-ridden, Angelo figured he had a world-class Vidalia on his hands and calculated that 30% of whatever the mark was spending on twelve hours of nonstop, billable, *a la carte* sex acts had to be in the thousands of dollars.

Angelo was so giddy that he kept calling me and his wife every fifteen minutes to brag and daydream about what he'd do with all that money. I had seen enough to be skeptical, but Angelo's kitchen-rhino wife did not know any better and actually believed that Angelo would be bringing her the mink coat he promised over the phone.

Well, after twelve hours of blowing kisses through the window, that old rag doll hooker stumbled out of the motel room, laid down in the parking lot, and went to sleep. She was followed outside by her drug dealer, who had just taken every cent of his favorite junkie's spending cash. There had been no Vidalia, no trick; Angelo had been used as a hooker's free taxi ride to her drug dealer.

Why she kept him waiting outside that long I'll never know.

When Angelo slumped through the door of his home penniless and minkless, his grumpy old lady packed her bags and left him for good. That's what that dummy got for selling that big-ass diamond without me! If he had let me sell it, he could have paid some coonass to slaughter and skin the 5000 minks it would have taken to fit around his wife's fat ass.

The fate of poor Angelo Pecorara reminds me of the equally sad fate of another hyperactive, penny-ante hustler named Tippy Toe. As far as I know, "Tippy Toe" was on his birth certificate; I never heard him called anything else.

Well, it was the same story for Tippy Toe, only with a different ending. He waited twelve hours outside of the Lafayette Hotel for one of my girls to turn a trick. Tippy Toe had already spent weeks making fun of poor Angelo Pecorara, so he was dying of nerves as the hours piled up.

Tippy Toe kept tiptoeing over to the nearest phone booth to bug me, asking what he should do, asking if the girl was a junkie, asking if we could trust her. I told that hack "She's a good girl...stop calling me, I'm a busy man!" Well, Tippy Toe couldn't wait any longer, so he called the house detective at the Lafayette and had him break down the door. Tippy Toe ended up crying in the street: the girl was found gagged and tied to the bed in a puddle of piss; she had been mugged and left alone for ten hours.

The hacks were sort of like the Keystone Kops in yellow cars. The driving obsession of just about every cabbie's life was the pursuit of get-rich-quick schemes. Since I knew so many hacks, just about every night I got to watch one of them strike it rich on a scam — and then shit it away so quick on rounds of drinks, $100 cocktail waitress tips, and card games that they would be deeper in debt than when they started their workday.

As much as I liked to watch the hacks' self-destructive behavior, in the end I was the only one hurting. To maintain my hold over their affection, it was inevitably me that had to call off Carlos' loan sharks and pay their gambling debts. I had no choice because the other pimps got out of jail soon enough and came a-calling to steal back their hacks. Not that they did a particularly good job: Mike Roach and Sherman Keaton both got the bright idea of handing out rolls of quarters to the hacks and saying, "Why dontcha gimme a call, sometime?"

I ended up getting about 200 rolls of quarters that week as tokens of the hack's loyalty to me and the far more generous lagniappe I provided.

The hacks were notoriously fickle, but not when it came to old Frenchy. Not at first, at least.

"Nellie Gaspar, the daughter of a London innkeeper, came to New Orleans in 1866 as a performer in Smith's European Circus. She was ruined by a smooth-tongued New Orleans scoundrel, who then put her in the Dauphine Street brothel."
Herbert Asbury

Sometimes, I think the only people that get a worse rap than pimps are the call girls.

This is what people need to understand about prostitutes and their work: a blowjob is just a job like any other, and it often blows. Hence the name.

The average sex worker is no dumber, sleazier, or more dangerous than any other woman from her particular background and class. It's all about the class. Back in Gasper Gulotta and Norma Wallace's golden age, a call girl was a *lady*. Since they had nothing to fear from the cops, and the job was basically the highest paying, easiest job a New Orleans woman could get, it attracted the wildest of the best and brightest.

This all changed when call girls started facing arrest; that's when you saw the "outlaw" element — junkies, con women, petty thieves, desperate losers, and crooks — begin to take over because only crooks would risk jail time. That's why it's unfair to say "hookers" are more likely to be petty criminals and junkies; the truth is that the police have made it so that only petty criminals and junkies are willing to take the risk of being hookers.

Don't get me wrong, high-quality girls have always been and always will be around. I've had graduate students turn tricks to pay for tuition, and rich high-society wives who set up out-of-town "dates" just for the thrill of being rotten. I once had to call a rich old Mississippi River pilot-ship captain and tell him that his devoutly religious, cocktail-party hosting, pillar-of-society wife was in jail for prostitution. "And who are you?"

"Uh," I answered, "Officer Frenchy, baby."

Classically stylish ladies still dominate the top end of the sex rackets. The by-appointment-only, high-class call girls who only work in nice hotels with steady dates are, if anything, smarter and smoother than the average professional woman. After all, their entire job is to be more charming, hip, sexy, and classy than their john's blue-blooded, college-educated wives.

Since they are almost never arrested thanks to their powerful clients, these women have very little of the criminal element in their makeup. To a few of these all-star call girls, the real lifers, prostitution is practically their dream job. In fact, I know some call girls who love the job so much that they'll never leave it — even if they become millionaires, even after they become eligible for Social Security.

I have a specific call girl in mind: the lady I call the English Queen, whose real name I will not mention since she will have me killed if I do. The Queen stomps on every stereotype about hookers. Though there's no one else like her, I've known many call girls who are just as unique and charming in their own way.

Prostitutes are just human, baby.

The Queen would probably be upset with me for calling her human; the bitch is positive that she is superhuman and knows it and won't let anyone forget it. She was a born businessperson, which means you'd be better off setting your head on fire than doing business with her. No one makes a penny off of her. I'd be hard-pressed to say that anyone I've ever met is a smarter or tougher entrepreneur.

Carlos Marcello made more money, but he damn sure wasn't as disciplined as the Queen, and I can't honestly tell you who I would be more scared of as an opponent. Carlos had more power and more henchmen, but the Queen had a death glare that could make a man's dick shrivel off at twenty yards. If Carlos and the Queen had ever settled down for a staring contest, I think they would've both melted.

The Queen is a half-Gypsy, half-English girl who came to New Orleans as a showgirl in the circus. Figuring that she'd rather stay in a stationary circus than a moving one, she stuck around in the French Quarter as a camera girl at the legendary French Quarter bar Pat O'Brien's.

One day I was driving my Pontiac Convertible down Bourbon Street with Satan in the passenger's seat when I spotted the Queen on the sidewalk on the way to work. And, take it from me, this girl was *walking*, throwing around a busty figure that would make a plastic surgeon lay down his scalpel. The Queen's long, soft, strawberry blond hair fell down to the small of her back, leading my eyes right down to an ass that convinced me that we should become friends.

I pulled my beautifully polished Pontiac alongside her on Bourbon Street. She was blinded by my jewels and by my good looks, which she compared to the "rugged, romantic" Hollywood star Victor Mature, but that was not what won her over. Lucky for me, the Queen was a dog nut in more than just the obvious manner.

As the chocolate-eyed Gypsy stopped in her tracks to make

goo goo faces at the uncommonly friendly Satan, I struck a relaxed pose and threw on my most rugged, romantic voice. "Baby, how 'bout some drinks?" I asked like a hunk who always gets what he wants.

Well, let's just say I was lucky to have that goddamn dog in the car to protect me. This pretty little thing with pretty huge breasts swung a high-caliber, double-barrel scowl at me that made a murder of crows fly away from a nearby oak tree. Lucky for me, the Queen, like Carlos, took a pitying fancy to me.

"No," the Queen said with the most goofy and self-consciously proper English accent I had ever heard, "*but...you may* buy me a hot dog!" To this day, the bitch loves a hotdog on a hot summer day.

Figuring that a stop at a Lucky Dog would not give me enough time to form a lasting bond with my gypsy princess, I took her instead to a restaurant I knew that made hot dogs. As we sat down at the table, barely having said more than a couple sentences to each other, the Queen focused that stare on me again and asked without embarrassment, "You look like the sort of man who could procure my friend an abortion."

Interesting small talk, I thought to myself. Of course, I *was* that sort of man, but it wasn't the sort of thing I necessarily wanted to be obvious just from one look at me. It was also the first sign that, no matter how good looking I was, this broad evidently wasn't too concerned with impressing me. I was just a way to procure a hotdog, an abortion, and some quality time with a German shepherd.

As we were chit-chatting about abortion, which naturally unnerved a choir-boy-at-heart like me, New Orleans's most notorious pimp Snake Gonzales busted into the place like a five-foot-tall giant, only to stop dead in his tracks the moment he saw my dinner companion. Snake was not the sentimental type — to say the very least — but from the moment he saw the Queen, he was *punked,* baby. This swarthy, violent little man who took shit from no one fell in love at first sight with the English Queen, and he was her mark for the rest of his life.

Snake was never a flashy or stylish pimp; the fashion statement he made was the terror he inspired and the blade he carried. With his drab clothes and unimposing physique, Snake did not look like someone who would appeal to a freakish beauty like the Queen, but that wasn't going to stop him. "Son," he said to me, using the nickname he used for all men, "where in the *hell* did you find *her*?" He threw the Queen a look that left nothing unsaid and would have been a felony in Mississippi.

I looked over to the Queen as if to apologize for the interruption of our conversation, but that girl had a look on her face that I never expected. Somehow, that incredibly perceptive girl looked past Snake's unimpressive exterior and saw the devil underneath. The man within the schlubby wrapper was a ruthless, merciless, power-hungry predator — terms that pretty much described the Queen. She just happened to hide her little Napoleon within curves and cream.

Technically, it was bad form for Snake Gonzales to steal my date that night, but I made a habit of letting Snake's bad behavior slide. That man didn't get the name "Snake" from being a reasonable sort of fellow. He got it from being the sort of vengeful reptile who would take anything I said the wrong way, stew on it, and then stab me seventeen times in the liver when I wasn't looking.

So I never said anything. And I'm still alive, so I think it was the right move.

Romance wasn't one of the first words that occurred to you when you heard the name of Snake Gonzales — vicious, paranoid, bitter, jealous, violent, and short were all more likely candidates. But Snake could sense very quickly that, beneath her layer of soft and luscious flesh, the Queen was every bit the cobra that he was. He appreciated and respected that.

The result was something no one in the French Quarter had ever imagined possible: Snake Gonzales in puppy love, stumbling dumbly after the Queen with hearts in his eyes. The Queen had reduced the most cutthroat, coldhearted player in the sex rackets to just another mark. Whenever Snake was not around, the other pimps had a good laugh.

The FBI was not so amused. While the feds did their best to ignore Carlos Marcello, they were balls-to-wall public servants when it came to apprehending and jailing Snake Gonzales. And when the feds want something, they play dirty.

First, they tried to pressure me into ratting on Snake, which was pointless since I didn't commit crimes with him — I just ate at his restaurant, The Snake Pit. I could have given them nothing but the same unsubstantiated rumors they already had. Still, I was threatened with countless federal charges if I didn't make up some crime I committed with Snake to send him to jail.

Next on their list was the Queen, who was still as square and proud as she could be; she naturally refused to testify against Snake. The feds made her suffer on Snake's behalf. They walked into Pat O'Brien's and told the owners to expect nightly visits from the FBI as long as the girlfriend of a known pimp worked on the premises as a waitress. The FBI got the Queen fired from every job she could get using this routine until she was left with no legitimate means of employment.

Like me, the Queen was backed into the sex rackets by circumstance, but she was too much of a survivor to be too bothered by lying on her back to make a living. No matter what profession she pursued, the Queen would have retired rich. She would have made millions selling peanuts at the Fairgrounds, if it came to that.

The Queen did not suffer by becoming a call girl — far from it. She was a real winner in the sex rackets. The only losers were Snake, who lost his girl, and New Orleans, who lost the one woman who could have built a Fortune 500 company in the French Quarter.

To the Queen, prostitution was a revelation; it had been inconceivable previously to her that she could make so much money for comparatively so little work. Once a man took a look at the Queen, they were three quarters the way to climax; she'd finish off her average client in less time than it took her to eat a hot dog.

With Snake covering her everyday expenses, the Queen banked every single cent she made as a call girl, and she hooked many of her clients for life. Once you went with her, you were just about close to ruined for other women. The Queen has rich clients that haven't paid another working girl since around 1965.

Yes, the Queen still turns tricks — occasionally. She's a multimillionaire now, and older than all of *The Golden Girls* put together, but she'd still sucker punch a child to get to a penny left on the street. She's beaten a bill at every restaurant in the state of Louisiana, and there isn't a department store in New Orleans that hasn't seen thousands of dollars of inventory disappear into her purse. That was the Queen's secret; anything she touched turned to money. After a date at a hotel room, everything from the curtains to the bedsheets would end up leaving the premises in her gigantic hammock purse.

That reminds me of one of my favorite Queen stories. One day, her richest client offered to give her and two friends a free trip to Acapulco. The Queen accepted the offer of three round-trip plane tickets and three hotel rooms in Acapulco for a week. As soon as she received the money for the tickets and hotel reservations, she put the money in her bank account and took her friends down to Acapulco on a bus. Instead of hotel rooms, the Queen packed three hammocks in her luggage, which she hung from the palm trees on the beach.

Any businesswoman this smart obviously was not going to kick up cash to a pimp. As the underworld watched in shock, the Queen fearlessly stole half of Snake's girls and became the first female pimp in New Orleans memory. Snake didn't do a damn thing besides wish her luck.

Once news of the Queen's pimping of Snake Gonzales got around, the Queen earned a new admirer: Norma Wallace. After getting released from jail, Norma went straight and opened up the

Tchoupitoulas Plantation restaurant, where she held court as the most charming hostess in all of America.

The news of Snake's defeat inspired Norma to invite me to bring down that "charming gypsy girl" to see her. Norma and the Queen sized each other up real quick, and they became fast friends. Since Snake Gonzales was Norma's absolutely least favorite person because he had stolen and then abused many of her girls over the years, the woman who stole *Snake's* girls and played him like a mark had her boundless admiration.

I always have shared that admiration for the Queen. I could never decide whether Carlos was lucky that the Queen and Norma were born women so that they could never be competition — or if the ladies were lucky that they were born women since Carlos would have whacked out any man that dangerous without hesitation.

Thanks to her worship of money, I trusted the Queen as my bank. At one point, she was holding over $50,000 for me, which I'm sure she was loaning out for interest. I can't tell you the number of times I've been in a bind, only for the Queen to swoop me up on her broomstick and remind me that she was holding just enough cash to get me out of trouble.

Even when I had no cash at all, the Queen took care of her oldest friend. Once, the feds put me in jail right as my precious dog Malcolm X was out of town on a week-long training and grooming package. Since the feds had seized everything before locking me up, I had no way of paying the $750 tab for the course. Without hesitation, the Queen drove over, paid the entire tab, and took care of Malcolm X for the next couple of years for free. That remains the second nicest thing any call girl has ever done for me.

The Queen and I are still double-tight, even if we've both lost our looks. She's more impatient with me as a homely old drunk than a hot young drunk, but she's still got my back. The woman is worth tens of millions of dollars, and she has a small business where her clients include presidents and royalty. One recent

President of the United States bought a gift for his mistress from the Queen — a story I sure wish I could tell you, but I *would* like to live to see this book published. Let's just say it wasn't Bill Clinton.

I just saw the Queen a few weeks ago for dinner. She had just jumped off her scooter, an overheated and sweaty old lady, bragging that she had made $400 for a date across town. She suggested we get some steaks, which I thought was quite generous of her. I thought we were going to Ruth Chris or Dickie Brennan's or some other local steakhouse; nope, we headed over to the supermarket, where the multimillionaire Queen boosted two huge porterhouses in her purse.

And let me tell you what she said as we sat down to eat. "Frenchy," she said with that same pretty Mary Poppins accent, "don't you agree that stolen steaks taste better?"

"On the day my uncle was to be baptized, his wife and small boy sat on the bank of the creek happy over his conversion. As my uncle was led out into the water by the preacher, there floated out of his pocket face up, the ace of spades, and a few moments later, the king of spades. As the preacher was just getting ready to take hold of him, there floated behind those cards the queen and jack of spades, and then out came the ten of spades. His wife saw the situation and screamed: 'Don't baptize him, Parson, my husband is lost...my husband is lost!' But the young boy on the bank yelled out excitedly: 'No he ain't, ma! If pa can't win with that hand, he can't win at all!'"

Huey Long

Since I've given the positive spin on working girls, I might as well do the same for all of the johns out there. I think you can figure out by now that I'll get to the horror stories in due time, but I don't want to start off on that foot because it would be misleading.

Most johns are honestly not perverts or sex maniacs. Almost half of the johns in my experience are not even really looking for sex. Between the guys who just want some freaky fetish role-play and the husbands who just want a pretty girl to talk with without being nagged, a call girl can make thousands a day without ever having sex. I've known girls who quit sex completely and made their livings by having their feet worshipped or giving rich businessmen shoulder massages.

Of the men who do want sex, most just want some relief at a price they can afford. The number of johns who are abusive, violent, or psychologically sick is under 1%, and, back in the day, I could fix those shit-asses with one phone call. I wouldn't waste time calling Carlos; I'd dial Joe or Sammy Marcello, my favorite customers of all time.

The Marcellos' relationship with prostitution was always positive as it could be, even though Carlos *never* had any interest in partying with a hooker himself. Tooling around with girls just seemed like something that was beneath a tycoon like Carlos.

With that said, Carlos did plenty of business in the sex rackets. He really had no choice; you can't be the crime boss of a port and tourist city without making peace with the prostitution racket. When Carlos originally bought the Town & Country, the plan was to use it as a wide-open house of prostitution protected by Jefferson Parish sheriff "King" Clancy. When that deal fell through, Carlos made arrangements first with Norma and Mike Roach and then with me to have a crew of girls available at a single phone call.

I'd pick up my phone and hear, "Hey, Frenchy, it's Mr. C!" in a low, teeth-gritting grumble at least once a night. "I need two girls on da double, and don't send me no bums!" Within minutes, a limousine would pull up outside of my apartment to take Carlos' order away. Two of Carlos' drivers, Slim and Ralph, were always available to transport girls from me to Carlos' clients across Louisiana and then back.

Carlos gave me so much business that I didn't want to bother him when someone got out of line. I'd call his two most powerful and lovable younger brothers, Joe and Sammy, to deliver the message. Joe and Sammy loved working girls - hell, they just loved girls. They didn't like to hear that some asshole was taking liberties and ruining some pretty young thing for the rest of mankind.

As Carlos' underboss for decades, Joe Marcello really is one of the most influential and least understood figures in Mafia history. Joe was intensely aware of how little credit he received in proportion to his massive role in the family business. Besides Carlos and Silver Dollar Sam, New Orleans never had a more powerful gangster, but that was not good enough for Joe. Living his entire life in his big brother's shadow, Joe was always insecure and second-guessing himself.

That's one reason Joe could never be his brother; Carlos was not a second-guesser. If Carlos killed John F. Kennedy, I guarantee you it never disturbed his sleep or bothered his ego.

The other thing that Joe lacked was Carlos' discipline and obsessive drive to obtain power and money. Joe, to be honest, had an obsessive drive to eat, party, and flirt with beautiful women. That's how he became my friend — one of my closest friends. Joe was really my sort of guy, a nonstop party.

I became close to Joe thanks to his insecurities. Joe was a big Jackie Gleason kind of guy whose smile and money girls loved, but his slim and charming younger brother Sammy made him insecure over his looks. So Joe hired a trainer at the New Orleans Athletic Club to get him into shape, but no trainer was going to crack the whip on a Marcello. Ask Neil Gautier: I hooked him up as the trainer of Carlos Marcello's son, and that boy never ended up a muscleman, either.

So, Joe Marcello was always at the gym but never working out, looking stupid doing nothing. I was always there trying to concentrate on lifting heavy things over and over again to improve my looks. New Orleans wiseguys were not exactly known for their physiques, so I was the only guy in Joe's entire social circle who was ever around the gym for him to talk to. Just about every day, I'd end up cutting my workout short to go eat lunch with Joe and tell funny stories about the local tricks.

Joe had a fascination with call girls, and he ended up becoming a terrible gossip, always asking me about the latest antics of his favorite crazy hookers. His brother Sammy did him one better: Sammy hired my girls by the hour and, unlike Joe, never did anything with them besides talk. Sammy paid them top-dollar simply to answer his questions about what it was like being a call girl. These interrogations could last hours. I could never figure out if thin, balding Sammy with his big, black nerd glasses was getting off from these interviews, or if he just had an innocent sociological interest.

After all, Sammy was a weird one. One of his hobbies was raising the Marcello herd of goats on the family farm on the north shore of Lake Pontchartrain. A buddy of mine who lived nearby would wake up in the morning to the *bah, bah, bah* of dozens of goats by his window. Sammy would be standing outside, smiling proudly as the goats devoured my pal's vegetable garden. With no choice but to humor a Marcello, he would ask, "So dey gotcha herdin' goats now?"

"Yeah, man, dese some hungry sons of bitches today," Sammy would respond with a shrug. Your typical millionaire wiseguy wouldn't choose to spend his early mornings with livestock.

Though Joe and Sammy were my cumulative favorite clients, they were not the favorite trick. In my mind, I've never been part of anything I'm proud of other than the time I got a man I'll call Papa John laid. Papa John was the father of a very good friend of mine named Dale, who will become a big part of my story.

Papa John was an icon of the New Orleans Italian community. Never before or after has a guido been that connected while keeping his nose that clean. John was honestly the squarest man I ever met in the French Quarter, yet at the same time you couldn't find anyone that the New Orleans Mafia loved more.

As a young man, this good-natured, quiet, and harmless gentleman had been perfectly situated to become a wiseguy, if he had had a single malicious thought in his head. As a young Italian laborer who worked around the French Quarter and the immigrant-dominated French Market, John was based in what was the stronghold of Silver Dollar Sam's Prohibition-era Mafia. Somehow or another, the personable little guy became a close friend of both the gun-slinging bootlegger Silver Dollar Sam and a young French Market vegetable hauler named Carlos Marcello.

Despite being as violent and unpredictable as a rattlesnake, Silver Dollar Sam had a well-known soft spot for humble, hardworking, honest, and meek Italians—real peasant types. Silver Dollar Sam was the sort of bloodthirsty bully who gets off on teaching other bullies a lesson, and he bragged that he enjoyed nothing more than blasting away some Irish or black or cop hood who thought he could mess with poor Italian immigrants. Naturally, in Little Palermo and the other guido ghettos of Louisiana, every Irishman, black, or pig that Silver Dollar Sam shot just added to his popularity.

To take care of his good friend John, who was barely getting by as a petty plumber, Silver Dollar Sam handed him the plum job of French Quarter "hot gas liner." The gas liner was the plumber who crawled into the sewers and rigged each mobbed-up bar in the Quarter with pipes that delivered "hot gas," illegal booze, directly from the underground breweries.

It was ugly work, but there was plenty of it in the booze-mad French Quarter during Prohibition. Soon enough, John saved enough money to open up his own restaurant, The Marketplace, at 45 French Market Place in the very belly of Silver Dollar Sam's turf. Silver Dollar Sam must have owned a piece of the place since he installed a full off-track betting parlor upstairs, complete with tellers behind a cage, a loudspeaker with live play-by-play from the fairgrounds, card tables with dealers, and a row of Frank Costello's Indian head slot machines.

John's restaurant was greatly benefited by his popularity with

New Orleans's brotherhood of perpetually hungry wiseguys since he was a real *paisan* and a lovable guy who they could tell in an instant was trustworthy.

There's a great story about how Papa John was drinking in a bar when he struck up a friendship with a clever-looking young stranger. He impressed the young man so much that the stranger invited him to his car to show him something special. When they reached his car, the stranger pulled back the front driver's seat to reveal a loaded tommy gun. As panic swept across Papa John's face, the stranger smiled and told him not to worry.

The stranger introduced himself as Alvin Karpis, the world-famous public enemy and bank robber. As the former leader of the Ma Barker gang, Karpis was the FBI's Most Wanted fugitive. John shook Karpis's hand and wished him luck, and Karpis sped off, secure in the knowledge that this practical stranger could not possibly be a rat.

A few days later, J. Edgar Hoover himself appeared in New Orleans to arrest Karpis in person. The master cop forgot to bring handcuffs to his big publicity-stunt arrest and was forced to restrain Karpis using a necktie. The rumor on the street was that Silver Dollar Sam's family had traded Karpis's whereabouts for continued immunity from investigation. Karpis was sent to prison for decades, where he taught Charles Manson how to play guitar. John always talked about how sad he was that his nascent friendship with Karpis was cut short.

Before John settled down for good with some nice Italian girl, he had an affair with a nice young lady named Marguerite Claverie. Though their love affair was short, John always had the nicest things to say about Marguerite, a troubled girl who disappeared from his life suddenly.

At the age of twenty-two, an already six-months-pregnant Marguerite Claverie married an older man named Robert Edward Lee Oswald, who promptly died. A couple months later, a child baptized Lee Harvey Oswald was born in New Orleans to the single mother. All I'm going to say about the supposed dead man's child is that, from the right angle, I always used to tease Dale that he bore a certain resemblance to Lee Harvey Oswald.

Unable to marry Marguerite, the blameless John instead married into a Mafia clan with close ties to Silver Dollar Sam and deep roots in the Black Hand criminal society in Cefalu, Sicily. The product of this marriage was my best friend, the humorously named Dale.

Anyway, after a long and happy marriage, John's wife died. This broke the sentimental old man's heart worse than anyone could have expected. Known as one of the most social people in the most social city in America, Papa John became a recluse, rarely going out and never going on a date for over a decade. John's depression was impenetrably black, taking the light out of one of the most lovable personalities I had ever met. Finally, I had enough.

John had made it to the age of sixty-eight without ever getting a strange piece of ass. That was *the* problem as far as I was concerned; no friend of Silver Dollar Sam should be that uptight. It was time for John to come out of mourning and enjoy the life he had left.

If there's anything that Dr. Frenchy is capable of curing, it's a bad case of celibacy. I prescribed my secret cure-all for depression: a fat joint and a naked bubble bath with a young hooker. I told my best-looking, twenty-two-year-old bombshell to draw a warm bubble bath, drag the old man into the water, and roll that old guido a gigantic, spaceman spliff.

By the time Papa John emerged from that bathroom, the weary old man didn't look a day over thirty. All the wrinkles on his face were smoked and balled away. With sleepy raccoon eyes and an astronaut smile blasted across his face, John was too happy to speak. When his son finally got him to comprehend that we were asking how his first hit of marijuana made him feel, Papa John slowly turned his face, raised his eyebrows, and barely mustered a single word.

"*Sexy...*" he droned on for what seemed like twenty seconds, knocked loopy by the wonders he had just experienced. The old man would live for another quarter century, and I don't think a smile ever left his face.

That's what I've been saying – I've always been a real humanitarian.

Papa John was rare — a prestigious and well-respected client who wasn't a stone freak. There's a world of freaks out there, and the freaks like to congregate at the top of the social pyramid.

The differences in the tastes of poor and rich johns have always interested me since I regularly alternate between life as a broke hobo and street rich millionaire. Regardless of their class, there are a number of tricks who just like sex with beautiful women. However, I find that they are usually the minority. With working-class folk, the john usually is coming to me just to relieve stress, to get a break from his shitty job, nagging wife, bitching kids, and financial difficulties.

One of my best clients of all time was a hard-working man who paid top dollar to come to my house, sit in my recliner, take off his shoes, and have one of my girls ask him about his day. As long as he could relax, air out his feet, and have a nice lady to talk to, there was nothing else he wanted in the world. He would have been offended if one of my girls asked about sex. That was the furthest thing from his mind.

The rich and powerful, on the other hand, have easier lives, and, when they order up a trick, it's usually to service an addiction to some outlandish kinky shit that their stuck-up wives and high-class mistresses would not even begin to entertain. If Jim Garrison was typical in any way, it was that he was a well-known pillar of the community who would have ordered up an orgy of centaurs, mermaids, and midgets if they had been on the menu.

Okay, midgets were occasionally on the menu.

The more education, power, money, prestige, and religious standing a customer has, the more likely he wants *anything* but normal sex: he wants to have his dick slammed in the door and his nipples set on fire; he wants a dog to eat sausages out of his ass; he wants to dress in women's lingerie and be pegged in the ass with a strap-on; he wants to watch a tranny ravish his wife; to role-play being raped by his mother; he wants to cry uncontrollably while a call girl insults him and jerks him off with a dirty stocking; he wants to suck on a hooker's big toe for an hour while wearing negligee.

There's no end to kink, baby — it extends in every direction, forever. As Mr. New Orleans, I think I have had a unique position over the years to observe the secret fantasies and fetishes of all of America since the Big Easy is where every lily-white professional from the rest of the country comes to fulfill his darkest, raunchiest longings. From experience, let me tell you, just about every man from Alaska to Key West wants something in the bedroom that he's ashamed of, and the shame is what makes it sexy. Most Americans are deviants by their own definitions.

After a while, you get jaded listening to all the stories of men asking to be violated with elephant tusks or kicked in the balls with steel-toed boots. Nothing really shocks me anymore except the really subtle and strange fetishes — the ones that hint that something else far weirder is going on that remains hidden.

For example, I once had a client who was the manager of four local banks. The man was a pleasure to talk to and a complete and total gentleman. He had no interest in sex. All he wanted to do was pay me thousands of dollars per week to set up his office in my living room so that he could come over in his business suit and tie every weekday morning and conduct major financial business surrounded by half-dressed, nodded-out hookers. For some reason, this was the purest ecstasy to him.

Once, the bank manager invited me to one of his banks and snuck me into the holy of holies, the vault. As he unlocked one of the safes, I was itchin' to see piles of cash and pyramids of gold bars, figuring I was due for a gift. Instead, when the safe door opened, it revealed the single largest sack of pure uncut cocaine I have ever encountered. The bank manager shoved his hand into the potato sack and came up with an enormous snow cone of coke that he messily hoovered up his nose and mouth. Prior to this display, I never would have believed the man had so much as a cocktail after work.

The bank manager would always be hanging around my place with another weird client of mine, Andre, the top salon hair stylist in New Orleans. Andre paid me $2000 a week for the honor of coming over and doing my girls' hair for free. Andre only had one request: that whomever he spoke with had to argue with him over whether he was gay or not. Andre's opinion on his own sexuality changed from moment to moment, but he expected you to take the opposing side, whatever that was.

That was the man's kink: arguing over whether he was gay.

As I said, there is a world of freaks out there.

Chapter VIII

Mr. Lucky Dog

<u>1960s</u>

"Let he who is without sin cast the first stone."
<u>Jesus Christ</u>
(In one of his more reasonable moments.)

IF YOU ASKED THE USUAL SUSPECTS WHAT THEIR FAVORITE FRENCHY BROUILLETTE STORY WAS, THOSE NO-GOOD JACKASSES WOULD PROBABLY TELL YOU ALL ABOUT "MR. LUCKY DOG."

Since I know better than to hope that this story won't get out, I feel like I might as well tell you myself. The Mr. Lucky Dog story is the Monica Lewinsky to my term as Mr. New Orleans, the one little indiscretion that overshadows a lot of good work. Take it from me: trifling with a celebrity is enough to ruin an honest crook's reputation.

If there's anything I've learned as a criminal, it's that the most crooked people you are ever going to meet are the ones who make the biggest production about how good and holy and straitlaced they are. For example, one of my call girls' best clients was the high-and-mighty priest presiding over St. Louis Cathedral in the French Quarter, the basilica where I married Isabella.

This fraud would deliver sermons that would convince gullible teenagers not to use birth control or condoms — saddling them with wives and children, and me with new clients — and then he'd call me up and order up a trick. To compound his sin, the bishop once invited me into the cathedral and made sure that I saw that he was paying with money straight out of the "Poor Box" at the front of the cathedral. I guess the old fuckface got off on showcasing how low he had fallen.

I assume there was a similar dynamic with the celebrity I will call the Holy Roller, or the Roller for short. Trust me, baby, I've been waiting for this jackass to die for decades so I could print his name. I'm sorry – this religious SOB clearly isn't in any apparent hurry to see his Redeemer. He's older than Methuselah now, and he's still hustling.

This gentleman was a sneaky horndog like the rest of us, only he made his millions pretending that he was anything but. This phony pipsqueak had the cleanest-cut, holier-than-thou Christian reputation in all of show business.

I ran into the Roller early in my career as a pimp. I was still living in my penthouse apartment above the Chez Paris, playing kindergarten teacher to the dozen squabbling girls who were idly sitting around my apartment waiting for a date. With only a dozen girls left, that meant dozens more were already out making money; this was a great night for business. I didn't need any trouble, and I didn't need to take any risks.

As I was counting an admirable stack of cash, my phone rang. It was the doorman at the Fairmont Hotel, who was overly excited, even for a doorman looking to make a commission. "Frenchy, man!" he shrieked into the phone. "We got a celebrity here, [the Roller] is in our place tonight, and, man, he need a boy as quick as you can send 'im. Can you believe he's a fairy?"

Baby, trust me, I've been to court enough times since that night to know better than to assume anything: as far as I know, the Roller never even talked to that doorman. Even if the Roller did ask for male companionship, I can't tell you why: maybe he wanted a boy for sex, or someone to read him a bedtime story, or a bridge partner. It's my business to keep it none of my business, really. All I know is that I got an order in to provide a client with a boy, and, because of the circumstances, I chose to deliver.

In those days, I did about thirty percent of my business in boys, usually for threesomes with a man and his wife — a lot of guys in those days liked seeing their wives get thoroughly worked over by a professional. This used to be the specialty of Pershing Gervais, Jim Garrison's lead investigator, who could "ruin" wives for any normal man with his "night stick."

I was comfortable with selling boys for threesome business — it was like a marital aid — but I usually told gay guys who wanted a pop to take a walk. I was still pretty Catholic about all of it and still am, but it was mostly a business decision. In those days, it could be dangerous if word got around to Carlos Marcello or any of those other Sicilian bastards that I was half-queer or somethin'. New Orleans was more relaxed than other cities, but not *that* relaxed.

Of course, I was always willing to make an exception if it was made worth my while. I would grant a pardon for man-on-man clients who were powerful or rich enough to be worth the risk — people like the Roller or the Mickey Mantle of the DA's Office, Jim Garrison. Jim was the sort of client who wouldn't have surprised me too much if he made an order for a kilo of cocaine, two girls, a boy, an elephant, and fifty yards of heavy-duty barbed wire.

So, before I agreed to send the Roller a boy, I asked my girls who the hell he was, and if he was rich enough to be worth the risk. They told me he was a real goody-goody, pastor-approved type of guy, a heartthrob for all the girls in Oklahoma City or Utah. The girls, who were all gossip hounds, told me stories about how the Roller's holiness was used to further his career — and how he was rich as a sultan.

"Listen up, Frenchy, that boy looks like such a wimp, he can't *possibly* be nah trouble!" one of my brilliant female employees advised. I would soon learn that a gaggle of New Orleans prostitutes doesn't necessarily make the best jury of a man's character.

I tracked down one of my regular boys, a hot dog street vendor who hustled for me from his Lucky Dog stand. He'd ask every guy that passed, "Hey, Mac, want a hot dog? Or d'ya want a girl?" In those days, it was said that any man willing to stand over hot sausages in the French Quarter heat all night long, boiling up and being sucked dry by mosquitoes, was probably willing to sell some sausage in the bedroom as well. Like many others, this particular Lucky Dog vendor did plenty of tricks for me on the side, girls and boys alike. He had a reputation as a jackhammer-of-all-trades; he'd do damn near anything for a dollar.

Figuring that Mr. Lucky Dog would be capable of handling anything the Roller sent at him, I told my boy to go up to the Fairmont and take the man's business. I counted on making a good commission off this celebrity client since he'd be so gullible and nervous that he would accept any price Mr. Lucky Dog named for his services.

Well, it didn't quite work out like that. What exactly happened has never been clear to me, and I guess I'll never know unless the Roller calls me one day before one of us dies and decides to finally clue me in after all these years.

Mr. Lucky Dog disappeared off the face of the planet shortly afterwards, thinking I had put a contract on his life and that I had Carlos' guys running after him. Though I never tried to kill the kid, I probably should have tried in retrospect. I knew dozens of crooks who would have done it for me, but I'd have never lived that down: "Frenchy, got any more sissies or hot dog vendors you need us to protect you from?"

All I know is that a couple hours after I sent him on the date, Mr. Lucky Dog came to my penthouse apartment with thousands of dollars in designer watches. I don't know if the Roller was queer for boys, but I know for goddamn sure that he was queer for watches.

Mr. Lucky Dog handed over a share of the literally dozens of wristwatches he supposedly received as a "gift" from the Roller, which was as likely of a story as John F. Kennedy politely asking Carlos Marcello to arrange for a bullet to be placed in his head. Either way, I hadn't personally dirtied my hands with the business, so I accepted the watches, figuring I could buy a new convertible from all the money I'd get from fencing them.

A few days later, the cops caught Mr. Lucky Dog hocking his share of the stolen watches at Canal Jewelry, which marked the first time in Louisiana history that someone actually got arrested for pawning stolen merchandise at that jewelry store. The only explanation is that the Roller had some friends in the police department — I wish I knew who! Considering how much I was paying the cops in bribes, I would've asked that bastard for a refund. I can guarantee you that whoever it was in the NOPD, he never expected to put *me*, of all cash cows, in jail over it.

The cops were nice enough to make sure that Bernie, one of my favorite crooked cops, was included in the goon squad sent to pick me up. It was their way of protecting their investment in me. When the police arrived, I wasn't exactly prepared. Like a real asshole, I was actually wearing *two* of those flashy stolen watches, one on each hand, which goes to show you that flashy gangster behavior didn't start with rap music.

When the police were cuffing me, I saw Bernie and whispered to him under my breath, "Hey, Bernie, baby, can you loosen these cuffs? They're real tight around my wrists." Bernie, who had been around the block more times than the St. Charles Avenue street car, knew what I was saying; not only were my cuffs loosened, but those two watches disappeared. Bernie probably made a few thousand hocking them the next day to Canal Jewelry.

At the police station, the cop in charge told me that the arrest was just a publicity stunt. They needed to show the out-of-town VIP that New Orleans was an on-the-level city where justice mattered. They downplayed the whole thing: "Frenchy, it'll blow over. It won't be nuthin'. There ain't no celebrity who gonna press charges on a pimp and a fag prostitute. Can you imagine what the papers'll say?"

Well, it turns out the cops knew just as much about the Roller as my girls. That evangelical grump insisted on pressing charges and going to trial. That says a lot about the Roller's courage, or his stupidity, depending on how generous you're feeling. Like a lot of good Christian folk, the Roller wouldn't listen to reason; he insisted on going to trial and staking his career on my silence. To old New Orleans hands like us, police and criminals alike, it seemed like the Roller was acting in poor taste, like he was pushing a joke too far.

So I went to trial — on the street. News spread, and I suddenly became Frenchy, the beefcake-selling, queer-pimping gangster. I became Mr. Unlucky Dog: "the man who sold the wiener without the bun." Luckily for me, I had built up enough of a reputation that it was mostly joking, locker-room teasing sort of stuff like Joe Gold used to indulge in.

As usual, my attorney Dean Andrews promised that I'd never see the inside of a jail cell. Dean was my blood brother, my on-and-off roommate depending on the state of his marriage, and the best attorney I could obtain for barter. A large part of Dean's legal practice was done in exchange for party essentials: I paid him in girls and drugs; Carlos paid him by letting Dean use his name wherever he went to get the VIP treatment; when he eventually returned from Italy, Silver Dollar Sam paid him in free food at all of the restaurants he owned in New Orleans.

Food, even more so than hanging out with gangsters or playing street-side jazz or taking sleeping pills, was Dean's greatest love. Dean was a ridiculous glutton who just kept getting fatter and fatter and fatter, to the point that even his wife, who didn't have high standards to begin with, couldn't stand the sight of him. Mrs. Andrews called me up and convinced me that it would be in both of our best interests if I installed a steel lock and chain around the family refrigerator and gave her the only key. At 2 a.m. that morning, Mrs. Andrews was woken up by the sound of one of Carlos' contractors taking a bolt cutter to the chains around the refrigerator.

"Frenchy, it was either dat or buy a new fridge, and, baby, I don't have that money," Dean told me.

As one of New Orleans's foremost publicity chasers and fame-whores, Dean was tickled pink that he would get to defend me at the Roller trial. The proximity to celebrity and scandal gave Dean a buzz.

Unfortunately, our trial judge turned out to be the Honorable Herbert Christenberry, a humorless hard-ass who talked down to you like he was Moses and thought he could shoot lightning bolts out of his gavel. Christenberry was the last judge in New Orleans you wanted to get for a criminal case. He was just as crooked as the rest, but he wasn't as social and reliable, and he wanted to make sure you knew that he was better than you before he'd let you off. Dean and I, the two sleaziest guys in all of creation, knew we would be surrounded by preachers and hypocrites in this courtroom.

The frustrating thing about uptight Judge Christenberry was that I could see through his pompous act. This man was a client. Another lawyer friend claimed that he had made a shady deal with Christenberry to free one of his clients in exchange for the lawyer's promise to secretly obtain a whore for Christenberry at the time and place of his choosing. Of course, the girl came from me, but I was sworn to secrecy — I had to just sit there as one of my own clients lectured me about how immoral and depraved I was.

Luckily for us, the prosecutor didn't have much of a case since the Roller obviously couldn't tell him what really happened. All they had was the absentee testimony of Mr. Lucky Dog — who was recast as a cat burglar — who swore that I, of all people, put him up to the crime. Obviously, this sort of phoned-in hearsay was not going to convict me by itself, so Dean motioned to dismiss the case.

Unfortunately, Christenberry wasn't going to let pass an opportunity to look like a pillar of morality in front of a celebrity.

The old bastard refused to dismiss the case and instead prolonged the proceedings by repeatedly embarking on verbal rampages against my shameless exploitation of a tourist. The old coot ranted and raved about how the Roller had come to the city to perform for a charity event and how sad it was that a godly man had been fleeced in such a good Catholic town.

If you ask me, I bet the Roller was making up that boo-hoo story about the charity gig; that's the sort of jury-prejudicing cover story Dean Andrews would make up for me all the time. I was always buying teeth for toothless orphans and rescuing kittens from alligators and things like that whenever I stood in front of a jury.

Unfortunately, Dean Andrews didn't even bother to cook up any bullshit stories for this trial. He realized that the case against me was so weak that it didn't matter what he did; I'd get acquitted anyway. So Dean decided to use my high-profile trial to go into business for himself. He wasn't going to waste an audience full of reporters, rubberneckers, and gossips in attendance. Halfway through the trial, Dean — the fat ridges on his forehead drizzled with sweat, his cheeks wet and red — decided he was ready for his close-up.

Looking to attract attention, Dean pretended to clear his throat at an enormous volume, sounding like a rusty motorboat engine kicking into gear. Once the attention was focused on him, Dean loudly kicked up his fine Italian shoes onto the defense table. This couldn't help but be seen as an act of flagrant disrespect for Judge Christenberry's court, which was exactly what Dean intended.

"Mr. Andrews, what exactly do you think you're doing?" yelled Christenberry, his jowls wiggling in the air with outrage.

"Oh, sorry 'bout dat, ya'honor," Dean said with a yawning tone as if he was tuckered out and ready for bed. "I just bought these new shoes, so I want to keep 'em clean."

"Mr. Andrews, what on Earth are you talking about?" Judge Christenberry asked in his senile tone, squinting at Dean like he had lost what little mind the Judge had credited him with having.

"Oh, the prosecutor, ya honor, the prosecutor's talking so much bullshit that it's pilin' up pretty high in this here courtroom, and I can't just sit here and let my expensive new shoes get buried beneath a tidal wave of shit!" This put the courtroom in hysterics, though Christenberry wasn't too amused. He warned Dean to behave himself.

But the laughter gave Dean a wild bug up his ass; he was past saving, long past behaving. When the poor, flustered prosecutor tried to recollect himself and continue talking, Dean began to cackle with hysterical laughter and started performing a flamboyant, flailing gesture with his hand.

At first, I wasn't sure if Dean was having an overdue stroke or a seizure or something, but then I started to see the patterns in his movements. Once I figured it out, I wished the cocksucker *had* been having a seizure. In full view of the court, my attorney Dean Andrews was impersonating what it would be like to masturbate the world's largest penis.

Dean was letting everyone know what he thought about the prosecutor's case and how it was wasting his valuable partying time. The Judge had to call a recess just to restore order, once the jackals in the spectator benches began to hoot and holler in support.

Thanks to Dean's antics in front of the most uptight judge in New Orleans, the gay prostitute trial I wanted to live down would become famous French Quarter folklore. I would be asked about the Roller and his penchant for Lucky Dogs for years — thanks Dean!

By chance, Dean's antics turned out to be a brilliant courtroom tactic. After my attorney had made a total mockery of the proceedings, Judge Christenberry lost interest in further prolonging this vanity trial and dismissed the case against me. The Roller seemed downtrodden, but he went on to have a long career as a religious conservative icon with gigantic toilet-bowl-porcelain teeth.

✦ ✦ ✦ ✦ ✦

"You're not drunk if you can lie on the floor without holding on."

Dean Martin

If the Roller was easily the worst celebrity client I ever had, let's just say I had plenty of other celebrity friends who were delightful. For example, I remember Danny Thomas and Dean Martin very fondly.

Danny Thomas was a television star on the 1950s sitcom *Make Room for Daddy*, which was later renamed *The Danny Thomas Show* in the '60s due to his popularity. Behind the scenes, Danny was a powerful Hollywood producer who worked on *The Dick Van Dyke Show* and *The Andy Griffith Show*, which itself was a spinoff from his show. Danny was a savvy operator, and he leveraged his connections to make his daughter, Marlo Thomas, famous.

Danny was also a world-class partier and heartthrob, and he loved New Orleans. Whenever he came to town, I was the first person he called. Thomas had so much fun with me one weekend that he pulled me aside and handed me a card with his private number. "Frenchy, baby," he slurred in an impersonation of me, "if you ever need anything, just call this number. I'll take care of it."

Despite being pants-shitting drunk, Danny took on this very serious tone as he gave me the card, as if he were Frank Costello or John F. Kennedy granting an all-powerful favor. I kept the card, figuring I'd never have any reason to use it — I was a friend of Carlos Marcello ... what the fuck use did I have for Mr. *Make Room for Daddy*?

A couple years later, I finally had a problem that even Carlos Marcello couldn't solve. One of my old ladies, Ronnie, had run off with her estranged husband and gotten pregnant. Let me tell you, nothing is more humiliating than being dumped for your girlfriend's *husband*. That means you've proven to be more boring and unfulfilling than the man she was already sick to death of when you met her. It's worse when your old lady's husband is so gay Liberace would give you "Can this guy tone it down?" looks in his presence.

The fact that Ronnie managed to get pregnant by her ex is one of the great wonders of the world. However miraculous the conception, the child was born with some rare, congenital disease that required organ transplants and blood transfusions. There was nothing anyone in New Orleans could do for the kid, so Ronnie, who was a helpless and hysterical little thing in the best of times, came back to me begging for another miracle. I told her that I wasn't really a well-known miracle worker (and if I was, I would've mastered the water into wine trick first), but I would at least make a phone call on her behalf to the one person who might have a suggestion.

Figuring "Fuck it, can't hurt," I called Danny Thomas. Maybe Mr. Hollywood would know a doctor who could bump Ronnie's kid up the waiting list. Little did I know, but Danny was a great American philanthropist: he had built St. Jude Children's Research Hospital in Memphis, which became one of the best-funded, high-tech hospitals in America. I had stumbled onto a miracle.

Within an hour of leaving a message for Danny, he called to tell me that he was going to get Ronnie and her kid on a plane to Memphis that day and no later; he'd charter a plane if necessary. The very next day, the little kid was getting full, on-the-house treatment from the best doctors in America, and Ronnie was staying in Memphis at Danny's expense.

Ronnie disappeared shortly afterwards, so I don't know what happened to the kid —only that Danny Thomas took care of him as best he could. Danny could have very easily never returned my phone call; instead, he spent thousands of dollars to do a favor for some whore's kid he had never met. Danny was a saint as far as I am concerned.

Dean Martin was the best sort of client: the rich drunk who is so past coherence that he is preposterously generous, perhaps without realizing it. Of course, over the years, I've been the senseless jackass tipping waitresses a $100 bill far too often to count, so I'm not judging.

The first time I met Dino was typical. I got a call from a bellboy saying that he had Dean Martin "waiting for company" at the hotel bar, so I headed over with my cutest girl —only the best for Dino.

When I arrived at the hotel bar with the girl, Dino figured out I was his man on sight; he had had plenty of experience identifying mobsters and pimps. Granted, considering my Mr. T gold chains, sparkling array of jewelry, fine Italian suit, and almost totally unbuttoned silk shirt, I can't quite figure what else I could have been besides a pimp or a mobster.

As soon as I entered the hotel bar, Dino waved me over. "Frenchy, man, been waitin' for ya!" he hollered in his unmistakable voice. Everyone turned to me like I was a superstar, too, which was a great feeling at first. Apparently, someone had been telling him Frenchy stories, so he started hitting me with all sorts of questions and jokes. To all the rubberneckers in the bar, we looked like old friends.

The spotlight felt good for a moment, but then my shyness kicked in something fierce, and I began to sweat and lose my breath. All those eyes on me started playing havoc on my brain. Fumbling for air, I decided to compliment Dino to put the attention on him. Picking at random, I told him he had a nice coat.

In the best who-gives-a-damn drunk style, Dean Martin said, "What? This thing? You like it, Frenchy? Then it's yours; here, take it!" I got the feeling he did this routine *every* time he received a compliment as a showcase of his generosity and wealth.

Before I could say no, Dino was up and stumbling in his shirt sleeves, waving the coat in my face like it was the white flag of surrender. I took it; it *was* a nice coat. I looked on the inside to see what designer made it, but instead all I saw was a tag that said, "From Son to Daddy, Father's Day."

Dean Martin had given me his Father's Day present from his kid! I didn't even know Dino had any kids, and now I had one of their precious family heirlooms.

And a lot of good it did me: it turns out that the height disparity between Dean Martin and me prevented us from sharing clothes. Instead of keeping the damn thing as an investment, which would have meant that a Vice Squad raider would have stolen it sooner or later, I decided to follow Dino's example and give the jacket to my bodybuilding buddy Swede, who was a Dean Martin fanatic.

Unsurprisingly, Dean was too drunk to perform later that night with my girl, though he lavishly tipped her after he gave it a game try. Afterwards, as she was getting dressed, Dean apparently blacked out, and when he woke up, he seemed convinced that they *had* made love and that he had performed fabulously. Dean Martin paid the call girl two or three extra times, once for each time he blacked out and lost his memory and could be woken up and told, "Dean, by the way, you haven't paid."

That call girl had the magic touch with celebrities — she never had to work for the money! Her next celebrity client came from Hyp Guinle, who rushed over to my penthouse so fast you'd think he had a firecracker shoved up his ass.

"Frenchy, man, you wouldn't believe it, man!" Hyp rattled off at me without even greeting me. "I just met Edward G. Robinson at the Lafayette Hotel. They's filming *The Cincinnati Kid* — Ann-Margret, Steve McQueen, and *Little Caesar* himself, man!"

Like a lot of gangsters of the '30s, Hyp idolized Robinson for playing some of the first great gangsters in film history, so it was an earth-shaking thrill for Hyp to meet the old bullfrog at the Lafayette. Figuring that Robinson was a shameless ole sleazeball like himself, Hyp decided to do him the greatest tribute a pimp could.

"Frenchy, baby," Hyp bellowed so that my entire apartment

could hear, "I want to take *care* of The Cincinnati Kid on behalf of the city of New Orleans! I want that man *treated!*" Later, it turned out that Edward G. Robinson didn't even play the title character in *The Cincinnati Kid*, but we didn't know that yet.

I tried to talk Hyp out of sending a call girl to Edward G. Robinson for the simple reason that the man seemed not a day younger than 112-years-old to me, and I figured sending a priest over to perform the last rites would have been a more appropriate gift. Hyp was insistent, however, that, no matter how old, Little Caesar would appreciate the gift of a fine young woman. I bet Hyp that Edward G. Robinson would prefer to tell old high school stories about Moses than bed a prostitute, and then I sent my prettiest call girl to see him at the Lafayette's bar.

My girl barely got to chatting with Robinson before the old man picked up what was going on and lost the bet for Hyp Guinle. "Look, darling," he said as he laid a hand on my girl's knee, "it's not that you're not beautiful, but I'm just too old for this type of a business."

When she returned to tell the story to Hyp and me at the Famous Door, my pimping mentor was genuinely disappointed, even deflated. His idol had proven a limp dick; time was passing him by. With a pout on his face, Hyp stuffed two $100 bills in my girl's cleavage and slumped away. Like his never-ending arguments with Steve Valenti, I would never see Hyp Guinle for the rest of his life without hearing about how it was my fault for not sending a cute enough girl to "The Cincinnati Kid" – who, once again, was not played by Edward G. Robinson.

One celebrity for whom I could never find a girl cute enough was my good friend Liberace, the dazzling pianist and Las Vegas icon. Don't get me wrong, I tried; I don't think Liberace's mom tried to get her son to ball a girl more than I did.

Sincerely, baby, I worked my ass off trying to get that man laid; he was so nice to me, and it was the only way I knew how to express appreciation. I was like the cat that keeps bringing its owner dead mice, thinking that it's the best gift in the world and not knowing any better.

After he died, some mean-hearted cocksucker told me that Liberace was gay and then laughed at how shocked I was. It never really occurred to me — in my presence, he didn't act like the stereotype at all, and I never met anyone who attracted more female attention. Sure, he dressed up in outlandish outfits and wore a ton of jewelry, but so did I! Shit, for years I walked around with a fucking parrot on my shoulder; I'm not the best judge of flamboyant fashion choices.

I met Liberace at the Acme Oyster House in the Quarter, where I was sitting at the bar, eating fresh oysters shucked as fast I could eat them over a pit of ice. He was sitting by my side, anonymous in everyday clothes. He tapped me on my shoulder and very politely asked, "Your nose?" he said, pointing to the splat of cartilage on my once perfect face. I felt like this asshole was itching for a fight, but I waited to hear him out.

"You're a former fighter, right? I used to be a boxer myself," he said with a strange note of pride in his voice. I guess he might have been hitting on me, but I was oblivious.

I told the stranger — who looked vaguely ethnic and sorta tough, believe it or not —that he was right. "That's wonderful," he said with glowing eyes. "I'm a huge boxing fan, and I've always had so many questions about the local fight scene down here."

I was always happy to have an excuse to tell my stories about Pete Herman and Junior Conforto, so we started chatting and having a good time. Liberace wasn't bullshitting; judging by the obscure questions he started firing at me, that man watched more boxing than anyone I knew in the city. When I started talking about the Confortos, he gasped. "Frenchy, I tell you, if you introduce me to the Confortos, I'll be your friend for life!"

Figuring he was a wealthy out-of-town Vidalia who might make a good client, I did him the favor and introduced him to the Confortos. I can't tell you how shocked I was when he introduced himself as goddamn Liberace! I hadn't recognized him even though he was, at that time, the highest paid performer in the world. Looking back, between the bodybuilding, Mr. Lucky Dog story, and hitting the town with Liberace, I can't believe I didn't get more shit from my wiseguy friends for being queer.

Then again, nobody in the '50s and '60s thought Liberace was gay. We just thought he had style! I mean, shit, look at how Elvis dressed.

You wouldn't believe how girls would throw themselves at Liberace everywhere he went; he made Neil Gautier look like the Elephant Man. I loved hanging out with Liberace because he'd attract the girls and then generously steer them right into my bed. Liberace was the best wingman I ever met. I didn't suspect anything. I just assumed he had high standards; he seemed like he was the finicky, high-class type, y'know?

Liberace was true to his word; he was eternally grateful to me for introducing him to the Confortos and the other New Orleans boxing legends I knew. Until his death in 1987, Liberace would regularly fly me out to Vegas and have whatever hotel was paying him put me up for free in the Presidential Suite for a week. I'd take a few of my girls and make more money than you could imagine. The only problem with Liberace was he'd always make me take the tour of his stadium-sized closet full of those goddamn glittery suits every time I'd visit, no matter how many times I'd seen it before. Sometimes, even a pimp has a limit to how much gaudy clothing he can stomach.

✣ ✣ ✣ ✣ ✣

"'Tis not such a time as that Proud Homo is worth looking at
But rather see him, minus hat,
Homecoming from some midnight bat
In owl car snoozing, bald and fat.

"For then he hath a pendent cheek,
A lip that hangeth, flaccid weak,
Where shadows play at hide and seek,
A tilted nose with crimson peak—
The ambient with booze doth reek!"
R.B. Mayfield
The Times-Picayune
New Orleans
6-24-1914

My career was such a success that I was confronted with the worst problem a gangster can have: too much cash flow. If you think I'm joking, remember that it was tax fraud charges that finally jammed up invincible gangsters like Al Capone, Mickey Cohen, and Meyer Lansky. It's easy to fix a murder trial with a limited number of witnesses, but it's damn near impossible to explain in court how you live like a king without a legitimate job.

I consulted with my friends in the Marcello family, and they told me that one of the favorite money-laundering schemes for the New Orleans Family was to open up a gas station. A gas station was an easy way to report any legitimate income I wanted: there was nothing to stop a gas station owner in 1962 from claiming that he sold as little as $4000 or as much as $40,000 in gas in a month.

I purchased a gas station at 1300 North Rampart, right across the street from where Papa John's twenty-two-year-old kid Dale ran a service station for another New Orleans Mafia associate. That way, if someone actually needed a legitimate service, I could just send them across the street. Dale used to laugh because, whenever he took a break, he'd come back to find me under the hood of a car in a $500 suit and $5000 worth of jewels.

Dale was New Orleans's version of Johnny Cash's "Boy Named Sue." As I told you earlier, every boy of our generation idolized Hollywood cowboy Roy Rogers— whose wife on-screen and off-screen was unfortunately named Dale Evans. My buddy Dale grew up being called "Dale Evans" in the post-war suburb of Lakeview, and he had no choice but to learn to become one tough motherfucker. Dale kicked so much ass that no one dared to call him Dale Evans anymore, and before he graduated from high school, he was recognized as the boss of the Lakeview Boys street gang.

When you weren't calling him a girl's name, Dale was a quiet and humble kid who, like me, spent his teenage years studying all of the degenerate gamblers and outlandish Mafia characters of the 1950s French Quarter. Thanks to the Mafia betting parlor above his dad's restaurant, Dale was treated as a favorite nephew by the old-timer wiseguys and as a sheepish little brother by the younger generation of crooks.

I'd like to think that Dale's favorite underworld older brother was a startlingly handsome Hercules who looked like he should have worked for Zeus instead of Dutch Kraut. I took a shine to Dale during my daily visits to the betting parlor to pick up Sam Saia's cash. Since I was only a few years older than him, Dale reminded me of the shy, simple, and ornery kid that had once run way from Marksville with stars in his eyes. Though I was barely into my twenties and had yet to learn to pull my own head from my ass, I figured it was time for me to mentor my gas station neighbor, like Dutch Kraut had done for me.

Dale was stubborn, though, and he initially took after his sane, respectable, law-abiding father. No matter how much I spiked the punchbowl of Dale's head with awful advice, the boy stayed sober. It would take a far worse bad influence than me to turn Dale dirty.

Frustrated, I decided to screw with the boy's head. Since I was always sending him customers from my gas station, the easiest prank to play on him was to refer a client from my *other* business to Dale and let the straitlaced boy figure it out slowly. One client I sent my unsuspecting buddy was a classic New Orleans freak named David Ferrie.

David Ferrie was a hairless homosexual boogeyman who flunked out of the seminary and went on to become a pilot, a half-ass private investigator, and a heavily armed wing nut mercenary. Ferrie was an authentic stone-fucking-crazy crank, and he damn sure looked the part.

Thanks to a skin condition that rendered him as hairless as a Sphynx cat, the buzzard-faced Ferrie felt compelled to glue some dirty, red, diner carpet on his skull and paint gigantic Groucho Marx eyebrows on his forehead. Neither of these substitutes even remotely looked like hair, and they were always crooked, peeling or rubbing off, or in the wrong place. It seemed like the world had cursed him, beginning with being born queer with the name "Ferrie." That must have just been *swell* in high school.

Rendered an outcast by his freakish appearance and his closeted homosexuality, Ferrie was a deeply wounded and insecure guy. Always paranoid that people were mocking him behind his back, Ferrie fought back against the world by acting hyperactively aggressive, babbling an obscene torrent of assertions, come-ons, and threats to everyone he encountered. Ferrie seemed to be trying to preemptively fuck off everyone and save himself the pain of rejection. He was a weird cat who only had one setting: coming on *way* too strong.

When Joe Pesci played Ferrie in *JFK*, all of the wiseguys were impressed by Pesci's uncanny performance. I remember this only because of one misunderstanding with a New Orleans gangster who confronted me at a restaurant and screamed, "How 'bout dat Joe Pepsi?!" I could have sworn I knew some small-time crook nicknamed "Joe Pepsi" who had disappeared, so I started ramblin' about how I thought he was in jail, and the gangster responded about how he was making big Hollywood movies about Jim Garrison, and we both ended up completely confused.

Anyway, Ferrie was just about my least favorite person in New Orleans in 1963. Ferrie was always dropping by my gas station to order up a gigolo. I was okay with your average, polite, homosexual john as long as they had money or power, but Ferrie was a pain in the ass and a groper. I still serviced his business for one simple reason: he was employed by Carlos Marcello as a private investigator at the time, and anyone with Carlos got my respect.

As soon as he saw me at the gas station, Ferrie would rush over to me like a queer Jake LaMotta and start pawing me all over for no good reason to feel my muscles. "Hey man, Frenchy, hey, c'mon, can I get a boy or what? I'm way overdue man, ready for a boy-on-the-double, know what I mean? Hey, are *you* available?" Ferrie would say as he squeezed my biceps like a grandma testing out fruit at the supermarket.

"Man," I'd growl as I recoiled from his oily touch, "get out of my face with dat shit if you know what's good for you." Asking me out once was an honest mistake that every queer man with taste should have made; asking me every time we met was just disrespectful. If I hadn't known that this goofy dipshit was somehow a close confidant of Carlos, I would have booted him into the street. Instead, I'd usually call up "Mr. Lucky Dog" or his successor and get him to take care of the freak.

One day, however, I got an evil idea. I told Ferrie, "Baby, you know who would take care of you? That young boy at the service station across dat street. Just ask for Dale!"

I thought it was a mighty funny joke, but apparently Ferrie took a liking to Dale and his good-looking black assistant and told his queer buddy, Clay Shaw.

Shaw looked like he deserved a better cruising pal than David Ferrie. A well-dressed war hero, businessman, and playwright, Clay was as charming and elegant as my friend Liberace. Shaw was also so tall that he and Jim Garrison basically lived in their own world far above the rest of New Orleans's swarthy, short, Mediterranean, white community.

Shaw visited my service station shortly after it opened and asked if he could park his car — I believe it was a mint green Ford Thunderbird in immaculate condition, but don't hold me to that — at my place every night and pick it up in the morning. Though I could not imagine why he needed to leave his car overnight on Barracks and Rampart St. on such a regular basis, I agreed as long as he tipped the wetback who did odd jobs around the station.

Despite his queer proclivities, I developed a very high estimation of Clay Shaw, which Dale unfortunately ruined. One day, Clay drove across the street to see the boy Dave Ferrie probably told him about and to get his car serviced. Shaw politely asked Dale to have "his head black boy" drop the car off at his place when he was done. When Dale's handsome, young, black mechanic returned to the gas station after making the delivery to the Shaw residence, his skin was as white as Mother Nature would allow it to be.

"Mr. Dale," the mechanic said, "if I gotta bring anything to that man again, I quit!" Apparently, Shaw had invited the mechanic into his house — and offered to tie him up and whip him in the secret S&M torture chamber that he tucked away on the premises. "Mr. Dale, there was whips and chains and paddles and bats and hooks and everything else you can imagine all hanging from the wall. It was horrible! The man is sicko!"

That story solved the mystery of why a respectable queer like Shaw would pal around with a sick fuck like David Ferrie. Unfortunately for poor Clay, the harmless kink he was into was considered so outrageous in 1963 that he could only confide his secret to a sick fuck like Ferrie.

And a few years later, these two harassers of gas station attendants would be investigated for the murder of John F. Kennedy by two more sexual free spirits, Jim Garrison and Pershing Gervais.

Chapter IX

JFK Reloaded

"The time has come for all good men to rise above principle."
Huey Long

ONE OF MY FRIENDS KILLED JOHN F. KENNEDY.

Don't get too excited, baby; I played no part in killing the man. I'm just the victim of an exciting social circle.

If you've ever wondered why the supposed conspirators in the Kennedy Assassination were such a bizarre circus crew of misfits, cranks, and mobsters — well, baby, that's my social circle. That's New Orleans. If that old fraud Jim Garrison claimed to be "On the Trail of the Assassins," then I was "On the Christmas List of the Assassins."

Just about every poor sonofabitch who has ever been fingered in the conspiracy to kill Kennedy was my buddy, my roommate, my business partner, or my customer. I knew them all — and I judged damn near every single one of them crazy enough to be credible suspects in just about anything besides a square deal.

That's also the obvious reason why it's been impossible to untangle the mess of claims, lies, schemes, and confessions and find the absolute truth about what went down. Baby, I can't get my friends to agree on which of them kidnapped a $20,000 pair of breeding ostriches from a legendary Louisiana sheriff, let alone exactly how they committed the most notorious crime since Jesus was crucified.

Among my acquaintances are a number of characters who have confessed, at one point or another, to have been a party to the conspiracy to kill Kennedy. One of my best friends and roommates actually confided that he was the gunman on the Grassy Knoll, and another of my buddies was a young man named Lee Harvey Oswald — whom once enjoyed a lovely afternoon with me and Carlos Marcello.

But who knows?

Maybe everyone was lying.

I guess you're just going to have judge for yourself.

You've heard the government's side of the story. Here's what the hoods had to say. Take it for what it's worth.

"I was unfortunate in buying [the Hotel Nacional in Havana] about seven months before the bearded, mongrel, Communist dog took it over. [Castro] stole it from me about a year later, in addition to other lands and businesses I had in Cuba."

Mike McLaney
Testifying for a gambling license in the Bahamas, 1967

As far as I can figure, the conspiracy to kill John F. Kennedy started with my best friend, Dale, and his beloved father John. Dale personally played no role in the murder, but, like me, he sure as hell knew how to situate himself to invite suspicion.

Though I tried to be a sincerely bad influence on the boy, I botched the job of ruining Dale. I tried to teach him to be crooked, but he insisted on being square and nearly got himself killed. Dale took one wrong step and planted his foot deep into a pile of matrimony.

Right when his social life was really getting in swing, Dale gave into sentimentality and married his childhood sweetheart – a thin, flat-chested brunette with an angelic face. Like my beautiful Isabella, Dale's first wife was a Catholic schoolgirl who modeled on the side. Dale, like me, was a born-sucker and a wannabe choirboy.

Our marriages had something else in common: unhinged in-laws. Unfortunately for Dale, he took more after his Mob-groupie dad in his choice of a new family. Instead of marrying into a miserably normal family, Dale had to go and hook up with a clan of stone-crazy Irish mercenaries and casino racketeers.

In case you don't see where I'm going, it's time to meet the first suspects in the Kennedy assassination. It's time to "Meet the McLaneys."

Dale's young wife Elizabeth was the niece of Michael and William McLaney, the pride and terror of the New Orleans Irish underworld. I'm being a bit unfair; Bill McLaney was generally recognized as pretty funny and laidback for a gangster. Mike McLaney, on the other hand ... well, Mike was pretty much the world's biggest asshole. He made Carlos Marcello look like Santa Claus.

The best way to picture Mike is as the most popular and conceited jock in high school, who, instead of slamming kids into lockers, topples the governments of banana republics using his private mercenary forces. Mike was like a demented Jimmy Buffett with his own private Caribbean army, navy, and air force.

The problem with Mike was that he was an athlete. In the sex rackets, you run into enough jocks to know they're just about the worst group of folks you're ever gonna find outside of political parties or organized religion. They have all the worst traits of stuck-up gorgeous women who have spent their lives being catered to, mutated and worsened by freakish levels of testosterone.

And Mike was a great athlete – great enough to really ruin someone's personality. Because Mike could beat just about anyone at any sport, it was only natural that he developed the opinion that everyone else was inferior to him in *everything*.

As a young tennis player, Mike shredded numerous future world champions. Mike built his fortune mercilessly scamming every degenerate sports gambler in Louisiana. Since most people didn't expect to find Olympic-caliber athletes at the local athletic club, Mike made crazy cash punking rich civilian athletes by performing various seemingly impossible feats of agility, strength, and tennis prowess.

Though tennis was his great love, Mike McLaney's greatest racket was golf. Tennis was more fun, but golf was the ultimate athletic con: a sport played almost exclusively by the high-muckety-mucks, the rich and powerful. Soon, Mike's tennis celebrity and uncanny talent attracted golfing partners like Joe Kennedy and J. Edgar Hoover, and his weekly gambling winnings reached tens of thousands of dollars.

While Mike set local tennis and golf records and did a short tour of duty as a deputy sheriff in the Orleans Parish police, his lovable brother Bill McLaney went on to serve honorably as one of the most decorated and beloved flight instructors in the Army Air Corps during World War II. Unlike his brother, Bill was apparently a decent and charming guy, a sweetheart, and he must have been embarrassed by Mike's overbearing personality and crooked behavior.

However, Mike ultimately held some type of psychological power over Bill that never wavered. No matter how much Bill McLaney resented or even hated his brother, he always acted as the respectable and likable front man for his disreputable and unlikable brother's schemes. Bill took the Hells Angels' attitude when it came to his brother: right or wrong, he had Mike's back to the death.

This made Mike and Bill a deadly combination: a master pilot and a gambling genius with elite government connections. It is not surprising that Carlos Marcello and Frank Costello headhunted the McLaneys.

Between Mike's huge bankroll, gambling acumen, and federal contacts and Bill McLaney's piloting and weaponry skills, Carlos and Costello had discovered the foundation for their own personal CIA. With vast gambling and drug interests in Central America, Cuba, and the Caribbean, the two Mafia bosses were in desperate need of a team of all-purpose "fixers" who could topple a fragile government, smuggle a ton of heroin in a hurry, whack out a troublesome generalissimo, take over a fledgling casino, or fly to Washington, D.C. and subtly purchase a shift in foreign policy.

The McLaneys could do it all. And it is my understanding that they did. They did whatever dirty work was required, not only for Carlos and Costello, but also for the entire national Mafia syndicate. The McLaneys were "specialists"— elite Mafia associates who were so good at a specific sort of job that they were loaned out and shared between families in times of need. Marcello and Costello introduced the McLaneys to Mob bosses like Tampa's Santo Trafficante, Iowa's Luigi Fratto, Cleveland's Moe Dailitz, Chicago's Sam Giancana and Tony Accardo, and New York's Albert Anastasia.

To better situate themselves, the McLaneys relocated their operations to the Miami area, which in those days was the administrative seat of Costello's gambling boss Meyer Lansky, who managed numerous Mafia families' Caribbean interests. They quickly earned Lansky's trust and thereby became the elite fixers for just about any problem the Mafia needed to handle from New Orleans to Bermuda.

The McLaneys were the scariest gang of freelance muscle since Jean Lafitte's pirates. Purchasing or stealing a fleet of airplanes, ships, and helicopters, the McLaneys boasted incomparable firepower and reach. By the late 1950s, the McLaneys had moved so far up in the world that they were fixing NFL championship games and purchasing the most notorious casino in Havana.

In 1958, the McLaneys, along with some criminal partners and Baltimore Colts owner Carroll Rosenbloom, bet somewhere between $1 million and $3 million on Johnny Unitas and the Colts in that year's NFL title game. Since the McLaneys and Rosenbloom needed a touchdown victory to cover the spread, the Colts inexplicably refused to kick a field goal to win the game in sudden death overtime and instead drove the ball down the field for that spread-covering touchdown.

The Baltimore Colts' grateful owner repaid the McLaneys the next year when he provided the financing for the brothers to purchase the 450-room Hotel Nacional casino in Havana from Moe Dailitz. Bill and Mike were now the owners of one of the crown jewels in the underworld gambling empire.

Practically overnight, Mike McLaney had risen from nothing to become the paymaster of stars like Frank Sinatra, the business partner of Meyer Lansky, and the dinner companion and golfing buddy of Cuban dictator Fulgencio Batista. The obscure Irish brothers from New Orleans had risen so goddamn high that I'm pretty sure even a meathead like me looked no bigger than an ant.

I can't help but feel you already know the punch line to this story: what goes up must come down. I'm not exactly breaking news when I say that American gangsters who made huge investments in 1959 Havana were not great gamblers. Those broken investors also tended not to develop high estimations of the Kennedys, either.

While guys like Mike McLaney and Meyer Lansky were distracted by fawning celebrities and showgirls, Fidel Castro and his communist guerillas swarmed into Havana, sent Batista into exile, and closed down the Mafia casinos. Mike McLaney was taken hostage. Bill McLaney's wife managed to escape by hiding her identity and sneaking aboard a refugee ship — with around $250,000 cash hidden under her blouse, along with, some say, a photo of her posing with a tommy gun next to Meyer Lansky.

The McLaneys were fucking wild, baby.

And if you can't guess what happened once Mike McLaney bribed his way back to America, then you don't have any imagination.

The CIA was furious that there was now a hostile communist dictatorship ninety miles from Florida. The Mob was enraged that its enormous gaming empire in Cuba had been stolen by the natives. Both parties saw only one solution: a coup that would replace Castro with a puppet dictator who would protect American interests.

And who do you think Joe Kennedy's kids hired to quietly topple a Caribbean dictatorship?

That's right: Dale's new in-laws.

"I spent that first night [in Guatemala] sharing a side of a bed with a secretary of a friend in her apartment. When I saw boots and a lumber jacket in the room, I said 'that's it!' I couldn't sleep all night."

<u>Carlos Marcello</u>
Testifying before Congress

Baby, if you ask me, there was no finer successor to JFK than Jim Garrison. The Jolly Green Giant followed in JFK's footsteps like an apostle chasing after any opportunity to get crucified like Jesus. Like JFK, Jim was a degenerate, sex- freak politician who used his underworld connections to get elected and then went on a bat-shit, self-righteous rampage against his old underworld friends once in office.

If you're wondering why the Kennedys died so young, and Garrison lived to be a rich old cocksucker, well, there's a simple answer: the devoted apostle Jim Garrison saw JFK get crucified and decided at the last second that the life of a martyr wasn't for him. No matter who else he pissed off, Jim Garrison always steered well clear of Carlos Marcello's bad side. He stayed clear of Carlos on *all sides.*

The Kennedys were not as smart.

To talk plain, the Kennedy Family was a Mafia dynasty — you can't understand their story if you don't come to terms with that. The press likes to say that old Joe Kennedy made the family fortune as a "bootlegger," which is a nice way to say that he dealt drugs with the Mafia during Prohibition. Long afterwards, Joe

Kennedy maintained close ties with the Mob through friends like Mike McLaney, and Joe's kids were close pals with Mob flunkies like Frank Sinatra.

When Joe needed a little help electing his son president in 1960, he called his old buddies in the Chicago Outfit for a favor, and they rallied just enough votes from the cemeteries of Cook County to steal the presidency for John Kennedy.

So far, business as usual — this is just how America was run in 1960. Kennedy's opponent, Richard Nixon, was heavily indebted to Carlos Marcello, so there was no clean contender in the race. The only difference is that one cheater was honest: when you bought Nixon, he stayed bought.

The Kennedys were not as honest as Richard Nixon. As the heirs of a Mafia dynasty, John and Bobby were cliché young mob princes. When it came time to succeed their larger-than-life father, the spoiled brats suffered what I like to call the Baby Kingpin Meltdown.

You see it all the time on the street: untested young guns who talk a great game as they wait *decades* for their old men to step aside who immediately flame out in a tantrum of paranoia, insecurity, and fear when they become boss. Once baby kingpins begin to shoulder the awful responsibility of controlling life and death, they discover, to their horror, that they're not up to withstanding the pressure.

Jack Kennedy started suffering his baby kingpin meltdown before he was even elected. Judging by the poor Irishman's constant partying and drug intake, he had no business running for any office higher and more uptight than my cousin Edwin's freewheeling gig as Governor of Louisiana. It's hard to avoid thinking that JFK was a man better suited to the Absinthe House than the White House.

I can empathize. I'd definitely have ended up turning to booze and drugs if *my* dad forced me to make Percy, *my* bratty, self-righteously Catholic, pathologically jealous little shit of a brother Attorney General. Hell, I turned to booze and drugs anyway.

That's why I don't think you can hold JFK's meltdown and crazy decision to make RFK Attorney General against him. Take it from someone who lived the same lifestyle as JFK in the early 1960s –that man could not have *possibly* been in his right mind. Look at this man's daily routine: he was constantly popping speed pills, chasing whores, shooting up with steroids, hobnobbing with mobbed-up celebrities, vainly trying to suppress Catholic guilt, and engaging in sibling warfare with his prick brother.

He was Mr. President while living like Mr. New Orleans!

JFK couldn't help making insane, self-destructive decisions because he was living an insane, self-destructive lifestyle. While on his multi-year, orgiastic bender of speed and steroids, JFK ran the country with appropriate amounts of paranoia, unpredictability, and raging aggression.

It's not a surprise that Kennedy's two years as president were so stuffed full of crises and scandals. That roided-up speed freak was in a rush, baby! Kennedy invaded Cuba, played nuclear chicken with Khrushchev during the Cuban Missile Crisis, maniacally tried to cripple the power of the CIA and the FBI, cooked up a top-secret operation to kill Castro, belly flopped into Vietnam, tried to topple Hoffa and the Teamsters, and went on a rampage against the same gangsters that stole the presidency for him — *all at the same time.* If you look at this way, it's almost surprising that this rabid dog wasn't put down quicker before he got us all killed.

Kennedy did not wait long at all to give very dangerous men *very* good excuses to whack him out. In April of 1961, only a couple months into his presidency, John Kennedy made more enemies and alienated more allies in a shorter period of time than any president since Abraham Lincoln.

The first betrayal came with the kidnapping of Carlos Marcello. JFK's deal with the Chicago Outfit that had won the election of 1960 included a mutual hands-off clause. Yet, only a couple months into JFK's term of office, the Department of Justice suddenly deported the boss of America's oldest Mafia family, just because the grumpy bastard made disrespectful faces at RFK during the McClellan Commission.

To add insult to injury, RFK did the deed dirty: like the half-ass gangster he was, RFK did not play by the book and wait to win the ongoing court cases concerning Marcello's naturalization status. Nope, RFK just sent his men to illegally detain Carlos, manhandle him onto an empty military cargo plane, and fly him without warning to Guatemala. Insecure like a real baby kingpin, RFK did not have the balls to finish the job and deputize some CIA killer to whack out the dangerous sonofabitch after publicly humiliating and kidnapping him.

Instead, a maniacally enraged Carlos was left to stew in Central America without friends, supplies, or a change of clothes. Eventually, the porky refugee waddled on foot through miles of jungle to reach El Salvador and an illegal plane flight back to Louisiana. Lawsuits were filed challenging the deportation, and the government indicted Carlos for defrauding the government with his fake Guatemalan birth certificate. Now, Carlos' ability to reside in America would rest on the outcome of a court case — which the government could have filed from the beginning.

Carlos was allowed to stay in New Orleans until the legal proceedings concluded. With Carlos back in America within weeks, all RFK's ridiculous scheme had accomplished was making his most recklessly aggressive enemy feel cornered and backstabbed.

After double-crossing one of their family's most dangerous allies, the Kennedys decided to aim a little higher and set about double-crossing the most dangerous people *on Earth* — the CIA. The method that the Kennedys chose of pissing off the CIA was the sudden and inexplicable sabotage of the Bay of Pigs Invasion, which, as a bonus, made blood enemies out of the McLaneys and the rest of the Mob as well.

The original plan for the Bay of Pigs operation was conceived by Eisenhower's CIA as a way to repo America's investment in Cuba and rub out Castro's Communist regime without grinding up a bunch of US ground troops. After assembling, arming, and training a marine force of Cuban exiles in Florida and Louisiana, the US would transport the exiles to Cuba under a cover of naval and air support.

Naturally, the CIA enlisted the support of the McLaney family, who were Cuban-friendly mercenary trainers already conveniently based in Louisiana and Florida. One of the McLaneys' closest friends, CIA agent and future Watergate burglar E. Howard Hunt, was deputized to construct the puppet government that would meet the shared requirements of the CIA and "expatriate business interests" like the McLaneys, Meyer Lansky, Santo Trafficante, and Carlos Marcello.

It was a prepaid deal: the Mob knew the plan long before even JFK was informed, and they provided whatever logistical support they could.

When Kennedy took office, he authorized Eisenhower's invasion of Cuban exiles. At the last second, however, Kennedy probably took a dose of painkillers that bummed him out and compelled him to poutily call off the planned air support. Without the Air Force's cover, this half-cocked raid ended with most of the CIA's Cuban pals getting helplessly slaughtered.

Mike McLaney, Santo Trafficante, and Joe Kennedy's friends in Chicago watched as their dreams of reclaiming their Havana casinos and their teenage Cuban cocktail-waitress girlfriends disappeared, all thanks to a sudden inexplicable loss of balls on JFK's part. This was not how they expected the President they put in office to act.

The Kennedys wasted no time rubbing in their outrage. Seeing that the CIA and the Mafia were becoming enemies, the Attorney General sloppily intrigued behind the scenes like a jealous hooker to destroy them.

I wish I could have seen the incredulous look on J. Edgar Hoover's face as he listened to RFK give him the order to investigate and prosecute their mutual friends in the underworld. Special attention was to be paid to crooked Teamsters Union president Jimmy Hoffa, who just happened to be the special servant of the same Chicago Outfit that had elected Kennedy in the first place.

It was not exactly a secret that Hoover was extremely angry that he was being forced to make an ass of himself by pursuing the Italian gangsters whose existence he had been steadfastly denying going back to the days of flappers and Model T Fords. Hoover was quick to spread word that this about-face change of Bureau policy was coming directly from RFK — not him.

Godfathers like Carlos Marcello received the news from their completely compromised local FBI field offices that RFK was gunning for them within a day of that initial meeting with Hoover. The national Mafia syndicate went apeshit as the news spread, and you could not talk to a wiseguy for more than fifteen minutes without hearing threats against the Kennedys.

As far as the CIA's reaction to the Kennedy brothers' bragging about their plans to "cut the Agency's balls off," well, let's just say I don't think it was particularly wise to threaten the manhood of the government's professional team of assassins and coup-planners.

That sounded like more of the Kennedys' typical, amateur-hour, baby kingpin behavior to me — the last thing you do is *talk shit* about killers. In my experience, there are two ways to deal with killers without getting killed: you flatter them, or you keep your mouth shut and kill them before they suspect anything. You definitely don't give them a warning that you mean to do them harm and then *take your time.*

I personally knew many of the people the Kennedys were fucking with — knew them like brothers. I knew that I would have expected to get shot if I dared to treat them in such a shitty manner. In street terms, the Kennedys were begging for it. It was as if they meticulously set about doing everything they could to get shot.

Maybe that's wrong to say. After all, I'm just a humble French Quarter hood. What do I know?

✤ ✤ ✤ ✤ ✤

"'Match made in heaven,' said a man who knew Joe [Kennedy] and Mike [McLaney], 'both of 'em bigots, gamblers, golfers, Irish Catholics, and right-wingers.' [...] In the fall of 1961, Joe Kennedy, John, and Bobby met with Joe's close friend [...] Mike McLaney to discuss "getting rid" of Castro. [...] Months later [...] the president himself met at McLaney's nearby Miami villa with McLaney, along with [Johnny] Rosselli representing [Chicago Outfit boss Sam] Giancana and [Florida Mafia boss Santo] Trafficante."

Sally Denton & Roger Morris
The Money & The Power

If you think I'm being cruel to the memory of JFK, reserve your judgment for a little while longer. The stories I've told you were just the beginning. The man had a death wish.

The next step in the Kennedys' kamikaze campaign was to collect all the former friends they had already backstabbed into a single group, hand them money and military-grade weaponry, and give them full authorization to train teams of assassins.

If a president paying to arm his most dangerous enemies and train them in assassination techniques seems insane, then, baby, *hold on to your hat*. The next step in the Kennedy's plan was to wait for their enemies to organize into a formidable paramilitary force — and then backstab them all over again without disarming them!

If you're starting to suspect that the Kennedys were the dumbest politicians in human history, then you're coming around to the view that has prevailed in the New Orleans underworld since 1961.

This brilliant plan was called Operation Mongoose. Mongoose aimed to make peace with everyone the Administration double-crossed in the Bay of Pigs fiasco by giving them the under-the-table authority to topple Castro themselves.

The scheme started with Mike McLaney, who was still fuming from the loss of the Hotel Nacional. Though McLaney still had enough money to last an average person decades, he was no average person. With his mint condition Rolls Royces, fancy clothes and jewelry, and month-long reservations in the presidential suites at the nicest hotels, Mike McLaney had the spending habits of an Arabian prince. Soon, the McLaneys were claiming to be perilously close to bankruptcy; they needed to get back their Cuban assets as quickly as possible.

Right when Mike McLaney was at his most desperate, he received a visit from his old golfing buddy Joe Kennedy. In secret, Papa Joe asked for the McLaneys to arrange an alliance between his friends in the Mafia, the CIA, and the Cuban exiles to covertly kill Castro and furnish Cuba with a pro-America government. In return, the Administration would recognize the Mob's gambling rights in Cuba, provide immunity from prosecution, and supply all of the weaponry, explosives, and information needed to get the job done.

Mike McLaney was weary of the Kennedys, whom he blamed for his continued exile from Havana, but he was too desperate to say no. The equally weary Mafia families took the same risk, hoping that their cooperation with an illegal plan to terrorize and assassinate a foreign head of state would give them blackmail leverage to keep the Kennedys "in pocket" from then on. Even Carlos cooperated, with the hope that his deportation case would be quietly squashed.

Obviously, they assumed that no sane president would dare to double-cross allies who could disclose such sensitive information. There was one problem: you can't blackmail folks who are too crazy or high to know better.

The McLaneys opened up paramilitary training bases in south Florida and in Lacombe, Louisiana, for the survivors of the first wave of Cuban exiles. Carlos Marcello, Santo Trafficante in Tampa, and Chicago gangsters Sam Giancana, Johnny Roselli, and Tony Accardo all provided funding for these camps and a grab bag of other anti-Castro militant groups, lobbying organizations, and radical publications. The Department of Defense supplied plenty of weaponry and explosives, and the CIA laundered millions through dummy corporations in New Orleans to finance the effort.

Within a few months, Operation Mongoose was wreaking havoc. The McLaneys had organized commando "sabotage teams" of hardcore exiles, armed them with excess World War II guns, ammunition, and explosives, and transported them by speedboat from the Everglades to Cuba. While visiting the island, the McLaneys planted bombs on anchored ships and blasted away Red troops patrolling the coastline.

The teams of Cuban commandos trained by the CIA and the McLaneys attempted to assassinate Castro on numerous occasions and supposedly came close to succeeding. Mike and Bill bragged that one near-miss C-4 explosion in Havana Harbor came so close to its goal that it left Fidel partially deaf.

"That cocksucker won't hear us comin' next time!" Mike McLaney hissed to anyone who would listen. "And that shit-for-brains knows who we're workin' for. There's only one government in the world that has C-4 explosives!" In the New Orleans underworld, the McLaneys' and Marcellos' operations against Cuba were hardly secrets. Everyone was bragging.

The pride of Operation Mongoose was veteran pilot Bill McLaney's improvised air campaign against Cuba. Utilizing six ramshackle airplanes, a volunteer crew of fifty amateur pilots, and a few airfields around Miami, Bill threw together some jerry-rigged shock and awe. The McLaneys conducted countless bombing runs from Miami, utilizing homemade napalm bombs: 55-gallon oil drums rigged with flares and filled with gasoline and a thickening agent.

Bombing foreign countries with Soviet military bases was not without its risks. During one flyover in 1962, Russian anti-aircraft guns opened fire and riddled the planes. The McLaneys' air fleet stayed airborne thanks to the efforts of the crews, who used their fingers to plug just enough bullet holes to maintain sufficient air pressure. The next day, almost all of the volunteer pilots reconsidered their devotion to the cause of a free Cuba and quit.

The excitement and ego boosts that come with daring adventures like these have a way of healing the resentments in a gangster's soul. There's no disagreement between wiseguys that a chance to tag-team a couple mutual enemies won't temporarily fix. Just as the Italians and their allies started to get comfortable with the Kennedys again, the final betrayals came. The Kennedys became radioactive.

While the Mafia was spending its money, and the McLaneys and various CIA agents were risking their lives to take down Castro at the Kennedys' request, the brothers never halted their crusades against Carlos Marcello, Teamsters President Jimmy Hoffa, and the CIA.

The worst betrayal of all came against Mike and Bill McLaney. The close family friends of Joe Kennedy had been risking their lives to do JFK's bidding, yet that did not earn them a single drop of loyalty. When some senators approached the White House after hearing scandalous rumors about the Administration funding the training of Cuban exiles by organized crime figures, the Kennedys denied everything and offered the McLaneys up as a human sacrifice to prove their innocence.

The FBI raided the home of Bill McLaney in Lacombe, which was fully stocked with forty-eight cases of dynamite and fifty-five gallons of napalm prior to a major bombing run over Cuba. Bill was crucified in the press for illegally possessing the explosives *the government had given to him*. It was like that scene in *Shane* where Jack Palance tells some innocent shepherd to pick up a gun and, after the hick reluctantly follows orders, shoots him dead for brandishing a pistol.

For the first time in their careers, the McLaney brothers — one a decorated war veteran, the other a local sports hero and ex-deputy sheriff — were publicly outed as gangsters and even potential traitors to the United States.

At that moment, Operation Mongoose unofficially came to a close. The question was whether all that meticulous planning that went into killing Castro was going to be wasted.

"Mike McLaney had a world-class Napoleon complex. His goal in life was to rule an island in the Caribbean as a dictator. He gave the boats, helicopters, and planes [Bahamas politician Lynden] Pindling needed to win his first campaign in return for the gambling rights and a piece of the island.
Then Pindling put the screws to him and cut him out. Mike then put out a hit on Pindling like it was nothin'. That was Mike; he'd pull off a coup or whack a president over nothing. He just didn't give a shit. He was nuts."
Anonymous Louisiana Police Official

It was at this point in the spring of 1963 that the plan to kill JFK supposedly took shape. The architects were the McLaneys, their Mafia patrons Carlos Marcello and Santo Trafficante, Jimmy Hoffa and his Midwest Mob protectors, and various rogue elements of the Cuban exiles and the CIA who were left disgruntled from both the repeated failures to topple Castro and the attempts to undercut the CIA's power.

If it sounds farfetched to you that this large and mismatched group would conspire to kill President Kennedy, remind yourself that it is public record that this *identical* alliance was already working together to assassinate Castro in 1962 and 1963. That's a fact. There is nothing about the Kennedy assassination that is more farfetched than the plain facts of Operation Mongoose. The only thing that changed between Mongoose and November 22, 1963, was the target and location.

I have my own personal reasons for believing that this group conspired and succeeded to kill Kennedy, which I will get to in time. For now, let's act like lawyers and agree for argument's sake that we know the people who ordered and planned the assassination. But who executed it? Well, to answer that question, it's time to pick up the story of my best friend Dale again.

In 1964, Dale had been left by his pretty little model wife, who he suspected of tooling around on him with some local characters. Heartbroken, Dale hitchhiked to Las Vegas to get away from New Orleans and beg for a job from the new owners of the Carousel Casino on Freemont Street. He had reason to hope that the Carousel's owners might give him special consideration: they were, after all, his former uncle-in-laws. Maybe they would do right by the boy whom their niece had done wrong.

That's right, only a few months after the Kennedy assassination, the deeply in debt Mike and Bill McLaney *somehow* found themselves the owners of an extremely expensive casino in Mob-dominated Las Vegas. And guess who was installed in the lounge downstairs? Sam Anselmo, an associate of Carlos Marcello who had previously run the Dream Room on Bourbon Street; Sam joined the McLaneys and Mario Marino at The Sands as the New Orleans Mafia's representatives in the new Sin City. Draw your own conclusions.

Any red-blooded Louisiana Catholic boy has plenty of opportunities for distraction in Las Vegas, and my protégé Dale's mind aimlessly wandered away from the McLaneys, once he saw the bright lights and pretty girls. After booking Room 1216 at the Mint, which was next door to the Carousel, Dale hit the lounges and used the seduction skills I taught him to pick up a beautiful girl. Dale dragged his catch up to his room at the Mint, opened the door, and found three tough-looking characters in suits waiting for him.

The handsome man standing in the middle of the room with a cigarette in his hand seemed familiar. Examining the smiling gentleman more closely, he saw a Bobby Darin look-alike with a Marine's haircut, more muscles, and a flashy collection of jewels. Finally, he recognized the stranger, and about a millisecond later recognized that he was in deep shit.

Dale had seen the man many times before, dating back to three years earlier in the run-up to the Bay of Pigs invasion. The stranger was always around Bill McLaney's house in Lacombe, which Dale had helped build as the able-bodied teenage beau of the McLaneys' niece. Though they had never spoken, Dale had watched the visitor in his hotel room train the Cuban exiles in the use of a variety of weapons and exclusive devices. The man was a marvel with just about any tool that could do someone harm, and he always wore a smile on his face.

The smiling stranger nodded first to Dale and then to his girl. "Dawlin', why don't you get along now and shut that door behind ya," he said with a quiet, polite voice marred by a heavy backwater Mississippi accent. "Trust me, you don't wanna be gettin' involved in none of dis."

Dale was shaken. The McLaneys' weapons specialist stood there with this calm, unflappable attitude that he remembered from Lacombe, where grenades would explode nearby without eliciting the slightest flinch from him.

Dale knew he was in danger; there was no *innocent* reason for the McLaneys' men to be lying in wait in your hotel room in 1964 Las Vegas. Shooing the girl out the door, Dale knew better than to act scared. Unarmed and alone in the McLaneys' city, Dale's only leverage was to play it cool and unflappable, like someone with nothing to hide and powerful friends to hide behind. Dale mustered a squeak, "Hey, man, what you guys mean by all this?"

The mystery man looked to his left and right, smiling at his goons. "We had a question for you," he said in the same friendly voice as before.

"Uhh," Dale moaned, subconsciously backing himself into the closed door. "What ya wanna know?"

"Well, we just heard that you like to beat on women," he said casually as he inspected the cuticles on his right hand. "Now, is that true, *Dale*?" As the stranger finished pronouncing Dale's name, the look on his face changed to something cold, doglike, and vicious, and his men crouched and charged towards the door.

With admirable reflexes, my boy Dale leapt to a nearby coffee table and brandished a chair in the air like a lion tamer. He knew damn well the trouble he was in: to explain why she had divorced him, his crazy ex-wife had lied and told her Catholic uncles that Dale had abused her. The McLaneys naturally put a bounty on his head throughout their criminal network, but Dale had made it easy by obliviously driving right to Las Vegas and booking a room right next door to the Carousel.

Within minutes of signing into the Mint, using his own name, some concierge or bellhop had collected on a reward and tipped off the owners of the Carousel that their target was in town. And now Dale was going to die.

But he wasn't going to go easy. "Man, if I'm going out that window," Dale cried as he sharply jabbed at the two thugs with the chairs' legs, "I'm not going by myself. And for the fuckin' record, I ain't never beaten any girl! Man, kill me if you want, but that's the god's honest truth!"

Lucky for Dale, he had inherited his dad's aura of trustworthiness, sincerity, and decency. As soon as the two thugs were about to disarm Dale of his chair, the smiling stranger called out.

"That's enough, boys," he said with a laugh and a wave of the hand. All three men in the corner turned to him in shock and confusion; even Dale seemed more perplexed than relieved. "I think the boy's right; he don't look like no woman beater to me. Somethin' 'bout him."

Walking over to Dale, who was still cowering against the wall with his chair, the stranger extended his hand. "My name is Farish Cody. People call me Tex. Let's go get a drink and sort this out."

Dale warily put down the chair to shake Tex Cody's hand. After that first handshake, they would be inseparable for the next eighteen years.

Allow me to introduce you to Tex Cody, the most dangerous motherfucker I have ever known and ever care to know.

"Farish Cody was a man's man and a gentleman.
By that, I mean that he would kill a man with his bare hands,
but be too discreet to ever talk about it at the bar.
Tex let his reputation speak for him."
Anonymous Gangster

Baby, I've got to be honest with you. Farish Cody scared the shit out of me as a man, and he scares me even worse as a storyteller. I've been dreading the moment when I would have to tackle the story of Tex Cody.

Given my record, I know that credibility is not necessarily my strong suit, so I can't help but worry that it will be hard for anyone to take me seriously when I relay the truth about the stone-craziest badass I've ever known. I know it will be hard to believe that Dale and I were the best friends and roommates of a man who was tougher, wilder, and deadlier than any Hollywood action hero, but I can't help the truth. That's always been my problem, the truth in all its unbelievable peacock feathers.

It's really history that's putting me in this bind by ignoring Tex Cody until now. It's one thing for me to talk about outlandish characters like Silver Dollar Sam, Carlos, or Mike McLaney since history has already gotten around to discussing how *shittin'-ass* crazy they were. You don't just have to take my word for it; you can plug their names into an encyclopedia or a computer and see that I'm not lying.

With old Tex Cody, on the other hand, I'm unfortunately breaking new ground. All I can do is ask for you to hear me out, so settle in and get ready to hear about the tallest tale ever to come to life.

Farish Lamar Cody was born in Pike County, Mississippi, on July 30 of 1929. Baby, if you think Marksville is a lame place for a gangster to be born, you should take a look at Pike County, Mississippi. I was born into a community of marks and Cody into a community of pikers.

You might think that's the reason Farish Cody and Frenchy Brouillette were both at one time nicknamed "Tex"— we were born 100 miles away from each other in the mercilessly deep South and had accents to prove it. Since Italians figured that all redneck accents came from Texas, I became "Tex" thanks to my countrified manner of speaking, a nickname I lost only when someone noticed I sounded more Cajun French than redneck and became Frenchy instead.

The story was different for Tex Cody. Though he sounded like a hayseed, he got the nickname "Tex" because of a run-in with a wild crocodile. While working for the McLaneys down in Miami, an acquaintance called up Mike because he needed someone to kill the crocodile that had slipped into his pond. Farish Cody was sent to whack out this crocodile, but he had a different plan. After asking the homeowner for some rope, Cody fashioned a makeshift lasso and lassoed that croc, yanked it out of the pond, tied it up good, and threw it in his trunk. Knowing Cody, he probably barbecued that fucker.

Due to his unexpected lasso skills, Cody became "Tex" — a nickname he wore proudly, unlike me. I can't blame the guy; if I had been nicknamed "Tex" for a cool reason like my ability to lasso crocodiles instead of my tendency to talk like an idiot, the name might have grown on me too. The only associate who chose a different nickname for Cody was Frank "Frankie One-Ear" Fratto, the acting boss of the Iowa Mob in the '70s, who preferred "Hillbilly."

Tex Cody grew up in backwater Mississippi in a house his extended family rented for $20 a month. His father was an engineer at a creamery. Tex grew up poor and tough during the height of the Depression, a real shitkicking redneck. You could see that penniless coldness and Okie cynicism in his eyes; life was cheap to Tex. He had that look of a farmer who no longer even notices the squeal of a pig when he slits its throat.

I was told by people close to Cody that whatever was wrong with him as an adult was wrong with him as a child. As a juvenile, Tex built up a considerable reputation as a cat burglar and thief, a quick thrill that turned out to become his lifelong addiction. No matter how much cash and how many connections Tex Cody obtained, he never could resist the buzz of a spur-of-the-moment house robbery or carjacking. It used to drive the McLaneys wild; they needed Tex for million-dollar bounties and casino jobs, and he was off jimmying a Cadillac's lock for fun.

Looking at Cody, you could never tell that he was so wild. He was as mild-mannered as you could hope to meet at a church social. This peaceful personality could evaporate in a second, however; if pushed too far or given orders, Cody was an absolute devil with his fists and any imaginable weapon. The country boy had a deep reservoir of rage and aggression that he could tap into at any moment.

According to his family, Tex's dad was a real louse, a drunk and an abuser. Little Farish took his beatings and beratings like a little saint, never saying a word — until one day he calmly grabbed a knife and stabbed his father a few times to shut him up. Wild and fearless, Tex hit the road as a highwayman at a young age to ditch his miserable home and hometown.

Tex was the scariest "yeggman" anyone had seen in decades, a quiet, mild-mannered, own-business-mindin' Southern boy who would take on the most suicidal jobs without hesitation and shoot a man within a split second of being crossed. Tex was a crook of all trades: burglar, bank robber, safecracker, hired muscle, gambling cheat. He was polite and handsome enough to act as the front man, and more than tough enough to act as the enforcer.

Tex traveled far and wide, building a reputation that would reach nationwide underworld proportions. Dale slowly learned that, to the most legendary gangsters in America, the real legend was Tex Cody. His name was unknown to squares but larger-than-life to gangsters. Though Tex would occasionally tell his own stories, Dale heard more than his share of tall tales about Cody from guys with Italian names that rang out across the underworld.

For example, in New York, Dale was told by wiseguys about the time Tex had used a crane to pull off one of the most incredible safe burglaries in the city's history. Tex climbed up the crane's arm to a third-story window on a crowded city street, locked the crane's hook to a wall safe in the room, and then shouted down the order to his accomplice to yank the safe clean out of the building and down to the street. Realizing that he no longer had a way out of the building, Tex carelessly hopped out of the smashed window and crashed onto the building's awning. He somehow bounced off and landed in his convertible unharmed.

"Man, I never would have believed that story if Tex told me himself," Dale told me.

Another Tex story from New York involved a high-stakes Mob card game. Tex had been hired to stand at the door as muscle and protect the game against stickup crews. Tipped off by informant testimony, two off-duty cops kicked down the door with the intent to shake down the game. Tex was having none of that; he shot both of them and then took their bodies down to the trash dump. Supposedly, one of them lived, which must have created some interesting political problems for whoever played political fixer in New York.

By his thirtieth birthday, Tex had racked up at least fifteen felonies in numerous states and served six years in prison in New York. The police in NYC had leaked to the prison authorities that Cody was a cop-killer, so he was mercilessly abused in jail and housed in solitary for enormous stretches with nothing but a dictionary and a bible. From these two books, Tex built himself a chess board, and he convinced one of the guards to slip a paper, with a code he devised for playing chess via taps on the wall on it, to the prisoners in the cell next to solitary.

During his thousands of hours in "the hole," Tex became such a brilliant, self-taught chess player that he rarely met anyone that could beat him. Tex could not resist challenging and defeating the chess hustlers that we saw sitting in public parks, and he occasionally showed up at the New Orleans Athletic Club chess tournaments to crush the competition of chess coaches and semi-professional players. Tex really was some sort of demented genius; he could also do MacGyver shit, like making weapons out of spare motorboat parts or hot-wiring a limo to blow up when put in reverse.

When Tex and the McLaneys met in the late 1950s, it was clearly a match made in heaven. Tex was a perfect fit for the McLaneys: a fearless weapons expert with ironclad ex-con credentials and a professional appearance perfect for Mike's con man schemes. For Tex, the immensely connected McLaneys represented the ability to work anywhere in the Americas with any crime family he wanted.

Tex became the full-time enforcer and bodyguard of Mike McLaney throughout his Havana, and later Las Vegas, heydays — if you subtract the short stints he did in jail servicing his burglary addiction. If you need any further proof of how incredibly dangerous Tex Cody was, just think of what sort of street bona fides you needed to be hired as the top killer for government-toppling soldier of fortune Mike McLaney. Mike McLaney was always bragging that Tex was the only hitter he knew who would happy whack a guy with his bare hands by request. This sort of thing makes one popular in the underworld, and, on his off-time, Tex let the McLaneys loan him out as a specialist to countless crime families across America for whatever particularly grimy jobs they couldn't source locally.

Born with a particularly healthy sex drive, Tex became one of the most notorious players in Havana in 1959. His entire body was decorated with jewels that he stole himself, and he picked up broads at a rate that would make Neil Gautier jealous.

During his travels with Cody, Dale was always astounded by the respect Cody commanded from Mafia godfathers. During one visit to Florida, Tex Cody took Dale to meet with Joe Fischetti (an elder statesman and consigliere in the Chicago Outfit), Tony Amato (a Mob kingpin from the Wisconsin Family), and Santo Trafficante, one of the most powerful Mafia bosses in history. All of these Mafia powerhouses treated Tex Cody with such over-the-top respect and kindness that it became almost unnerving to Dale. Halfway through one meal, Tony Amato gave Dale a beautiful jade ring circled by diamond baguettes, just because Tex liked him.

As Mike McLaney's paramilitary expert, Tex was intimately involved in training Cuban exiles for both the Bay of Pigs Invasion and Operation Mongoose. Among the Cuban exiles who trained with the McLaneys, there was a lot of gossip that Tex had to be CIA or something worse —no one "normal" was that fearless of repercussions, that violent and aggressive. Dropped behind enemy lines in Cuba, Tex supposedly just missed whacking out Castro on more than one occasion.

By the time Dale met Tex at The Mint, the McLaneys had Tex working as their all-purpose Las Vegas lieutenant. When out-of-state Mafia leaders visited, Tex picked them up in Mike's turquoise limousine and guarded them closely during their visit. On off-nights, Tex managed the "eye in the sky" surveillance teams that watched table gamblers from rafters in the ceiling of The Carousel. A veteran degenerate gambler and cheat himself, Tex had an expert's eye for spotting cardsharps and cheat team, and he knew exactly how to handle them when they were escorted by security "to the back" of the premises.

Why such a stone-cold, redneck hitter took such a liking to meek and mild and middle-class kid like Dale I'll never know, but there's no doubt that Tex became closer to Dale than anyone else in his life. Wives and children came and went in Tex Cody's life, but Dale was a constant for two decades. It must be something genetic in Dale's family that makes them so likable to remorseless gangsters.

Hell, I love Dale and his old man myself.

After their first meeting, Tex drove Dale in his red Cadillac convertible with the white top to meet with the McLaneys, who reluctantly accepted that he had not beaten his ex-wife and, as a peace offering, put him on the payroll. Dale managed the McLaneys' parking lot properties in Vegas, worked in "the eye in the sky" at the Carousel, and assisted Tex in executing the "debt collection" gigs that all of the Mafia casino owners gave to him.

Within a few months, Dale and Tex had become such good friends that they bought matching red Lincoln convertibles, proclaimed themselves full-fledged partners, and hit the road as highwaymen. Life under Mike McLaney was too stressful and constricting for them. They wanted to be free.

After engaging in a cross-country rampage that would have made Jesse James or John Dillinger proud, Tex and Dale eventually returned to New Orleans, where they worked for Carlos Marcello and me for years.

But forgive an old boozer: I'm getting off-task. I will get to all of that in good time. Right now, it's time to discuss the role Tex Cody allegedly played in the Kennedy Assassination before either Dale or I knew him — and what he had to do with my little buddy Lee Harvey Oswald.

⚜ ⚜ ⚜ ⚜ ⚜

"On November 1, 1963, a Cuban man entered the Parrot Jungle gift shop [...] and initiated a conversation in which he stated 'that he had a friend named Lee who could speak Russian and German and was living in Texas or Mexcio, and that Lee was also a sharpshooter.'[...] The Cuban exile was identified as Jorge Martinez, who [...] 'had been brought to the United States by Mike McLaney, one of the old Havana gambling bosses.'"

<u>Dick Russell</u>
The Man Who Knew Too Much

Like many New Orleans gangsters, I came to know Lee Harvey Oswald in 1963. Oswald was something of an underworld curiosity that summer and fall.

I would be lying if I said I didn't like the guy, though he unnerved me. Talking to him, you would look in his eyes and feel like something seemed to be missing. He was one of those guys who just seemed "not quite right" in that way that you can't put your finger on.

The kid was weird. Though he was far better read and better traveled than I was, he still had the air of a teenager about him. I was three years older, yet felt a decade older, which is funny since I'm about the most immature person in the world.

A lot of wiseguys who knew Oswald called him a "punk," which in retrospect I think is unfair. Oswald certainly looked like a punk, but he was damn sure not weak or stupid. I don't know any weak Marine sharpshooters, and he couldn't have been too stupid, or otherwise they wouldn't have given him security clearance when he was still a teenager.

Also, it had to take some wits to pull off the international hijinks that made him infamous in New Orleans long before the assassination. No one's ever been able to explain to me how a nerdy high-school dropout and twice court-martialed Marine from the Big Easy convinced the KGB to let him defect to Moscow and *then* managed to convince the CIA to let him defect back. Clearly, that was some level of double-dealing there that we don't know about.

That has to take some type of talent — the closest comparison I can make is when I used to go back and forth bedding sisters. Convincing a woman to take me back after I left her for her sister was always a challenge, and the girls I screwed around with had to be less vindictive than the CIA and KGB.

As soon as Oswald returned to New Orleans in April of 1963, he became the talk of the underworld since his uncle was Charles "Dutz" Murret, an ex-boxer who worked as a bookmaker in Sam Saia's network and had worked in fight promoting with Gasper

Gulotta. Even for a crew that included such clowns as Dutch Kraut and Frenchy Brouillette, the idea that a nephew of a wiseguy was a Marine turned international double-agent was surreal and fascinating. The story of Oswald became hot gossip to all the old guidos, who liked eating and gossiping above all else.

Men like Carlos Marcello and Mike McLaney, who set up intricate networks of underworld informers throughout the South to be on the lookout for any unusual characters, knew about Oswald within days of his return. After all, the former Marine and international double-agent also had close ties to Sam Saia and Carlos' private investigator David Ferrie, which meant that Carlos had reason to fear that the double-agent Oswald could get close enough to become a snitch.

I met Oswald for the first time during the summer of 1963. I was walking to the pharmacy to buy 25¢ leeches, which I did whenever I got bruised in a fight and wanted to suck the blood out of the inflammation. It was an old boxing trick taught to me by Gasper or Pete Herman, I don't remember which.

As I was walking, Oswald spotted me from his perch in front of the store. After briefly making eye contact, he started coming my way with a smile. I sighed, figuring he was one of the many fellows I had met on a drunk night out on the town and forgotten. I then noticed the pile of flyers in his hand, which, when combined with his sweat-stained, short-sleeve, white dress shirt, convinced me I was dealing with a Mormon missionary or a Jehovah's Witness. I had enough trouble resisting Catholic guilt trips, so the last thing I needed was someone else throwing their bullshit on me.

I was relieved when Oswald started yapping about Cuba and Castro and Lord knows what else in his *Forrest Gump* voice. At least this spiel had nothing to do with religion. Granted, I had heard enough bitching about Castro to suffice for a lifetime in the New Orleans underworld, but I would prefer anything to a sermon.

One of the worst quirks of my shyness is that I'm a helpless mark for panhandlers. Without thinking, I started responding to Lee's Cuba jive, which was unfortunate since he was talking way above my head, and I had no interest in the subject. Finally, I was able to switch the subject to the weather, and we bullshitted for a little bit about, what else, the heat and humidity. He seemed nice enough, very eager to be liked.

After a polite chat, I shook his hand, introduced myself, and managed to commit the name "Lee Harvey Oswald" to memory when he told me. The name was familiar from all of the talk around town, but I had not paid enough attention to remember the details at that moment. All I recalled was that he was a freak of some variety, harmless enough by the looks of him.

I wished Lee luck with his political bullshit and walked away, happy that I had established friendly relations with a panhandler.

A few days later, I was saddened but not surprised when Oswald made citywide news for getting into a public scrap with some anti-Castro Cuban who got upset at Oswald for handing out flyers on behalf of Fidel. One of the things I learned from Edwin is that there is no greater waste of time in the world than worrying about politics, and Lee apparently is one of those tiresome people who will ruin a good day arguing over irrelevant bullshit over which he had no power. Clearly, this sort of guy would never go far in New Orleans.

That turned out to be a premature assessment — the next time I saw Lee Harvey Oswald was in Carlos Marcello's office.

I know that sentence will come as a surprise to many investigators of the Kennedy assassination, because apparently there is some dispute whether Carlos knew Oswald. That should be taken as a testament to Carlos Marcello's talent at picking people, because *everyone* in Carlos' inner circle had seen them together. I saw Carlos and Oswald together a few times in 1963, and I didn't see Carlos nearly as often as the Italians around him.

My first Oswald sighting came in Carlos' office at the Pelican Tomato Company, a small vegetable-wholesaling company run by his close Mafia confidant Joe "Baby" Matassa. Carlos' official profession as a "tomato salesman" was one of the jokes that showcased his dark sense of humor; the poor, barefoot boy who sold tomatoes in the French Quarter had grown up to be a millionaire Mafia boss. It also showcased his power: his biggest customer was the United States Navy.

Carlos started hanging out at the Pelican Tomato Company, which was situated next door to his friend Papa John's restaurant, after his temporary deportation to Guatemala — which incidentally was where Pelican bought a lot of its fucking tomatoes. As soon as I heard that Carlos was killing hours every day in the office of a tomato company, I started taking lunch in the neighborhood so that I could drop in and entertain him. Since I was not Italian and still had a completely clean record, I could visit him without worrying about potential federal surveillance.

Carlos loved my visits since I was always good with a funny story, and he could live vicariously through my tales of sex, drugs, and rock 'n' roll in the Quarter. The serially monogamous Carlos liked hearing call-girl stories almost as much as his far looser brothers Joe and Sammy. When I strutted into Carlos' office in August or September of 1963, my mind was fixated on just how I would word some crazy hooker story, so I was unprepared for the shock I felt when I found Carlos sitting there with Lee Harvey Oswald.

Oswald was startled by my careless, unannounced entrance into Carlos' office and looked at me nervously, but Marcello didn't miss a beat. In my experience, the only person who could make Carlos uncomfortable was Silver Dollar Sam, and I was no Silver Dollar Sam. "Man, you stomp in like a fuckin' china bull cabinet," said Carlos, mangling his phrases as usual. "Hey 'dere, Frenchy, lemme introduce ya to someone. This is Lee — Lee, Frenchy."

Lee looked nervous, as if he did not know whether to mention that we had met, but I shut him up. "Hey, baby, Frenchy Brouillette, nice to meet ya, man," I said with a firm squeeze of the hand.

It was out of bounds to ask Carlos *anything* about his personal affairs with another person, let alone the pro-Castro kook from the newspaper, so I kept my mouth shut. We made small talk for a while, and, though Lee was clearly a little nerdy for this room, he gradually seemed pretty at ease with Carlos. That might have been that boy's downfall.

After that meeting at the Pelican Tomato Company, it seemed like I couldn't go anywhere without running into goddamn Lee Harvey Oswald. Over the next few months, he seemed to be hanging around the diner at the Town & Country Motel just about every time I went to visit Carlos there. There was nothing fishy about that to me — Carlos was always collecting new flunkeys of every stripe and background. You never knew what sort of work he was planning. My understanding was that Oswald had become a runner of some sort for Carlos.

One day in early fall, I went to visit my attorney and on-and-off roommate Dean Andrews at his office. When it came to his buddy Frenchy, "attorney client privilege" definitely did not exist. Dean would slip me the info on every divorce case he received so that I could send girls to the aggrieved husband.

There was one client of Dean's about which he was anything but forthcoming: Lee Harvey Oswald, whom I ran into at his office. For once, the manically talkative Dean seemed nervous and awkward — his body language clearly told me to get the hell out. I did not need to be told twice and made my excuses to leave.

Later, when we were alone at my place, Dean confided in me that he had been setting up business between Carlos and Oswald, and he didn't want to make Oswald nervous. Around the same time, Carlos' visits to my place shot up precipitously, which was *very* abnormal; Carlos did not typically drop in unannounced at the Brouillette residence. In the fall of 1963, Carlos was always looking for me to ask where he could find Dean for discussions about his upcoming "deportation case."

At the time, I did not think twice about why Carlos, with the best and most connected immigration attorneys in D.C. on his payroll, would require Dean's services. I just took it as a sign that I had stumbled into a relationship with a world-class attorney, which was not exactly the estimation of Dean you get from interacting with him.

After all, one of Dean's favorite tricks was to go to all of the courthouse libraries and rip out all references to any case that set a bad precedent for his client. When the opposing counsel tried to cite precedent at trial, Dean would ask for clarification; when the clerk or opposing counsel came back after recess and announced that they could find no record of the case anywhere in town, Dean would laugh.

Then again, besides Dean, Carlos had a habit of employing extremely bizarre and disreputable characters on his deportation case. Another client of mine that Carlos was always seeing in "preparation" for his November deportation trial was David Ferrie. As crazy as Dean was, the hairless-wannabe-priest-gay-mercenary Ferrie made him look like Sigmund Freud.

Even for a New Orleans Mafia boss, Carlos was flying his freak flag pretty suspiciously high in the fall of 1963 with a crew like Ferrie, Andrews, and Oswald constantly around him. In the middle of the legal fight of his life, I had to conclude Carlos had an extremely pressing reason for consorting with these crackpot circus carnies so often.

I wish I could tell you that I suspected something extraordinary was going on, thanks to Carlos' strange associates that fall, but I'd be putting you on. My ability to sniff out something strange in the air was handicapped by the fact that I was in no position to be suspicious.

After all, I was yet another strange associate of Carlos Marcello — a redneck Cajun pimp who Carlos inexplicably entertained regularly in his office at the Pelican Tomato Company. How could a freakshow like me look at the rest of these freakshows and proclaim them unworthy of Carlos Marcello's company? If I were normal, then strange was *very* relative.

As strange as I was, I was still close enough to the Marcello family that I was invited down to the courthouse to hear the verdict on whether the godfather of New Orleans could stay in the country. Though I desperately did not want my benefactor and biggest bulk client to leave town, I realized that my presence in a courtroom stuffed full of crying, histrionic Marcello family members would be an unneeded distraction. Besides, I did not want to see what happened if they decided to deport the Little Big Man — that courtroom was liable to get shot up.

In retrospect, I regret not attending the last day of Carlos' trial. I would love to be able to tell you what the look on Carlos' face was when it was announced in the courtroom that John F. Kennedy had been shot and killed in Dallas, another city in Carlos' network. From friends who were eyewitnesses in the courtroom, Carlos did not so much as raise an eyebrow when he heard of the sudden and spectacular murder of his mortal enemy, the President of the United States.

I was around the Marcellos the day after, when Chicago and New Orleans Mob associate Jack Ruby shot Lee Harvey Oswald. Though Ruby was a friend of Peter Marcello and well known throughout the Quarter as an owner of a Dallas strip club that frequently used syndicate showgirls, none of the Marcellos seemed surprised when he popped the assassin of Carlos Marcello's arch-enemy. No one even brought it up.

Baby, you'd have to be a government employee to doubt that this sounds like a conspiracy. I've beaten around the bush — and no, that was not a reference to former CIA head George Bush — long enough. Let's throw the rest of the cards on the table.

"Look at Jack Ruby's phone records for the days before he shot Oswald. From Jimmy Hoffa's Teamsters: a conversation with Hoffa aide Murray Miller and three calls from Barney Baker, Jimmy Hoffa's enforcer, the man RFK called his 'roving ambassador of violence.' Well, guess what? I was extremely close with Barney Baker. Barney Baker told me outright that he was in on the crime and hinted that he may have even been in Dallas that day. And who else does Jack Ruby talk to? Nofio Pecora, a top lieutenant of Carlos Marcello. Then, when Ruby is on the news for shooting Oswald, I'm in the room with [a Mafia boss] who knows Ruby well, who's talked about him in the past in front of me. Well, guess what? When his buddy kills the most famous assassin in history live on TV, [the Mafia boss] does not say a fucking word. I'm watching him at that very moment. He does not even act surprised. Wouldn't you think he would say something like, 'Holy shit. My friend just shot Oswald?'"

<u>**Anonymous Mafioso**</u>

Farish Lamar Cody died in my home in 1983. Before he died, this is what the top enforcer of the McLaney gang and freelance violence specialist for Carlos Marcello, Santo Trafficante, and various branches of the Chicago Outfit told me.

The conspirators against Kennedy were the same conspirators who were already working together on Operation Mongoose: the New Orleans Mafia, Tampa Mafia, Chicago Mafia, Mike McLaney, Hoffa, and the Cubans. The involvement of rogue CIA elements with the McLaneys was implied. The decision was made after the Kennedys double-crossed the McLaneys and kept putting the screws to Carlos and Hoffa.

Tex Cody told Dale and me how the assassination was conducted in detail. To paraphrase my departed friend:

"The security around Kennedy was a joke, man. We took triangulated positions to ensure that there was a shot from every angle: one in the book depository where they said Oswald was, one on the grassy knoll, and another coming from the manhole on Elm Street. I was the gunman on the grassy knoll, though it was closer to the boxcars [the railway overpass] than people say.

"The shooting went without a fucking hitch. Afterwards, we fled according to the plan: the guy who came out of the manhole dropping back down into the sewer and the guy in the book depository going out back and fleeing down through Mexico. Trust me, you don't wanna know who the other two shooters were. One was a professional assassin who I know had done similar work before.

"As far as Oswald, he was just a patsy. A wannabe the Marcellos knew with a Marine background. They had assurance that they would be able to get rid of him real quick since Dallas was Carlos' town and, besides, it's not like the people in the government wanted a messy trial. Jack Ruby was the perfect solution: a Chicago Mob guy with ties to Carlos who was a police station hang-around. Ruby was already deeply in debt and had ass cancer [rectal cancer] and was gonna die anyway. They pay him off, lean on him a bit, and he whacks out Oswald. That ties up everything with a bow, and the next year Mike and Bill McLaney own a casino in Las Vegas and I'm helpin' to run the show."

Yes, you read right. Farish Cody, a man not known for concocting stories about his exploits, claimed credit for the most infamous unsolved crime in American history. That he was capable of and qualified for committing such an act is beyond dispute, and there is no more logical shooter than the top rifleman for Mike and Bill McLaney, the architects of the campaign to assassinate Castro. Tex Cody had all the necessary bona fides: he had a track record as a trustworthy enforcer and "specialist" with Carlos Marcello, Santo Trafficante, and the Chicago Outfit — and he was intimately involved with the CIA during Operation Mongoose and possibly earlier.

If anyone would have known if the McLaneys and Cuban exiles were involved in the Kennedy assassination, it would have been him. He was the perfect shooter.

Do you remember when I said nothing with my friends was simple? Yeah, Tex Cody makes a perfect JFK assassin in every way. Every way except one: according to penal records, Farish Lamar Cody was in jail in Indiana on a short bid for burglary on the day that Kennedy was assassinated and for months afterwards.

Seemingly, Tex was full of shit.

Or maybe not. When I did bids in state and federal jail during the golden age of the Mob, I was able to use my connections to get out of jail whenever I needed to. Cody definitely could have escaped, if the task was important enough, and I can't think of a better alibi.

Even if Tex did not actually pull the trigger, he would have been in a position to know if the McLaneys and the Cubans had been involved. I have other good reasons to believe his scenario. The first one is the simple fact that Dean Andrews, Carlos and Lee Harvey Oswald's attorney, later confided in me, after I pushed him hard enough, that Oswald was a patsy for the crime and that he had reason to believe that Carlos set him up for the trap. When I asked for more details, Dean got stuffy, as if suddenly realizing how foolish it was to be talking about this topic at all.

But then again, Dean Andrews was *definitely* a bullshit artist.

The next reason is that someone close to me, who was also very close to Carlos, came to me in a panic about a year after the assassination. According to this person, Carlos lost his temper when discussing Bobby Kennedy at the Town & Country and vowed to, "take care of him like we did his brutha."

On the same tip, Santo Trafficante's attorney, Frank Ragano, has come out and admitted to being an eyewitness to conversations in which Trafficante, Marcello, and Hoffa all implicated themselves in the conspiracy. According to Ragano, Trafficante specifically admitted to having Kennedy killed in a conspiracy with Carlos and Hoffa.

There's one more story I'd like to share that to my knowledge has never been published, though it was well known enough in the underworld that my writer for this book also heard it in interviews of Mafia associates outside of Louisiana. I myself have heard it from a member of the extended Marcello family. I cannot confirm or deny it, though I figure the fact that it's been in circulation in these circles makes it worth reporting.

The story goes that right before Oswald began hanging around Carlos Marcello, he met a woman who went by the name Katherine Hidell or Lidell in the Quarter. Knowing the Quarter, it was likely not her real name.

This woman happened to be the mistress of Peter Marcello, Carlos' most dangerous and vengeful brother. According to this story, Kathy took a liking to Oswald — the intensity of it is in some dispute. The Marcellos believed they were screwing, which Pete, being Italian, took quite personally.

This supposedly was the impetus for the closer attention paid to Oswald and was one reason why the Marcellos were so eager to set him up for a bloody fall. This story also offers an explanation for one of the great mysteries of the Kennedy assassination: why Oswald or someone pretending to be Oswald used the name "Alek J. Hidell" when ordering the mail-order rifle ostensibly used in the assassination. "Alek Hidell" is, of course, one letter off from being an anagram of "Kate Hidell."

Whether Oswald chose this name as a tribute, or whether it was chosen for him as one of Carlos' dark jokes, or whether the entire story is bullshit — don't ask me.

"We have been in repeated public conflicts with Orleans District Attorney Jim Garrison, who denies the existence in our city of probable organized crime. He and his staff have blocked our efforts to have grand juries probe the influence of the Cosa Nostra and other syndicate operations."

Aaron Kohn

Head of the New Orleans Metropolitan Crime Commission

I have one last loose end to tie up. Let's talk about good old Jim Garrison, the crusading hero who selflessly chased the truth about the Kennedy assassination.

What a crock of shit! How that transparently sleazy cocksucker got away with laundering his record I'll never know. I know that I will be dismissed as a CIA operative by Garrison's fans for the crime of exposing him as a fraud and a con man, but, trust me, baby, there ain't no conspiracy less believable than the idea that Frenchy Brouillette is a CIA spook.

To those of you who believe that Jim Garrison was really an honest crusader for the truth, here are a few questions that you can answer for me:

Why did Garrison hire publicly-disgraced dirty cop, gigolo, and gay bar owner Pershing Gervais as his lead investigator?

Why did Garrison keep Gervais as his investigator despite constant reports that Gervais was collecting bribes and payoffs from vice operators across the city — including me? Why did Garrison just shrug when I told him that the money Gervais was demanding was extortionate?

Why, in Garrison's eleven years as DA, did he not bring a single case against Carlos Marcello, one of the biggest criminals in American history?

Why did Garrison refuse to prosecute one of Diamond Jim Moran's sons when he shot a police officer over a parking ticket? Why was Garrison allowed to run up a bill worth thousands of dollars at La Louisiane and never asked to pay?

To get right to the point, Garrison was a crooked, lazy, and sloppy district attorney who was owned wholesale by Carlos Marcello. I know for a fact that Garrison was corruptible because I paid him off myself. In return for access to call girls and occasionally callboys, old Jim Garrison dropped or slow-pedaled a number of cases which involved me or my friends.

The jive rap on Garrison's crusade against fellow New Orleans homosexuals David Ferrie and Clay Shaw for the murder of JFK was that it derailed his bright future in politics. Nothing could be further from the truth. The Kennedy Assassination trial saved a doomed career and fulfilled some of Jim Garrison's dearest dreams.

Garrison's term as DA had been a catastrophe. Elected on promises to reform the city and fight crime and corruption, Garrison instead let the DA's office fall into disarray while he attempted to raise his profile with a petty media feud against the NOPD. Since they both refused to take on Carlos Marcello, Garrison and Superintendent of Police Joe Giarrusso instead engaged in tit-for-tat raids of each other's favorite underworld campaign contributors. The damage this feud did to the French Quarter, which practically became a slum, discredited Garrison forever as a major political figure.

The feud with Giarrusso also sealed Garrison's legal fate. Every powerbroker in New Orleans besides Carlos Marcello became determined to clip Garrison's wings and bring him up on corruption charges related to the protection racket Pershing Gervais operated on his behalf. The fix was in to stuff Garrison in a jail cell on corruption charges.

Faced with certain electoral and legal doom, Garrison had an epiphany. If he rebranded himself as "the one DA fearless enough to bring Kennedy's assassins to justice," then he could redeem his credibility as a reformer and discredit any future charges brought against him as a retaliatory propaganda campaign — all thanks to single publicity stunt.

If this sounds like a wild plot, remind yourself that his ridiculous scheme worked! Garrison went from a joke, a publicity-chasing huckster DA, into an American hero, and he escaped the eventual federal prosecution for bribery despite strong evidence.

I don't know, maybe Garrison also sincerely believed David Ferrie and Clay Shaw were involved in the crime. It is impossible to know. It seems fishy to me that Garrison believed the murderers of the president both came from his and Gervais's underground queer French Quarter circle. Perhaps there was bad blood there, or perhaps Garrison intentionally selected two patsies who he knew he could instantaneously discredit if they fought back.

My bet is that Garrison initially had no idea that this publicity stunt would in any way lead back to Carlos Marcello. As his stint in the DA's office proved, the Jolly Green Giant paid very little attention to Mafia affairs, and he knew nothing of Carlos' plots. Garrison most likely had no idea about Ferrie's affiliation with Carlos in 1962 and 1963 because, when that fact became public knowledge, the Jolly Green Giant made sure to relentlessly deny the possibility that Carlos had anything to do with the assassination.

Shortly afterwards, Ferrie died under extremely suspicious circumstances. According to the coroner, Ferrie wrote two suicide notes and then, once finished, coincidentally died of a wholly natural brain aneurysm. I always thought that was a pretty amateurish hit: halfway through the murder, whoever did it apparently changed their minds from "suicide" to "aneurysm" without getting rid of the suicide notes.

Now that Ferrie was out of the way, Marcello had every reason to *encourage* Garrison to continue his witch trials. With Garrison in charge, Marcello was guaranteed that the final outcome would be an expensive, exhaustive, high-profile investigation into the Kennedy assassination that — just like the Warren Commission, overseen by good old J. Edgar Hoover— would pronounce Carlos

Marcello a humble tomato salesman who was cleared of any involvement in the crime.

Whoever else Garrison implicated would be just one more patsy to deflect attention away from Carlos and his confederates. Likewise, if any prosecutor ever did try to indict Carlos for the assassination, he could rely on Garrison's findings and call on Garrison as an expert witness to provide reasonable doubt. More likely still, after Garrison's comically failed prosecution of debonair dungeon master Clay Shaw, no district attorney or state's attorney could touch the Kennedy assassination without immediately being painted with the same kooky conspiracy theorist brush as the Jolly Green Giant.

Far from breaking open the Kennedy assassination, Jim Garrison made it practically impossible for the real culprits to ever be indicted and convicted. The title of one of the most famous books to ever bestow sainthood on Jim Garrison's watermelon head was all too appropriate: *Farewell to Justice.*

Chapter X

The Notorious Vice Operators

1964-1974

"Police made a series of lightning raids early today and said five of the most notorious vice operators in the history of New Orleans were arrested. Charged with pandering and public bribery, police said, were Mike Roach, a bar operator [...] Kenneth [sic] Brouillette, 29, a service station operator [...] and Sherman Keaton, a taxi cab driver and owner of a Jefferson Parish lounge, The Black Door."

Corpus Christi Times
July 22, 1965

BABY, IT TOOK A FEW TRIPS TO JAIL TO TEACH ME THE SECRET OF A GOOD LIFE: DO EASY TIME AND NEVER LEAVE HATING. If you follow those two old convict rules, you'll always get the most possible out of life.

Those were the days when a prison sentence could be a fondly remembered rite of passage for a gangster. Young crooks really don't know what they're missing. The American prison system once was designed with a gangster's general comfort in mind. That was one of the great benefits of working hand-in-hand with the government — on the off chance that you were accidentally arrested like a common perp, the prison system was designed to treat the organized criminal like the VIP you were until you could obtain pardon or parole.

Carlos Marcello always used to brag to me that punching an

FBI agent and getting sentenced for a short stay at the Springfield Medical Center for Federal Prisoners in 1968 was a great benefit to his health and peace of mind. When Carlos arranged for his early parole, he came home fifty pounds lighter and as tan and fit as a fighter. No one had ever seen the man more relaxed, easygoing, and energetic; he looked like he was returning from a health spa vacation. It's no coincidence that, in those days, the slang dealing with jail sentences sounded like a vacation: "going on a trip," "stopping off at Club Fed," "takin' a break," "headin' upriver."

The threat of imprisonment did not cast much of a shadow over the New Orleans Mafia of the 1950s and 1960s. We understood that we were breaking the law, but so was everyone else. Often the cops were our accomplices. The chance of doing serious time seemed remote and generally *was* remote for the simple reason that the police stood to lose money if we were jailed. You could get away with the most ostentatious crimes in the French Quarter right in front of the police. I once saw the Quarter beat cops cheering as one Conforto brother held down a civilian so that another Conforto brother could jump off the bar and hit a flying knee drop onto the civilian's head.

By 1964, I was rolling in so much cash and popularity that I felt like one of America's most beloved celebrities. That's how cool it was in those days to be a gangster — no one was treated better. I hung out with the highest paid entertainer in the world, Liberace, and that man did not receive the respect and treatment I did in New Orleans. And don't forget, in the scheme of things, I was just the top pimp in the South; I was *not* a Carlos Marcello or Frank Costello or Mike McLaney, men who lived their lives as if they were dictators who answered to no one.

Still, I had no trouble convincing myself that I was a big deal. I could not walk down any major thoroughfare without hearing shouts of "Hey dere, Frenchy!" and "There's Mr. New Orleans!" and "Hey, good lookin'!" Thanks to my hacks and jewel thieves hookups and the connections I made at Dutch Kraut's old

Bourbon Street tailor shop, no one in New Orleans was more stylish. I usually won the annual Best Dressed Man on Bourbon Street contest in a walk. My girl Satan was renowned as the toughest dog in the city, and, with my powerful biceps, I was the undisputed champion of the New Orleans Athletic Club's regular chin-up contests.

My social circle contributed to my big head. I really can't tell you how easy it was to convince yourself that you were some sort of demigod when you were always tooling around with Carlos or Joe Marcello. The treatment you received was just sick, baby — *everyone* was your friend and admirer.

I also got a kick out of visiting Norma Wallace at her restaurant and stopping the party dead. The moment I entered, Norma forgot her other customers and focused all of her attention on me like I was Frank Sinatra stopping to say hello. All the VIP politicians and tycoons in the place, who came to get a voyeuristic buzz from being so close to an underworld legend like Norma, would be craning their necks to get an eyeful of me and my jewels as they whispered gossip to each other.

Even actual celebrities massaged my ego. When singer Aaron Neville and his brothers first became local stars, their family would send me free tickets to all of their concerts — not because they were clients, but because I was such a local icon that my attendance would give the shows buzz. I struck up such a friendship with the Neville Brothers that every year for Jazz Fest they would send me twenty free backstage passes to the event. When I arrived backstage, one of them would run to grab coffee for me to enjoy.

Fats Domino was another admirer of mine. The Fat Man would joke with me that I was his style guru, that I even had the black folk beat when it came to being on the cutting edge of Cadillac and jewelry appreciation. One year, for my annual new convertible, I purchased a hot pink Cadillac like no one had ever seen. Within a week, Fats rapped on my door like a maniac, screaming through the wall, "Frenchy, I need dat car, boy! Let me have dat pink Caddy, or I'm-ah gonna take it!"

"Okay, okay," I said as I opened the door, probably shirtless and groggy from a long night. "You want it, Fat Man, then you take it. Make me an offer, and make it fair." The Fat Man paid me a fair price, and I bought myself a new Pontiac convertible as a replacement. That deal sealed a close friendship with the Fat Man ever since, and he had the good taste to tell that tale all around town, building up my legend as the baddest New Orleans soul brother ever born white.

Cadillacs really were my lucky brand when it came to making celebrity pals. It was thanks to another Cadillac —this one red— that I got hooked up with rock icon Jerry Lee Lewis and his sleazebag televangelist cousin Jimmy Swaggart.

I was driving with two girls to some high-paying gig when I came to a wild-looking honky-tonk called Blue's Red Devil. In the parking lot was a mint condition, gorgeous, red 1959 Cadillac convertible. The only other person I knew with a red '59 Caddy that pretty was me, so I swerved off the strip and into the parking lot to find the owner and shake his hand.

I waltzed in with a girl on either arm and said to the barman, "Baby, point out the owner of that 1959 red Caddy. I want to buy that man a drink."

"It's that asshole over there," the grumpy barman said with a scowl. To further show his disgust, the redneck spit on the floor and accidentally lost hold of the toothpick he was chewing on, which made him look like a bit of a geek. I looked down the bar and saw that the target of his disgust was a very sweaty man with red eyes and a curly blond pompadour dressed in outrageous pimp clothes. I instantly recognized him as one of my idols, Jerry Lee Lewis, who became one of the most famous rock stars in the world despite growing up poor only a few miles away from Marksville.

Just by wanting to talk to Jerry Lee, I had unintentionally done the great man a great favor. After it came out that the "Killer" of rock 'n' roll had scandalously married his thirteen-year-old cousin, he became a pariah in most of America. Though the news was hardly fresh by the time I met him, he had apparently done nothing but drink and take shit from bullying locals at Blue's Red Devil all night before I came along. "Man," he said to me in a slow drink-shot voice, "you are the first man to talk to me like a person all day!"

We became fast friends and partied the night away. He appreciated that I was not the judgmental type, and I appreciated meeting the only white boy from the backwater parishes who had ever figured out how to be stylish, sexy, and cool without being born to Edwin's and my family. In return for befriending him on one of his loneliest nights, Jerry Lee did me the service of hooking me up with his cousin, radio-minister Jimmy Swaggart, who he promised would be a great client.

Jerry was right; Swaggart would carelessly throw money at me for decades until he was finally caught on Airline Highway with a working girl and lost his multimillion-dollar televangelism empire. Jerry and I always have a good laugh about that old hypocrite whenever we see each other.

My reputation grew to such legendary proportions that even the press came calling in the person of my old best friend, Bill Elder. Bill was not yet some muckety-muck TV anchor, just a hard-luck young journalist looking for his break. Playing on our old camaraderie, he offered me his entire savings if I would grant him a tell-all interview about my incredible rise in the underworld or give him the rights to my life story. I graciously declined, though I *was* happy to see the envy and confusion in my old buddy's eyes.

"Kent, I have to tell ya," Bill said as he looked down in his coffee, feeling inadequate. "I don't know how you've done what you've done. Making the money you're making, you must have millions stashed away. You could probably retire tomorrow."

"Far from it, baby!" I said with what I thought was dead-cool indifference. "I live one day at a time, and I live the shit out of every one of those suckers!"

"Man, you're telling me you don't have *anything* stowed away for a rainy day?"

"Not a single red penny, Bill," I said with the same fool's confidence. I should have recalled that Bill was always much smarter than me and figured that maybe he had a good point, but I had grown too arrogant to second-guess myself. "Who needs savings when there's new money to be made every day?"

"Aren't you afraid of what might happen if you go to jail? Don't you think it would be wise to have some money stashed in case the police come and take everything?" Bill asked with that squinting leer that I remembered all too well.

It was the same leer that Bill gave me in Marksville when we were kids, that look he got whenever he wondered to himself if I was afflicted with some form of mental retardation.

"Baby, trust *me*," I said, getting testy, "I know the ropes. I know how dis goddamn town works. I ain't seen the inside of a jail cell in over a decade on the streets, and I don't think I ever will. People like me, people who know who to talk to and how to talk to 'em, baby, we don't go to the police station unless it's to drop off a bribe."

Bill Elder may not have been as rich as me, and he may not have been as popular as me ... but Bill was *always* much smarter than me.

"In the old days, you couldn't open a whorehouse, you couldn't open a lottery shop, you couldn't even beg on Canal Street. . . unless the police said okay. That was crime that was organized."
Pershing Gervais

Baby, if you told me beforehand to think of the least likely charge that I would ever get pinched for, *bribing a NOPD officer* would be number one without question. I'd have said, "Are you kiddin' me? Who is going to arrest Old Frenchy for paying a cop? *Another cop?* I'm bribing all of 'em!"

My first trip to jail began when crotchety old Mike Roach came to me in July of 1964 with an offer. Ever since Garrison's election, the NOPD Vice Squad had been acting up, hassling the hacks, roughing up bellboys, and pinching working girls to make a show of enforcing the prostitution laws that would have crippled the New Orleans economy if they were actually taken seriously.

The Vice Squad would do PR stunt shit like this just to get space in the *Times Picayune* and neutralize Jim Garrison's attacks against police corruption. They'd occasionally stage "sting operations" by sending a plainclothesman around to ask each operator for two or three girls who could eat a charge and spend a night in jail. It was a real low-class operation, and Mike Roach decided to see if he could bring it to a close by working out a new payment plan with the Vice Squad. In return for the established pimps' agreement to make larger bribe payments, Mike asked for the Vice Squad to lay off the hacks and tip us off as to what hotels were under surveillance.

Unfortunately for me, Mike Roach was no seasoned political operator like Gasper Gulotta. The old pimp's first mistake was to give the vice cops a low-ball bribe offer. Nothing raises a NOPD officer's temperature more than a low-ball bribe; it's an insult to his dignity and manhood. That's why Carlos was so ridiculously generous with the cops — he knew from experience that one short payment could cost him a nickel or dime behind bars. The Vice Squad was so incensed by Mike Roach's cheapness that they decided to make an example of him.

I should've stayed out of it, but Roach had convinced Sherman Keaton and a couple minor players that he had brokered such a sweet deal that anyone who was not a party to the agreement would be run out of business by the cops. That sounded like bullshit to me — I made too many cops too much money to get run out of business — but I decided to chip in just to be safe.

"What the hell," I told Mike, "it's just 'nutha bribe. I'll help pay your way. Jus' keep my goddamn name out of it until we see dat the pigs are gonna keep their word."

Well, a week later, I received a phone call from the Vice Squad. "Hey, Frenchy, thanks for playing ball. Stay away from the Hotel Monteleone this week." Apparently, "keep my name out of it" was a request that hard-of-hearing Mike Roach loosely interpreted.

Roach's second mistake was to showboat by arranging for the meeting with the vice cops to "seal the deal" at Carlos Marcello's Churchill Farms swamp camp. As the former house pimp for the Marcello family, Roach was able to convince Carlos to let him use his camp for the cash handoff to impress the vice cops and intimidate them into keeping their side of the bargain. All Roach actually managed to do was make a lifelong enemy out of Carlos when the bust came down.

Since I was a named party to the deal whether I liked it or not, I decided to go to Churchill Farms to make sure that Roach didn't say something so stupid that I would end up paying for it. This proved to be *my* mistake. When my wrists were put in bracelets for the crimes of pandering and public bribery, I had the added pain-in-the-ass of being arrested on Carlos Marcello's property.

True to form, that shameless cocksucker Jim Garrison went peacocking for the press when the bust was announced. Though I know for a fact that the NOPD Vice Squad kept the undercover operation secret from his office since they knew of the S&M DA's close ties to the sex rackets, Garrison did his best to claim all the credit. To ensure that he was the one quoted by the journalists, Garrison went over-the-top in blackening our names, calling us "the most notorious vice operators in the history of New Orleans" and "the kingpins of prostitution."

I was featured in a big photo spread in *The New Orleans Times Picayune*, taking a perp walk with four other pimps. At the time, I thought I was very clever for impersonating crooks in the movies by covering my face as the cameras snapped; I thought of saving my family in Marksville the embarrassment. Of course, now that I have this book, I sure wish I would have smiled big for the camera so I'd have that photo to show off how pretty I once was.

From my jail cell, I sent word through Dean Andrews that I didn't appreciate the irony of a DA, whom I regularly pandered to and bribed, prosecuting me for pandering and public bribery. Garrison sent word back that the bust was not his doing and that he was going to offer us all a sweetheart eighteen-month plea deal, which was the best he could do without giving the Vice Squad ammo to blast him in the press.

I told Dean Andrews to tell Garrison to go fuck himself. I was going to fight the case. Eighteen months was at least a year-and-a-half longer than I ever planned to spend behind bars. Gangsters like me didn't go to jail; at that point, I had never seen Carlos or Joe or Sam Saia or Dutch Kraut do any time at all, so why should I? I was going to trial just like I did with Mr. Lucky Dog and the Holy Roller.

"That's true, Frenchy," Dean said, smiling since he was in on a joke that I had not been let in on yet. "There are just two problems with you going to trial. One is that you will ruin the universal plea deal with the other guys; that means, if you're not down, Mike Roach and Sherman Keaton are going to be facing major jail time with their prior convictions. You might be responsible for getting them ten-to-twenty."

"Fuck 'em," I barked, furious at those fat old shitheads for getting me in trouble. "Those shit-for-brains can eat it."

"One other problem, Frenchy," Dean said, barely able to contain his laughter. Dean was always a giddy little weirdo when bad things happened to his friends. "I had a talk with a friend of ours. And let's just say that friend of ours doesn't necessarily want to see his vacation home be the subject of a major public bribery trial. Our friend doesn't like bad press."

Carlos. The man was very touchy about his 6400-acre spread in Jefferson Parish. He had a history of making his friends take the fall to protect Churchill Farms from bad publicity.

My buddy Woody worked for Carlos on Churchill Farms, killing and skinning alligators in the surrounding swamps. Since it was illegal to sell Louisiana alligator skins, Carlos would send Woody's hides to one of his import-export companies, where they would be packaged in old wooden boxes stamped with Spanish company names and sent to clothing companies as completely legal caiman alligator imports from Latin America. When the feds latched onto this scheme, Woody was pressured into "voluntarily" taking the fall and exonerating Carlos of all knowledge of the scam. Without a trial, Churchill Farms was protected from further bad press.

Shielding Churchill Farms from outside publicity was worth millions of dollars to Carlos. Carlos had a plan to turn the land into the site for a sports stadium that would host the home games for the NFL team that Carlos was diligently working to get for New Orleans, through Mike McLaney's contacts. When the New Orleans Saints finally came to town, the first owner was a buddy of Carlos Marcello's who could always be seen hanging out with Sammy Marcello and Diamond Jim Moran's kids at La Louisiane.

So, I took the plea deal. Before I went to jail, I visited Carlos and let him know what I was doing. Carlos was looking particularly troll-like and grumpy that day, mostly because he partially blamed me for Mike Roach's fuckup even though Dean had made it clear to him that I was just an incidental party. Nonetheless, I was taking one for the team, so he promised to "take care of things" for me in the joint. I had no earthly idea what he meant.

After entrusting my movable belongings to the English Queen, asking Snake Gonzales to look after two of my old ladies, and lighting a couple hundred candles at St. Louis Cathedral in an attempt to bribe the Virgin Mary into sparing my mom all knowledge of my incarceration, I reported to Orleans Parish Prison. I was frankly terrified; being a pretty social animal ever since I arrived in the French Quarter, I thought I might die of boredom and alcohol deprivation in the clink. You might think I would have been worried about the lack of women in jail, but, after a few years of living with a few dozen oversexed broads, I was happy to detox my rocks.

Not since I first arrived in the French Quarter or lost my virginity did I ever enter a situation with less of an idea of what to expect. Within minutes of being booked, I was called into the warden's office. The fat old warden lit up when he saw me. "So *you're* the boy known as Frenchy!" he said as he damn near shook the knuckles off my hand. *Shit*, I thought to myself, *I'm even famous in jail.*

"Well, Mr. Broo-lay, you sure as hell have some powerful friends. If you ever have any problems here, you come straight to me, and I'll take care of it. Let me know if you need *anything* to make your stay more comfortable."

Now I understood what Carlos meant — I had the warden as my servant! Testing the length of my leash, I made a request right away. "You know, Mr. Warden, there is something you can do for me. I'm mighty hungry, and I've got a hankering for fried chicken. And a drink."

"Shit, boy, that's no problem!" The warden picked up the phone and told his secretary to send in a guard. A guard appeared in a nervous hurry, which impressed me; I liked a man who ran a tight ship. "Take this boy out to get some fuckin' fried chicken and booze on the double. And make sure he brings back some for the prison gate captains, and he brings me back a girl." Less than an hour after arriving in prison, I headed right back out the door to grab lunch and a piece of ass for the warden.

This just about set the tone of my first stay behind bars. I never wanted for booze, fried chicken, conjugal visits, or strolls in the sunlight while in Orleans Parish Jail. To my surprise, I came to really enjoy the stress-free ease of life in the concrete jungle. I had all the time in the world to lift weights, sip hooch, and bullshit with other crooks, so all I needed was a dog, and I would have been in heaven. When I got horny, I called the warden, and he escorted Ronnie, my old lady at the time, to come see me in my cell.

The only downside to life in jail was the awful cafeteria food, but I figured out quick how to solve that problem. In addition to our prepared meals, inmates could buy snack food from the *zuzu*, a little concessions cart that would be wheeled around once a day. I had Ronnie bring me in a fat wad of cash during one conjugal visit, and afterwards I went to the warden's office and bought control of the zuzu.

The zuzu was the source of all power in the can. Now, I could order absolutely anything from the outside world to stock the zuzu, and I kept a veritable supermarket in my cell with me at all times. I also had the ability to place a zuzu embargo on any inmate that pissed me off, which made me the ruler of the yard. To get the most out of my investment, I increased the prices on everything for sale and skimmed the difference.

Since I could take anything from the zuzu for free, the cash I skimmed was worthless to me in jail, so I put it to use on the outside. I sent weekly payoffs to the sheriff of Orleans Parish, who then sent word to the warden that I could have my own phone and complete freedom of action. With a phone line and ready spending money, I had everything I needed to go back into business. I had Ronnie get the gang back together at my apartment, and she circulated my number in prison to all of my favorite hacks and bellhops.

Soon, I was making a thousand dollars a night pimping from my jail cell. The best part of this equation was that I made all that money without actually having to deal with any call girls, hacks, or johns myself; all I did was answer the phone. Life was pretty much perfect. For a while, I considered beating up an inmate to extend my sentence, but then I got a visit from the sheriff, who regretfully informed me that the FBI had tapped my phone line and that I would have to quit pimping.

For that reason alone, I was relieved when Dean Andrews

visited a few days later and told me that he had secured my early release. Like Carlos a few years later, my few months stay in prison had returned me to the street a healthier, happier, and rejuvenated man. If my prison stay was supposed to deter me from resuming my life of crime, it definitely failed. If my prison stay was supposed to get my physique in tip-top condition for the 1965 Mr. New Orleans contest, then it definitely succeeded!

> "What the fuck do you think you're doing?
> You stupid son of a bitch, you Uptown asshole,
> what the *fuck* do you think you're doing?
> If you and your men are not out of here in the next minute,
> you and every goddamned cop in here is *fired.*"
> **New Orleans Mayor DeLesseps "Chep" Morrison**
> On the occasion of having his stag party raided
> by Superintendent of Police Provosty Dayries in the 1950s
> As quoted by Christine Wiltz

My next brush with the law was probably my favorite since all of the crooks escaped serious punishment while a judge wound up in a pretty tight bind.

The judge in question was my client Edward A. Haggerty, a slobby old Irish drunk with a quick wit, a volatile temper, and a healthy appetite for hookers. Haggerty became one of my favorite clients when he called a recess during a murder trial solely to order a hooker from me, which I thought showed a proper New Orleans attitude towards his job and the law. Where else would a judge get so horny during a *murder trial* that he could not wait any longer for relief?

Haggerty attained fame as the criminal district court judge who presided over Jim Garrison's circus sideshow trial of Clay Shaw for the assassination of JFK. For those counting, that means just about *everyone* in the most famous trial in New Orleans history was a client of mine: the DA (Garrison), the defendant (Shaw), the judge (Haggerty), the most embarrassing witness (Dean Andrews), and the accomplice in the crime (David Ferrie). I sure got around in those days.

Nine months after that silly show trial ended in the acquittal of Clay Shaw, I was having dinner with big-time bookmaker Hank Lumberg when Judge Haggerty strolled over to our table. Despite his irascible personality, I had always liked Haggerty because he was corruptible and disreputable. The man would always show up late to court, looking disheveled, unshaven, and hungover — my sort of jackass. I also liked that Haggerty made no secret that he thought Garrison was on the verge of exploding from being so full of shit.

Haggerty leaned over the table in front of Lumberg and whispered into my ear. "Hey there, Frenchy, real glad to see ya. You see, we're having a bachelor's party, and we need as many girls as you got. The chairman of the girlie committee flaked out on me, so I mean it, just send over *as many as you got.* Send them to the DeVille Motel on Tulane Avenue, alright?"

This was known as a "get out of jail free" gig. Stag parties were one of the grand traditions of New Orleans political life, an illegal ceremony that sealed political and business alliances among the elite with mutually incriminating blackmail material. Just about every faction in the city's judicial, political, and law enforcement community would get together every couple months to toast their bond by congregating in a hotel suite or government conference room for a night of food, drinks, porno, and, occasionally, orgies.

While a crowd of rowdy men in business shirts guzzled beer and yelled out lewd commentary, an aide would play grainy, illegal, European porn reels using a wall projector. Afterwards, the best parties would conclude with a live sex show between hookers followed by "one-on-one" performances in the bathroom or closet.

Besides working for Carlos Marcello, the highest form of prestige that a New Orleans pimp could attain was being hired as the entertainment provider at one of these elite stag parties. Any pimp who sold hookers to a room full of judges, politicians, business tycoons, and police officials came into possession of a bona fide *fuckload* of political capital. Each stag party you handled was usually good for one felony that you could get squashed.

I sent three downright beautiful girls to the DeVille, which was owned by some of Carlos' buddies, in the hope of securing Haggerty's lifelong loyalty. At the party was a nerdy-looking man with a microphone and radio transmitter hidden under his tie. After some food and porno, Haggerty stood up and yelled, "Why go on watching films when we can have the real thing? Who's going to go with the girls first?" Haggerty asked as the room erupted into cheers and whistles. My three girls stood before the ten drunk, chain-smoking, leering New Orleans powerbrokers and prepared to strip down.

As they got down to business, newspaper and TV reporters got into position along with a detachment of the NOPD Vice Squad. Right as the action was going to get good, the Vice Squad stampeded into the motel room.

Haggerty did not go calmly; the tubby, silver-haired, eyeglasses-wearing, old Irishman bull-rushed outside and assaulted three police officers out of spite. It turned out that the alcoholic judge was in even worse shape than the NOPD officers because he was soon tackled and handcuffed. As blood spilled from his forehead onto the asphalt, the furious NOPD officers called over the TV cameramen to get a good look at the squealing, foaming, bleeding judge in his moment of humiliation.

Now, you may be asking why there was already an army of newspaper and TV reporters at the scene of the bust. Well, that's how Jim Garrison did business; if he was in on a bust, you better damn well believe it was going to be televised. For Judge Haggerty, it turns out the cost of disrespecting the Clay Shaw monkey show was public humiliation and charges of obscenity, soliciting prostitution, and resisting arrest.

Garrison wore a shit-eating grin for weeks afterwards.

If there's one thing a devoted perv like Garrison should have realized, it's that nothing unites New Orleans judges, politicians, and police officials better than the defense of the unholy rite of stag parties. This was just one more example of the Jolly Green Cocksucker not playing by the rules, injecting chaos into an otherwise stable system for his own selfish reasons.

Jim Garrison be damned, the people that mattered in the Big Easy were not going to let pass a precedent that normalized raids on innocent good fun orgies. "You might as well ban beignets, Mardi Gras, café au lait, and raw oysters if you're going to do away with stag parties," one politician said to me.

Within twenty-four hours of Haggerty's public disgrace, the word was out that the fix was in and that he would be fast-tracked to redemption — no matter how many cops he assaulted. The cops should have known better than to disrupt an innocent motel room stag party and orgy. Just over a month after the arrest, Haggerty found himself acquitted of all charges in record time.

Operating on Carlos Marcello's suggestion to leave town while Haggerty was in the news, I temporarily relocated to Houma, a modest town southwest of New Orleans, and opened a brothel. Houma was one of those outlying, generally quiet spots where Carlos was God. He had long-entertained the notion of opening up "a wide open house" in Houma since it was only an hour away from New Orleans, yet the cops and politicians were much cheaper to bribe.

For the rock-bottom rate of $300-a-week, Carlos secured full immunity from the sheriff to run as many call girls as I wanted from a nice suburban home. To encourage me to stay, Carlos made out-of-the-way trips to Houma, saying over and over again how often he came down this way and how much we'd be seeing each other if I stayed put. Thanks to Carlos' shameless campaign to butter me up, the girls who were with me in Houma thought that Carlos was the happiest, sweetest, and friendliest man they ever met. That grumpy little guido practically bounced through the door when he visited me in Houma.

I was hesitant to inform Carlos that I was a French Quarter boy at heart and that Houma could never keep me. So, in early 1970, I just cooled the heels of my alligator-skin boots in my suburban bordello, which more closely resembled a poorly maintained frat house than Norma Wallace's elegant bawdy house. One night, my most reliable girl came to me and whispered, so that no one else could hear, that she saw the owners of a local fruit shop stashing wads of cash in their washer and dryer at the back of the store.

Since I completely owned the police out in Houma, this gig seemed like a no-lose proposition. I called a team of highwaymen based in Oklahoma whom I trusted, and invited them down for an overnight job. I then visited the sheriff and slipped him a few hundred to close the roads with patrol cars to and from the store at midnight on the night of the crime. There would be no interruptions.

At midnight, my two highwaymen kicked down the door of the fruit shop wearing black ski masks, black turtleneck sweaters, black jeans, and black jackboots. Unfortunately, they ruined their nighttime camouflage by carrying burlap vegetable sacks. Anyway, these two seasoned professionals hurtled over the cashier's counter and rushed to the washer and dryer in the backroom. When they opened the appliances, they discovered that the girl's information was correct: both machines were filled with money — pennies, nickels, and dimes. That's small towns for you.

Making the best of a ridiculous situation, the boys filled their bags to the brims with small change and shuffled slowly back into the night. By the time they returned to my place, the highwaymen were completely empty-handed: their heavy-duty potato sacks had popped under the weight and spilled the change into the street. Feeling responsible for their wasted time, I handed them a few hundred apiece, which, when combined with the police bribes, put me down nearly a thousand dollars on the job.

At least someone was robbed successfully.

After this escapade, I decided that my time playing for small stakes in small towns was done. I returned to New Orleans and did my best to expand my business to Chicago and New York.

"Mr. Brouillette gave his occupation in the past as illegally training racing horses; he stated, however, at this time he was not employed. Mr. Brouillette jokingly stated, however, that he knows every prostitute in New Orleans and the Jefferson Parish area; he would not give any details relative to his knowledge of so many prostitutes."

FBI Document 31-8777
Filed February 8, 1971

It is my duty to regretfully inform you that you are reading a book co-written by a man convicted of violating the White-Slave Traffic Act of 1910. Yes, according to the United States government, I am a slave trafficker, and, more specifically, a trafficker of white slave bitches. This idea, of course, is a gigantic load of bullshit, but it makes for great cocktail party chitchat. "Oh, you went to Harvard? That's nice, baby; I'm a federally - convicted slave trafficker."

You would think that, at some point in the development of our country, the government would have found the chance to rename the statute that prevents trafficking women across state borders for prostitution to something less outdated, but I guess the politicians had other pressing business. Some people call it the "Mann Act," but that's not how that charge appears on a federal rap sheet.

You can imagine the response of Carlos and the New Orleans Mafia wiseguys to this conviction. "Goddamit, Frenchy, we had newfound respect for you until we heard the color of the slaves!" When I tried to explain that it was not a real slave-trading charge, but just a Mann Act violation, I worried Carlos might get confused with the term and think that I had gone queer on him like Jim Garrison.

At least I got this bum rap thanks to my greatest client of all time — it would have been a real bitch to ruin my reputation over a penny-ante score. Nope, this score was *the big one*: Avondale Shipyards, one of the few companies that built the United States Navy's fleet and the largest employer in the state of Louisiana besides Carlos Marcello.

Based in the Marcello family's ultimate stronghold, Westwego, Avondale was one of Carlos' most powerful business allies in the state. It's no coincidence that Pelican Tomato's top multimillion-dollar client was the same U.S. Navy that gave Avondale hundreds of millions of dollars in government grants. It was also no accident that, when Avondale decided to hire a sex-rackets operator to help corrupt admirals, Department of Defense bureaucrats, government contractors, and politicians, they retained the services of Carlos' sex rackets lieutenant, Frenchy Brouillette.

For eight years, I received at least $2000-a-week from Avondale, eventually totaling around a million dollars. The money came in a variety of ways, some of it sent via check to my shell company, Bayou Catering. In return, I was on constant call; at any time, I would be required to send as many girls as they requested to anywhere in the world where Avondale representatives were meeting with people who had the power to help obtain lucrative contracts for the shipyard.

The girls' job would be to dress up as prim and proper Avondale secretaries who the Avondale big wigs would introduce to whomever they were trying to charm into diverting money to the company. While supposedly never revealing themselves as call girls, my little secretaries were supposed to find a way to organically tumble into bed with their marks. The next day, you wouldn't believe how well-disposed all those admirals and government bureaucrats would be to Avondale Shipyards without suspecting that they had been worked over by a professional.

"But tell the girls not to be too easy," Avondale President Henry "Zack" Carter told me. "I don't want it to be suspicious."

This is not necessarily as easy as it seems; getting prostitutes to act like prim and proper corporate secretaries was a pretty tall acting order by itself. Sometimes, the girls would focus so intently on playing a secretary that they would forget to play a slut, and the night would end without sex. I'd get an irate call from Zack Carter, "Frenchy, I said don't be easy, but I didn't say play hard to get! Those girls need to make sure they get got by the end of the night!"

In spite of a few missed connections, everything went beautifully for Zack and me for eight years. I made a cool million, Zack got more government contracts than ever, and a shitload of sexually repressed admirals fell in love with shy secretaries with the bodies of bikini models. It was a great time for everyone.

It began to come to an end in late 1970, when one of my call girls turned rat on me. I should have known better: she was an airline hostess on the side, and I always had bad luck with stewardesses. I slept around the French Quarter for years without catching so much as a single crab, but one night with an airline hostess got me a full-blown dose of gonorrhea. From that time on, I swore never to trust stewardesses.

I made an exception for the girl I called Brains, due to her college degree, whose good looks earned my trust quicker than good acts ever could have. I took one look at her face and body and said, "Well, clearly *this* airline hostess is trustworthy."

Unfortunately, poor Brains got the silly idea to use her book learning to forge checks and got caught by the FBI in Baton Rouge. Instead of doing the honorable thing and eating a tiny jail sentence, the girl gave up Avondale Shipyards, shitting away a $2000-per-week check for me. I would have preferred for her to just rat me out and leave poor Zack Carter and his millions of dollars alone.

Brains, my old lady Jackie, and another girl took a trip to Chicago and then another to New York in early 1971 to meet

Avondale clients. They were busted in New York to prove that the crimes crossed state lines, and I was facing federal racketeering and white- slavery charges. The FBI came to me and offered to give me a free ride like Brains if I flipped on Zack Carter. I may not have any brains, but I definitely had balls; I told the G-man to fuck off.

So I went to prison, and Avondale relied on its congressional power to have the investigation squashed. My FBI file contains a letter, covered in scribbles, which was sent directly to J. Edgar Hoover from Congressman Patrick Caffery (D-LA) regarding the Avondale mess. I'm sure the savvier Louisiana congressmen and senators left no paper trail of *their* conversations with Hoover about the importance of protecting the dignity of the U.S. Navy and Louisiana's largest employer.

Naturally, I sought again to use my influence with the Marcellos to protect me from the horrors of the criminal justice system, and luckily their reach extended well into the federal system. Instead of some grimy dungeon, I found myself deposited in ritzy FCI Texarkana, a minimum-security federal prison seventy miles north of Shreveport. Texarkana was a great place for me to land, since I was immediately installed in a cell with Frank Caracci, a fellow French Quarter legend and close associate of Carlos Marcello.

Besides Carlos and Joe Marcello, and Silver Dollar Sam when he returned, no one in New Orleans had more juice than Frank Caracci. As the owner of the iconic 500 Club burlesque joint on Bourbon Street, Frank gradually inherited Gasper Gulotta and Diamond Jim Moran's role as the reigning kingpin of the French Quarter. Whenever I saw Frank in the Quarter, he was a deadly serious pain in the ass, always jockeying to steal an extra penny or two on every deal, always pushing for more respect and more power in every relationship. Frank was relentless — a jackal.

Frank's only topic of conversation was Carlos Marcello's cheapness. Oddly enough, whenever I brought up Frank around Carlos, his only topic was how cheap *Frank* was. It was a never-ending loop with those two, forever crying that the other guy was "a cheap, Jew, penny-pinching, pick-pocketing asshole." Finally, a Louisiana bookmaker who was doing time with Frank and me in Texarkana walked up during one of Caracci's "Carlos is cheap" speeches and lost his temper.

"For *fuck's sake*, Frank, cut the shit!" the bookmaker cried. "*Both* of you pricks are too cheap. There's no room to make money with *either* of you cheap motherfuckers. Get over it, already!" I thought Frank was going to flip his lid in response, but instead he just smiled the most self-satisfied smile in the world. That was all Frank wanted: confirmation that he was every bit the cheap, thieving, impossible-to-scam prick that Carlos Marcello was.

From the moment he heard that he was as cheap as Carlos, Frank Caracci did not have a care in the world. The merciless ball-buster became a pleasure to be around. He had received the respect he was looking for. You would think such a powerful and wealthy guy would do real hard time, but Frank did the easiest time I've ever seen.

Frank was always telling me, "Frenchy, just remember: don't worry about hard time. It's out of your hands. Just do the time as easy as you can and don't leave hatin'; let it go when you walk through that prison door!" This advice, to do easy time and never leave hating, has stuck with me ever since as being the most profound advice I've ever heard.

Frank Caracci was no "do as I say, not as I do" hypocrite. Every day in prison was a vacation to him, a reprieve from Mob politics and stress and financial wheeling and dealing and comparing himself to Carlos and coming up short. Frank would walk into the recreation room in the middle of the day, crawl onto a billiards table, and fall fast asleep with his big fucking belly hanging out — not a care in the world. He had not a single fuck to give.

Speaking of that big belly, I tried to teach that goombah how to eat well and exercise. I used a beautiful stratagem: I reminded him how much everyone admired Carlos for losing all that weight and coming out looking so much healthier after his short jail sentence. That got Frank rarin' to go, and I started dragging his panting, side-grabbing carcass from one end of the yard to the other, back and forth every day. I felt like a trainer taking his prizefighter out for his morning jog bright and early every day, only my prizefighter never reached any speed that could be even charitably classified as a "jog."

Nonetheless, after a couple weeks, Caracci looked exactly the same despite the mandatory exercise and revolutionary changes I prescribed in his diet. Finally, I figured something must have been up, so I searched our cell for contraband food and only found the fresh fruit I instructed him to buy.

Baffled, I redoubled my training efforts. After another two weeks of hard training went by without any obvious weight loss, I decided to go back to our cell when Frank was away and turn the place upside down.

Again, I found nothing besides fruit. Then I realized what was off: the watermelon under Frank's bed sure as hell looked like the same watermelon he had originally bought a month ago. I pulled that fucker out from under the bed and turned it over; the watermelon had been hollowed out. Inside the empty husk was an enormous quantity of candy, plus fried chicken special-ordered from the kitchen.

As you might be able to tell by the fact that Frank and I had a cook delivering a la carte meals to our cell upon request, Texarkana was pretty kind to two New Orleans gangsters. Still, it wasn't *that* nice; I actually had to order my fried chicken from the kitchen as opposed to walking right out of the jail and getting it myself, like at Orleans Parish Prison. Dissatisfied with Texarkana's culinary services and fully stocked recreational room, I called Joe Marcello and asked him to take care of me.

As always, my buddy Joe came through. I was transferred from Texarkana to the luxury prison camp at Eglin Air Force Base in Florida.

Eglin was the palatial resort that originally inspired the nickname "Club Fed." Housing mostly millionaire business criminals, crooked politicians, and dimwit celebrities, Eglin fancied itself a country club more than a prison. It was not coincidental that almost all the inmates were white folks who belonged to actual country clubs. The mere fact that they had committed horrible crimes was no reason for the better sort to have to live side by side with blacks and petty criminals.

You could walk around the grounds of Eglin without seeing anything that would have seemed out of place in Audubon Park in New Orleans. Instead of barbed wire or guard towers, Eglin was covered by beautifully mowed emerald lawns, lush gardens, moss-covered oak trees, and countless sports opportunities. If you wanted to play tennis, baseball, or football, there were beautifully maintained facilities ready for you at any time.

Best of all, Eglin boasted *two* incredible weight rooms, and the guards made sure that their lockers were well-stocked with protein products and steroids. I dried out, put on mass, and dumped of all my bad drug habits, devoting myself to attaining my all-time best physique. By the time I left Eglin, I could have competed professionally in any bodybuilding competition in America.

Joe Marcello took care of my company in Eglin, as well. I stayed in the same dorm as longtime Louisiana Attorney General Jack Gremillion, a Cajun boy from Ascension Parish who made good and then made bad. Stuck in jail with me due to securities and mail fraud, Jack didn't seem to notice and lived as if he was still on the campaign trail. Every day, he would go around shaking hands and telling funny anecdotes; the crazy bastard would even run around the visitors' area kissing babies.

The guards loved Jack and me since, unlike a lot of the condescending, country- club prick inmates, Jack and I were just working-class Cajun boys who treated everyone as equals. The guards appreciated our attitude so much that we received preferential treatment even for Eglin.

Every Friday, Jack and I received two bottles apiece of Johnny Walker Red scotch, giving us plenty of booze to stay drunk all weekend. On hot days, the guards would take Jack and me out to swim in the Gulf of Mexico, and I'd tan to a golden brown on the beach. On Christmas morning, we'd wake up to find stockings of fresh fruit next to our bed.

After only a few months at Eglin, Joe Marcello's attorney arranged for me to be paroled. When I left, one of the old convicts came to me and reminded me that the secret of recovering from life in jail was to not leave hating.

Chapter XI

Silver Dollar Sam &
The Silver Fox

"Silvestro 'Sam' Carollo, an Italian alien, was deported from the United States in 1947. [...] On August 22, 1929, Carollo is alleged to have shot U.S. Narcotic Agent Clarence V.B. Moore, when Moore was attempting to place Carollo under arrest. [...] The state case against Carollo was *nolle prosequi* [refusal of the district attorney to prosecute]."

FBI Document 94-337

BABY, LET ME TELL YOU MY FAVORITE STORY I EVER HEARD IN THE UNDERWORLD.

Sometime around 1969, a passenger ship left Palermo, Sicily, with an old Catholic priest onboard. The priest was just a quiet, short, well-dressed, little old man. He did nothing to draw attention to himself.

Whenever anyone spoke to this priest in Italian, he responded in a rough street dialect of Sicilian that sounded anything but appropriate for a man of the church. Up close, the passengers noticed that this priest's handsome, dark face was marred by what appeared to be a knife-fight scar on his lip. When the priest walked, he did not walk humbly; he walked like the entire world made way for him.

Gradually, the passengers drew out the Father's teasing,

mischievous personality, and he became the star of the cruise. To the lily-white American biddies playing cards on shaded, deck-side tables, the priest was a source of amusement and gossip. He spoke fluent English and, though polite and halfway proper, could not help flustering far younger women with his flirtatious Latin charm.

One young American was so taken with the priest that she begged him to conduct an impromptu marriage ceremony for her and her fiancé in the middle of the Atlantic. With ill-disguised amusement, the priest agreed and damn near kicked the couple down the aisle. As a number of passengers looked on, the priest improvised a very unorthodox marriage ceremony, afterwards blessing the new bride and calling on her to be fruitful and "bring plenty of pretty lil' babies into the world!" as the Bible taught.

Landing in New Orleans after a pleasant trip, the Father disembarked into the torridly humid, Louisiana swamp air that he knew all so well and passed through the inspection booth maintained by the Crescent City's infamously lazy custom agents. Chauffeured in another black limousine from the Mississippi River waterfront to a smoky Italian restaurant in nearby Jefferson Parish, the man of the cloth was greeted by a raucous welcoming party of fat old guidos.

Looking down at his priest's outfit with incredulous eyes, Silvestro "Silver Dollar Sam" Carollo smirked and announced, to riotous applause, "Man, I can't believe dis bullshit worked!"

Raising his right hand, Carollo made the sign of the cross over the crowd, tears of laughter pouring down his cheeks. The twice-deported godfather of the New Orleans Mafia Family, exiled for over twenty years, had returned for good.

Still clad in his priest's costume, Silver Dollar Sam laughed until he was red-faced and hyperventilating as he told the story of the young couple he married aboard the cruise ship. To Sam Carollo, it was unbelievably hilarious that the "newlyweds" would never suspect that they, in reality, were living in sin and that their future children would be illegitimate.

"I made the whole lot of 'dem bastards!" Sam rasped, trying to catch his breath as his adoring audience of fellow wiseguys hacked up their tobacco-tarred lungs and splattered pasta sauce over the tablecloth.

"Mack the Knife, the creation of Kurt Weill, never lived in old Storyville. But as Louis [Armstrong] puts it, he grew up with a lot of characters just like Mack the Knife [and] played at a lot of their funerals."
TV Announcer for 1956 Louis Armstrong Performance

That was Silver Dollar Sam for you, baby, a real New Orleans original. While the other cruise passengers of his generation played shuffleboard and bridge, Silver Dollar Sam amused himself by desecrating the sanctity of the priesthood, making a mockery of the sacrament of marriage, and bastardizing an entire family. For the last two years of his life, Sam regularly brought up that young couple with a wistful smile and, before choking on a wheezing cackle, speculated over how many illegitimate children they would shit out.

Without a doubt, Silver Dollar Sam was the greatest boogeyman and hero of the Italian underworld in New Orleans. Stone-cold thugs like the Confortos would speak of Silver Dollar Sam with terror, like he was a demon.

Though I never met Silver Dollar Sam in my early French Quarter days, I could not help but know him by reputation from the stories told by his longtime lieutenants like Diamond Jim Moran. When Louis Armstrong covered "Mack the Knife," the old tune about a fearless, dagger-wielding murderer, and made it a big-time hit in 1956, all the gangsters began to request the song in the French Quarter lounges. I don't remember if it was Diamond Jim Moran or someone else, but one of those crusty, old-school gangsters came up to me as the song was playing and nudged me in the side.

"That Mack dah Knife, man, you'd swear they were fuckin' talkin' 'bout Silver Dollar Sam, man. Old Silver Dollar Sam was just like Mack the Knife. I bet that's where Louis Armstrong got the idea for that song! You didn't cross Sam; no one did and lived. You got the fuckin' knife. You fucked with Sam and you got the knife. That fucker went to jail for shootin' a fed; he didn't give a shit 'bout nobody and nothin'. That's why you'll never hear Carlos say a goddamn word about him."

Sam was downright cinematic, a Hollywood villain on Bourbon Street. They say Sam received his nickname due to his resemblance in both looks and dress to George Raft's stylish gangster in the 1932 version of *Scarface*. Since Raft's character constantly flipped a silver dollar, his look-alike Sam Carollo became "Silver Dollar Sam," the New Orleans underworld's most *GQ*-ready killer.

For all his looks and charm, Sam nonetheless inspired absolute terror — even in his own family. When Sam's sister-in-law Francis and his cousin Michael Carollo dared to get engaged against his wishes, the young couple, fearing for their lives, had no choice but to flee to Detroit with the help of some friends in the Detroit Mob.

Silver Dollar Sam eventually tracked the terrified couple down after attending a wedding as a guest of Detroit kingpin "Black" Bill Tocco, who was born within months of Carollo in the same village in Sicily. In order to honor his host, Sam made peace and told Francis and Michael that he had "called off the hit." A moment later, Silver Dollar Sam unexpectedly pulled out a NOPD-issue pistol ... and gently handed it to Michael. "Use dis to defend yo'self in case the word didn't get out fast enough," Sam said with a smile.

Eventually, Francis and Michael would send their son Vic to stay with his uncle in New Orleans. The oblivious Vic thought Sam was the finest fellow he had ever met until he happened to encounter his uncle at the wrong moment in the kitchen of Sam's

St. Charles Tavern. Silver Dollar Sam was in a wild, pistol-waving rage — cursing and swearing that he would shoot another in-law dead for an act of infidelity.

Though Sam was deported back to Sicily first in 1947 and then again in 1950, it was common gossip when I started in the French Quarter that Silver Dollar Sam was always in town, hiding in plain sight, keeping a close eye on everyone who thought he was gone. Even kingpins like Diamond Jim or Sam Saia would shrug uneasily if asked where Silver Dollar Sam was at the moment, as if he could be right behind us, waiting for one of us to say the wrong thing.

Sam was supposedly always lurking in the swamps and slipping through the back alleys and walking in the shadows and smoking cigars in the backrooms of restaurants. Silver Dollar Sam sightings were like UFO or Sasquatch sightings, and sometimes you'd hear that the man was one day in Tijuana, the next in Cuba, the next in Sicily, and then he'd be back in Louisiana before you noticed.

When my buddy Dale was a teenager, he went to visit a Sicilian uncle at their vacation home in Abita Springs, Louisiana. In addition to his Uncle Frank, Dale was awestruck to discover that the house was occupied at the time by the supposedly deported Silver Dollar Sam and New York Mob boss Frank Costello, whispering together at the kitchen table.

French Quarter MC Frank Pirelli had another chance run-in with Silver Dollar Sam. As the top comedian on Bourbon Street, "Frankie Ray" was so often told stories about Silver Dollar Sam that he began to assume they were all bullshit. One day, Frank heard that Carollo had just arrived in Brownsville, Texas, and was renting a car to drive over and visit his family. Frank laughed it off, but a couple days later he received a visit from the sheriff, who looked as nervous as if he had just seen the devil in person.

"Hey, Frank, I don't how to tell you this," the sheriff said with a wavering voice, "but we got Silver Dollar Sam in lockup at the jail. The feds pounced on him in Slidell. And, I don't know why, but Silver Dollar Sam told me to come get you and bring you to him. He doesn't want to see nobody else."

Considering Frank was just a Bourbon Street comic with no relationship at all with the mysterious Silver Dollar Sam, the poor guy almost died of terror on the spot. Why on Earth did Silver Dollar Sam need to see *him*? How did Silver Dollar Sam even know that he existed? Was he being "called for" in the dreaded Sicilian sense of the word?

"Maybe the man just wants a good laugh now that he's getting deported again," said the sheriff, trying to make Frank feel better.

At the prison, an entire floor had been beautifully furnished and given to Silver Dollar Sam and Salvatore "Kansas City Sam" Guarneiri, another deported gangster caught by the feds. Frank was escorted into an open jail cell where Silver Dollar Sam was pan frying a marlin. "Nice to meet ya there, Frank," said Silver Dollar Sam. "Youse about to eat the best goddamn fish in yo' entire life."

As Frank sat down, he sniffed the air and became instantly queasy. You see, Frank, despite being Italian, is severely allergic to garlic, and that marlin that Silver Dollar Sam was preparing for his enjoyment was, like most things cooked by a Sicilian, coated in garlic.

Clearly, turning down the hospitality of the most feared Mafia boss in Louisiana history was not an option, so Frank found himself slowly choking down searing bites of marlin, pouring sweat and breaking out in hives as he half-listened to Silver Dollar Sam's disarmingly friendly small talk.

"How 'bout dat marlin, huh?" Sam asked him.

Frank nodded dumbly as he tried to get his eyes to focus and his lungs to work. After a few minutes, Silver Dollar Sam took Frank for a fool and cut the bullshit and got to the point. "So, Frankie, here's why I asked for ya to come down 'ere. Kansas City Sam and me need to get a message to Chicago, to [former Capone enforcer] Sam Hunt and his people, and we was told that you are good with 'dem people, being from Chicago yahself. We heard you was a trustworthy sort and could do it quiet and keep a secret. You can handle dat?"

Frank nearly spit up the marlin in relief. The two soon-to-be-deported gangsters needed a clean, unsuspicious messenger who could get admitted into the prison and then send word to Chicago without raising anyone's eyebrows. And here he was, a dweeby little comedian who knew the Chicago Outfit well from working in their clubs. It was a perfect match. Frank sent the message for Silver Dollar Sam, and he never spoke with him again. Within a couple months, he started hearing the same rumors again that Sam was back in America.

As a young man, I believed in every Silver Dollar Sam legend I heard — except for one. I could not accept the idea that my hero Carlos Marcello truly feared Silver Dollar Sam. Carlos was treated like God by everyone; there's no way he feared any mortal man.

Carlos would rail for hours against *anyone*, cursin' and spittin' and making lewd hand gestures about the Kennedys, Frank Caracci, and "that cocksucker Vito Genovese in New York," the new godfather who had tried and failed to kill Carlos' mentor Frank Costello. Surely, Carlos would tell Silver Dollar Sam to go fuck himself like all the rest.

A few years later, I got the chance to see with my own eyes how Carlos talked about Silver Dollar Sam. Someone brought up Sam in conversation, complaining about how the old man was greedy and stomping on the Marcellos' prerogatives as the ruling family of the Louisiana Mafia. This was just the sort of talk that got Carlos raging under normal circumstances, but that hawk-like face just scowled and stared off at nothing. Carlos didn't say a word, and the matter was dropped. When it came to Silver Dollar Sam, even Carlos worried that the walls had ears.

According to my buddy Joe Marcello, at no point did Silver Dollar Sam resign his title as godfather of New Orleans. Though Sam had been absent more or less since 1950, according to the traditional rules, Carlos ran the Family in his place only as the "street boss," and Joe confirmed to me that Carlos regularly sent Silver Dollar Sam token "tribute" payments throughout his years in Sicily. The specific amount Carlos owed Sam was a constant source of guido bickering for decades. I asked Joe why Carlos didn't simply wipe out Silver Dollar Sam, and I wish I could have taken a snapshot of the bug-eyed face that guy made back at me.

Apparently, you didn't just "wipe out" Silver Dollar Sam.

After seeing first-hand the respect the Marcellos gave to Carollo, I simply could not turn down my attorney Dean Andrews' offer to introduce me to his larger-than-life client once he returned to America as a priest. I needed to make sure I saw the legend with my own eyes in case he disappeared again.

Dean had promised Sam Carollo's remaining New Orleans family that, if the old man could manage to return from Sicily to Louisiana, he could guarantee that he would never be deported again. Dean wasn't sure if he could win Carollo's immigration case, but he felt confident that he could prolong the proceedings until the old man died. In return, Dean asked for no money — only the right to eat for free for the rest of his life at the Carollo family's various restaurants. Not knowing Dean, the Carollos happily agreed to what they figured was a bargain.

Since I *did* know Dean, I was reluctant to go out to dinner with him at one of Silver Dollar Sam's restaurants. I knew that Dean's hog-wild gluttony would end up embarrassing the appetite out of me. Still, I could not walk away from a dinner with the most mysterious godfather in American history.

As Dean promised, we were ushered right to the best table in the restaurant like VIPs, and before we knew it, a slender old man with a round face appeared out of nowhere and nimbly slipped into the chair next to me without any fanfare. Silver Dollar Sam had sleepy pothead eyes and one of those fat-lipped smiles that's always open and a little crooked, like he's frozen halfway into starting to laugh. He was just about the most happy-go-lucky-looking old man I have ever met.

Before I even had the chance to get nervous introducing

myself, Dean took the offensive and embarrassed the shit out of me. First, he called over the waiter and ordered three appetizers and three entrees; considering the size of Louisiana Italian restaurant portions, I thought this sounded like way too much food for the three of us. But I was wrong; Dean wasn't ordering for the table. To my horror, after ordering six dishes, Dean started to cackle and swung his head to Silver Dollar Sam and me, "That was just for me. Whatta you guys having?"

That bulbous-bellied bastard actually downed three appetizers and three entrees of Italian food, one after the other without pause, all by himself. While dumping sixteen pounds of pasta and sausage down his throat, my slob attorney never thought to close his mouth or stop his incessant talking as he chewed, spraying the table and Silver Dollar Sam with marinara-colored spittle.

It wasn't wise to impose on Silver Dollar Sam and make a fool out of him like some Chinese all-you-can-eat buffet owner, but nothing Dean did was wise.

Silver Dollar Sam was just an Italian ghetto boy himself, so I don't think he even noticed Dean's atrocious table manners. He was more interested in *what* Dean was rambling about: the usual tales of mayhem and perversion surrounding Frenchy Brouillette. What I didn't know was that Silver Dollar Sam had risen through the ranks as the enforcer for the French Quarter branch of the Mafia, so, like most French Quarter gangsters, he had a deep affection for stories of crazy pimps and their decadent lifestyles. Like Carlos before him, Silver Dollar Sam took a liking to me, and Dean and I began to have dinner with him occasionally.

After a while, Dean finally convinced Silver Dollar Sam to share some of his stories about his life as a twentysomething Mob boss during Prohibition and later as the top narcotics-smuggling godfather in America. Sam was so nonchalant and easygoing that it took a while to realize that he was being honest when he would start talking about how, even as a godfather, he preferred to "do my own heavy work, y'know, by myself. I didn't want no one messing it up."

In street slang, that meant that, contrary to all precedent and tradition, Silver Dollar Sam, as the godfather of New Orleans, had gone about committing his own murders all by himself. According to the old timers I knew, Sam was famous for walking around in broad daylight with a sawed-off shotgun hanging from his shoulder. Sam didn't need any bodyguards; you could take up your problems with him one-on-one if you dared. The man was stone cold.

In 1930 alone, Silver Dollar Sam was personally arrested for three shootings, including a drive-by of the top Irish bootlegger in New Orleans and the point blank attempted murder of a federal narcotics agent. Sam's power was so great that the local authorities refused to prosecute him for *trying to kill a federal law enforcement agent.* If the guy was willing to kill a narc, what was to stop him from taking out a judge or a district attorney?

"Man, them guys up North hated me somethin' wild over that agent," Sam said. "One time when they deported me, they didn't even drop me off on the mainland. They marooned me on a fuckin' oil rig or some shit off the coast of Sicily. I had to wait for a passing ship to save me from starving."

As Sam got to trust me, he opened up and shared more of his stories from the old days. My favorite was the showdown between Silver Dollar Sam and Al Capone. Sam was reminded of the story when I told a story about how crooked the NOPD was at the time.

"Man, today is nuthin'. I'll tell you crooked. Now, get dis, Frenchy. So, back in Prohibition, we were distributing alcohol all the way up the Mississippi since we could get the stuff straight from Cuba with no problem, just sailin' it right in.

"Well, we were doin' so much business up north that it pisses off that guy Capone up there, who's gotten to thinkin' that he's the Father, Son, and Holy Spirit over the entire country. He sends word down 'ere for us to knock it off and stop sellin' our hooch up there, but I jus' ignored 'im. Fuck 'im, y'know? Talk is cheap, and this wasn't Chicago last I heard.

"Well, this crazy bastard gets mad that I'm ignorin' him, so he sends word through some friends that he wants a sitdown and that he expected me to meet him at the train station at so-and-so time on so-and-so morning. The guy jus' bought some tickets for New Orleans and got on a train. That's how cocky the sumbitch was then.

"So, I met him at the train station," Sam says in his scratchy voice, suppressing laughter. "Jus' me and about fifty fuckin' NOPD cops in their finest dress blues all lined up. It looked like a fuckin' military parade. As soon as dat tub of shit Capone gets off the train with a couple goons, the cops pounce on them, take their guns, and slam them hard against the side of the trains.

"As Capone's gettin' his face mashed into the steel, I walk up all slow like in my nice expensive suit and whisper in his ear, 'Ain't ya heard this is a closed town? You better get permission next time you come down here, dontcha ya think?' and sent his ass right back up to Chicago on the next train."

Silver Dollar Sam was laughing and slapping his knee throughout this entire story, but his pleasure could not come close to matching the sheer ecstasy that Mob groupie Dean Andrews was experiencing from being the guest of honor at this underworld legend's table.

And Dean kept his word to Silver Dollar Sam, just as he did for Carlos. Carollo died on Louisiana soil a free man. Unfortunately, my buddy Dean did not live to starfuck the assembled gangsters at Silver Dollar Sam's funeral. Only a few weeks after our last dinner together, Dean finally died of heart disease.

✣ ✣ ✣ ✣ ✣

"Edwin's father, Clarence, known as 'Boboy,' was half Cajun, a stern Presbyterian who gave up sharecropping to open a country store. His mother, Agnes, who is still living, was a Brouillette, 100 percent Cajun, who brought up her five children as Catholics and hid her disappointment when Edwin took out a license as a Nazarene preacher in his late teens."

Hugh Mulligan
Associated Press Story, March 29, 1987

Growing up in Marksville, I heard a lot about my brilliant, charming cousin Edwin Edwards, who just about everyone in Marksville figured would become a great man one day. It was obvious from the start: this kid could charm *anyone*. With his round, red cheeks and clever eyes, the boy had the look of a Cajun Dennis the Menace, but it was impossible to stay mad at him. In school, they used to say that little Edwin would flirt his way out of schoolwork, and even his dowdiest teachers would be competing with the young girls for his attention.

Since I was, in comparison, such an unimpressive and unheralded Brouillette, the golden boy Edwin did not get to know me in Marksville. Instead, he started traveling and making a name for himself statewide. At first, Edwin wasn't sure *which* of the sleaziest professions on the planet he wanted to pursue: he tried roving evangelical minister and lawyer before deciding to shoot for the highest rank on the sleazeball career ladder, Louisiana politician. By the time I was released from Club Fed down in Florida, my forty-five-year-old cousin had been elected the Governor of Louisiana.

The secret to Edwin's political appeal was that he did not act like a politician: he acted like a pimp. With his jewelry, beautifully barbered hair, silver silk suits, deep tan, pretty mistresses, and brand-new cars, Edwin did not run for office; he *swaggered* into office. Edwin was cool, man. Like a pimp picking up women, Edwin did not pander or beg for votes; he showcased how much cooler he was than everyone else and let the voters come begging to vote for him.

Edwin had the epiphany that, in the TV age, voters would naturally choose the *cooler* candidate. It was just a high school popularity contest, and, as he did back in Marksville, Edwin used his style and wit to make himself the coolest bad boy in school. Unlike other politicians, Edwin made no attempt to hide that he gambled hundreds of thousands of dollars at a time or that he tooled around with *Playboy* playmates and swimsuit models; he wanted everyone to see what a high-roller he was. He knew that the ultimate candidate would be the man whom every woman wanted and every man wanted to be.

If you have ever seen the pro wrestler Ric Flair, then you know what Edwin Edwards was like in the 1970s. That's where Ric got his routine, I bet.

When Edwin was interviewed, he did not try to ingratiate himself with the voters; instead he concentrated on establishing that the other candidate was a dork. Edwin said that Republican candidate for governor David Treen was "so slow it takes him an hour and a half to watch *60 Minutes*," and, in another election, bragged that he would have to be "caught in bed with a dead girl or a live boy" in order to lose. The voters of Louisiana mobbed Edwin like a rock star rushing from the backstage exit of a club to his tour bus.

Edwin was *cocky*, man, more Ric Flair than Richard Nixon, and he was every bit as clever as his nickname, "The Silver Fox," would indicate. Knowing that he had an ethics problem, Edwin embraced it like Bill Clinton on an 8-ball of cocaine, making a big joke of how crooked he was to anyone who would listen. Edwin's honesty completely disarmed the opposition; it was impossible to turn his lawbreaking into a news story or scandal since everyone already assumed Edwin was guilty. Edwin got elected running on the crooked ticket, so it was impossible to use his sleaziness against him in elections, either.

Edwin reassured his audiences by saying that he had no choice but to be honest because, considering how incompetent the previous officeholders had been, "There would be no money left to steal!" When Edwin finally had bribery charges pinned on him, he laughed and told reporters that, "It was illegal for them to give, not for me to receive!" Edwin even endorsed bumper stickers that read "Vote for the Crook!"

I should have realized that, judging by Edwin's behavior, we would become a regular old mutual admiration society. While Edwin was fulfilling my childhood dream of reveling in the praise and admiration of our family and all of Marksville, I was fulfilling his childhood dream of being a New Orleans gangster. As soon as I got out of jail, I received a phone call at my old lady's place.

"Is this Frenchy?" asked a friendly voice.

"Yeah, baby, what's it to ya?"

"This is the *governor*," the voice said emphatically. "I hear we're cousins." I had made a career out of answering freaky, unpredictable phone calls, but this one took the doberge cake. I briefly considered that I was talking to a prank caller, but then I realized that no one in New Orleans had the slightest idea that Edwin and I were related because I never discussed it since I was embarrassed that we didn't really know each other.

"Uh, I hear that too," I said without particular inspiration. I was on the spot, so I was just happy that I managed to make sense.

"I also hear that you're in the same business I'm in," Edwin teased, displaying his usual honesty about his political career.

"I guess you can say dat," I responded, instantly won over.

"Would you like to have lunch with me at Antoine's today?"

"I'd love to, baby."

That's classic Louisiana: the most powerful politician in the state inviting an ex-con fresh from a federal bid for white slavery for lunch at the fanciest, highest-profile restaurant in the city. As you can probably guess by now, Edwin wasn't worried that the Governor would be seen with a gangster; in fact, he booked a table at the one place in town where we would be *guaranteed* to be seen together. The report that he was partying with me would actually *help* the image he was trying to portray.

"Hey there, country cousin, heard a lot about you!" Edwin called out across the restaurant as I walked in, drawing every goddamn eye in that place to me. Those eyes didn't stay there long; I may have felt like a celebrity most places, but I was a completely nobody sitting next to Edwin. I've sat down with people like Dean Martin, Liberace, and Jerry Lee Lewis, and none of them came close to projecting the aura of fame and glamour that my slender cousin from Marksville did. Antoine's is an enormous, sprawling restaurant, but the entire place was filled to the ceiling with Edwin's charm.

Within seconds, Edwin and I were thick as old cellmates, and we both laughed over how ridiculous it was that two men from our country-ass family were able to build reputations for debauched city-slicker cool. By the end of the meal, we were sharing war stories of parties and broads, trying to one-up each other; Edwin won, but, then again, he's a bold-faced liar.

Anyway, at the end of that meeting, *someone* made a proposition to me — I won't say who. That person informed me that an interested party was throwing Edwin's campaign staff and advisors a big weekend-long party at the Hotel Monteleone, where they had booked the entire top floor of rooms. To get going properly, this party was going to require the services of fifteen girls for the entire weekend. Finding fifteen girls willing to work a three-day hotel bender was tough on me, since I had just gotten out of jail and was low on resources, but I called the English Queen, and we put together a crack crew of eleven girls that we dispatched to the hotel.

The stories that were telephoned to me from the hotel rooms were incredible: political aides and state senators throwing around stacks of hundreds, kilos of cocaine piled atop coffee tables, bags of weed the size of lawnmower sacks sitting unnoticed in the corner. No matter the time of day, I could barely hear my girls when they called because of the raucous party in the background; it sounded like ancient Rome was being pillaged.

All of the girls came away with thousands of dollars in cash from the weekend; Louisiana politicians are usually so well bribed that they can afford to be stupid-generous. On Monday, a very weary, red-eyed Edwin called me to his suite at the Monteleone. Without explaining, the robed Governor sighed, looked at me for a moment, and grumbled, "I hear I might owe you money for some services to my campaign."

After making a big show of reluctance, Edwin smiled and whipped out a cheese wheel of hundred dollar bills. Edwin counted off seventy and asked, "Is this enough, country cousin?"

"Damn right it is. Lunch is on me, baby!"

"Ah, they always say the Brouillettes are generous people," Edwin teased as he handed me the cash.

Within a few days of meeting Edwin, I got a phone call that I should have been expecting. "Frenchy, it's Mr. C.... Come see me on the double."

I hurried over to the Town & Country, where I was greeted by the absolute friendliest Mafia boss I've ever encountered. "Now, Frenchy, we don't keep secrets around here," said the man who kept a sign reading, "Three people can keep a secret if two of them are dead" over his door.

"Why didn't ya tell me that you were double-tight with Edmund?" Carlos was a busy man, apparently too busy to ever figure out the four-term governor of Louisiana's first name.

From that day on, I became the Marcello Family's official political fixer. I don't mean to say that Edwin Edwards was corrupt and did favors for the Mafia — far from it. I almost never spoke to Edwin about any favors or any requests from Carlos Marcello, and I never gave him cash.

Nope, things worked very differently; we were both completely blameless. First, Carlos would tell me a problem — a body found in a landfill, a state contract given out to the wrong company, a convict that deserved a pardon — and then I would take that problem and a briefcase full of cash to my attorney in Baton Rouge.

My attorney just *happened* to be a fellow Brouillette: Nolan Edwards, Edwin's brother, who was tragically murdered in 1983 by a drug dealer. After a discussion that was legally protected by attorney-client privilege, I would pay my cousin Nolan for his legal services and refer a female friend to him who might be interested in certain extralegal services.

Later, it occasionally turned out to be true that Edwin Edwards and Carlos Marcello, so different in so many ways, would come to the same conclusion on how to solve the original problem that caused the Mafia don to reach out to me. As far as I know, Edwin never received a penny from Nolan; maybe Carlos was paying me just for an imaginary service. We'll never know.

Once the news started spreading that I was Carlos' boy in Baton Rouge, I was given a crash course in Louisiana politics. I thought that I had seen the dark side of human nature as a New Orleans pimp, but Louisiana politics slapped that delusion right out of my head. I had seen *nothing.*

Barely a week went by when some blameless public figure or company did not approach me with a briefcase of cash asking for a favor. Sometimes, the money was staggering; a union for Mississippi River ship pilots once introduced themselves to me with a briefcase containing $100,000. Stunned, I drove over to Nolan's office in a greedy frenzy, hoping to get some information that would help me tap deeper into the goldmine.

Nolan sniffed with disgust at the $100,000 I showed him. "I suggest you return that, Frenchy."

"Why? Is it hot?"

"Nah, man," Nolan said, laughing. "They're low-balling you. There are much bigger bidders playing on *this* deal." From that point on, I never wondered how Edwin and Nolan could afford to toss away hundreds of thousands of dollars at Las Vegas casinos. There were always big bidders playing on their deals.

Though not as charismatic as his brother, Nolan was twice as freaky and charming in his own blunt way. Edwin was witty and sly, a fox, but Nolan just didn't give a fuck. I once sent my highest-class call girl to him as a present, and the girl took one look at the disheveled, partied-out nut-job, stumbling around the hotel room in holey socks, and smelled a rat.

"Now, before we do anything, honey, show me ID. I want to make sure you're Mr. Nolan Edwards," my girl said with disbelief, leering at him up and down.

"Girl, I ain't carrying no ID, are you fucking kiddin'?" Nolan slurred.

"Sorry, hun, I'm going to need ID!" my girl snapped, figuring for sure that she was being conned.

"Alright, babe," Nolan said as he dug for something buried within his coat, "how's about *this* for ID?" The girl stared in disbelief: Nolan Edwards had thrown the largest bag of cocaine she had ever seen onto the hotel room coffee table. "Take a hit of that and tell me if I'm fucking Nolan Edwards, okay?"

My girl came back to me the next day and said that the family resemblance between Nolan and me was uncanny.

A few days after that, the girl started gossiping about the Edwards's blood relationship with me, and somehow just about every low-level character in the French Quarter concluded from that loose talk that I was lying about being related to them. This put me in a bind because, as much as I hated being called a liar, I knew that, if I proved myself to be Edwin's cousin, then every pimp, peddler, hack, and whore in New Orleans would be crawling all over me looking for a pardon. So I let it ride and hoped that Carlos' people would keep quiet.

Unfortunately, I didn't count on Edwin blowing my cover. I was having breakfast at a local hangout, Morning Call, with the usual cast of characters, when Edwin Edwards slipped through the door with a couple political aides. Before Edwin or I had a chance to notice each other, a loudmouth hack seized the opportunity to embarrass me and call bullshit on my family relationship with the governor.

"Hey dere, guvnah! Look, it's yo cousin!" this idiot yelled so that the entire Parish would hear.

You could not fluster Edwards; his face did not register a single twitch, as if it had been possible for *anyone* not to hear the hack.

"I *said*, hey dere, *guvnah!* It's yo cousin, Frenchy!"

With perfect timing, the governor quietly started making his way in my direction, without making eye contact or giving away that he knew who the hack was yelling about.

"I *said, EDWARDS!*" screamed the hack, standing up out of impatience. He pointed his finger at me so there could be no confusion. "*That man's spose to be yo'* cousin!"

Finally, Edwards reached me, stopped, and turned to the hack. "He's not my cousin," he said in the calmest voice imaginable. Then, as if stooping down to check out the menu on my lap, Edwin reached out, grabbed my hand, and lifted it into the air so that the entire restaurant could see the sparkling, six-karat diamond ring on my finger.

"He's my *rich* cousin.... Get it right next time!"

Chapter XII

Women Who Make It

1960s - 1970s

> "The truth is that prostitution is one of the most attractive of the occupations practically open to the sort of women who engage in it, and that the prostitute commonly likes her work, and would not exchange places with a shop-girl or a waitress for anything in the world."
> **H.L. Mencken**

"FRENCHY, YOU LIKE WOMEN THAT MAKE IT," BIG HENRY USED TO TELL ME, "BUT I LIKE GIRLS THAT ALREADY GOT IT!"

As always, Carlos Marcello's gigantic bagman Big Henry was talking about money. Big Henry was a con man and cash jockey who would tolerate just about any woman with money to spend on him, and he figured that I would tolerate just about any woman who made money for me to spend. Naturally, our priorities resulted in very different bed partners: I trafficked in the young and beautiful, and Big Henry was usually loving on some ancient eighty-year-old Garden District widow.

Though Big Henry only cared about the money — you should have seen some of the coffin-cases this pallbearer would drag around town — I never have been so simple. I've supported many working girls who don't work and moneymakers who spend more of my cash than they bring in. Unlike most pimps, I did not beat or kick out the girls that caused me the most trouble or lost me the most money; I usually fell in love and married them so I'd have an excuse to keep them around.

More than a few of my friends say I was tragically miscast as a pimp, that my generous and gullible personality could not be less appropriate for the gig. This is one of the favorite subjects of the English Queen, who to this day tells me that I live to get fleeced by untrustworthy hookers. If you listen to her, my greatest mistake was not letting her pimp me out as a high-class gigolo. With my looks and her savvy, the Queen swears that she could have made me the trophy husband of Louisiana Senator Mary Landrieu or TV newscaster Angela Hill.

According to the Queen, my downfall is that I am too nice and too careless with money. Granted, you have to take the Queen's opinion with a kilo of salt; this is a woman who thinks Snake Gonzales was a fine specimen. Unlike Snake, I never made "beating sticks" by wrapping bath towels around coat hangers, which Snake assured me left no mark whatsoever on a hooker no matter how badly you beat her. That was not for me; violence against women turned my stomach.

There were only two occasions when violence came into play with my relationship with my call girls. The first is when a team of lesbian hookers from Lafayette began to blackmail my clients; one would hide outside of the motel room while the other turned the tricks and subtly opened the blinds so that photographs could be taken. When I found out from one of my clients that these girls were ruining my reputation and making enemies for me, I didn't know what to do, so I did nothing. Then I heard from some of Carlos Marcello's hitters, regular clients like Big Pete or the enforcer, whom I will only refer to as "Number 8" because he's still alive, that these girls were pulling their shit with the wrong people.

Now that Carlos' people were involved, I had no choice; I had to make an example of these two con artists or risk that the Family would think I was in on the scam. My life was at stake. I talked to the English Queen, and she was characteristically blunt:

"You have to kill the dykes...or you're toast."

Baby, as you can imagine, this was a troubling piece of advice for a pacifist like me. As Mr. New Orleans, I was the friend of every killer in town, but I had never done anyone harm that extended past a friendly fist to the face. The idea of killing two *women* was completely impossible for me to entertain; I think I may have actually vomited after the conversation with the Queen.

But I had no choice. I told the women to jump into my convertible and come with me to visit a rich mark out in the country. The night was absurdly hot and humid, so my relentless sweating did not seem too suspicious. Though I was carrying heat, I felt like the heat was carrying me, carrying me away. I was frying.

I had no intention of pulling a trigger on these two broads; I have the sort of finicky stomach that cannot handle the idea of hunting jackrabbits, let alone lesbians. I had no specific plan in mind. I just told myself that, one way or the other, these two women were going to go on a ride with me and never return.

As I was driving along Bayou St. John within the city limits, I remembered that Carlos was thought to dump the bodies of his enemies in the swamp. Of course, it was also said that Carlos dissolved the corpses in lime first — and he also tended to pick bayous that weren't in the middle of the New Orleans metropolitan area. But Carlos was an expert at that sort of thing.

I parked my car over one of the tiny bridges over the tiny bayou; this bridge couldn't have been more than four or five feet above the water. I got out of my convertible and walked to edge, saying with the enthusiasm of a small boy, "Holy shit! Did you see those fish?"

Now, these girls must have been pretty stupid not to suspect that something was fishy since it was pitch-black night when I made this comment. I couldn't have seen the fucking Loch Ness Monster if he had been lounging in the bayou, let alone some guppies beneath the surface of the water. My naturally goofy behavior must have lent credibility to this ploy because the dykes indulged me and came to the edge of the bridge.

"Do you see 'em?" I said with a wavering voice. "Look down deep!"

As these two Einsteins leaned over to try to see fish when we honestly could not even see the water, I tried to breathe and still my frantically panicking heart. It felt like my heart was not beating so much as having convulsive, bubbling diarrhea. Speaking of which, my bowels felt like they were about to liquefy and splatter all over the bridge; my eyes were clouded, and my brain was overrun by wave after wave of molten hot sand.

"Nah, Frenchy, I don't see nuthin'," said one.

"Me neither, Frenchy," said the other.

"Well, take a closer look!" I said as I pushed them both off the bridge.

I was quicker than the Flash; I was back behind the driver's seat and twisting my key in the ignition before those bitches even hit the water. I was terrified that I would hear the sound of gargling screams or the snap of an alligator's jaw — sounds that would torment me for decades.

Instead, a couple hours later I heard the sounds of police sirens. My assumption had been that Bayou St. John was deep, and that these girls from Lafayette, who could not swim, would just sink to the bottom. It turned out that I had dumped them into roughly three feet of water.

They probably bruised their asses pretty bad, though.

All they had to do to avoid drowning was to sit up and inhale. The girls sloshed out of the Bayou and walked right to the police station. I was arrested for attempted murder, but my method of attack was judged too silly to prosecute. My crime was about as threatening as a teenage boy horsing around with his girlfriend and tossing her into the shallow end of the New Orleans Athletic Club pool.

Naturally, renditions of the "death by kiddie pool" story joined similar recitals of the Mr. Lucky Dog story as the favorite way for New Orleans wiseguys to bust my balls. If nothing else, this fuckup cleared me of any suspicion of colluding with the lesbians' blackmail campaign, and it achieved the miracle of making the deadly serious English Queen laugh.

You might think this would be the last time that I would be arrested for ineptly drowning a hooker, but you would be wrong.

"You call her 'the scarlet woman' now;
yet, how can you do it, I ask you, how?

"She was a girl once, all in bloom;
Just like a bird once, all in tune;
She was a flower, sweet and fair;
Just a little girl, sun in her hair. ...

"You call her 'the scarlet woman' now;
But how can you do it, I ask you, how,
When you have a mother, sister, a child
Who may go a foot or may go a mile
On the road of wrong, the road so gay
The road of night--the scarlet way?"
<u>Anonymous</u>
The Macon Daily Telegraph
4-10-1922

The relationship between an operator and his old lady is one of the strangest in the world. When I broke in, the first rule was that a pimp is never a "pimp" and a whore is never a "whore." It was considered bad form to call a spade a spade in those days.

In my generation, it was a relationship between an operator, manager, steerer, agent, old man, boyfriend, or daddy and his girlfriend, model, working girl, call girl, old lady, or bottom bitch. The word "pimp" was as offensive and demeaning to me in those days as "madam" was to the great "landlady" Norma Wallace. As far as "whore," I fucking dare you to call the English Queen or most working girls of that generation that word to their face.

Things have changed, baby. Ever since rap began to dominate street culture, the word "pimp" has seen its stock skyrocket. Nowadays, the most pussy-whipped, mark-ass accountant will call himself a pimp as a compliment, and young women of good families will brag to friends that they are "complete hos in the bedroom."

When I started talking to my writer for this book, I could not wrap my head around the idea that calling myself a "pimp" would actually make people *more* interested in my story. I thought it would render me a complete untouchable. If anyone asks me if I'm Frenchy the famous pimp, I throw on an offended face and righteously inform them that I am just a humble horse trainer from Marksville, Louisiana, thank you very much.

If there's any question I am asked most, it's why call girls choose to work with a pimp in the first place. Though the high-end call girl makes far more money with a pimp or madam with direct connections to the local rich folks, the average whore in the old days would have made more money leaving me and working on her own out of Lucky Pierre's, the infamous haunt of the "outlaw" call girls who paid no pimp or madam. One hundred percent of the money made at Lucky Pierre's was generally more than getting to keep thirty percent of what they made for me.

As best as I can tell you, the reason working girls accept less money to be with a pimp is simple insecurity and loneliness. The outlawing of prostitution is to blame for this sad state of affairs; the insulting stereotypes about hookers would have no truth whatsoever if it wasn't for the police driving the normal girls from the profession. If you outlaw and discredit a profession, it attracts outlaws and discredited people. Most hookers nowadays are generally lonely, troubled, insecure, and unemployable, and they thirst for the stability and approval a lot of broken women can only find in a strong man. If they can't find a strong man, someone like me will have to do.

These jaded and heart-heavy girls take on a pimp in an attempt to make them *forget* that they are hookers. Because I could give them hot jewels and boosted designer clothes, reserve the best table in any restaurant, and introduce them to powerful clients like Joe Marcello or Jim Garrison, it was a common occurrence for one of my girls to convince herself that she was the trophy bride of a celebrity, not a whore. This is where language like boyfriend or old man becomes too-close-for-comfort; I often found myself in a relationship with a hooker who was desperate for the affection, attention, and sex normally given to a wife.

Living with a hooker who has tried to convince you that she's really your wife can become pretty tiring, especially if you're living with up to *twenty* hookers at once, who all have convinced themselves that they're your wife to one degree or another. Every second of a pimp's day is spent fulfilling someone else's needs and, usually, breaking up catfights between women with unfulfilled needs. That's why I always say that a pimp is nothing more than a whore for whores; in return for selling their bodies and time, I sell them *my* body and time.

To be honest, I'm not a particularly sexual or emotional person when it comes down to it; I'm more of an alcoholic person. After the initial sex spree I embarked on in the French Quarter following the exorcism of my Catholic guilt, my sincere interests really only extended to drinking, eating, bodybuilding, and palling around with dogs, horses, and other gangsters.

I honestly am not equipped to be a single woman's boyfriend, let alone the mack daddy to a dozen women. There have been many days when satisfying the sexual and emotional appetites of a couple dozen women was nothing short of torture. Thank God I had sex freak Neil Gautier on call to pick up the slack at any time.

The pressure of managing what is basically a polygamous marriage with numerous needy female outlaws is one reason why so many pimps become violent. You just get tired, exhausted, annoyed. To be honest, most pimps only have limited reservoirs of love, reason, and attention to give; to keep order, they must resort to the "pimp hand."

Instead of violence, I used the silent treatment to keep order. I gave my respect and friendship to women who treated me with respect and friendship. If you stole from me or cheated me or double-crossed me, I placed you under emotional embargo, and most working girls are too needy to stand the idea that they are being shut out and rejected. For most of them, it is a replay of the childhood rejection they suffered with their actual daddies. My ability to keep my pimp hand strong without using violence or terror only increased my prestige among my women.

Still, a minority of my girls took my peaceful manner personally — as an insult. Some girls would bitch and moan because I never slapped them. They wondered if I didn't hit them because I didn't *care* enough about them. Snake Gonzales always used to tell me that, to a working girl, a thorough ass-beating was taken as affection, as a more meaningful sign of love and personal investment than a date at a fine restaurant.

Naturally, this made, and continues to make, no sense to me. To an extent that you probably won't believe, all women remain a mystery. Still, I have drawn some conclusions from nearly fifty years living and working with call girls. I have found that there are three sorts of prostitutes in the world: workers, old ladies, and bottom bitches.

The vast majority of hookers are just workers, women who turn tricks without forming deep and lasting bonds with their pimp. "Worker" also has a double meaning; "to work" is another way to say "to con" on the street. The average worker will call you her "daddy" and her "man" and tell you she loves you, but when you turn your back she will swipe your valuables and cash them in for crack rock.

For decades, I paid a driver $50 per trick just to follow my girls around and make sure that both they and the money made it back to me without incident. The driver also tipped me off if a bust went down since just about every worker will think about ratting you out if you don't get a lawyer to her immediately to tell her not to say anything and shush the cops away.

The second type of girl is the old lady, a woman who is sincerely in love with her pimp and judges herself solely by her ability to win his approval over the other girls. An old lady is a lifer, totally devoted to the sex rackets and almost as devoted to you. She will stick around for years, defend you against other underworld characters, and handle your books and watch over the other girls. Though she will eat a charge and jail time for you, an old lady will also stab you in the throat with a fork the second she thinks you love another call girl more than her. That is the old lady's mortal weakness: jealousy—and her vanity, which needs to be validated by preferential treatment. An old lady is just a pain-in-the-ass wife that also balls for money on the side.

The last and rarest type of prostitute is the almighty "bottom bitch," which is frankly the strangest breed of human I've ever encountered. A bottom bitch is something like a female suicide bomber or kamikaze devoted to your cause. Her world begins and ends with her man. The bottom bitch loves her pimp with a love that is unconditional, unlimited, infinite, and intense. It is a sacred love, bordering on the religious, like she's the wild-eyed high priestess of some sort of secret pagan cult.

You can leave a bottom bitch at home with ten million dollars cash, and when you get back she'll have counted and banded the cash for you and hustled an extra $200 to add to the pile. The thought of stealing it or even spending it without permission would not have even crossed her mind.

As long as you promise to remain her "big daddy," a bottom bitch doesn't give a damn if you screw other women, kill babies, or set churches on fire. A bottom bitch will eat a life sentence for you, and a bottom bitch will kill a man if he criticizes you — even if what he's saying is accurate! *Especially* if it's accurate!

In my life, I've had a couple dozen old ladies, three or four or five wives, and maybe one or two bottom bitches. As much as I could deal, I loved all of these women in their own way. I miss all of them — only one or two are alive and even distantly in contact with me today. We shared more tears and laughter than any family, and we made so goddamn much money that you would think my name is Frenchy Rockefeller.

"The women here are extremely ignorant as to the means of securing their salvation, but they are very expert in the art of displaying their beauty."
<u>Sister Madeleine Hachard</u>
New Orleans Ursuline Nun in 1727

One secret of the sex trade is that it is not looks that count. Take it from me: some of the greatest moneymakers of all time were outright *dogs* by normal superficial standards. What sells sex better than anything is not a pretty face or shapely body ... it's *personality*. An ugly woman who can screw with authority and confidence is better than any shy Playboy playmate. A top-dollar trick can look a strong man in the eye and say the most perverse, dirtiest, raunchiest thing imaginable with a smile on her face and the man's balls in her hands. That is a real moneymaker: a woman who can take charge.

I had one broad named Peggy who was older than dirt and looked like Ed McMahon after a Tijuana sex change. But Peggy could walk up to *any* straight man — Steve McQueen, Fidel Castro, Jimi Hendrix, didn't matter — and convince him to rush to a hotel room with nothing more than a ten-second whisper in his ear.

Baby, if you got the personality *and* you got the looks, then you can't be beat. You're worth your weight in gold. That's why the English Queen is richer today than the actual Queen of England: she had the personality to please the brain and the body to please the eyes. The only thing she lacked was the good taste to be my old lady.

Another girl who seemed to have it all at first was Mickey Medina, and it is one of my great regrets that I only had her for one week. Mickey was the last franchise girl for the legendary landlady Dora Russo. When Dora retired, Mickey came to me as the number- one call girl in the city, and she looked the part. Mickey was hotter than any Hollywood celebrity or Bourbon Street showgirl, and she was as charming as a princess. I was excited to have her on my team until I spoke to her ex-boyfriend, John, who looked way too happy for me to have her.

Suspicious, I asked John how he had broken up with Mickey. "Aw, Frenchy, it was no big deal," John said, laughing at me. "The goddamn woman asks me if I was enjoying my pancakes one morning, and, after I said they were fine, she showed me the pancake mix. In that goddamn tub, Frenchy, was smashed up dog turds. The bitch fed me dogshit for no reason!"

I kicked Mickey out of my penthouse apartment the moment I got home. No matter how much money Mickey would have made me, I could not stand to sacrifice my peace of mind. I preferred the enjoyment of a good hearty breakfast to an extra thousand dollars a day.

My next near-miss was my second wife, who had all the looks with none of the charm. I'll call this, ahem, "lady" Cheryl Lee. I first met Cheryl in the early 1960s when I was managing the Chez Paris, and she was working at the Sho-Bar for Frank Caracci as a tap dancer. Caracci would send Cheryl over to warn me when the heat was in the Quarter, and I got to flirting with her since she had a dancer's body honed from years as one of the dancers in Bob Hope's traveling review, a beautiful face, and the type of pushy personality that can be mistaken for "moxie" when a woman's attractive. Cheryl also was Jewish, which continued to hold an exotic appeal for me.

Cheryl Lee gradually became my girlfriend and, when she discovered that I had become a pimp, told me that she wanted to become a prostitute too. "What, you think I can't do this too, Mr.

Tough Guy?" Before I knew it, she had moved herself into my apartment, pushed out the other girls, and forced me to sign marriage papers. I didn't even tell anyone that I was married; I was being held hostage by this pushy battle-axe and was too scared to speak. For the short duration of our marriage, I was under constant surveillance, and there was not a working girl in the city who didn't get hassled by Cheryl Lee over her suspicions that they were *all* having sex with me, no matter how old or ugly.

Luckily, Cheryl Lee was so pushy that she pushed herself right out of my door. Absurdly greedy, even by hooker standards, Cheryl started shaking down my clients with sob stories and protests of love, looking for big cash gifts and trips to the jewelry store. When Cheryl took a good friend of mine, who happened to be a multimillionaire, to the cleaners, I had no choice but to get a divorce. I may have been afraid of her, but she wasn't worth losing a multimillionaire client over.

Cheryl left to marry a crooked, jukebox-business operator named Harry, and, on her way out, she went to my safe deposit box and stole half my cash and half my stash of jewelry. The note she left in the safe deposit box perfectly captures her personality: "ASSHOLE! I could have took it all!"

My next old lady was my first working girl who had both the looks and the personality, but only briefly. Beverly had it all until she found drugs, and then she lost everything and took a lot of my stuff, as well. After Beverly ran away to live with her dealer and stole my washer and dryer on the way out of the door to sell for drug money, I decided to play a prank on her by putting up an Old West-style "Wanted" poster with her face on it in all of the city's Laundromats. This earned me a visit from a pair of FBI agents, who told me with straight faces that they believed I was hiring a hit team to kill Beverly through a Laundromat poster.

"Well, if so, you got a pretty strong case, don't you, gentlemen?" I said, incredulous.

Apparently, Beverly bought the FBI's theory that the way to assassinate a hooker was to put up novelty-style flyers in public places. Beverly showed up at my penthouse a couple weeks later, shaking and obviously terrified, with a beautiful young woman she introduced as her sister-in-law. Beverly told me that the sister-in-law was a peace offering who wanted to work and could "take my place as your old lady." Since the sister-in-law, Ronnie, was undeniably younger and more beautiful than Beverly, I happily accepted the gift and freed Beverly from all of her debts to me for stealing my property.

Ronnie seemed finally to be the woman who had it all, looks and personality and even youth. She was pretty, sweet, and friendly, and I was getting ready to fall in love with her when she left me for her gay husband and sick child. She was another close call.

Finally, in the late 1960s, I met my dream woman: the woman with both the looks and the personality and the senselessness to marry me. Known to everyone simply as "Jackie," my third wife Joan Lee Clemens of Texas was easily the best Mrs. Brouillette in history and a bottom bitch to the core. She stood by her man no matter if I was rich or poor, free or jailed — as long as I was hers, it made no difference to Jackie.

Befitting the wife of Mr. New Orleans, Jackie claimed to be a descendant of Mark Twain, which I could not imagine was true since that would mean her crazy-ass sons had some Twain genes in their mix. Jackie was a busty, raven-haired beauty who loved hooking but loved her man Frenchy even more. What I did for her I'll never know; she was just wild over me. She pressured me into marriage, and I told her that, as long as she didn't get any ideas about monogamy, I'd sigh and say "Oh, what the hell?" and go through with the ceremony.

Not a week after our marriage, Jackie nonchalantly mentioned that the famous New Orleans trumpeter Al Hirt asked to be her sugar daddy. Seeing that I was getting excited about tapping into those jazz millions, Jackie flipped on me and shook her head with disgust. "You don't mean to think that I'm going to say yes, do you? We're married now!"

That was typical of a hooker: give her a marriage certificate, and all of a sudden she thinks she's become a professional homemaker! So I told her, "Baby, marriage don't mean anything. Dale has a friend who gives him stacks of pre-stamped marriage certificates; he can legally marry an oak tree and a dildo in the state of Louisiana if he wanted to! Don't take that piece of paper to heart!"

Jackie quickly came to her senses, and she continued to bring in tip-top clients. Joe Marcello, in particular, was damn near in love with her. Because of the Mafia rule against divorce, Joe was trapped in a loveless marriage with a woman who was cheating on him with an FBI agent.

This betrayal left Joe lovelorn and vulnerable, and he burrowed into Jackie's considerable tits whenever he saw her. Joe's woe only deepened when the fed that cuckolded him had the balls to mouth off to Carlos, who, like Silver Dollar Sam, never considered government employees off-limits. Carlos knocked the FBI agent on his ass and earned himself that six-month stay at the health spa federal joint that I mentioned earlier.

I asked Carlos why he would not give his poor brother permission to divorce, but he just snorted at me like a bull. Later, I heard that Carlos was afraid that Joe would embarrass and disgrace the family by marrying Jackie, which is one reason Carlos encouraged me to take her officially off the market. His wedding gift was uncharacteristically generous that time around.

If I had a single complaint about Jackie, it was her hasty decision to give birth, years before she met me, to Steven, whom I simply called The Asshole. The Asshole was a long-haired string-bean with a pissy look permanently on his face and a tattoo of the devil on his arm. The boy must have been born with great potential — he was a mechanical genius and could talk the panties off the pope — but he was a weak sister psychologically thanks to his troubled childhood. Like most bottom bitches, Jackie was too obsessed with having fun and doing right by her man to ever raise her child. The boy grew up feral, and he suffered throughout his short life from violent mood swings, unpredictable temper tantrums, and all manner of paranoia and random rage.

I first suspected that this young man would be trouble when he beat up and kidnapped a FBI agent. Though I appreciated the sentiment, this sort of thing just was not done. The Asshole had gone on a car-stealing spree, and he told the FBI agent that visited him never to bother him again. Since The Asshole went on merrily stealing cars, the agent visited again, so The Asshole beat the shit out of him, hog-tied him, drove him to a cornfield, and tossed him behind a row of crops for a farmer to find.

This was a pretty deep pile of shit by any man's standards, but Jackie brought the kid to me and asked if I could fix it. I said I would do what I could. I went to see Nolan, and, since this was during Edwin's prime, he was able to argue the plea down to six months' probation for beating and kidnapping an FBI agent. When I told The Asshole about the fucking miracle I had just performed for him, he scoffed, threw his hands in the air, and screamed, "I thought you had connections!" as if I had committed him to serving twenty-five years in Angola.

This sealed the deal for me: this kid was going into my book as "The Asshole." The funny thing is that I received a phone call from Nolan the next day. "Man, you won't believe it! We coulda got the boy off in that kidnapping case!"

"What the fuck are you talkin' 'bout, Nolan?" I was pretty grumpy and had even been thinking about going to Nolan to get the plea deal squashed so that I could send The Asshole to prison.

"Frenchy, that FBI agent went back to the cornfield to show the investigators where everything happened, and, right there in the middle of the same cornfield, he was fucking struck by lightning and died! The prosecutors had no witnesses to bring to the stand; they would have had to dismiss the case."

In retrospect, I think Nolan might have been puttin' me on, but I'll never know for sure.

Because Jackie was my bottom bitch and the overseer that

allowed my businesses to run without me paying attention, I more or less had to let The Asshole hang around. Naturally, this hyperactive petty crook nurtured ambitions to become my successor, so he did his best to interfere with my rackets and ruin my life.

One day, a twenty-five-year-old call girl made the mistake of asking The Asshole to pose in a picture with me. I knew the girl was sentimental, but The Asshole got the idea that she was taking photos of us to give to the police for identification purposes. This was asinine — the police had millions of photos of me, and no one had trouble recognizing me either since this was during my phase where I walked around with a fucking gigantic red parrot on my shoulder — and I told The Asshole so.

Unfortunately, The Asshole took matters into his own hands and "punished" this "rat" by trying to drown her. And where did he try to drown her? If you said "anywhere but the place where I notoriously failed to drown two other women," you'd be wrong. That's right, The Asshole decided to prove that he was the better man by "besting" me and showing how to *properly* drown a hooker in Bayou St. John.

I'm sure you can guess what happened. The 140-pound hulk failed to drown the hooker, and she too escaped and went right to the police station. Though it turns out she was no rat before, she definitely became one now, and The Asshole was arrested for kidnapping and attempted murder, and I was arrested for prostitution.

To add to my problems, the *Baton Rouge Advocate* reported that *I* had been arrested for trying to drown the hooker in Bayou St. John. Though they issued a correction the next day, the entire underworld became convinced that, undeterred by my previous humiliation, I had tried and failed *again* to use shallow Bayou St. John as my own personal aquatic cemetery.

I seriously considered letting The Asshole fry on the murder charges, but I made some calls, patched up some hurt feelings, and got him released from jail. In gratitude, The Asshole broke into my house, stole my pet parrot, and fled to the Carolinas, never to be seen again. Luckily, I was able to negotiate the return of my precious parrot through The Asshole's stepmother.

That parrot was another one of my bottom bitches, but it took me a while to find out. I named it Napoleon because it was short but pushy. Napoleon was only about three feet tall from the tip of its tail to its head, yet he dominated my goddamn life. Napoleon was a beautiful scarlet macaw, and though that species is not known for mimicking human speech, my speech is so redundant and inhuman that it picked up a single, all-important word that it would pronounce with a gruff, scratchy Cajun accent. Sometimes I'd pick up the phone and just let Napoleon squawk, "BABY!"

I thought it was inhumane to keep a big-ass parrot in a cage, so I let the macaw take over my house. When he felt like it, I'd let him jump on my shoulder and take a walk around town with me, introducing him to everyone as my "best friend." One day while we were at home on the couch, Napoleon hopped off my shoulder, clopped onto my coffee table, squatted, and shit out an egg.

Well, it turns out that Napoleon was a girl — though Jackie suggested that she may have been a transsexual parrot of some sort. I renamed her Josephine and gave her full status as my new bottom bitch, which Jackie took in stride. I also sternly told my other best friend, Satan's son Malcolm X, that he'd better not turn bitch on me.

"Malcolm, if you get the feelin' like you gotta lay a fuckin' egg, please keep it away from me! I can't take any more surprises like that!"

"BABY!" screamed Josephine.

"Judges, lawyers, and politicians have a *license* to steal. We don't need one."
Carlo Gambino

Before I was paroled from Club Fed, an old crook pulled me aside and told me a piece of wisdom that would save my life. If it wasn't for this old man, I never would have survived the past three decades.

"Let me tell you a story," the old convict began, though I was clearly showing no interest in his ramblings. "There's an old gangster. Someone asks him what he would do different if he could do his life over again. The old gangster thinks for a second, and then says 'I'd do everything the same — only this time, I'd get a license for everything.'

"Think about that for a second. It makes perfect sense! If you're a bookmaker, it's illegal to take bets from a degenerate gambler, but not if you're a licensed stockbroker! The average joe can't legally hold a friendly poker game, but, if you have a casino license, you could have 100 card tables running at once! If you're a pimp, it's two-to-five every time you introduce a hooker to a john, but if you get licensed as an escort agency you're all set! No one can fuck with you."

Escort agency ... this was a phrase I had never heard before. I made some collect calls to New Orleans, and apparently no one there had heard of the idea either. For once, I was on virgin territory. After many hours of patient questioning, the old man was able to get me to understand what the words actually meant. It seemed too good to be true.

Some brilliant pimp had discovered the loophole in the law that said that it was legal for a businessman to sell a customer the company of a female escort for a certain period of time. As long as this transaction at no point mentioned sex, then it was wholly legal; the escort agency owner was just selling the right for the customer to be *escorted*. Any further deal negotiated between the escort and the customer regarding sexual acts was exclusively between them and could not rebound on the owner of the agency.

This setup seemed foolproof. Not only would I receive steady hourly agency fees in addition to my commission on the girls' services, I could also excuse myself from negotiations with clients. Naturally, the girls would underreport whatever deals they negotiated to screw me, but the immunity from prosecution would be worth it.

Theoretically, if I found some discipline somewhere, I could report enough legal taxable income to own homes and cars in my own name, which I had repeatedly neglected to do. Even when I had my service station, I could not bring myself to launder enough money to fabricate a respectable taxable income with which to support myself; instead, I bought everything with dirty money and promptly lost it all to the cops and petty crooks as soon as I was arrested.

When I was released, I returned home to Mrs. Jackie Brouillette, and we talked it over and decided that the escort agency was too risky. After all, if it was such a good idea, why hadn't someone cleverer than me thought of opening one up in New Orleans? Having just been released from federal prison, I was feeling pretty cautious and unwilling to take wild, ambitious risks. So I returned to the pimp game.

That did not last long. Besides Jackie, my most reliable girl was a tame sweetheart named Sunny Lynn. As far as I could tell, Sunny was not an addict, an alcoholic, a pervert, or a lunatic; she was just a mellow college girl with a thing for comic books. As long as I gave her the opportunity to make enough turning a few tricks at night to vegetate for the rest of day, all Sunny Lynn wanted from me was a fresh batch of comic books once a week since she was too embarrassed to buy them herself.

This was no problem: I cut a deal with the local kids to buy their old comic books for a nickel apiece. I was so crooked I couldn't even bring myself to buy something as innocuous as comic books anywhere besides the black market.

I used to tell Jackie, Malcolm X, and Napoleon/Josephine that Sunny was the sanest hooker I had ever met. The comic book obsession was nerdy but harmless. It was simply a pleasure to do business with her. She didn't ask for anything emotionally, socially, spiritually, or financially — she just wanted to work and read some fucking comic books. She was always friendly, polite, reliable, and to the point. No robot could have been programmed to do her job better.

So I was happy to have Sunny back on my team when I got back on the street. To reward her, I cleaned out the comic stashes of all the little boys and drove over to her apartment at 2 a.m. to give her the gift and pick up my share of the night's proceeds. I used my key to open the door since I paid for her place and called inside, "Hey, baby! It's Frenchy Claus with some presents for ya, dawlin'!"

I walked over to the couch to see Sunny sleeping peacefully — or at least pretending to sleep. I had made such a racket coming in that I knew she would have been woken up; unlike my other girls, she wasn't an opiate girl. Since I could see her breathing, I knew she wasn't dead. I put down the box and leaned over. "Hey, baby, cut the shit, I can see you're ..."

I was distracted for a moment by the pile of money under her ashtray, which she left for me every night to pick up. As I lifted the ashtray, I could hear a rustle on the couch. I was right; Sunny was faking sleep.

Sunny's eyes flung open like the gates of Hell, and the mad she-beast sprung off the couch in a buck-wild fury, squealing like a piglet set on fire. Before I could move, I felt extraordinary pain in my right thigh and my stomach. I looked down and saw that my sanest call girl had just plunged two picadors deep into my body for no reason. I looked up at Sunny's face for an explanation, and the blood-covered bitch was laughing and sticking out her tongue like Gene Simmons.

After I tied the bitch up with a telephone cord and got it out of her that she had guzzled some pills a john gave her, I called my crooked doctor and had him come over and stitch me up. As I patiently waited for the doctor and stained the entire apartment red, I kept asking Sunny why she had planned to ambush and kill me. She just laughed and laughed and laughed.

I thought about setting her up on a date with Jackie's son so that they could duel it out with picadors in Bayou St. John, but I decided not to get carried away. Sunny was also an attempted murderer, but she didn't deserve to deal with that parrot-stealing Asshole.

The doctor told me that Sunny had been one inch to the right of landing a fatal blow in my stomach. At that moment, I decided that it was time to give the pimp game a vacation. If Sunny could go picador-stabbing-spree mad, no one besides Jackie, Napoleon/Josephine, Malcolm X, and the English Queen could be trusted.

So I talked with my council and asked for input. Malcolm and Josephine were no help, freeloaders as usual. Jackie was against leaving the sex rackets, so I told her that I would open up The House of the Rising Sun Escort Agency as long as she did the leg work with the hookers. Since I foolishly counted on the Marcellos to invest in Frenchy Inc., I talked about launching another "legitimate" business in case the first escort agency in New Orleans failed.

I was not confident that I could voyage too far from the sex rackets and still make money, so I told Jackie to think of another legal business that sold sex. "Well, shit," she said, "you could always open up a go-go joint."

I knew there was a reason I married Jackie.

"I have a lot of friends convicted of felonies...
A lot of people are uptight about that. I'm not."
Jefferson Parish Sheriff Harry Lee
Testifying as a character witness for Frank Caracci

After twenty years of unabashed criminality, I decided to impersonate going straight. It was around 1973, and I was a twice-married, thirty-seven-year-old teenager with a great physique and a fabulous alcohol habit. Other than being harder to scandalize, I still felt fundamentally unchanged from Marksville; at any moment, I worried that I was going to be arrested and carted back to the countryside in the back of a pickup truck. I was improvising as I went along, and it was a continual surprise to me that I made so much money and won so many friends.

The escort business proved an easy and painless success. The novelty of the idea was so strong that, as soon as word got around, my phone line was jammed with new straitlaced customers who would never have called a pimp but had no problem dialing up an escort agency. Scared johns knew what they were getting with a pimp, but with an escort agency they could cautiously feel their way through the deal before doing anything too daring.

I paid $5000-per-month in ads in the Yellow Pages telephone directory, the most they would allow, and then answered my phone as I normally would as a pimp. The only difference was that I now received a regular, legal, hourly payment from the customer (the "agency fee"), and I had Jackie and later my "agent" run around and pick up the cash from the girls at the end of the night.

It was easy, stress-free money, and I never had to touch the cash or the crimes myself. Opening my strip club turned out to be almost as easy — as you might guess, *everything* with me is pretty easy, or it just never gets done.

My original idea had been to replicate the old French Quarter-style burlesque clubs I knew so well from the 1950s. From my years with Dutch Kraut, I knew everything there was to know about the burlesque club business. It was a straightforward gig: you appeal to middle-class folks and easily scandalized tourists by offering an "all-star revue" of an MC, a band, a couple variety acts, and most importantly some hyped-up showgirls. You could charge just about anything you wanted for food, cover charge, and drinks, and the lure of naked tits would keep wealthy customers lined up around the block.

That's at least how it was in the 1950s. But at this time, in the

1970s, the French Quarter was a toxic, impoverished mess of junkie dives, bathhouses, and shithole strip clubs full of mustached trannies and 200-pound biker bitches. Clearly, I was not going to head back to the Quarter to get hassled by the local beat cops with their competing protection rackets.

I decided to follow in Carlos' footsteps and relocate to Jefferson Parish since I was pretty *simpatico* with the Marcello's pet sheriff's office. I originally got a promise from Sammy Marcello for a $100,000 loan to build my place, but Sammy always was a pushover, and I'm sure Carlos told him to give me the Conforto runaround. After waiting a couple months, I was able to secure a smaller loan from a jukebox company.

Since I was dealing with a much smaller budget, I scaled down my ambitions. I didn't have the cash to build a large theater for a big Vegas-style, multi-act revue; I'd barely have money to buy a tiny place and pay strippers. Thus was the first modern strip club in Jefferson Parish born.

I rented a tiny building just off Veterans Highway in Metairie that was once home to the Holiday Drive-In restaurant back during the 1950s and '60s when bobby-socks and poodle-skirt joints like that were popular. The building was truly bizarre looking, a futuristic shack with a roof like a stealth bomber and an attention-grabbing, A-frame tail. Someone had redesigned the drive-in as a bar simply by piling ugly bricks over the windows. Due to its microscopic size and flamboyant 1950s look, the home of my future strip club could not have looked less appropriate.

Nonetheless, I decided to make a jerry-rigged go of transforming this dump into a go-go joint. I sent word out through my extensive network of burglars, boosters, and scammers that I was looking to stock my new club on the cheap. Between the hacks and the gangsters, I knew every petty thief in Louisiana, and they all came to see me.

Shortly after I sent the open call out to my thieves, a hack gave me a phone call one night, immediately after I had reached the peak of Shit-faced Mountain. "Hey, Frenchy, boy you should score this. Right down on Veterans, there's a gigantic roll of the prettiest carpet you've ever seen behind dis building just takin' a sit on a loading dock. This thing would be perfect for your club, real fine oriental-style shit with a big, fuck-off dragon on it."

That's all I needed to hear; what was a strip club without dragon carpeting? I grabbed two more drunk friends, and we snuck over to meet the hack at the loading dock. I was so drunk that I did not recognize the location, and we did not even attempt to hide that we were stealing this goddamn thing. Since this carpet roll was far too long to transport in a car, we just carried it across busy Veterans Highway like four ants lugging a giant French fry back to our pile.

The day after that, international highwaymen Dale and Tex dropped by to discuss my new club. Dale and Tex had spent the last five years on a multimillion-dollar tear in the Midwest, traveling in their matching red Lincoln convertibles from town to town on an unending robbery and burglary spree. Dale and Tex traveled with only one essential: a glass furnace for melting down gold and silver jewelry into untraceable bars of pure gold and silver. Tex was such an expert at spotting vulnerable jewelry stores, mansions, banks, and warehouses that it was not uncommon for them to completely fill two Samsonite briefcases with gold and silver bars in a week.

Once they had a briefcase of gold or silver ready, Dale would take it down to the bus station and register it as luggage on a Greyhound bus to a town where they had a reliable Mafia fence. A few weeks later, Dale and Tex would swing back around to visit their fence and pick up tens of thousands of dollars in cash. Whenever they wanted to visit New Orleans, I'd act as their fence and meet Dale at the airport; sometimes, his Samsonite briefcase would be so heavy with gold that the handle would be bending.

Luckily for me, I was released from jail right when Dale and Tex had chosen to move down to New Orleans and stay for a little while to work for Carlos, who wanted a surveillance and counter-surveillance team. Using God-knows-what contacts,

Carlos bought Dale and Tex some government night-vision cameras and a "hound dog" radio frequency detector to check for bugs.

After the Kennedy fiasco, I don't think I ever dealt with a more paranoid and meticulously careful gangster than Carlos. Words were unnecessary — Carlos' face could communicate just about anything that words could say. More and more often, Carlos would insist on taking walks out in the Louisiana heat to have a discussion, which greatly pained him as an old, fat-ass Italian. Though Dale and Tex regularly searched Carlos' offices and hangouts for bugs, he was still too suspicious to enjoy a conversation anywhere close to an air conditioning system.

For causing him this discomfort, Carlos wanted revenge on the FBI. He had a dream that, by having Tex and Dale hide at the apparently empty Town & Country in the dead of night with their night-vision equipment, he could possibly rack up a couple of "free kills." The theory went that Tex and Dale would catch the FBI during an attempt to break in and plant new bugs in Carlos' office. Naturally, Tex and Dale would be heavily armed, and Carlos' plan was for them to wait until the agents were trespassing on private property before opening fire and legally slaughtering the unannounced federal agents.

When no agents turned up after multiple stakeouts, Carlos' paranoia festered. He decided that there must have already been bugs planted that Tex and Dale had somehow missed, so my two buddies restarted the search of his office from the top down.

After that second search once again turned up no bugs, Tex and Dale drove over to visit me in my empty barroom with the beautiful oriental dragon carpeting. Looking around, Tex asked what I needed most. "Ah, man, I think the bar is probably going to be the most expensive pain in the..."

"Don't buy nothin'," said Tex with that enigmatic smile that meant felonies were about to be committed. "I'll have what you need tomorrow."

The very next afternoon, Tex and Dale drove up to the front

of my soon-to-be strip club with a moving truck carrying a *fully stocked* bar, complete with a cash register still filled with money.

Thanks to friends like these, my strip club was ready for its grand opening in a couple of weeks without a single legitimate purchase. The newly dubbed Body Shop was nothing to look at: a tiny, smoky, dimly-lit club with brick walls, low ceilings, ornate Chinese carpeting, and a bar that looked like it belonged in a nice seafood restaurant. My back office was just large enough to fit my muscles inside before closing the door.

Topping off this Frankenstein joint's ambience was one of those *Saturday Night Fever*-type lighted disco platforms that Tex Cody somehow stole, years before I ever saw another one in New Orleans. It may sound like a dated idea to have a girl dancing on a glowing and blinking floor, but at the time it seemed insanely futuristic and over-the-top.

If the escort agency hadn't been bringing in so much money, I may not have even gone through with the opening. Looking at this mess of a strip club, I figured I could have given off a more classy impression by just holding the festivities in a circus tent.

My marketing campaign for the debut of the Body Shop was simple: call every gangster, hack, pimp, drug dealer, whore, and crooked cop I know and invite them to attend opening night. Since the characters figured that Carlos, Joe, and Sammy would likely be there, just about everyone *besides* Carlos, Joe, and Sammy attended. It was a huge success.

Right as the party got wild, my friend Harry Lee arrived. Lee was a big, fat Chinese attorney at the U.S. District Court of New Orleans whose family owned the fabulous House of Lee Chinese restaurant right by the Body Shop on Veterans. Harry was a real good ole boy, smart as hell with a shit-kickin' redneck "who gives a fuck?" sense of humor. Harry walked over, shook my hand, and said, "Frenchy, this place is..."

Harry paused and his face went pale. I followed his eyes down to the object of his shock: my carpet. Finally, I realized where the fuck we had stolen that carpet from: the loading dock of House of Lee! I had stolen an extremely expensive, custom Chinese carpet from my friend's family restaurant and stuffed it into a strip club only a few yards away.

Now would be an appropriate time to inform you that a couple years later, Harry Lee was elected as the new Sheriff of Jefferson Parish — a job he would hold for twenty-seven years.

Luckily for me, Harry Lee was a player who understood the rules of the game in Louisiana. After the initial surprise let go of his tongue, Harry gave me a friendly punch on the shoulder and laughed. "Nice fucking carpet you got there, Frenchy. Nice dragons!"

Like Edwin Edwards, Harry Lee would become the sort of friend whose family members coincidentally did me a shitload of favors. I rarely talked to Harry himself besides to smooth out the problems caused by a particularly troublesome family member of his with illegal habits. That same troubled and troublesome family member, however, was always calling me up with surprisingly detailed instructions on how to avoid upcoming police raids, vice busts, and drunk-driving roadblocks.

Nice family.

The opening night at the Body Shop brought in a few thousand dollars. The legendary cast of characters I assembled that night established the Body Shop's reputation as the hottest and wildest men's entertainment venue in Jefferson Parish. It had an air of danger and secrecy as the place where the underworld rulers of the parish hung out and partied. I raked in $700 to $1000 in 100%-squeaky-clean nightly profit from the Body Shop for almost a decade, which barely even hints at the dirty profits I made from the joint.

Frenchy Brouillette was now a successful legitimate businessman.

"[William "Canada Bill" Jones] made enormous sums of money, but he lost it all ashore, for while almost every professional gambler was an arrant sucker for some particular game, Canada Bill was a sucker for all of them... [A]fter diligent search Canada Bill found a faro game and began to play. His partner urged him to stop. 'The game's crooked!' he declared. 'I know it,' replied Bill, 'but it's the only one in town!'"

Herburt Asbury

Until the Body Shop's success forced me to keep it open at all hours, my established habit was to pass out drunk, rich, and happy behind the bar. Usually, I woke up slumped over the counter to the sound of one of my employees knocking at the door at 5 p.m. looking to enter and get ready for work.

One morning, I woke up to a very different sound — the sound of a chainsaw revved up and started a couple feet from my resting spot. Opening my eyes, I saw that my ears were not deceiving me: some lunatic was approaching me with a whirring chainsaw lifted above his head. Before I could say anything, the chainsaw swung down towards me and shredded through the spot on the bar where I had been napping like a turkey breast.

I was halfway out the back door when I realized who the *Friday the 13th* madman was: Tex Cody. Though Tex undoubtedly qualified as the sort of guy who would behead you with a chainsaw, he definitely wasn't the sort of guy who would behead *me* with a chainsaw. Nonetheless, I took precautions, crouching down and skulking back inside my strip club as Cody laughed uncontrollably with the chainsaw still chugging in his hands.

After a lot of hysterical body language, I convinced Cody to turn off the chainsaw and explain why the fuck he had just cut my bar's counter in half. "Frenchy, you should've seen the fool face you just made." Tex was panting, his face dripping with tears of laughter, as if pretend decapitations were a normal *Candid Camera*-style prank.

"Baby, I'm going to start fucking attacking *you* with chainsaws when you sleep! Man, why did you destroy my bar?"

"Ah, don't worry man. You're going to make a ton more money once I finish turning your bar into a horseshoe-shaped bar."

Tex was right; I doubled the nightly booze profits after he finished reconstructing the bar so that it sat twice as many people. It helped that Carlos' people got me a hookup with Falstaff Brewery for damn near free beer, which I served to all of the customers from the tap regardless if they ordered the $3 glass of the tap beer or a $7 pint of imported German lager.

I got real creative inventing expensive, exotic imported beers to offer to my customers while pouring Falstaff into their glasses. Soon, my profit margin was so high that I had no choice but to keep the bar open twenty-four-hours; closing it at all would have been like walking away from a malfunctioning ATM machine spitting $20 bills.

To make up for the heart attack he almost caused with his chainsaw stunt, Tex and his partner Dale went out of their way to save my life on two occasions. The first near-death experience happened at Snake Gonzales's bar, where I was busting out a mark using Snake's magnetized dice table. After I wrung him dry, the mark told me that he'd get the cash to pay me from his car. Dale tagged along with me to the parking lot, suspecting that I was walking into a trap. Sure enough, the mark jumped into the driver's seat, revved his engine, and gunned his car right at me.

Dale barely managed to pull my booze-heavy, thickly-muscled frame out of the way at the last possible moment. Before I knew what happened, Dale was firing his Derringer through the car's back window, dusting the street with glass but failing to kill the driver or stop his escape. "Nice shooting, Dale," I grumbled as I pulled myself off the ground. "I appreciate you saving my life, but it'd be nice if you got my money, too."

The other lifesaving gesture came at the Body Shop, where I was generally short-staffed when it came to muscle. I started slipping Tex some cash just to hang around since, between myself and the bartender, there was very little we could have done by ourselves to break up a big brawl among my rowdy customers. On the other hand, Tex could singlehandedly win any fight, so I felt much more secure having him around to oversee the proceedings.

Sure enough, one night two six-foot-six, corn-fed, redneck gorillas snuck behind a girl playing pool and ripped off her skirt as she bent over to shoot. As a Cajun gentleman, I could not allow this sort of thing, so I courageously threw my body into action and quickly learned the meaning of an ass-beating. I felt like I was in the middle of a grizzly bear gangbang. Just when my soul was getting wrung free of my immaculately sculpted body, Tex and Dale came in swinging pool cues like Reggie Jackson and Willie Mays on a speed binge.

By the time the cops arrived, the entire floor of the Body Shop was covered in teeth, blood, and tears, and Tex was almost finished wedging an entire pool cue up one of the gropers' asses. Like me, Tex was a traditional Southern gentleman: as far as he was concerned, you could ignore and screw around on your old lady, but you made sure to be polite to female strangers at bars.

The cops dragged Tex, Dale, and me in for assaulting and damn near killing those two giants. They had to drop the charges at the arraignment because the heavily bandaged gorillas refused to look down at us — none of us a centimeter over 5'8" — and admit to the entire courtroom that we beat their asses only after they started it.

Whenever Tex was not around to even the numbers, I was still practically defenseless behind my bar as the Body Shop filled up with fifty or sixty wannabe Jefferson Parish toughs. I decided to increase the criminal element in the bar to provide backup in case I ever needed it. Following Snake Gonzales's example, I installed a secret backroom gaming parlor complete with magnetized dice tables, a fixed roulette wheel, and card tables manned by cardsharp dealers. With the table set, I invited the crossroaders over to dinner.

Crossroaders were elite gambling cheats and affiliated boosters, safecrackers, jewel thieves, burglars, and con men who worked in traveling crews. I gave the crossroaders an impressive venue to do business. My smoky, secretive, high-stakes gaming room was just the sort of place to attract a rich mark looking to waste his money while feeling dangerous, and the crossroader would have no trouble fleecing his Vidalia using my crooked tables and dealers. After they finished bankrupting their marks, the crossroaders gave me a cut of the loot and then spent the rest on my strippers and booze.

Thanks to the ideal conditions, The Body Shop became the accepted headquarters of the crossroader brotherhood in Louisiana, and every night a new cardsharp or jewel thief would arrive from Kansas City or Jackson or Houston to look for local gigs, fence some jewels, and waste thousands of dollars in loot on strippers, whores, and booze.

The money I made from the crossroaders' business was obscene; at one crooked card game, I actually won ownership of a bank in Houma. My attorney bullied me into giving it back; I had not been careful enough at laundering money to justify my overnight ownership of a major financial institution to the IRS. The bank owner was so grateful that he visited once a week for years to drop off a couple hundred dollars at a time, paying off his debt in dribs and drabs.

The arrival of the crossroaders marked the last golden age of my criminal career. For the second half of the 1970s, I made maybe a million dollars a year between the Body Shop, the escort agency, and my lobbying with Nolan Edwards; none of this would rise to the level of a job in my mind. My cousin Edwin ruled Louisiana politics, and my friend Carlos was the unchallenged king of the Louisiana underworld. My bottom bitch Jackie was cool, calm, and devoted, and every pretty outlaw girl in the state flocked to work for me as a stripper, escort, or both.

Though I regularly got hit with the usual minor booze, drugs, and pandering charges, I made out without serious jail time thanks to my friends in the judicial system. Every day, I tried to wake up early enough for lunch at Mandina's, the noon hangout for all of the district attorneys and judges. Today, I would put every lobbyist in Louisiana on the payroll of a shell company registered in the Caymans, but at the time I lobbied those in power by picking up the tab at every table I visited.

To seal the deal, I'd send each judge who smiled at me a case of Chivas Regal scotch along with a bottle of Crown Royal whiskey. I also took after Carlos and memorized how everyone "liked dey coffee." I knew every judge's taste in women and sent them a "present" every birthday.

Thanks to meticulous efforts like these, by the late '70s I had achieved a level of gangland success that I had literally never conceived possible for someone like me, someone without work ethic, self-control, financial know-how, discipline, an education, a good background, the ability to stay sober, or even an Italian last name. It was clear to everyone around me that I did not deserve the financial bonanza I was enjoying.

My obscene wealth could not possibly have a long lifespan. I tried my damndest to bankrupt myself at least once a day, emptying my wallet like it was full of bad memories. I spent about $300-per-day on lunches at Mandina's and another $300 on dinner for myself and friends, $1000-per-week on various bribes, $2000-per-month on an apartment I never visited, $25,000-per-year on cars I never drove, and tens of thousands of dollars on diamond rings that I had no free fingers for and clothing items that might never see daylight. Since I always had a superabundance of it, money meant nothing to me; it came too easy to be respected.

The ultimate story from the Body Shop era involves my buddy Dale. He came into my office during the strip club's peak hours and found me passed out drunk at my desk. Drool was pouring down my silk suit, and I had wads of cash spilling out of every pocket and a bag of hot jewels damn near setting my desk on fire. To teach me a lesson, Dale snuck over and snatched every dollar from my body without coming close to waking me.

"How ya doin', Frenchy?" Dale asked in a chipper voice when he called the next morning.

"Not worth a shit, baby. Someone took $20,000 off me last night," I said, sounding a little groggy and hungover but hardly heartbroken.

"You fuckin' liar, it was only $16,000!" Dale teased with a laugh. "Goes to show you, you need to stop drinking and take better care of your money."

The sad thing was, as soon as Dale let me in on the joke and told me that he would return the money, I wasn't even relieved. Honestly, I should have told Dale to keep the money. I just didn't care. I had never cared in the first place. I didn't give a fuck if I lost $16,000 or not. It was just money. It would be there forever, and it didn't do anything for me anymore.

All I wanted was another drink to start the day off right, and I spent twenty-four-hours-a-day within walking distance of my own personal bar. This was the sort of heaven that starts to feel like hell after a while.

Chapter XIII

Don't Leave Hating, Baby

1980-Today

> "We may not pay Satan reverence, for that would be indiscreet,
> but we can at least respect his talents."
> **Mark Twain**

BABY, THE SECRET OF LIFE IN FEDERAL PRISON BEARS REPEATING: DO THE TIME YOU'VE GOT EASY, AND DON'T LEAVE HATING. We've all got sentenced to do time down here on Earth, and we have little control over the rules, conditions, or our fellow inmates. The only thing we have control over is how we do our time: easy or hard.

As far as I can tell, if you walk through the door on the other end with a smile on your face and no regrets, you've won. All the pain and suffering and guilt that you can feel doesn't add up to a single damn thing in the end; it just evaporates away like a bad hangover. If you did your time on Earth easy, you've won.

That's been my philosophy with this book, too. There's no point in giving you folks a hard time when there's an easy time to be had. I could have concentrated on the thirty years when the good times rolled, or the thirty years after that when the good times repeatedly rolled off a cliff and landed on my head. Naturally, I gave you my years as an unbeaten, pretty boy heavyweight instead of the twilight of my career as a beaten-up, uglied-up, ring-worn veteran struggling just to give as good as I got.

Taking a beating is just everyday life; walking through the punches like they're nothing is the definition of greatness.

Look at my boxing mentor, Pete Herman. Pete lost his eyesight from the glory he achieved in the ring, but, to me, all that matters is the glory that he won and the fact that he did not buckle when the bill for that glory came due. Pete Herman didn't pity himself; Pete didn't leave hating. He died old, blind, and ready to punch any shitass that gave him an excuse.

That's not as easy as it looks, to be honest. Some of the toughest men and women I ever met fell apart under the pressure of getting old, passé, and soft. You don't have to look any further than my heroine, Pete Herman's ex-wife Norma Wallace.

My girl Norma did some hard time on her way out, before pardoning herself from the old woman's body she was imprisoned in. After that fraudulent dildo Jim Garrison started the turf war that killed off the French Quarter and all the old bordellos, Norma had to do her time. She lost her rackets. For a while, she held up; she breezed through jail, married a young, redneck beefcake one-third her age, and held court as the glamorous hostess of Tchoupitoulas Plantation. She even received the official key to the city of New Orleans in a big ceremony – she had become respectable and respected, a legend.

She had become Ms. New Orleans.

Norma could handle going legit, but, in the end, she could not handle growing old. As a loose-skinned, dried-up, white-haired old lady, Norma could not keep her trophy hunk interested. Deprived of her sexual allure, Norma grew to hate herself. She used to say that she was born the wrong sex, the wrong body, but she did easy time for decades anyway. She was tough, but, baby, one thing I've learned is that tough doesn't necessarily last forever.

When her sex appeal and young trophy husband — the only good things about being a woman — disappeared, Norma could not take it any longer. She hid her old fat body far away from New Orleans, out in tiny bayou towns that no one ever visited. After a while, she got tired of listening to the crickets and watching her body droop more and more by the day. She wrote a self-pitying, passive-aggressive, pathetic note to the dummy who had abandoned her and fired a shotgun into her head.

Norma Wallace left hating in 1974.

So did my third wife and best bottom bitch, Jackie. As she aged and lost her looks, Jackie got infected with a bad dose of Jesus in the late 1970s. Suddenly, her adventuresome, daring life was over. It was time for the guilt, the shame, and the flight. She buzzed away to parts unknown, and I never heard from her again. I loved that woman, and I was sad to see her go. I was also hurt that she left that parrot-stealing Asshole behind in New Orleans for years longer. Jackie got nothing out of hating herself. She left hating, and her poor son eventually hung himself with a dog-training collar.

Even the toughest man I ever knew went down hating. Farish "Tex" Cody was a man that Mike McLaney claimed could kill anyone with his bare hands, and I saw evidence of that in many Body Shop brawls. Tex was so fearless that, after he was bailed out of jail, he would hunt down and beat up cops that had arrested him. But Tex got old, and Tex got weak.

Tex's downfall began when he came down with a middle-ear infection after a deep sea scuba-diving expedition. Since Tex was too macho to head to the doctor, the infection developed into mastoiditis — a serious, potentially fatal infection of the bone behind the ear. Tex was rushed into emergency surgery, where some half-ass doctors hacked away at his skull, haphazardly chipping out bone and draining the infection.

Dale and Tex had made a promise to each other that if either one ever became mortally ill or hooked on drugs, the other would perform a mercy killing. Dale had no doubt that Tex would fulfill his end of the bargain if given the chance, but unfortunately the test came for Papa John's boy, instead.

The agony of having his skull mangled with a rock hammer sent Tex into a tailspin of painkiller addiction. The doctors made the mistake of giving my buddy injectable liquid Demerol to treat his pain, and soon the toughest man in the world was more lifeless and pathetic than any heroin junkie. Dale came over to my place, where Tex was shooting up and slowly dying, and found himself unable to pull the trigger as he had promised. Dale apologized to his best friend.

Tex did the deed himself, and he was bitter about it. Tex thought he deserved to die with a bullet in his head like a real man and felt ashamed to go out otherwise. Finally, Tex slammed down the plunger and overdosed in October of 1983.

Tex left hating, all right.

I think of Tex all the time, and I always settle down on one memory that captures him perfectly. I remember he once came over to my house when I had a full gaggle of call girls, and he walked into that room like he owned the hearts of every one of them. In his signature white jeans and a tight shirt, Tex came over to me and pulled out a black velvet sack the size of a cabbage. He stuck his hand in, pulled out a handful of perfect diamonds as a sample, and asked for me to set up a sitdown with a buyer who could move weight. As Tex was leaving, I noticed that he had dropped four or five diamonds on my carpet and told him so.

"Ah, Frenchy, they're just diamonds. Let the girls fight over 'em!" Before Tex slammed the door, six or seven wild banshees were piled in front of me on the carpet, wrestling and choking and pulling hair and gouging eyes. When a five-star character like Tex Cody ends up leaving the world bitter and hating, you know life is a bitch.

That's why you have to respect the men who did their hard time like it was easy and went out laughing, not hating. It's no secret that my friends Carlos and Joe Marcello were tough motherfuckers. They went down in flames with their middle fingers raised like Joan of Arc, whose statue they passed every time they went to Pelican Tomato Company or Papa John's restaurant. Both upheld their Sicilian honor.

By the late 1970s, it became clear to Carlos' friends and family that he was going prematurely senile. The extraordinarily cautious godfather, who had impressed Dale with the high-tech precautions he took against the FBI, grew soft as a splat of mashed potatoes and nearly as careless over what he said as I was. His lips got loose, and his ideas lost their focus.

In past years, this wouldn't have mattered. As I said earlier, besides the Kennedys, no one in the government was really ever after Carlos. Unfortunately for him, the good times stopped rollin' for the Mob. The Mob's protector, J. Edgar Hoover, died in 1972, and Carlos' favorite politician, Richard Nixon, the man he proclaimed "the greatest president of all time," resigned thanks to the Watergate burglary.

Watergate also sent a couple CIA hands to jail who were close to Mike McLaney from their work on the Bay of Pigs and Operation Mongoose. When E. Howard Hunt had his funeral, some of the McLaneys were there to hear the CIA adventurer's last testament announce that he *still* hated John F. Kennedy. Before he died, Hunt recorded a confession claiming that he was involved in the conspiracy to assassinate Kennedy.

Under Jimmy Carter, the FBI finally woke up and decided to give the Mafia house of cards a little flick. The entire organization in Louisiana imploded. A couple undercover FBI operatives tricked Carlos into trusting them over huge Italian meals that would have made Dean Andrews proud, and he bragged about his control of Edwin Edwards and countless other politicians and sheriffs. They also caught Carlos planning to assassinate a judge, which fit his character to a T.

They had Carlos dead to rights, and Carlos knew he was going to eat some hard time. They tried to get him to rat or cut a deal, but the old man, senile as he was, never wavered in loathing the ever-living fuck out of the American government.

There's a funny story about the last trial of Carlos Marcello in 1981. Shortly before the jury was set to deliberate, Carlos ran into one of the FBI agents that had busted him outside the courtroom. Carlos called the fed over and told him there were no hard feelings. With a convincing smile, Carlos invited the G-man to head down to Louisiana to one of the Marcello family's favorite Italian restaurants and enjoy a meal on him.

"I promise you," Carlos said to the agent with apparent good humor, "I'm gonna make dat chef make a sauce special jus' for you. It's gonna be the best sauce you ever ate. He gonna take his time, put just the right ingredients in, and, right before he serves it to you, *he gonna stir it with his fucking dick.*"

Carlos' smile slouched down into that intensely focused, feral scowl that I knew all too well, and the godfather of New Orleans turned around and went on his way. Facing sure conviction and the guarantee of spending the rest of his life in prison, Carlos Marcello didn't apologize, didn't beg for clemency, didn't rat, and didn't kiss the ass of the government he held in contempt.

Carlos Marcello died *at home* in Metairie, Louisiana, in 1993. His Alzheimer's disease became so advanced that the feds saw no point in keeping the brain-dead lump of mozzarella in prison hospitals on the public's bill and sent him home to die. To the end, his brother Joe said that Carlos never weakened, and "did as good as could be expected under shitty circumstances."

That's called doing good time, baby.

Joe Marcello had the right to inherit the role of godfather he had envied for so many years, but my fun-loving friend looked around and decided that it was a job for a fool.

For a man generally thought of as heartless, Carlos had done the brave thing by rejecting all tradition and intentionally refusing to "make" his younger family members into the Mafia. Ever since the Kennedys betrayed their agreement with the Mafia, Carlos refused to reserve suites at Club Fed for his son, nephews, and cousins.

Carlos wanted better for his family than a life that inevitably ended in paranoia, public disgrace, and imprisonment. Instead, he transferred millions in legitimate assets to the younger generation of Marcellos and let the New Orleans Mafia die out.

Seeing that there would be no good piloting a Titanic full of fat old guidos to the bottom, Joe Marcello passed up his chance to be godfather. Joe focused his energies on becoming the Italian Mr. New Orleans, throwing parties and running clubs and having a ball. He bought up the restaurants Lenfants and La Louisiane, Diamond Jim Moran's old haunt, to host his quarter-century-long goodbye party.

Living it up, Joe ceded the Marcellos' stake in the local rackets. He left my old cellmate Frank Caracci alone to run his French Quarter businesses along with his partner Nick Karno and son Vincent. The official title of godfather was handed to Anthony Carollo, Silver Dollar Sam's long-disrespected goofball of a son — this was like electing George W. Bush president and had similar results.

Together, Carollo and ancient Silver Dollar Sam loyalist Frank Gagliano rebranded themselves as the beyond-parody "Muffuletta Mafia" after the signature sandwich at Tony Carollo's sandwich shop. As you can tell by the name, these guys had no idea what they were doing, and most of the local Italian hoods impersonated Frank Caracci by spinning off and forming their own little crews.

Lacking local man power and prestige, the Muffuletta Mafia called up John Gotti's Gambino Family and invited them down to Louisiana to give them a hand in obtaining bribed video poker and casino licenses. If Tony Carollo had been a smarter man, he would have realized that the best way to catch the G-men's attention was to invite Public Enemy #1 down to your neighborhood. The Carollo Family had fallen: from booting Al Capone out of town to inviting John Gotti to come take over.

Unfortunately, Joe Marcello got roped in on the FBI indictment that almost immediately followed Tony Carollo's message to New York and wiped out the entire New Orleans Family. Despite this, Joe did not despair. He did beautiful time, came out rejuvenated, and immediately started engineering some complex crime revolving around the port of New Orleans and coffee. That was Joe: an elderly millionaire who saw no reason to quit breaking the laws he loved breaking. He was a Marcello.

Unfortunately for Joe, he was a Marcello, so the FBI was on his trail again. According to a friend of mine in law enforcement, the G-men prepared press releases for June 12, 1999, to announce the racketeering indictment of longtime New Orleans Family underboss Joe Marcello. When the feds knocked on Joe's door that day, they were told that Joe could be found at Memorial Medical Centre. When the G-men arrived at the hospital, they learned that their prisoner was already dead. They had to cancel the press releases.

Joe died beautifully, a jokester to the end.

Speaking of jokesters, we have my cousin Edwin, who gets no credit for almost saving the state of Louisiana. My country cousin took the rap for the collapse of the Louisiana oil industry in the 1980s, which crippled the local economy and the finances of the state government. As businesses fled from Louisiana to nearby Houston, Edwin Edwards had a simple, profound, and brilliant idea to save the state of Louisiana from permanent poverty and decline: legalized gambling.

Nothing could have been more historically appropriate and better suited to Louisiana than reclaiming our heritage as *the* gambling hotspot in America. How sad was it that the Mormons in Nevada had more freewheeling gambling laws than the Cajuns, Sicilians, and Creoles of New Orleans?

Since the entire state was illegally gambling anyway, why not open up the city to major casino development to suck billions of dollars more from the millions of hopped-up Vidalia tourists who were already gawking around the French Quarter? Since Edwin was a VIP, high-stakes gambler in Las Vegas, he had the connections and know-how to make the state flush with old-school gambling syndicate cash. The state had no other potential boom industries, and no politician came forward with a suggestion worth a solitary shit for investing in the economic future of Louisiana.

Edwin took his case to the legislature in 1986, and the forces of the uptight Marksville element in Louisiana prevailed. Gambling was struck down. A couple years later, the nearby podunk town of Biloxi, Mississippi, legalized casinos and within a decade could boast tens of billions of dollars in outside investments and a $1,000,000,000-a-year gaming industry. Suddenly, New Orleans residents were subjected to the indignity of driving to *Mississippi* to gamble in style.

My cousin was appalled. There was nothing more shameful than the idea that New Orleanians had to take vacations to Mississippi to have fun.

When Edwin was elected for his fourth term in 1991, he set about correcting this grave injustice. Edwin passed legislation legalizing riverboat gambling, video poker, and a single land-based casino. Edwin proved a savvy, competent, and shady administrator, just like always. The only problem was that he no longer had Nolan to shield him, and the good times had stopped rolling for him in the 1980s just like everyone else.

Edwin found himself indicted for the usual Louisiana politics bouquet of charges: bribery, mail fraud, racketeering, etc. He had seen it all before. He bragged to the press that it was no big deal. "People say I've had brushes with the law. That's not true! I've had brushes with overzealous prosecutors!" As always, Louisianans laughed, and the press figured that no jury of the Cajun Casanova's peers would convict him. Mr. Louisiana would keep on rollin'.

Well, Mr. Louisiana turned out to have less luck than Mr. New Orleans. Edwin was actually convicted by a Louisiana jury and sentenced to an outrageous ten-year term in federal prison. They dropped *a dime* on Edwin! I got a quarter of that on a *white slavery* charge!

As if you can't guess, my cousin was not going to show ass; he was not going to let anyone see him down and out. Hell, no! Bragging that he would be a "model prisoner as he was a model citizen," Edwin followed Jack Gremillion's example and swaggered into the jail, and he won over every gangbanger, drug dealer, and hard-core convict in the place.

Far from picking on the elderly politician, all of the convicts rushed to kiss his ass, beg for autographs, and ask for free legal advice. From his jail cell, Edwin put together an improvised law office for his fellow inmates, worked on a memoir, and organized a national bipartisan effort to convince the Tony Carollo of Washington, George W. Bush, to pardon him.

Edwin always was a gambler, and the push to get pardoned by Bush came up snake-eyes. Due out in 2011, Edwin swears that he will emerge unbowed, unchanged, and unapologetic.

So that just leaves me. You may think I've been talking about the humiliation and defeat of my friends to get away from talking about my own scrapes with Fate, but you'd be wrong. Damn wrong! Baby, I'm prouder of my hard tough-luck years than I am of my time at the top. It takes a real man to do the hard time easy. And baby, I've been easy all the way.

It's like Muhammad Ali, one of my great heroes. They say Ali was at his greatest when he was young, pretty, and unbeatable, but that's a young man's delusion. Ali only became great when the bill came due for daring to be fearless and reckless, and he paid it all with a smile. Ali does his hard time easy and without complaints or apology; he never backs down. Whenever I felt low and pathetic, I looked at Ali and said, "Fuck it, baby, if Fate throws haymakers, it's time to rope-a-dope."

> "Alcohol may be man's worst enemy,
> but the Bible says love your enemy."
> **Frank Sinatra**

As the 1970s drew to a close, I was a degenerate drunk millionaire. Inching into my forties, I was still living hand to mouth, owning nothing in my own name, and blowing thousands of dollars daily on whatever crossed my mind. I was still handsome, but I no longer had the perfect physique of a Greek god. Booze reduced me to somewhere around 30% or 40% Greek god, and more of me was slipping into human territory with each pint.

The bad days, the blackout and puking days, came more and more often. I liked prescription pills of all colors and flavors, which, when combined with alcohol, made for a very comatose strip club owner. There were still many nights when Dale would find me passed out behind the one-way mirror in my office, diamonds and rubies spilling out of my pockets, a pile of cash as my pillow on my desk. He tried to tell me to bank the cash and save up for a rainy day, but who ever heard of a rainy day in New Orleans?

Once Jackie started to phase herself out of my life, I had no one with any brains or reliability to take over the day-to-day affairs for me. Things got sloppy even by my standards. Bribes were paid late; sensibilities were offended. Consequently, I started eating stupid charges like Dean Andrews at a buffet, and so did everyone who worked for me.

The criminal justice system's renewed sniping caused a serious problem. If my crew of misfits was regularly getting sent to parish jail, I had to constantly shift the on-paper ownership of my assets to prevent the cops from seizing everything as an ill-gotten asset. To avoid that grave injustice, I was constantly juggling the Body Shop between various front men, all of whom were my good friends and therefore were shifty, shiftless, and constantly facing indictment themselves. It was a real hot potato.

I thought an angel had come to deliver me when my Jewish tap dancer ex-wife Cheryl Lee showed up and said that she had the perfect front man in mind: her husband, the nice jukebox company manager who had once been my client. His name was Harry, and I liked Harry well enough. He was a bookmaker and con man from a good family with ambitions to become something more — and he had the money to back it up. Since I was short on patsies, I agreed to give Harry the job.

Unfortunately for the nightlife scene of Jefferson Parish, I had forgotten what type of girl Cheryl Lee was — ballsy, dishonest, and thieving. I also forgot what type of man I was — drunk, high, and lazy. I was the last sort of person who should be entrusted with supervising a con man on the make.

Cheryl pushed Harry to treat his on-paper-only ownership of my club as a reality and hijack my rackets. After all, I was too pilled-up and booze-pickled to mount any resistance. They thought they could just squeeze me dry.

Harry started off by suing my former front owners for money they "owed" him that we had agreed they never had to pay. Next, he pursued outstanding "debts" from merchants that I had waived in exchange for favors and under-the-table barters. Alienating my most important remaining allies, Harry stomped on the crossroaders' traffic and demanded higher cuts of their winnings.

He even used the Body Shop as his local base to push his jukeboxes, slot machines, and pinball machines on other bars in Jefferson and especially the mobbed-up Fat City entertainment district, which was just on the other side of Veterans. This put him in *bad* standing with the local kings of the "amusement" industry, the Marcellos, and he didn't help by trying to shake down their tour bus drivers as well.

But the Marcellos were not alone. Harry pissed off just about everyone I worked with, which meant he pissed off every gangster in Orleans and Jefferson Parish. The entire time, he had Cheryl riding him like Roy Rogers, whipping him and digging her heels into his side; she wanted more diamonds, more fancy dresses, more fancy dinners and vacations. She wanted the high life.

And I was too high to pull that helium-filled heifer back down to Earth. I was too goofed-out to put the wannabe gangster Harry on ice, either; these two were hot, steaming hot, and they smelled money and power. They were rabid dogs making the entire neighborhood uncomfortable, snapping at anyone and everyone, following none of the rules and honoring none of the past agreements. They were like the Kennedys of Veterans and Causeway.

It's ironic that Jim Garrison started showing up at the Body Shop just as these two amateurs started their slash-and-burn campaign, especially since the former DA had only a few years earlier been indicted for accepting bribes from pinball operators connected to Harry. Shortly after Garrison fixed Judge Haggerty for a fall, Old Melon Head beat the bribery charges that were a long time in coming by convincing his old buddy, government witness Pershing Gervais, to flip again and turn on the government at trial. Afterwards, Garrison settled into a cushy judgeship of his own and began a lucrative career fleecing conspiracy marks by writing books that credit the Jolly Green Giant with solving the Kennedy assassination.

So when Garrison first ducked that big Easter Island head under the Body Shop's low doorway, I was happy to see him: he was, after all, rich as a sheik, thanks to the conspiracy marks, and a proven spender. Garrison wasn't coming to see me, of course; he was dating my cashier, a South American swimsuit model and former Miss Potchartrain Beach named Sue. Garrison kept his thoughts to himself about what a fine mess Harry and Cheryl were making, and I kept my thoughts to myself about what a shameful, destructive prick Garrison was.

Shortly before the Body Shop went into its final death spiral, Sue came to me crying while I was passed out on the bar. Even in my absentminded haze, I snapped awake at the thought that someone had hurt my sweet little cashier. "Whatsa matter, baby? Tell Frenchy now, dawlin'," I cooed as I pulled a drool-covered $20 bill off my face.

"It's Garrison, that asshole," Sue cried. "He left me for a boy, Frenchy! He went queer on me!"

I felt bad for a beautiful girl like Sue, who was so good-looking and sweet that she never deserved to have a man go queer on her, but I couldn't help but laugh. "Honey, you'll soon learn that Jim Garrison's gone queer on *everybody* in this city at one time or another. Just be thankful he didn't charge you with killing John Lennon."

After Jim Garrison stopped coming around, so did most everybody. Thanks to Cheryl Lee and her boyfriend, the club became unpopular; everyone with money to spend had a bitter memory about being shaken down. A lot of people blamed it on me, which was their right; I should have been more proactive in stopping these baby kingpins from running hog-wild on my friends and customers.

But I was in no shape to offer a fight. Soon, the Body Shop closed. These two idiots had taken a cash cow and a goose that laid golden eggs and threw an impromptu barbecue.

That's the thing about New Orleans, though; there's *always* someone else ready for a fight. The entire city is like Murray's Tavern, always itching for a brawl for any old reason. Since I had failed to do my duty and chain up the two rabid dogs prowling the neighborhood, someone else took extreme measures. They put those dogs down.

Just like JFK, Harry and his hard-driving RFK Cheryl had gone out of their way to give everyone with the power and personality to whack Harry out a *reason* to whack Harry out. I was like that governor in the Cadillac with the Kennedys; I didn't know it was coming and was unlucky enough to be caught in the crossfire.

One morning in March of 1983, the police pulled me out of my stupor with a dose of the rough stuff that I usually never received since I was such a friend of law enforcement. I did not have the slightest idea why they were being so rude. I regularly committed crimes, but nothing so bad as to justify *this* behavior.

I was not surprised by the news that Harry had been murdered, but the style of the murder sure gave me pause. This wasn't a bullet in the back of the head — far from it. This was some gruesome voodoo shit. Someone was really looking to put on a showcase.

According to the police, who could have been making it all up, Harry got a steak knife in each eye, a steak knife in the back, and his dick chopped off and shoved into his mouth. They claimed that witnesses saw a man in a black jogging suit running away from the scene of the crime.

Needless to say, the cops fingered me for the murder. I wanted to ask them if that gruesome crime sounded like the work of a man who thought a three-foot drop into Bayou St. John was the perfectly executed crime of the century, but I held my tongue. I knew they couldn't pin it on me because I hadn't done a goddamn thing to Harry — shit, I hadn't done a thing *at all* for years besides get wasted and high.

And that was really the problem. I never was charged with the murder, but I was already finished. The Jefferson Parish police let me know that, with Carlos in jail and a gruesome murder like Harry's hanging over my head, the era of free rides was over.

My bill was coming due. The time was about to get hard.

> "No doubt exists that all women are crazy;
> it's only a question of degree."
> **W. C. Fields**

As I was getting older, it made sense for me to balance things out by dating younger and younger. With Jackie and the Body Shop gone, I hooked up with the first of my two young loves, Renee. Renee was a perfect companion for my circular journey down the drain; after all, she had just come from New Jersey, so she met me on the way up.

Renee was the beautiful, blacked-haired daughter of a New Jersey wiseguy named Primo. Primo had given his daughter the usual Italian Catholic hard-ass routine, driving her to embrace life on the wild side. A high-school friend dared Renee to go on a date from an escort agency, and that was all the excuse Renee needed. After she turned some tricks in Jersey, her dad found out and went wild with threats, swearing to whack out everyone who gave his daughter work.

Renee escaped to Biloxi and eventually made her way to New Orleans. I met her in Port of Call on Esplanade Avenue, and we quickly hit it off. There was no mistaking that I was a pimp, and my expert eye keyed in on Renee right away. She had that wild look in her eyes and that dead-giveaway inability to keep herself from laughing at things that weren't funny. Real call girls are always laughing like teenagers who think they've figured out that the entire world is a joke. At the time, I probably agreed with her.

Renee was just the breath of fresh ether that I needed in the Reagan years: an extremely ambitious, young, and wild broad who wanted to make big-time moves on the street. It had been so long since I had a truly crazy, untamable, wild bitch that I felt twenty years younger almost immediately. Ever since I dated Latashma in the 1950s, I have been a sucker for the dangerous ones, and Renee was damn-near fatal.

I assume one of the New York wiseguys who started showing up around Louisiana after Carlos' incarceration ran into me at one of Joe Marcello's clubs and recognized the pretty little guidette on my arm. Without doing the gentlemanly thing and having a personal talk with me, he made a call to New Jersey. Within days, I started hearing through the grapevine that Renee's father Primo had "ordered a K" on me — put a bounty on my head. The young Italians around the Caraccis and Marcellos who didn't know better started looking at me a little funny.

Baby, if I had gone to New Jersey, I would have been a dead man. Unfortunately for old Primo, I wasn't in New Jersey; I was in New Orleans, and no New Jersey guido was going to be able to out-maneuver Mr. New Orleans on his own turf. I dragged my drunken carcass over to Joe and Sammy Marcello at La Louisiane and introduced them to my pretty Italian fiancée.

As you can guess, Joe and Sammy took a shine to Renee that

proved quite valuable. Sammy arranged to pay me $1000 every Saturday in exchange for the right to take Renee to a hotel room with a rich friend of his. As always with Sammy, it wasn't about sex; the multimillionaire New Orleans tycoon that Sammy brought to the hotel room wanted to interview Renee because he had fallen in love with a New York call-girl and wanted an insider's perspective on how to seduce her away from the rackets. This was a true fool's errand, but Renee and I received $1000-per-week for the work, and Sammy got to get his rocks off listening to Renee talk for free, so the rest of us put up with the charade.

After a few months, the tycoon hung himself in despair. His New York working girl had refused to be his wife and kept right on turning tricks.

Joe Marcello had an even greater gift to bestow than Sammy's $1000-per-week: protection. As loudly and widely as possible, Joe advertised that Renee and I were to be his special guests at his restaurant/club Lenfants for our wedding. It was a beautiful, raucous affair. The remnants of the entire Marcello network came out to pay their respects, handing wads of hundreds to the wife according to tradition.

Joe dragged me in front of everyone and gave me two unopened bottles of 1984 vintage Château Lafite Rothschild, the finest red wine in the world. "Frenchy," Joe called out with everyone watching, "you better not let me drink a drop of that wine, because I promise you I will drink *all* of it."

Joe didn't have to worry; Renee and I drank all of it. We drank so much that we forget her purse, filled with all of the cash gifts, when we left Lenfants that night. When we came back from our honeymoon, I went to see Joe to thank him for the party. "Don't thank me yet," my best friend said, grabbing me by the shoulder and pulling me into his office. "I've got another gift for you." Hidden away in his office was Renee's purse — with $17,000 cash still inside.

Joe's wedding celebration had the effect he intended: word got back to New Jersey that I was off-the-fucking-limits. Soon, I received a phone call from my father-in-law, who was, of course, younger than me. He asked if he could come down and meet me for dinner, which I graciously said was a wonderful idea.

Then Primo asked again — it became clear that he was asking if he had *permission* to even visit Louisiana, just like the New York wiseguys used to have to get permission just to visit as tourists in the days when Carlos ruled the town. I laughed and told him times had changed. He came down, gritted his teeth through a dinner that wasn't quite as jovial as we would have liked, and flew back home.

The drawback of saving my life was now I had a crazy-ass wife again. Renee was completely irresponsible and beyond teaching — a girl with a bottomless appetite for drinking, snorting cocaine, setting up elaborate orgies, getting into fights, and running from the cops. She was always laughing and smiling, teasing the entire world by what a *bad, bad little girl* she was; she got off on the entire lifestyle. She was a nut-job, and that made her completely irresistible to me.

It also damn near killed me. This bitch was no wife for a pimp approaching retirement age. She was always bullying me to be wilder, crazier, more adventurous, more ambitious; she was trying to turn fifty-year-old Frenchy into the wild man that twenty-year-old Frenchy never had been. Like most fools who want to feel young, I tried to keep up, and I paid the price.

The first goofy indictment that I racked up with Renee was over my Thanksgiving party. Of course, with a young girl to impress, this couldn't be your average Thanksgiving party; I needed to throw a bash that would have befitted a joint party for Rick James and King Louis XIV.

I leased a gorgeous mansion with a swimming pool from a widower for almost nothing since the place had memories of his wife's death attached to it. Then I rented three large restaurant tables and made a catering deal with some of my favorite local restaurants. When my seventeen guests arrived, they found the tables decorated with full roasted pigs, three turkeys done different ways, sixteen or seventeen side dishes, three unopened bottles of Dom Perignon — and complimentary dishes full of coke, speed, pills, weed, and everything goddamn thing else illegal in the world.

I'm lucky I had such degenerate friends because, by the time the police busted our Thanksgiving orgy, most of the drugs were already in my friends' bloodstreams. Still, this was a devastating arrest for me. The cops had always given me considerable leeway solely because, unlike older pimps like Snake Gonzales and the new black generation of pimps, I tried to stay away from hard drugs. Being from Louisiana, the cops didn't so much mind hooking as long as it was between consenting adults and they could be sure there wasn't some drugged up teenager being exploited. Since my girls were comparatively sober, they went easy on me.

I used to get pimps mad at me because Jefferson Parish Chief of Police Beauregard Miller would lecture them, "Y'know, Frenchy Brouillette is the only man who should even be in this business because he don't fuck with drugs." After my Thanksgiving arrest, old Beauregard came to see me. "I thought you didn't fuck with this shit, Frenchy?"

"I don't, baby, I don't. Take my word!" Beauregard looked at me sly, but I assured him it would never happen again.

Not too long later, Renee caught me at a weak moment and convinced me to do the most fatal thing any younger woman can convince an older man to do: trying a new thing. Baby, old dogs like me get arrested or killed when they learn new tricks. The Jefferson police cuffed me a couple hours later on suburban 47th Street trying to lift cars off the street and twirl them above my head like Superman. It turned out drinking a bottle of Dom Perignon and "widening my horizons" by snorting some crystal meth put me in a bodybuilding mood, and, with no weights, I apparently thought I could perform a couple sets of overhead squats with a Lincoln Town Car.

Of course, old Chief Miller *had* to see me after this arrest. "Frenchy, I *thought* you told me you didn't fuck with this shit?"

"Baby, baby," I jumped up, way too eager to change his mind. I was still closer to Tasmanian Devil than man. "I swear, I swear, I *swear* I don't."

"Ha," scoffed the Chief, "looking at you right now — boy, I find that *hard* to believe."

That arrest marked the end of my police protection. I would still get tipped off every once in a while, but, now that I had the reputation as a junkie, more often than not I'd just get busted. And, with Renee carrying on, I got busted *very* often.

Don't get me wrong, Renee wasn't selfish; she took the fall too. The only difference was that the bitch was a bungee jumper: she *enjoyed* taking falls. Nothing tickled her more than having a room full of older men in uniform check her out in her hooker clothes and look at her like a naughty little girl. Shit, she'd get so worked up, she'd start making eyes at the guard from her jail cell.

My favorite Renee arrest actually involved the one brilliant idea of her entire criminal career. Early in our relationship, Renee asked if I would back her in opening an escort agency in Texas. Since I was already getting sick of keeping up with the crazy bitch, I happily handed her a stack of cash, a couple girls, and a car to drive her ass there.

This is where Renee suddenly stepped into some serious smarts. On her way, she heard the hit song "867-5309/Jenny" on an FM radio station, which was about a horny kid calling up a number scrawled on a bathroom stall hoping to get laid. "Hot damn," my wife thought, "that sounds like a good idea for an escort agency."

The next week, Renee registered the Call Jenny Escort Agency and paid off the local owner of the 867-5309 number. They couldn't wait to get rid of that number; ever since the song came out, horny teenage boys had been prank-calling their house and asking for "Jenny." That was bad for a quiet suburban family — but it was *fantastic* for an escort agency run by a "Jenny." Pimply teenagers would call up Renee, ask for Jenny, the fictional slut, and receive the following response, "Hey, baby, this is Jenny. You lookin' to have fun tonight?"

Let me tell you, those Texas boys thought that band had let them in on the secret of a lifetime! Renee went around telling all those rednecks that she had *paid* the band to record the song and that they were old clients. With tens of thousands of dollars coming in every month, Renee started acting like goddamn Norma Wallace, tooling around in new everything and sending me packages of cash that could have bought me a respectable retirement if I had had the inclination.

The problem with hitting on every teenager that prank-called the 867-5309 number is that some of those pranksters by the law of averages would be nerds who would tell their parents. It didn't take long for the son of a Texas Ranger (the cops, not the baseball team) to call up Jenny.

A squad of Texas Rangers blasted into Renee's house in full riot gear and arrested everyone inside. Though no one was committing prostitution, the Rangers did find a huge Ziploc bag of white powder and arrested everyone in the house. Renee was now the one dropping change into a pay phone, begging me to come to Texas and find a way out for her.

I didn't have the slightest idea who to call in Texas, but I wanted to see with my own eyes that the wild woman was locked up. I was in the courtroom pews looking suspicious at their arraignment, Renee craning over her shoulder with this look like she expected me to pull out an assault rifle, blow everyone away, and carry her out through the window. Maybe she should have called her father.

Anyway, just as the proceedings began, a cop walked into the courtroom and motioned to the prosecutor. Leaning over the railing, the cop whispered into the prosecutor's ear; you could see absolute horror cross over the lawyer's face. I leaned forward; I *had* to hear what had happened. I figured someone must have shot the president or the DA's wife.

"Um, y'honor, we have to apologize. The state withdraws all charges."

"Excuse me?" asked the judge.

"We just received word from the forensics lab that the bag of powder...." The DA couldn't find the words. His face was making tortured movements like someone was squeezing his tongue real hard, but there was no one there.

"Excuse me?" the judge said, looking around the room in confusion. He leaned forward just like I was doing.

"The powder is *not* cocaine. We withdraw the charges."

"No, no, no, counselor, you're not going to waste the court's time and not tell us what the powder was!"

"Y'honor, I rather not.... May I approach?" asked the queasy district attorney. The spectators actually started *booing* because they were so annoyed that they might miss out on the big reveal.

Reading the room accurately, the judge decided to make the DA squirm. "Absolutely not. You can tell the courtroom, or you will be held in contempt."

"Ahem, well, okay. It's douche powder. The bag was full of two pounds of douche powder."

I was crawling on the floor and panting with hysterical laughter, and I was not alone. Even the judge started waving papers in front of his face to cool himself down. Renee was jumping up and down, squealing "Thank you, Frenchy!" which made no sense to anyone in the courtroom, including me.

Apparently, this bitch thought *I* had called Carlos Marcello in prison and arranged for one of his guys to exchange the cocaine with douche powder. What really happened, I'm sure, is some cop just wanted some cocaine and didn't realize the coke he exchanged for douche powder in the evidence room hadn't been to the forensics lab yet.

Once the room had calmed down, the judge shushed Renee and told her to stop bouncing around like a cheerleader. "Listen, little girl, you got lucky this time," the judge cautioned, earning his title by accurately judging that Renee was up to no good regardless of whether that bag was full of cocaine or douche powder. "I suggest that, wherever you're from, you go *back*. Just go *back*."

Renee returned to New Orleans soon afterwards — but only after working a convention of Texas Rangers.

By the end of the 1980s, that judge pretty accurately summed up my feelings towards Renee. Wherever she was from, I was ready for her to just *go back*. Every day was a new stunt: a bad check cashed, a new drug dealer pissed off, a new car stolen. I was closing in on 60, and I wanted a chance to breathe.

I didn't dump her because I thought that would be unnecessarily confrontational; clearly, *someone* was going to arrest her sometime soon. They had to; a cop didn't have to go looking for crime in Louisiana very long before you stumbled upon Renee breaking four or five laws at once. Don't forget, the girl *got off* on getting caught; she didn't make it hard.

I never thought I'd accuse the police of playing hard to get, but in Renee's case they didn't want anything to do with her. She could have walked into the police station naked carrying a flamethrower, and no one would have even deigned to make eye contact with her. When they finally busted her, it wasn't even for a crime, just an honest mistake. She accidentally deposited a check that was addressed to our neighbor in our account. Once she heard that the police were looking for her on a mail fraud charge, she jumped town.

I never heard from her again.

❧ ❧ ❧ ❧ ❧

"A 'lotion technician' at a North Valley lotion demonstration parlor who reportedly lost a fight this week with a co-worker allegedly persuaded her boyfriend to get even. [...] [The boyfriend] Gonzales allegedly 'hit her upside the head with the pistol several times, knocked her to the floor and then kicked her in the face and upper torso area,' [Detective] Rollerson said. Rollerson said Gonzales also fired three shots. Two shots were fired inside the lotion parlor and one of those came close to hitting [Dusty] in the head. [...] According to the complaints, Gonzales told [Dusty], 'I'm going to kill you (expletive). Do you want to die, (expletive)?'"

Albuquerque Journal
August 14, 1998

Baby, it's time to talk about Dusty, the love of my life. I was looking forward to a little peace and quiet, but then I remembered that was for old people. I saw what happened to Norma Wallace when she got old and took the loss of a young lover too hard.

But my memory took a little jostling. The early 1990s taught me that the life of a sixty-year-old alcoholic escort agency proprietor with a Catholic conscience trends toward loneliness and self-pity. When I ran into Cheryl Lee at a breakfast joint, and she loudly accused me of murdering her husband in front of everyone, that made things worse. I've also been odd about guilt; I am ashamed of myself when someone's angry at me even if I know that I'm innocent of whatever they're thinking I did.

I felt the hard times overshadowing me, so I did what used to make my time easy — I partied, I hung around horse stables, I visited Joe Marcello and the English Queen, I bought new cars and jewelry — but eventually I had to admit that I was pretty lonely. I've never been the emotional type of guy, but old age makes you sentimental.

Even old pimps get sentimental. I had never grown up, and being an immature person drawing social security is a sad state of affairs. You get the worst of every age all at once — the body of an old man, the mind of a young man.

I was an old man who deep down just wanted a little love and friendship coupled with excitement, yet I had a reputation as the sort of guy who would toss lesbians into the bayou and cut off a man's dick and shove it into his mouth. That sort of reputation is actually a bonus with beautiful women when you have your looks, but, as an old addict with a busted nose, that reputation left me pretty hopeless of ever finding normal, decent companionship.

What I'm trying to get around to saying is that I was a vulnerable old man who was inching closer by the day towards leaving hating. I was reminding myself of Tex with his Demerol needles, Norma with her self-pity and isolation, Jackie with her affair with Jesus. Even when I was in the French Quarter, Bourbon Street started to feel just as drab and suffocating as Marksville. I needed an angel to save me.

She called.

"You hiring?" asked a pretty, youthful voice on the phone. I had always followed Norma's example and turned away girls looking for work, but I needed something, anything new.

"I sure am hiring," I responded, immediately regretting it. "Have you worked?"

"Yep," she said with a chipper, bright tone. "I worked Albuquerque, Florida, Las Vegas..."

"Baby, you're hired."

"Great, my name is Dusty."

I've always said that one horse is as good as a stable if it can really run. Trust me, this girl could *run*. Without ever laying eyes on her, without doing anything more than giving her a call and sending her an address, I started receiving $1000 or $2000 every day just in my agency fees from her work. I asked my "agent," the man who answered my phones and picked up the cash, what the story was. He told me that every single client he sent to Dusty became a regular, and they didn't wait long to see her again; they would order her *night after night after night.* "We got ourselves something special," the agent said. "You should take a look at her."

I wanted to — badly. As Big Henry always said, I like the women who make it, and this Dusty was a moneymaking bitch. Still, I played it cool like a pimp should. I let my agent make the phone calls and pick up the money, and I stayed back, way back in the dark.

It was all very calculated. I didn't have my looks, or my money, or my old friends anymore; all I had was my name and the mystery that came along with it. I knew damn well that any working girl who sends an operator $2000 a day without meeting him is thinking to herself, "How the fuck does this man not want to meet me? How much money is he making that he doesn't even call?" I knew she would come to me, if only to allay her own insecurity.

Finally, one night, my agent flaked off from work, and there was no one to pick up Dusty's agency fees for that night. Dusty called my house and got my friend on the line; she only asked two questions: where was I, and what did I like to drink?

When she walked into the room, a referee should have gotten in between us and waved everything off. There was no need to count to ten or call in the doctor; I was *done.* I looked out my window to see this black-haired, 5'7" knockout in four-inch heels and a designer cocktail dress swing her long legs out of her brand-new Corvette with a roll of cash in one hand and a plastic bag with two bottles of my favorite wine in the other.

The sight of Dusty getting out of that Corvette in her high heels was like a clip from a music video. She knew how to strut, how to kick her hips; her makeup was perfect and her hair salon-fresh. The woman knew how to make an impression. She was almost intimidating, like some vixen off of *Melrose Place.*

There was no hope; I was going to be the Vidalia in *this* relationship. Any woman smart enough to arrange her first impression to be a couple thou in cash, two bottles of wine, and a sports car is too skilled to be defeated. She knew her prey.

As Dusty walked into my living room, she was all bravado, a statuesque sex bomb with the swagger and the polished appearance of a movie star with a million-dollar hair, makeup, and wardrobe team. Not since my first meeting with Norma Wallace have I ever been so awestruck by a woman's ability to martial her sexual firepower. She was a real pro.

"Daddy," she said with a sweet voice, lifting the bag of booze, "these are the best bottles they have in this city. I hope you like 'em." I looked into the bag and was stunned to discover that here was a twentysomething prostitute who knew how to choose a nice bottle of expensive wine. This woman had true class, composure, and glamour.

And then, as soon as I invited her to sit on the couch and look me in the eyes and talk, this Hollywood dream woman melted away into a tiny, mousy, vulnerable little creature that was begging for me to be easy on her. Dusty slipped off her shoes, pulled her legs on the couch, and tucked them under her body. She immediately seemed familiar to me.

Dusty's badass image of the moment before disappeared, and she slumped down and became a teenage tomboy not sure how to dispose of her limbs and look adult. She was the sort of girl who is so pretty that it shocks you when she's nervous or hesitates before talking. Dusty had a look of vulnerability, of sadness, that touched me. I thought it was telling that she kept mentioning that she was a black belt in karate, as if she was so scared of being hurt that she wanted me to preemptively know that she was tough.

Baby, I had enough experience with damaged girls in this life to know *exactly* how to unlock this mystery with only one question. "Tell me, baby, how does a sweet, pretty girl like you end up turning tricks?"

"Ah, Frenchy, it's a sad story," she said, in the most predictable sentence of the 1990s. "My mom's boyfriend was an ex-state policeman who left the force to open up jerk-off massage parlors across the country. He had so much money that he owned two private jets, a real crook. These parlors were lotion studios, y'know?

"So, there was this strike with the lotion workers, and one of the shops my mom ran for her boyfriend was, y'know, understaffed. So my mom came up to me and asked if I wanted to make a little money filling in. I asked her what I had to do.

"Well, she looked at me like I was retarded. 'Bitch, you know what you have to do!' she barked. My mom was a tough woman. I worked at the studios for a while, and then I went on my own, and now I'm here," she said, rushing out the words. "Now, let's talk about something happier, okay?" she asked, putting her graceful hands with their beautiful nail polish onto my old, boxing-deformed claws. She was sincerely uncomfortable, having trouble speaking, tears in her eyes, snot catching in her nose.

I changed the subject, and we talked about lighter things. We laughed; she was a funny girl, a thrill seeker like me who afterwards felt a bit silly over the crazy things she did. She seemed as sweet and harmless as a Mormon on that couch, but I knew better from experience.

I could tell from Dusty's immaculate looks that she was no junkie, so that left only one option. She'd have no choice but to be wild. An emotionally immature woman like Dusty needs thrills, or drugs, to distract her from the pain she cannot handle in her life.

Everything that Dusty did was to numb that pain of her mom pimping her out. It was just an attempt to do the hard time she knew she had in store as easy as she could. Dusty would do just about anything. She was putting up a brave front –the $2000-a-day call girl front with movie-star clothes, shoes, cars, and jewelry as accessories. She lived fast because, if she slowed down, she'd fall apart.

Dusty's combination of style, glamour, sex appeal, and wounded vulnerability attracted me like nothing I had ever encountered before. I felt she was a lot like me, back in the days when I was young and beautiful and was living fast to distract myself from the guilt of breaking the hearts of my poor parents back in Marksville. Dusty could feel my empathy as I talked to her, and I bet that was a pretty rare feeling for her, to meet someone who looked past her appearance to give a crap about the girl underneath.

Dusty did not waste time getting close to me. Very soon after our first conversation, she came to me and said, with a look of a woman fishing for a compliment, "I've lost my place to stay."

"That's no problem," I said, happier than I had been since the 1970s. "I've got an extra bedroom."

"Are you serious?" she said with forlorn eyes, as if a girl like her really had a hard time finding a place to stay.

"Dead serious, baby. Don't think twice about it. Everything that's mine is yours."

Dusty took me at my word. I didn't have much in the world, but I did have cars. Lots of cars. I'd miss paying rent or a hospital bill or bail to buy a new car or an old collector's item. Ever since I was a kid, I was queer over cars, and now that I was a queer old man, I saw no reason not to indulge one of my few pleasures.

Within the month, Dusty had irreparably crashed two of my cars, used my money to buy a motorcycle that she also crashed, and damn near set my place on fire somehow or another. She was an equal opportunity hell-raiser, though; on the eighth day, she crashed that perfect, brand-new Corvette of hers into a fleur-de-lis light pole. There was no explanation for any of it since she wasn't a noticeable drug abuser yet; all I'd get was a shrug of the shoulders and a familiar refrain.

Guess the lady just couldn't drive.

"Frenchy, don't mind me," she'd say with a half-mischievous, half-embarrassed grin as I surveyed the latest destroyed possession of mine. "I run with the boys. I like to drive fast cars, break stuff, fight, get wild. I like to do boy stuff. I need a thrill to get me through the day. I think I wasn't meant to be born a girl. I like to destroy things."

As soon I heard that, I fell in love. I was reminded of my sweet old friend, Norma Wallace, who also had been turned out by her mom at a young age, spent an inordinate amount of effort on looking perfect at all times, and cursed God for making her a woman. The difference between Norma and Dusty was that Norma had the strength of character to persevere and build something out of her life. Dusty had just enough spark to flameout.

And I knew it, but there was nothing at my advanced age and state of decay that I could do about it. A sixty-year-old pimp with forty years of alcohol and drugs wear-and-tear on his mind and body cannot be the savior of a profoundly damaged young woman. I just didn't have it in me; I never had the maturity to save myself, or even to maintain a balanced checkbook. All I could do was nurse my wine bottle and be this girl's friend and supporter. I just wanted to enjoy being near her; she made me feel young, excited, and, above all else, loved in a way that I cannot describe. I was covered in a warm halo whenever she was around.

One of the great things about Dusty is that she helped alleviate my guilt over running the escort agency. Ever since crack cocaine devastated New Orleans and especially the sort of women who worked in the sex trade in the late 1980s, the business had gotten real dreary and sad. Half of my clients just wanted to use an escort as a crack delivery service, and the girls themselves had no interest in the job besides a grim, impatient determination to fuck their way to another hit. You rarely met call girls anymore who still had a passion for the business like in the old days.

Dusty was a throwback; every trick was a Mardi Gras celebration to her. When I took her out on dates to fancy restaurants or the movies, she'd only go if I promised that I'd send her on any call that came in, regardless if it was in the middle of a movie or the middle of our entrée. She didn't want to let a single trick pass her by. *That* was her crack. The thrill of dressing up in beautiful lingerie with stockings and a garter belt, doing her makeup, throwing on a designer dress, and strutting into a hotel room, with no idea what was coming, was the queen of all thrills for this girl.

A couple years into our time together, as Dusty was nearing thirty years old, my attorney called me up and told me that he had been tipped off that the heat was on; we needed to chill for a while. I looked at my savings and found that, even with Dusty's wasteful behavior, we still had over $100,000.

"Baby, I think it's time for you to retire," I told her, feeling like a Good Samaritan for letting my number-one moneymaker take it easy. "You're gonna get arrested if we keep goin' like this, and we have enough money for you just to take it easy and answer phones."

I thought she would appreciate the selfless concern I was showing for her, but her eyes were wet and wide. It was like I had sucker-punched her. "What are you trying to do, Frenchy?" she asked. "Take my livelihood away? I'm not getting old before my time, so don't you *dare* try to make me, because I'll get a plane ticket back to Albuquerque this minute!"

That was the end of that. I should have known better.

Heading out for a trick, Dusty felt like a movie star, a porn star, and a secret agent undertaking a dangerous secret mission all at once. She'd come out of that hotel room strutting like Lauren Bacall. I'd take her to Mandina's to help me charm all of the judges, and one judge was so enthralled by her that he'd bring a camera to Mandina's specifically hoping to see her so that she could do a photo shoot right on his table. Dusty even suggested that I bring an electric fan into the restaurant so that it could blow her hair out like at a real photo shoot.

I once took Dusty out to see a prizefight as a guest of boxing promoter Les Bonano. We were sitting in the front row when Les rushed up to me. "Frenchy, I need a favor."

"Anything, baby!" I said, my typical answer when anyone whom I'm even halfway friendly with asks for a favor.

"I need your girl to get into a bikini and be my ring girl

tonight. The other girl flaked." You should have seen the look of pure, badass pride on Dusty's face. The prizefight was awful that night, but I'd never seen a prettier ring girl. She knew it, too, kicking those long legs around the ring, reveling in the attention the crowd was giving her; she'd walk around the ring twenty times, in no rush to let the fight resume. You just couldn't *tell* this woman that she wasn't a movie star, no matter how many times she got on her knees for strange men.

And God forbid that you didn't treat her like a movie star, even if she was a prostitute. She never wanted anyone to forget that *she* was the one doing the favor. She asked one john who gave her some lip if he was into S&M and then gagged him, handcuffed him to the bed, took his money and clothes, and left.

Things weren't all beautiful with Dusty — far from it. This girl *did* have problems, and they seemed to get worse by the month. It was okay when she smashed up some of my newer cars, but I told her, "Baby, don't touch my '59 Cadillac. It's the only one like it in the state. It's irreplaceable...just like you."

Naturally, the next day she walked into my place without a care in the world and told me, by the way, that she was going to take my mint condition 1959 Cadillac out on the road. I told her no, but that wasn't a word that held any power over her. Within a couple hours, I was called to the scene of an accident: she was still in mint condition, but the Cadillac was folded like an accordion. When I started yelling, she shrugged, "Eh, I'll fix it."

"How the hell can you fix it?"

"What? I'll just buy you a new one."

"You can't buy a new 1959 Cadillac!"

"Sure you can, just go to the store!" The bitch was so flamboyant, I just had to laugh. When I started driving around a Lincoln Mark 4 in an attempt to find a car that wasn't glamorous enough for her to crash, she ridiculed me. "That's a girl car, Frenchy! It's gutless! No pickup! You should be ashamed of yourself." Soon enough, she crashed that car too. She demolished ten cars of mine, all told.

Dusty eventually started to feel bad about destroying the only nice things I had left. After a couple years, we were busted on a drug charge and taken to court, which gave her the opportunity to make up all the vehicle manslaughters she had committed. As soon as she entered the courtroom, she started screaming, "Y'honor, y'honor! The drugs are mine! Don't prosecute this innocent man! The drugs are mine!"

I've never been so touched in my life. I had a pretty rough record, so this move saved me from a few year bid. To thank Dusty, I called in my last big-time favor and had her sentence reduced to only a three-month stay in the prison hospital, which I thought would do her good and help her sober up. Instead, Dusty escaped and went on the lam for eighteen months, in and out of my life, a paranoid mess. I wondered to myself what could have possibly happened to her in previous visits to prison that made her that scared of an easy bid like the one I got her.

I never found out, but my movie star was never the same again. Her drug abuse intensified, and her psyche became increasingly strained under the threat of a prison sentence, any sentence. The wild ride of living with her became scary as opposed to funny, and I began to get paranoid, myself.

I've never been possessive when it comes to women; I've married my share of working call girls. Dusty changed that. As she spun further and further out of control, it was clear to me that I would lose her sooner rather than later. To compensate, I held on tighter than ever, becoming jealous and paranoid.

When one of Dusty's multimillionaire clients fell in love with her and volunteered to be her full-time sugar daddy, I made her quit him even though it would have put us on easy street. This guy was sending her championship horses and cars and nice jewelry and, contrary to the rest of my career, I made her send it all back. I didn't want her getting out of my grasp — which, of course, guaranteed that a girl like her would get rebellious and start running away.

The first time it happened, I nearly fell apart. We had been arguing all the time because Dusty hated money and would spend it on just about anything to get it out of her hands. I tried to tell her that I knew from experience the money would one day run out, but she didn't listen. "Life is too short," she'd say, which sounds ominous in retrospect. How did she know life would be so short for her?

Finally, one day Dusty had enough of my nagging and told me, "No problem, I won't waste any of your money anymore." She called up her family, had them send her a ticket back to New Mexico, and flew right the fuck home. I never spent a lonelier few weeks than the month or so it took her to show back up at my door, kiss me on the cheek, and walk back in like nothing had happened.

This happened fairly regularly from then on. Whenever Dusty would get a wild bug up her ass, she'd spend enough of my money to get me angry and then use my anger as an excuse to go on a cross-country bender with strange men. Sometimes, she wouldn't even wait to argue. I remember one time when I walked into our place with $2500 I had just been paid. Dusty asked to count the money to double-check since I wasn't good with numbers. I gave her the stack; she put one $100 bill on the table and then walked out the door with the rest. Moments later, I heard my white Cadillac convertible drive away at top speed.

I was pacing around my apartment, just livid. I knew she would come back in a couple hours and tell me that she had spent all of my money, *again*, and I knew that I would let her get away with it. Sure enough, she came home later that night with $2400 worth of new clothes *and* a look of profound annoyance on her face. I thought to myself, *Shit, this is the only girl on Earth that can go on a surprise $2400 shopping spree and come home pissed.* Before I could say anything, she turned on *me* like I was the asshole. "Hey, what did you do with that $100 I left here?"

"What the fuck are you talking about? I spent it!" I yelled, incredulous that this bitch could take $2400 of my money and then start quizzing me on how I spent the last $100.

"I can't fucking believe you!" she screamed, a smile cracking through. "I can't believe you wasted that $100! You need to be more careful with your money." That was it; I couldn't be angry with Dusty anymore. She was too flamboyant for me; I was being out-pimped.

Deep down, the girl felt guilty for outright stealing my cash and wanted to make it up to me. She didn't understand how, of course. Instead of being a little bit thriftier, she stole *another* $2000 of my stash and bought *me* a new wardrobe. I would have appreciated a nice suit, but this girl had been watching too many rap videos. She wanted me to dress up like a black pimp: baggy jeans, big t-shirts, the whole costume. I told her that I would look like a seventy-year-old minstrel and asked her to return the clothes.

Instead, I think Dusty may have just given the clothes to this young black pimp whom I had put in business. I know this won't come as a surprise, but this turned out to be a bad business move. The young black pimp figured that she was sweet on him and started to pursue her. I didn't worry about it; this kid was a friend and a protégé, and Dusty wasn't going to go out of pocket on me for another New Orleans pimp.

Soon enough, I ended up in jail again, unable to make bond thanks to Dusty's spending, and I asked her if she could compensate me for this inconvenience by simply living safely and protecting herself. Without me around to guard her, I asked her to move out of the Motel DeVille, where we had been staying, and lay low so that no one could find her.

It didn't take long for one of the guards to come to my cell door. "Frenchy, I hate to tell you this," the guard said, "but I just got word your old lady's in critical condition. She's on the endangered species list, man. She was stabbed. She's had emergency surgery; they had to remove her spleen. I'll let you know if she's okay."

The culprit was my protégé, the black pimp whom Dusty had gotten all worked up, who immediately went to our motel room once he heard that I was incarcerated. Dusty had ignored my advice and bragged to everyone we knew that she was so tough that she was going to stay right where she was. Anyone who had a problem with us could come see her.

Well, the pimp came to see her, and she lost her temper when he refused to take no for an answer. She forcefully kicked him out of the hotel room. In response, the pimp called a degenerate crackhead with a reputation for sticking people and paid him cash to come to Dusty's room and kill her. A knife plunged into Dusty's body the second she opened the door to see who was knocking.

Using her martial arts training, Dusty disarmed and knocked out the crackhead. The man at the desk didn't answer the phone, so Dusty had to stumble out, bloody and lightheaded, and crawl onto Tulane Avenue. Luckily, a car stopped to give her a ride to Memorial Hospital, where they barely saved her life.

By the time I got out of jail, the pimp was already locked up, and I couldn't settle that score. Dusty had been released from the hospital, but, just like Farish Cody, the pain she suffered recuperating from the surgery sent her into a drug-addiction tailspin. In the meantime, my lawyer had sued the motel for not answering the front desk call and won Dusty an $85,000 settlement. "Daddy, how much do you want?" she asked when I came home.

"Not a dime, baby. Send it home." Dusty sent it back to New Mexico to her family to take care of two young daughters she had left behind.

Between the threat to Dusty's life and her increasing reliance on drugs like crack to get up in the morning and heroin to go to sleep, I lost my mind with fear. I followed Dusty around every minute of every day like a nervous babysitter, reluctant to let her turn a trick even with familiar clients. I was positive that she would die the moment I pulled my eyes away from her. I had lost too many of my other friends already, and I had never had a friend I cared about as much as her.

Since she insisted on going out on dates, I refused to let Dusty rely on her karate for self-defense. I bought my increasingly insane drug addict a .32-caliber Beretta. A week later, she locked me out of our place and would not answer the door. Thinking that she may have overdosed, I kicked down the door and heard a gunshot. There was the love of my life, standing in front of me with a smoking gun. I looked down and noticed that my entire left pant leg was soaked red with blood. I hadn't felt a thing.

"Dusty...?" I asked, the pain in my voice coming from my heart.

She aimed the gun right for my mouth and pulled the trigger. The Beretta jammed. Usually, that's one of the drawbacks of Italian guns, but in this instance, that shitty guido workmanship saved my life.

"I can't believe this, you lucky bastard," she said with hatred in her voice, her eyes mad with drugs. "You must've stacked the deck." She threw down the gun and was gone before I could even say a word.

I was too distraught to even go to the hospital. Since the bullet had gone straight through my leg, I figured it would heal itself. I wrapped my leg in a towel and pulled the bullet out of the wall. This bullet was meant to kill me.

Sometimes, I think it should have. I spent the next few days in excruciating pain, rubbing the bullet between my fingers. No one called. No one visited.

Finally, two days later, my phone rang. There was no introduction, no apology. All she said was, "Can I come home?" in the loneliest voice in the world. I said, "Yeah, come on home," in the most tired voice in the world. She put that bullet on a necklace for me and said it was my lucky bullet.

"Baby, you're wrong there," I said as she examined my leg, which was purple-black from my groin to my toes, "the bullet that *jammed* was the lucky one. Look at my leg; *that* bullet ain't lucky from where I sit. I'm already broken down enough as it is, and now you got my old ass limping!"

Like clockwork, Dusty disappeared again. After a while, I heard from her family that she was detained on a drug charge in New Mexico. This wasn't surprising; she had gotten so bad that she was sleeping with the heir to a supermarket chain so that he would let her in the store at night to steal steaks and liquor to exchange for crack.

A couple months after that phone call, I finally heard from her. "Frenchy, send me two plane tickets to New Orleans. One way. One for me, and one for my daughter, Kai," she barked into the phone like I was her secretary. Before I could ask why her daughter was coming along, she yipped, "Delta, not Southwest! Remember, not Southwest!" and hung up.

The next day, Dusty's daughter called me and said that the love of my life had died of an overdose.

You might think that was the end for me; it sure felt like it. I fell into my own drug malaise. I couldn't find the energy to work out, to get out of bed, to take a shower, or change into shirts without dandruff on the shoulders. My teeth rotted; my hair started falling out; I never slept well, and I was never fully awake. Some of my friends called me "the zombie," and the few old wiseguys around at the beginning of the twenty-first century would look at me with disgust. "Boy, if I had been born with your looks, I think I would have taken care to keep 'em!" they'd tell me.

I shuffled through my days, almost a hobo, making just enough money to stay alive by referring customers to the few escorts I still knew. I pawned off the girls who needed some sex from their "old man" on Neil Gautier, who was the same horny little leprechaun he'd always been. Even at the age of 114 or 115 (I lost count), Neil still can satisfy any woman who gives him half a chance. I appreciated him taking those responsibilities off my hands, and I still love him for being so gullible that he'll rush to his car the second I tell him there's a 300-pound sex maniac in Oklahoma who needs to fuck by 5 p.m.

The years melted by, and my old friends died off one by one. Soon, the only people left were Neil, Dale, the English Queen,

Edwin in prison, a couple old wiseguys whose names I won't mention, and whatever passed for Frenchy Brouillette. I had only one steady old lady, Sharon O'Dell, a stone-cold Irish sex freak whose only purpose in living was feeding the sixty stray cats who lived around her trailer in the trailer park. Sharon named and developed a personal relationship with each one, and I think the only reason she used me as her operator was because she needed someone to dump fifty-pound bags of cat food in her yard once a week when she was locked up. I was her stray-cat insurance.

As I closed in on my seventieth birthday, I was on my way to leaving hating. I had done plenty of hard time in my old age, and a happy ending was not looking likely. Then, another angel came into my life.

A pretty teenage girl with dyed-black hair just like her mom's flew in from Albuquerque, New Mexico. She got into a cab and asked for Frenchy. In the old days, she would have been taken right to my place, but in 2004 things had changed. Being a smart girl, she told the confused cabby to take her to the nearest criminal attorney's office. That proved to be the ticket; she was delivered right to my doorstep. That almost makes me proud; my criminal career is so legendary that attorneys make a point to memorize my constantly changing address.

This pretty young thing came into my life long after I thought I had seen my last pretty young thing. She was beautiful, and before she said a word I knew who she was. "Hi, Frenchy, I'm Kai..."

"I know. I can tell. Your mother would be proud of how beautiful you've grown up to be."

"Frenchy, I want to move to New Orleans. I've heard all about you. I've been looking at apartments out here, and I think I can get a nice place. I ... well, I want to get *a job,*" she said with a wink. She was dressed exactly like her mom; in fact, I think she may have been wearing some of Dusty's old clothes. With her youth and her looks, she could have made $5000-a-day, potentially a lot more if she found herself a good sugar daddy. I would never have to worry about money again.

"Baby, I'm going to buy you lunch," I said, putting my arm around her shoulder, which felt so much like her mother's. "And then I'm going to buy you a one-way ticket back to Alba-kirk. You need to go to college, and you need to live a normal life."

"But..."

"Baby, *trust me*. I've seen more than you can ever imagine. Take it from me: you don't need to go down that path."

So I sent the prettiest girl I had seen in years right back home. It was what I had always done when new girls came calling, and the only exception I ever made was for Dusty. Deep down, I feel like that's why I'm responsible for what happened to her. It wasn't going to happen with her daughter.

A year later, shortly after my 69th birthday, another girl came to town to visit, but this one was a crazy bitch named Katrina. Yes, the Hurricane that sank the great city of New Orleans, the greatest storm in history, 175-mile-per-hour winds and almost 2000 people dead and 80% of a great city underwater. Overnight, I was stranded in a friend's house as the town I loved so dearly was submerged beneath the sea, and lily-white America did not lift a finger off of their TV remote controls to help us. When the floodwaters subsided, I was homeless, and all of my possessions and savings had been washed away. I thought I would die on the street.

But that's not how it worked out. Dusty's daughter sent me a one-way ticket to Albuquerque so that I could ride out the aftermath of the storm and get back on my feet. While I was over there, her family thanked me for my kindness to Dusty in her last years by giving me a piece of a local business, so that, no matter how badly I fucked up otherwise, I would still have regular cash to keep me from starving.

Over a half-century after I abandoned my first family, I had been accepted — warts and rap sheet and all — into a new one.

A few months later, I returned to New Orleans in style. My last old lady, Sharon, had tapped into one of the FEMA bigwigs who came into town, and he was spending $10,000 a week on sex, drugs, and multi-course meals at Antoine's. The out-of-town Vidalia business after Katrina was out of control, as it seemed like every lily-white Red Cross worker, FEMA bureaucrat, and devoted missionary was ordering escorts for their charitable stay in what was left of the Crescent City.

The locals were not as freewheeling; almost all of our native New Orleans calls were broken people just looking for someone to deliver crack, heroin, or guns to their bombed-out homes. A lot of them were looking to commit suicide; others, I feared, had other business in mind with their hot pistols.

A charitable friend loaned me his FEMA-purchased suite at the ritzy Hotel Monteleone, and I was living in style in the Quarter once again for the first time since the 1960s. None of the old characters were still around, and all of the old burlesque clubs had closed decades before. The bartenders still recognized me, though, and I could once again spend lazy nights listening to the characters chatter at the Absinthe House, where I met Dutch Kraut back in the days when Louis Armstrong would stop by to play sets on the house piano.

One day a couple years ago, I was sitting on my barstool at a high-scale cocktail bar. I was a little sweaty since I had just come from the gym, where I was slowly catching up with Neil Gautier's seventy-or-over weightlifting records. I still looked like hell, but I could walk ten miles a day without losing my breath, and my body didn't feel a day over thirty. My mind, of course, still felt seventeen years old, as it always has.

As I was nursing my cocktail, I noticed that a tall, beautiful young lady was staring at me. There are days when I'm ugly enough just to gawk at, but today I fancied that I was looking vaguely human. She must have recognized me, but I couldn't place her face. I knew lots of young women, but very few of them would be allowed into a nice place like this.

Just as I was about to leave out of nervousness, the barmaid called out, "Hey, Frenchy, would you like another?" I graciously declined, but, when I stood up to leave, the young woman was at my side.

"I'm sorry, but I couldn't help overhear your name," she said with a sultry voice, "and I have to ask. Are you Frenchy...or *the* Frenchy?"

"I don't know what you're talkin' about, honey, I'm just a poor horse trainer from Marksville, Louisiana."

"I know you, Frenchy. I recognize you." She introduced herself as a former hostess for an Italian restaurant owner in Metairie whom I had done business with for many years. "I know you're *the* Frenchy."

"I'm sorry, honey, I don't like to talk about that sort of stuff with strangers. It's one reason I'm still here, and no one else is."

"Don't worry about it, you can talk with *me*," she said as she placed a hand on my thigh. "I *understand.* I work, well, I work in *referrals.* I have six beautiful female employees who I refer customers to."

I'll be goddamned! I thought to myself. A real, honest, no-bullshit New Orleans madam in the 21ˢᵗ century!

"Baby, I thought we were a dying breed," I said as I motioned to the barmaid to let her know I had changed my mind and was looking for another drink. "That just goes to show you can never count New Orleans out."

"There are only two types of people: Italians, and people who wish they were Italians. Look at Frenchy's nickname, and judge for yourself which he is. All of his problems really come down to that one. He's a Cajun who got the silly idea that he could get away with acting like an Italian. Look at him now!"

Dale

I have one regret in my life, one that I intend to fix once this book is published.

As I have said, at a certain point in every person's life, there comes a time when they have to choose whether they are going to do easy time or hard time. The Church and the government and your parents tell you that life is about hard time — living a boring, tax-paying, law-abiding, squeaky-clean, safe life.

Growing up in Marksville carrying potatoes, tolerating school, and going to mass every weekend, I lived that life. At seventeen, I realized I was doing my time hard; I was hating — hating the responsibility of my family's expectations and the pressure of school and the guilt of Catholicism and the uptightness of that small-town world.

I looked at my big brother Percy and saw a boy who would always be doing hard time; he would never forgive himself his humanity or forgive anyone else for theirs. Though I didn't understand it at the time, I sacrificed everything for a chance at getting away from that. I wanted to do easy time, far away from the life imprisonment that most people call "being a responsible adult." Fuck that noise, baby.

Like millions of people down the century, I came to New Orleans in search of easy time, light time, lazy time, a good time! All we got is time after all, and no one has shown me a good reason why every single, solitary second should not be its own little Mardi Gras. That's been the entire point of New Orleans: the one place in America you could come —not in search of a righteous City on the Hill or land, liberty, and the pursuit of happiness —but in search of an unapologetic, shameless, easy time.

That's why I'm proud to say I'm Mr. New Orleans: there's no higher goal in the world than a free ride and a good time. Anyone who thinks otherwise is just being pretentious.

It's like they say about working girls: you don't pay for the sex; you pay for them to leave afterwards. You pay to avoid the awkwardness, the doubt, the guilt, the emotional responsibility, everything uncomfortable that comes with sex; you pay to put off reality. That $300 the john pays to the escort agency is for an hour where the rules of reality are suspended, and he can make all his responsibilities disappear. All he wants is the easy time without all of the hard stuff that's supposed to go with it.

That was my life for decades. I made money without paying taxes; I was a gangster without doing any of the dirty work myself; I committed crimes without doing hard time; I made millions without working; I grew old without growing up; I had sex without commitment; and I became Mr. New Orleans without winning an election or even a bodybuilding contest. I lived to defy the consequences of living. And that's what makes me Mr. New Orleans.

New Orleans for centuries was the city that consequence forgot. We built our city on a sinking mud pit below sea level...surrounded by water...in hurricane alley...embezzled the money set aside for building working levees...and got away with it for three centuries without paying the price!

We're the city that brought cocaine, casino gambling, absinthe, race-mixing, organized prostitution, *laissez faire* Mediterranean Catholicism, jazz, and the Mafia to a miserable, stick-up-the-ass Protestant country, and didn't see the backlash coming! We expected the WASPs and the Yankees and the Texas evangelicals to bail us out when the Great Flood came. We lived for today and prayed that tomorrow took its sweet fucking time getting here.

And tomorrow finally came — for me and for New Orleans itself. My generation, the last witnesses of the French Quarter and the Louisiana golden age, saw the apocalypse; we've seen the most glamorous city since Sodom reduced to ruins, first by the incompetence of our local government, and then by the incompetence of the federal government.

Now that I think about it, it makes hilarious sense that, along with the cockroaches and the snakes, just about the only survivors of the golden age are the Brouillettes: Frenchy and his country cousin Edwin. I'm Noah, stumbling naked and drunk off my ark back into a mud-covered world.

And you know what? I'm not changing a goddamn thing. Any god who would cause the pain and suffering that happened during Katrina to teach *me* a lesson picked the wrong mark. I'm not going to rat, and neither is Edwin.

That's why I'm Mr. New Orleans. And that's why Edwin is Mr. Louisiana. Unbowed and shameless to the end, my country cousin just put out a book talking about how great he is from his federal jail cell. And I just rented a room in the French Quarter. Next time you land at Louis Armstrong Airport, jump in a cab and ask that hack to take you to Frenchy. Maybe you might get lucky.

As for me, I'm going to give the English Queen a call. That multimillionaire Gypsy may no longer have her youth, but I've got a long memory, and she still looks good to me. She's asked me out to dinner because she's suspicious that my writer may be an FBI agent out to get her old ass, and I'll play on her paranoia long enough to get some wine and steaks out of the deal. When I'm done, I'm going to give Neil Gautier a call and try an experiment I've been thinking of for a long time.

I'm going to tell him the English Queen's address and say, "Neilly, baby, boy, have I got a find for you! Go to that address. There's a horny young woman who lives there who shared her deepest, darkest fantasy with me. She's always wanted to answer her doorbell and be greeted by a naked man!"

When it comes to sex, even at his advanced age, Neil is still that gullible. I'll be hiding in the bushes to see the look on the Queen's face when she sees Naked Neil, and, more importantly, Naked Neil's face when he sees the death stare coming from the Queen. Trust me, baby, I *have* to be there, or otherwise I'll have to find five other survivors from the Quarter to act as Neilly's pallbearer.

After I've had a good laugh, I'm going to call up Dale and have him drive me up to Marksville to take care of that last regret

I mentioned earlier.

I'll tell Dale that I want to introduce him to the man he could have been if he had stuck with the McLaneys: Billy Guillot, my dwarf pal who went from champion midget wrestler to the head of security at the luxurious new casino that the Indians put in the quiet, hardworking, religious hometown of the Brouillettes. I'll take in the sight of Dale looking down with envy at an elderly midget casino pit boss, and I'll enjoy it. "This coulda been you, Dale!"

Having killed as much time as I could, I'll finally drive by my parents' old house, and I'll say hello to my brother Percy. I'll tell him about Dusty, and how she paid me back for every motorcycle and car of his I ever wrecked. I'll tell him that I love him, and that I hope he's done his time as easy as he could.

Finally, I will walk over alone to the Marksville cemetery by that water tower with the painting of the wagon wheel missing its spokes. I owe it to my parents. I'll put a rose on each grave, and I'll tell 'em it wasn't personal. I'll tell 'em I'm sorry.

And when I leave Marksville this time, I'll do it right. I won't leave hating. First round at the Absinthe House will be on me that night, and the toast will be "To Marksville for making me, and to New Orleans for saving me! *Laissez les bon temps rouler,* baby! "

MRV's Thanks

Here's to you, Frenchy; I owe you a bottle of Château Lafite Rothschild.

My heart belongs to my wife Melissa and my mother Jeannie. Melissa is my inspiration and partner, and Jeannie is my biggest supporter. They both selflessly contribute their time, energy, brainpower, and love to everything I do. I owe them everything and thank them for it. My love also goes out to the rest of my family— Stevie and Cookie in particular.

I owe an immense debt to Jefferson Parish Clerk of Courts Jon A. Gegenheimer, chess grandmaster Malcolm Meyer and his lovely wife Jeanne, and Jefferson Parish historian Frank J. Borne, Jr. for their friendship and patient support. I also must thank Howard Hunter for sharing his love of Louisiana history with me.

Thanks to my L.A. ambassador Brian Gross for his patience, my dear friends Diana Lofflin and Chad England for their tireless work as editors, and Dr. Ranjan Chhibber for his constant support on all fronts. Also, I owe K. Thor Jensen for his forgiving nature and Jack Scovil for being the first person to believe in this book.

Obviously, I feel incredibly thankful to everyone in law enforcement, the New Orleans underworld, and American society at large who took the risk of helping me with a book as controversial as *Mr. New Orleans.* I must especially thank Dale and Jay for their help, as well as the many people whose names I cannot mention in the interest of everyone's safety.

Thanks to: Percy Brouillette, Sam Carollo, Vic Carollo, Quinetta Cody, Harry Connick, Sr., Rick DeLaup, The Dentist, The English Queen, Lenny Gail, Neil Gautier, Bill Huntington, Frank LaBruzzo, Sal Lentini, Patrick McLaney, KM, Betty Anne Mueller, Sharon O'Dell, Frank Pirelli, Mike P., The Restaurant Owner, Carrie Schwartz, Shirley Shipp, Irene Wainwright, Kitty "Evangeline The Oyster Girl" West, and everyone at the Jefferson Parish Sheriff's Office.

It is my duty to acknowledge the historians who have come before me in the study of the Louisiana underworld. Though dozens of books were consulted for *Mr. New Orleans*, a few deserve specific praise: *The French Quarter* by the immortal Herbert Asbury; *The Last Madam* by Christine Wiltz; *Mafia Kingfish* by John H. Davis; *Storyville, New Orleans* by Al Rose; *Every Man a King* by Huey P. Long; *DeLesseps S. Morrison and The Image of Reform* by Edward F. Haas; *The Money & The Power* by Sally Denton and Roger Morris; and *Bad Bet on the Bayou* by Tyler Bridges.

About the Authors

MATTHEW RANDAZZO V was born and raised in New Orleans. He is an investigative journalist and popular historian who seeks to discover extraordinary untold stories from America's underworld. He is also the author of four books, has written for the *New York Daily News,* and has appeared as an authority on the American underworld on E! Entertainment Television and over 100 radio programs around the world. More information can be found at www.MRVBooks.com.

FRENCHY BROUILLETTE has been the reigning Mr. New Orleans for over fifty years. With a record that includes over three dozen felony arrests, multiple gunshot wounds, and a 1,600-page FBI file, Frenchy is the most notorious Cajun gangster in the history of Louisiana and certainly one of the most colorful figures in the history of the Mob. Known as "The Keith Richards of the American Mafia," Frenchy was often a fugitive from justice during the writing of *Mr. New Orleans.*

CPSIA information can be obtained
at www.ICGtesting.com
Printed in the USA
BVOW06s0123021216
469575BV00008B/155/P